THE ART AND IMAGINATION
OF W. E. B. Du BOIS

Harvard University Press

Cambridge, Massachusetts, and London, England   1976

The Art
and
Imagination
of W. E. B. Du Bois

ARNOLD RAMPERSAD

Copyright © 1976 by the President and Fellows
    of Harvard College
All rights reserved
Printed in the United States of America
Publication of this book has been aided by
    a grant from the Andrew W. Mellon Foundation.

Library of Congress Cataloging in Publication Data

Rampersad, Arnold.
    The art and imagination of W. E. B. Du Bois.

    Includes bibliographical references and index.
    1. Du Bois, William Edward Burghardt, 1868-1963.
I. Title.
PS3507.U147Z85   301.24'2'0924   [B]   76-10295
ISBN 0-674-04711-7

He created, what never existed before,
a Negro intelligentsia, and many who
have never read a word of his writings
are his spiritual disciples and descendants.
   —NAACP

This stern prophet, this flaming angel.
   —James Weldon Johnson

Hope and Memory have one daughter
and her name is Art.
   —W. B. Yeats

Preface

WHEN THE DU BOIS papers at the University of Massachusetts, Amherst, are finally opened to scholars, the definitive biography of Du Bois will doubtless be written. It cannot be too early, though, to try to see his life and work in as comprehensive and exact a way as possible.

I write of Du Bois' "art and imagination" because it is clear to me that his greatest gift was poetic in nature, and that his scholarship, propaganda, and political activism drew their ultimate power from his essentially poetic vision of human experience and from his equally poetic reverence for the word. This sense of Du Bois increases rather than lessens the task of judging his achievement and demands more skills than many of us possess. But it is the accurate view.

To see him simply as historian or sociologist or propagandist is to overlook the heart of Du Bois' intelligence, just as to underestimate his contribution in each of these areas is to misrepresent the major ways in which his art and imagination functioned. Similarly, one cannot ignore his novels or verse and yet hope to understand or represent the complex gift of a man whose career as writer covered some eighty of his ninety-five years and whose contribution to Afro-American scholarship, intellectualism, and cultural identity has never been surpassed in scope and quality.

In starting out to write this book, I was helped immeasurably by the advice and friendship of Maurice J. Bennett, Lee Daniels, Lorna Ferguson, Robert Ferguson, Charles Hamilton, Paul Jefferson, Nellie McKay, Lenny Rieser, Susan Van Dyne, Antony Waddell, and Ernest J. Wilson. I also owe much to Zeph Stewart and Diana Stewart. Later on, many people directed and influenced my work either by reading and criticizing parts of the manuscript as it evolved or by sharing with me, in letters or conversations, their understanding of its subject. I thank Herbert Aptheker, Houston A. Baker, Jr., Warner Berthoff, Francis L. Broderick, David Du Bois, Shirley Graham Du Bois, Charles T. Davis, Irene Diggs, St. Clair Drake, Ewart Guinier, Alan Heimert, David Levin, Rayford W. Logan, August Meier, Raymond J. Nelson, Roger Rosenblatt, Andrea Benton Rushing, and Hortense Thornton.

I benefited from the support of the University of Virginia and Stanford University, and from a summer research grant from the American Philosophical Society. Thanks are due to the librarians of Atlanta University, Fisk University, Harvard University, Howard University, the Schomburg Collection of the New York Public Library, Stanford University, the University of Virginia, Yale University and the Library of Congress, where Mrs. Louis R. Harlan took time off from her own research to assist me. John L'Heureux and Susan Riggs kindly helped by reading the text in proof.

For permission to quote from Du Bois' works I am indebted to Kraus-Thomson Organization Limited, International Publishers, and Beacon Press. For photographs of Du Bois I am indebted to *Freedomways* Magazine, 799 Broadway, New York City; Archives of the University of Massachusetts at Amherst; and the Philadelphia *Tribune*.

Contents

CHAPTER ONE

The Making of the Man

In the folds of this European civilization I was born and shall die, impris-
oned, conditioned, depressed, exalted and inspired. Integrally a part of it
and yet, much more significant, one of its rejected parts . . . Crucified on
the vast wheel of time, I flew round and round with the Zeitgeist, waving
my pen and lifting faint voices to explain, expound and exhort; to see,
foresee and prophesy, to the few who could or would listen.   (Du Bois,
1940)

WITHOUT W. E. B. DU BOIS' first seventeen years in a New
England town, the history of Afro-America might well have been
different. By his thirty-fifth year, in 1903, he was ready to command
one of the two basic intellectual camps within the black community.
He would stress the beauty of the folk, the necessity of liberal learning, the value of culture, the importance of a leading class, the
spirituality of life, and by implication, the perfectibility of man. In
other words, he would bring to the racial question the force of nineteenth-century British and American liberal apologetics, that peculiar synthesis which brought to the service of diverse libertarian
causes various elements of the teachings of Calvin, Carlyle, Emerson, and Matthew Arnold. In the other camp would be the followers
of a man born in chains and reared in the grip of racism, trained in
schools far removed from liberal educational ideals, whose life had
been a struggle up from slavery. Du Bois' youth prepared him to
champion an ideal; Booker T. Washington's youth prepared him
for a life defined by the reality of oppression. The strength of Du
Bois' experience was that it opened a fresh and daring perspective
on the old Southern situation.

What Du Bois would come to realize only slowly was that the
peace of New England and the beauty of its ideals were also implicated in the disaster of the Southern black. The integrity of a small
town and of a persuasive tradition, he would discover, might not be

1

the most reliable analogue for dealing with the reality of the world. The culture he was raised to admire might be not only irrelevant to the necessities of a depressed people but actually harmful to their political progress and to the expression of their distinct identity. After 1910, when he joined the effort of certain whites to revive the liberal spirit of the abolitionists, Du Bois was to discover the distance between ideal and commitment, between what he would later call memory and deed.[1]

William Edward Burghardt Du Bois was born in Great Barrington in western Massachusetts on February 23, 1868. His mother's family had lived there since the middle of the preceding century, before the incorporation of the town itself. In Du Bois' youth, the family owned a little land and even some of their own homes. They never attained the middle class, but there was never any question that they belonged to the community of Great Barrington. Free men since at least the War of Independence, in which a black Burghardt had marched as a private with other Berkshire County soldiers, the family knew service but not slavery, some poverty but never destitution. They saw themselves as a small part of the tradition and history of the town, and believed that they were treated with fairness and respect. Like many of the white Protestant English and Dutch townfolk, the Burghardts were Episcopalian or, as in Du Bois' own time, occasionally Congregational. Thus the Burghardt religion and way of life were those of New England and its neighbors in the Hudson Valley.

Although Du Bois himself made the distinction, there was little essential difference of thought in the late nineteenth century between the two regions of New England and the Hudson Valley.[2] Their traditional religion shared the same diluted but still potent Calvinism, and their way of life was founded on the same rocklike principles of work, thrift, and the necessity for inner and outer discipline and restraint. Great Barrington was a community in which all men worked, though it was clear that some worked harder than others, and in which wealth was sometimes wolfish but always sheepishly garbed. There was no great difference between the lifestyles of the well-to-do and the working poor, so that the boy Du Bois could visit the houses of his wealthier schoolmates and still feel perfectly at home.[3]

Du Bois noted: "It was not good form in Great Barrington to

express one's thoughts volubly, or to give way to excessive emotion
. . . I am quite sure that in a less restrained and conventional atmosphere I should have easily learned to express my emotions with far greater and more unrestrained intensity; but as it was I had the social heritage not only of a New England clan but Dutch taciturnity."⁴ In such a setting, the work ethic took precedence. Work explained wealth and was often accounted the only reliable outward sign of existing inner grace. Shiftlessness was the unforgivable civic sin. Although Du Bois' engagement with the formal processes of the New England intellectual tradition would mature at Fisk University and bloom at Harvard, Great Barrington showed him early in life an ordered, civilized existence, against which he was soon to measure the squalor of much black life and the crude racism of the white world beyond New England.

Great Barrington taught him first, through its respectful treatment of a village eccentric who regularly disrupted town meetings while Du Bois looked on "furious," the meaning of democracy—a respectful consideration of all opinions and an independent exercise of one's own. Life in a county with one murder in ten years and a town with one unarmed, dozing policeman to preserve order must have seemed Athenian, in Du Bois' memory, compared to the slums he would later investigate as a sociologist. The remarkable persistence that he showed during the crises of his life, Du Bois felt, was a New England trait bred into him. And his personal dedication to the gospel of work sprang both from the famed New England pride in thrift and industry and from the attitude that to be dependent on public charity "was the depth not only of misfortune but of a certain guilt." Du Bois himself recognized and encouraged his apprenticeship to the spirit of the region: "In general thought and conduct I became quite thoroughly New England."⁵

In Great Barrington Du Bois had no experience of segregation and little of overt color discrimination. He excelled in his favorite subjects in schools otherwise white, and felt himself to be respected by his peers and teachers. When he and his mother joined the Congregational church as its only black communicants, Du Bois was confident enough to become the disquisitional—and, he claimed, popular—terror of the Sunday school. "I felt absolutely no discrimination, and I do not think there was any, or any thought of it."⁶ Eventually, of course, he discovered that he was black and

therefore peculiarly vulnerable. A classmate showed racist disdain
in one childhood episode, dramatized by Du Bois for *The Souls of
Black Folk*. Some of the rough Irish in their dangerous neighbor-
hoods called him "nigger" as he passed. And among the older Burghardts he heard talk of race and racial injustice. But there was little
sense of communal oppression in an isolated town whose white citizens believed that they had fought to set black men free.

Later in life Du Bois looked back and saw that there had indeed
been incidents, adjustments, and manipulations, clearly attribut-
able only to racial prejudice but invisible to his younger and more
innocent eyes. Yet the great fact of Du Bois' boyhood is that he was
apparently happy. He felt himself justly constrained by the mores of
his community. He was fairly, even generously treated and was
almost always accorded his deserts. His abilities were recognized.
His aspirations were often anticipated and encouraged. The philosophy that work could triumph over prejudice "saved me from conceit and vainglory by vigorous self-testing."[7] Far from being an
unfair disqualification, his blackness gave only a keener edge to his
sense of the competition of life.

Du Bois needed a spiritual father, for he knew little of his natural
one. Alfred Du Bois, extremely light-skinned, "a dreamer — romantic, indolent, kind, unreliable," came to town in 1867, married
Mary Burghardt, and soon disappeared.[8] He never returned. Mary
Du Bois deeply mourned her loss, but she mourned in silence, not in
open bitterness. No word was spoken against his father to William,
her only child. She worked where and when she could, mostly in
domestic service, and she suffered in later life from a paralytic
stroke. Du Bois remembered her gentle disposition and infinite
softness. She devoted herself to her son, stressing the virtues of dili-
gence, optimism, and religion. Du Bois grew up on the sunny side of
poverty, provided by his mother and her family with the essentials of
food and clothing. Mother and son were close to each other. Mary
Du Bois died March 23, 1885, after Du Bois' graduation from high
school, which freed him to leave Great Barrington for the wider
world.[9] There can be little doubt that Du Bois' remarkable regard
for all women, especially black women, had its roots in his deep
regard for his mother. In Great Barrington, Du Bois said, he never
stole and he never lied. He arrived at Fisk at the age of seventeen
knowing "nothing of women, physically or psychically, to the

incredulous amusement of most of my more experienced fellows."[10]

The basis of his moral fervor was the iron of Puritan ethics, initially instilled in him in the First Congregational Church of Great Barrington. "Mrs Mary Dubois" was admitted as a member in 1878, when Du Bois was ten. It was "the brilliant era" of the church's more than two-hundred-year life, a period of marked prosperity when the church attracted the business and intellectual leaders of the town. It is not clear why she turned from the Episcopalians, but the Congregational leader, the Reverend Evarts Scudder, was apparently a good friend. And Judge Justin Dewey, whose house on Du Bois' corner was open to the boy, was a deacon and taught Bible class. Du Bois was thus directly exposed to the fundamental doctrines of New England Puritanism. The Congregationalism of Scudder's church was deeply orthodox. In its doctrine, if not its style, it reflected the severe Calvinism of the first minister, Samuel Hopkins, emphasizing "the divine authority of the Bible, the sinful nature of man, the absolute dependence of man upon the Atonement of Christ and upon sanctification by Christ as the only hope of salvation, and the everlasting punishment of the wicked."[11]

There was scope for disquisition, but not dissent. In this post-Darwinian age the impact of Germanic Biblical scholarship was everywhere undermining the authority of the Bible and encouraging the backsliding agents of ecclesiastical liberalism, even in Great Barrington. The boy Du Bois was a witness to the drama of Rev. Scudder's public denunciation of Judge Dewey as a heretic for just such liberalism, and Judge Dewey's equally dramatic walk-out from the church—to the Episcopalians—on a Sunday morning in 1880. Even though Du Bois later scorned organized religion, these early Great Barrington years probably had a lasting impact on him and on the nebula of philosophic speculation surrounding his view of mankind.

The decisive factor in shaping Du Bois' philosophy was the seriousness and combativeness of the Calvinism in which he was tutored. In reacting against triumphant Darwinism and the new Biblical scholarship, Scudder's prestigious church was remaining faithful to a distinguished tradition of ecclesiastical dynamism. It was attempting to preserve the spirit of the Great Awakening and of those years when, in Great Barrington, the Rev. Hopkins had entertained his chief ally and close friend from the neighboring town of

Stockbridge, Jonathan Edwards. Although Du Bois did not take
long to discard such teachings as the divine authority of the Bible or
the need for the atonement of Christ, he would seldom escape the
influence and implications of the other articles of faith, such as the
sinful nature of man, which were endorsed by the evidence of his
experience.

Du Bois retained a formidable and lifelong grasp on the rules of
Puritan ethics. What has been said of Carlyle is equally and
relatedly true of Du Bois: "The dogmas of Puritanism he had indeed
outgrown, but he never outgrew its ethics."[12] Gifted with a poetic
nature, Du Bois remained influenced by the restrictive aesthetic
principles and attitudes that logically derive from Puritan ethical
premises, and their impact on his concept of the ideal political
world was equally strong. Essential Calvinism, according to Santayana, asserts three things: "that sin exists, that sin is punished, and
that it is beautiful that sin should exist to be punished." Calvinists
experience simultaneously a tragic concern for their "own miserable
condition, and tragic exultation about the universe at large." The
Calvinist thus "oscillates" between a profound sense of lowliness and
"a paradoxical elation of the spirit."[13] This definition accurately
describes Du Bois' basic spiritual and psychic temper. Although he
loved and pursued the pleasures of life, it was in this deep, dark
view of the human spirit, in this blend of humility and exhilaration,
that reposed the source not only of Du Bois' extraordinary moral
intensity and prophetic zeal, but also of what many have perceived
as his paradox, contradictions, and pointless ambivalence. The
sensuous black body was not the most hospitable place, he believed,
for the strict Calvinist conscience. Yet he insisted on giving his
heroes precisely such a conscience. His first novel, *The Quest of the
Silver Fleece* (1911), is about one such man, Blessed Alwyn. A character speaks for Du Bois' own bemused perception of his dilemma
when she slyly observes of Alwyn that someone "has gone and grafted
a New England conscience on a tropical heart, and—dear me!—but
it's a gorgeous misfit."[14] Out of this sense of paradox came Du Bois'
doctrine—extremely important in his earlier years—of the necessity
for cultural cross-fertilization and cultural pluralism. The tropic
heart, or blackness, "softens" the harsh tendency of the Calvinist or
white spirit, while the Calvinist element steels the tropical heart and
body into discipline.

The ordered life and simple beauty of the small New England town remained for a long time Du Bois' model of the civic polity. This modern secular version of the old theocratic order founded by the Pilgrim fathers rested, in spite of the overthrow of theocratic power, on a foundation in which Puritan moral elitism was an indispensable part. Moral elitism appeared to be simultaneously sympathetic and antagonistic to the democratic principles enshrined in the constitution by the Fathers of the Republic, whose deism was nevertheless hostile to the idea of a church-dictated state. The balance between moral elitism and liberal democracy seemed to Du Bois to be most brilliantly achieved in a small New England town such as Great Barrington. But in cherishing such a principle, Du Bois was honoring a model of political experience that had little application to the life of the masses of black people, suffering in the aftermath of slavery. The need for the recognition of moral superiority in a political community could easily be turned against them.

The imperative of moral restraint on the ambitious spirit often appears contradictory to true democracy. Du Bois spoke both of the necessity for submission and of that "anarchy of the spirit" which is the goal of human consciousness.[15] The Puritan sense of duty and of a guilt that requires special forgiveness demands humility. The dictates of the trained Puritan conscience seem thus to be opposed to democracy. Du Bois had to struggle to recognize what Ralph Barton Perry has called "the profound democratic implications inherent in the fundamental ideas of puritanism."[16] Du Bois' thought and work, particularly his fiction, reflect his attempt to reconcile the conflicts of these two basic ideologies. The Puritan hold on and expression of the personal conscience and its discipline needed to come to terms with that exhilaration which is the attraction of democracy. The view of mankind as lowly before God had to admit the perspective of human potential implicit in the appreciation of the democratic right. Self-denial had to live with the democratic need for social liberalism and generosity. And a full dedication to moral absolutes would, paradoxically, shackle the agitator and propagandist seeking victories in a political world. The history of this conflict is written on Du Bois' pages. It helps to account for his championing of the elitism of the "talented tenth" of Afro-America simultaneous with his demand that the fruits of liberal democracy be given to the masses of black folk.

The moral imperatives enshrined in the doctrines of the church were stressed in the secular environs of the classroom. Though the exhortations of the Great Barrington School Committee now seem quaint, they were nonetheless significant for the New England of Du Bois' youth. "We must everywhere teach morals," one annual report stated; "our school, especially, must teach in every possible way, *faith* in morals . . . The teacher must magnify the sense of truth in word and deed."[17]

The Great Barrington High School was actually younger than Du Bois himself, having been founded a few weeks after his birth in 1868. The school had no strong scholarly tradition. In Du Bois' day it usually graduated fewer than a dozen students and sometimes sent one or two of these to college. But teacher and student made the most of what they had. Du Bois responded eagerly to the challenge of college preparation, sensing early that his future lay in his studies. His affection for books grew. He began collecting a library and also preserving his private papers. In one respect the curriculum of the high school was deficient: it told him little or nothing of Africa or Afro-America. It is no wonder that he left Massachusetts with the impression, shared by most white Americans, that the African and the Afro-American were creatures without a distinct cultural future. In a sense, he was to spend the rest of his life correcting this one inadequacy of an extensive and varied education. But when he graduated from the Great Barrington High School in 1884, with high honors in a class of thirteen, he was largely unaware of either this failing in his education, or the complexity of his racial fate.

Nevertheless, by that time there had been clear and definite signs of the life to come. The first was provided by the slight encounters with racial prejudice in Great Barrington. He knew that he was different and might therefore be despised. Although the generosity and goodwill of many whites appeared boundless, the knowledge of his vulnerability, like the knowledge of an original sin for which he was not responsible but was still accountable, was there to haunt him. With all the wealth, education, and breeding in the world, the black man, he discovered, depended on the kindness of white strangers.

A different intimation came to him on a boyhood trip to Rocky Point in Rhode Island. There, for the first time, he saw hundreds of black people gathered in sportive mood to celebrate a holiday: "I was transported with amazement and dreams" at the sight of such "extraordinary beauty of skin color and utter equality of mien."[18] This experience confirmed the rapture he had felt on yet another occasion, when—again for the first time—he heard a choir of Southern blacks singing spirituals: "I was thrilled and moved to tears and seemed to recognize something inherently and deeply my own."[19]

The perception of a split in the black consciousness, the sense of two souls, black and American, warring in one body, of which Du Bois would write so perceptively in *The Souls of Black Folk*, had its personal origins in these fleeting apparitions of prejudice, on the one hand, and dark loveliness on the other. His loyalties were already dividing. His concept of what constituted his "traditional community" was being tested by the pressures of the world both inside and outside his small town. With the shattering of an apparently perdurable boyhood peace would come the contest between his learned values and the experience of black life, a struggle that would be of the deepest emotional and spiritual significance to him. He would soon recognize that his coldness and hauteur were poor defenses against the power of white people, "for the worlds I longed for, and all their dazzling opportunities, were theirs, not mine."[20]

Another more elusive foreshadowing of his future came to him on a vacation in New Bedford in the summer of 1883. The main purpose had been to visit his paternal grandfather, Alexander Du Bois, then eighty years old. In his grandfather's house he caught his first glimpse, in an "unforgettable" toast offered by the old man to a visiting black friend, of the elegant life: "I suddenly sensed . . . what manners meant and how people of breeding behaved."[21] There was more to the meeting than a lesson in etiquette. The Burghardts of Great Barrington were hale and hearty, often boisterous, and quite black. More significant for an aspiring boy, they had never risen in the social scale beyond performing essentially manual labor. The Du Boises, on the contrary, were the light-complexioned side of the family. Alexander's father had been a doctor, and there was a hint of aristocracy in his easily traced Huguenot ancestry. The grandfather himself was a man of property, a reader of Shakespeare, and a writer of poetry. He could tell a good wine; he kept an eloquent journal. And paradoxically, he was more militant than any black Burghardt.

As Du Bois related, "Always he held his head high, took no insults, made few friends. He was not a 'Negro': he was a man!"[22] His private verses recorded his sensitivity, but he kept a chilly exterior. He was thus a living forecast of his more gifted grandchild, and in this their only meeting he must have impressed his image on the boy. In 1887, Alexander Du Bois died. "Here my grandfather lies buried," Du Bois wrote of the cemetery near Yale, "and here I shall one day lie."[23] In thus seeming to cherish the light Du Boises over the black Burghardts, he was being consistent with notable aspects of his character and opinions: his less than settled sense of racial identity, his hunger for an aristocratic tradition, his basically inflexible, Western view of art and culture, and his sense of a peculiarly personal affront when faced with racism. These qualities underlay his struggle with Booker T. Washington as much as any purely ideological factor; Marcus Garvey would cruelly rake him over the question of his alleged racial ambivalence. There can be no doubt about Du Bois' militancy, about what he himself called his "chauvinism."[24] But his origins were so complex, his sympathies so broad, and the power of his reason so acute that he could not rest for long in dogmatism, or suppress admirations and affections that transcended race and politics. Thus he repeatedly left himself vulnerable to charges of inconsistency and ambivalence over matters of great importance.

His meeting with his grandfather came at an important juncture in his life. In April of the same year Du Bois began his public career as a writer when he became the area correspondent for the weekly New York *Globe*, edited by the then radical black journalist T. Thomas Fortune (in 1884 the *Globe* became the *Freeman*, then later the New York *Age*). Between April 14, 1883, and May 16, 1885, the teenaged correspondent published twenty-seven letters in the newspaper, articles that reveal something of the social life of blacks in western Massachusetts in the 1880s but more about Du Bois' precocious sense of himself as a leader of his people. In his very first piece he struck a characteristic note of authority. Black men should join the local temperance movement in its latest effort. He had not noticed many of them at the most recent town meeting: "it seems that they do not take as much interest in politics as is necessary for the protection of their rights."[25] The next letter urged the formation of a literary society as "the best thing that could be done for the colored people here."[26] Du Bois had begun his self-appointed stewardship of the fortunes of the race.

His job as journalist drew him into greater contact with black people, notably in the African Methodist Episcopal Zion Church, and thus at an intellectual and social level he commenced a double life. As the only black member, apart from his mother, of the First Congregational Church, and eventually the first black to graduate from his high school, he found a distinctly different milieu among the personalities and activities centered in the AME Zion Church. Composed mostly of Southern immigrants new to the town, the congregation became incorporated in the fall of 1884. The Zionists could not compare with the Congregationalists, whose grand new edifice Du Bois called in a September 29, 1883, letter "the handsomest church in the county," but it was black. Du Bois became secretary of the Zion Sewing Circle, participating in its monthly suppers organized by the women members and in its debates, including one on the question, "Ought the Indian to have been driven out of America?" Although the Zionists did not convert him, they affected his education. The important social role of the black church in America was exemplified by this Great Barrington institution; the Children's Mite Society was founded as part of its Sunday school effort and to aid in the building of the church; and out of members and others also came in 1884 "a club for literary and social improvement," the Sons of Freedom, of which Du Bois was secretary and treasurer. Comprising a number of young black men of the area, the club adopted as one of its continuing exercises the earnest study of "the history of the United States."[27]

The young correspondent enjoyed the role of society reporter at soirees, weddings, and other activities, and once or twice poked fun at himself as a gourmet equally interested in discussing a turkey or a serious topic, but he believed in his intellect. He "advised" readers intending "to replenish their libraries" to consult him before doing so.[28] Less tactless and more prophetic of his later political role was his analysis in September 1883 of upcoming local and state elections. Black men, he observed, "may well ask themselves how they have been benefited" by the governor they had helped to elect, "although he professes to be their friend." There was evidence in the town itself that whites excluded blacks from traditional political spoils in spite of party affiliation. Du Bois then stressed an idea that would be the focus of his approach to the American electoral system for many decades: "The colored men of Great Barrington hold the balance of power, and have decided the election of many officers for a number of years. If they will only act in concert they may become a power not to be despised."[29] Whatever his life may have been in the white Congregational church and the white high school, among blacks Du Bois at fifteen already understood the crucial terms of black progress: education, separateness, solidarity, and power. And he had already defined certain fundamentals of his character: a sense of duty, of moral and intellectual eminence, and of close kinship with the race of "colored" people.

Although his loyalties had begun to divide, Du Bois remained a favorite son of both races in Great Barrington. The New York *Globe* of July 12, 1884, carried the news of his graduation from high school and of his successful address on Wendell Phillips delivered as part of the exercises; the "colored people" of Great Barrington were "quite proud" of him. More important to his later life was the support of the local whites, especially his headmaster, who steered Du Bois toward college, and three members of the Congregational flock, including its minister, Evarts Scudder. Du Bois was penniless and, after the death of his mother in March of 1885, an orphan. He was advised to work and study for a year before college, and found employment as timekeeper on a local building project. A former Congregationalist minister solved the problem of additional financing by arranging a fellowship supported by four Congregationalist churches in Connecticut, where he had been pastor. A year after graduation from high school, Du Bois left home for Fisk University in Nashville, Tennessee.

In Du Bois' three years of college in the South, the Southern brand of racism was seared deeply into his unprepared skin: "No one but a Negro going into the South without previous experience of color caste can have any conception of its barbarism."[30] He soon developed, as he later wrote, "a belligerent attitude to the color bar." Simultaneously, he began to cultivate the sense of his identity as a black man: "I was thrilled to be for the first time among so many people of my own color or rather of such extraordinary colors, which I had only glimpsed before, but who it seemed were bound to me by new and exciting and eternal ties . . . Into this world I leapt with enthusiasm. A new loyalty and allegiance replaced my Americanism: henceforward I was a Negro."[31]

But perhaps the most significant period of his personal development at Fisk was the summer months after his first academic year,
when he taught school among the black folk in the backwoods of
Tennessee. The experience is recorded principally in "Of the Meaning of Progress" in *The Souls of Black Folk*. It was Du Bois' first sustained encounter with the residue of centuries of agrarian enslavement, with mass illiteracy and destitution. At Fisk and elsewhere in
Nashville he had been introduced to the children of the black
middle-class or to other blacks who had adapted to an urban situation. Around his impoverished country schoolhouse Du Bois met
for the first time the black peasant masses, who lived totally
removed from the impact of formal education. Whatever the pupils
may have gained, he wrote, "it was little to what I acquired."[32]

For Du Bois, the experience was significant and deeply compli-
cated. He saw illiteracy and immorality, but he also noted the struggles of moral heroism in a people incapable of vulgarity, although
they seemed primitive. Under the humblest conditions, he attempted to intimate to their children some of the lessons of his
liberal education, his faith in art and culture, and the structure of
his moral logic. But he was himself moved and instructed by these
folk, by the mystery of their innocence and their seemingly irres-
olute shifting between hope and fatalism, which often ended in
tragedy. These summer months brought home to Du Bois the reality
of the black masses. But he also saw that, although on common
ground, he was effectively separated from the folk he espoused.

James Weldon Johnson, unlike Du Bois, grew up in a Florida
town among black people; yet Johnson's first experience of the black
peasantry in their own setting, in a teaching situation almost identical to that of Du Bois, also marked his "psychological change from
boyhood to manhood" and the beginning of his knowledge of his
people as a race. Johnson saw the implications of the tension between his objective assessment of the black folk and his identity
with them: "I found myself studying them all with a sympathetic
objectivity, as though they were something apart; but in an instant's
reflection I could realize that they were me, and I was they; that a
force stronger than blood made us one." For both Johnson and Du
Bois, the white man suddenly became a severely powerful and arbitrary figure, with whom it was impossible to be even moderately
familiar. The most ignorant and debased white man was legally and
socially the superior of blacks. In areas remote from the university

and the city, Du Bois and Johnson each laid what the latter called "the first stones in the foundation of faith" in the black folk on which they afterwards stood. But each also perceived for the first time the peculiarly heavy burden for "the Talented Tenth," as Du Bois called the leaders of the race, in attempting to move the masses forward. Johnson, for example, was "puzzled and irritated" by the rich, spontaneous laughter of the black folk: he could not decide whether it sprang from "a mental vacuity" or from the will to survive. Both men shared with other members of the black leadership a concern that the "easy-going traits" of the black masses hindered progress.[33] At the same time, they recognized that these traits were also natural reactions to the harsh conditions of black life, as well as subtly exploitative of the preconceptions and prejudices of the white man.

Moreover, not only had the black masses survived without the aid of liberal education and culture, but on every side in the South the educated black man saw examples of untutored, energetic virtue. The black intellectual therefore asked whether his gifts to the folk were necessities for racial advancement, or whether they were luxuries that the people could not afford. The black man of culture stood before the masses as a figure embarrassed by his "riches." While separating him from the ignominy of the people, they also seemed to deprive him of the greater glory of the struggle of the folk for survival. Respected by the people, he himself could not completely respect them, for their way of life appeared to defy the cultural insistencies of his education, which in turn represented to him the proof of his own dignity and worth.

For Du Bois, that summer of 1886 marked both the end of an ignorant romanticism and the beginning of an almost romantic faith. After the restraining Congregationalism of Great Barrington, he was shocked by the emotional spontaneity of black worship. His first experience moved and troubled him: "A sort of suppressed terror hung in the air and seemed to seize them, — a pythian madness, a demonaic possession, that lent terrible reality to song and word . . . Round about came wail and groan and outcry, and a sense of human passion such as I had never conceived before."[34] He knew that he could never be an active participant in such a religious drama; he stood outside the folk, a psychic mulatto, an intellectual. He responded to this distance not by dissimulation and hypocrisy, but by using the opportunity for objectivity that it presented, especially when he returned to the South as a trained social scientist in 1897.

The drama which powerfully confused, then steeled, Du Bois' emotions and intellect consisted in the conflict between his memory of white benevolence in New England and the infinite varieties of racism he encountered as an adult. His life between 1885 and 1910, first as a student at Fisk, Harvard, and the University of Berlin, then as a teacher and researcher at Wilberforce University in Ohio, the University of Pennsylvania, and Atlanta University, coincided with the most repressive era in the history of the free black. Legislation designed to deny the vote to blacks was only the basis of an elaborate legal machinery to segregate and exploit the Southern black, developed in an atmosphere of pervasive intimidation and terror generally unopposed by judical restraints. Bent more on reconciling North and South than on serving justice, the U. S. Supreme Court between 1873 and 1898 handed down a succession of rulings that culminated in two decisions of extraordinary significance to blacks: *Plessy* v. *Ferguson* in 1896, which held that "separate but equal" facilities were constitutionally valid; and *Williams* v. *Mississippi* in 1898, which approved Mississippi's plan to strip the black voter of the franchise given him in the aftermath of the Civil War. "When complete," C. Vann Woodward has noted, "the new codes of White Supremacy were vastly more complex than the ante-bellum slave codes or the Black Codes of 1865 66, and, if anything, they were stronger and more rigidly enforced."[35]

Oppression stimulates as often as it stultifies a people. Young Du Bois met raw racism, but he also saw spirited attempts by black America to promote racial pride and unity through a variety of cultural, political, and economic associations that often foundered short of their goals but signified the determination of blacks to assert their legitimacy and dignity. Nevertheless, racism institutionalized in the law and reinforced by widespread lynchings and destructive white riots during the age took its toll on the collective self-regard of blacks, as well as on Du Bois himself as an observer of his people. He did not remain immune to the psychological subversions of white racism. The mixture of races in his ancestry was reflected in his physical bearing and occasioned more than one ironical reflection from the man himself and from those who surrounded him. To a magazine contributor in the 1920s Du Bois resembled "a sunburnt Jew," a Turk, an Italian, a Cuban, or a German, "anything but what you are: A Negro."[36]

Du Bois judged the lines of sufficient merit and accuracy to appear in a 1929 issue of the *Crisis*. While he could triumphantly assert, "I am a Negro and proud to be so," he felt that pigmentation was all that separated him from the world of the majority. From his youth he had known "that in all things in general, white people were just the same as I: their physical possibilities, their mental processes were no different from mine; even the difference in skin color was vastly overemphasized and intrinsically trivial."[37]

In attempting in 1921 to discredit Du Bois before the bar of black public opinion, Marcus Garvey, a color-conscious West Indian, struck at what he considered his most vulnerable point. Du Bois, he insisted, was "trying to be everything else but a Negro. Sometimes we hear he is a Frenchman and another time he is Dutch and when it is convenient he is a Negro . . . Anyone you hear always talking about the kind of blood he has in him other than the blood you see, he is dissatisfied with something, and . . . if there is a man who is most dissatisfied with himself, it is Dr. Du Bois."[38] Du Bois had picked up his sense of aristocracy, Garvey noted, on the streets of Great Barrington. These accusations, which contained slight truth, were only the liveliest variations of a theme sounded by Du Bois' opponents from the start of his career as a polemicist until his last days.

Although his reputation as a sensitive interpreter of the race drew many blacks toward him, he admitted only a few into what was often a warm, lively relationship. The rest he excluded, often rudely. Thus, opinions about Du Bois' personality often contradicted each other in striking ways. President Horace Bumstead of Atlanta University wrote of him as being "about the jolliest member of our Faculty."[39] Sinclair Lewis remarked in tribute that he was "the only man I have ever met in twenty countries whose sense of humor is equal to his scholarship."[40] On the contrary, Claude McKay spoke for many more people when he said that Du Bois seemed "possessed of a cold, acid hauteur of spirit, which is not lessened when he vouchsafes a smile . . . I did not feel any magnetism in his personality."[41] James Weldon Johnson saw the poles of his behavior: Du Bois, when "among his particular friends," was "the most jovial and fun-loving of men . . . but his lack of the ability to unbend in his relations with people outside the small circle has gained him the reputation of being cold, stiff, supercilious."[42] To this Du Bois replied quietly that "if, as many said, I was hard to know, it was that with all my belligerency I was in reality unreasonably shy."[43]

What Du Bois called his shyness was presumably more than simple embarrassment at making new friends. Du Bois' lack of tact, Francis Broderick has remarked, became "a Negro legend."[44] In part it was caused by the romantic idealist's extreme sensitivity to evil and to pain, mixed with the authoritarian idealist's desire to assert his identity through a lofty exclusivity. Du Bois was an emotional man, who delighted in the beauty of the natural world. He guarded his emotions from the indulgence of strangers because he was aware of his acute vulnerability. But in addition, Du Bois avoided broad conviviality and charismatic manipulation through his regard for the role in which he consciously cast himself—that of moral prophet for the people on the question of race. He learned to live with, even to cherish, the prophet's knowledge that honor is not to be expected in his own country. Though he liked wine, women, and song, Du Bois cultivated moral severity. He did not hesitate to strike swiftly and harshly at corruption in blacks and whites alike, and he became accustomed to and contemptuous of (as such men must become) accusations of arrogance and tactlessness. Adopting the moral severity of the Puritan—though, like the early American Puritans, he ate and dressed well—he did not often condescend to be political. Men must either rise to his mark or sink in his regard. He was confident of his exclusivity because of its moral flavor and because of his conviction that it was balanced by his Puritan sense of lowliness in the cosmic scale.

In talking about his white ancestry as often as his black forefathers, Du Bois was being perfectly consistent with his ideals. He would not accept the white racist convention that denied the truth of his mixed genealogy, of his identity, and which in this denial saw him as something called a "Negro." He did not subscribe to the self-deception that made some almost-white men deny their whiteness just as readily as others of the same mixture denied that they were partly black. Du Bois knew that, as a mulatto, he was born as a cultural metaphor both of the American nation, which was both black and white, and of Afro-America, which was both African and American. In the struggle for racial justice his arsenal included the very fact of his dualism: he was spy and counterspy; he knew two worlds and felt that he was therefore doubly powerful. He was committed to the defense of one world because the other had unjustly made itself inimical to the blackness he shared with Afro-America and which he came to revere. But Du Bois finally recognized only one set of ideals, which he felt to be common to humanity regardless of race and color, and which had been best articulated — but not invented — by the great white moral prophets with whom he felt completely comfortable, if only as a disciple: "I sit with Shakespeare and he winces not . . . I summon Aristotle and Aurelius and what soul I will, and they come all graciously with no scorn nor condescension. So, wed with Truth, I live above the Veil."[45]

CHAPTER TWO

The Age of Miracles

Consider, for a moment, how miraculous it all was to a boy of seventeen, just escaped from a narrow valley: I willed and lo! my people came dancing about me, — riotous in color, gay in laughter, full of sympathy, need, and pleading . . . I studied eagerly under teachers who bent in subtle sympathy, feeling themselves some shadow of the Veil and lifting it gently that we darker souls might peer through to other worlds.   (Du Bois, 1918)

Du Bois CALLED THE nine years spent as a university student at Fisk, Harvard, and Berlin "the Age of Miracles," because so many of his wishes came true.[1] His preparation for college enabled him to graduate from Fisk in 1888, after three years of study. He entered Harvard as a junior the following autumn and was awarded the bachelor's degree *cum laude* in 1890. He continued at Harvard as a graduate student in the field of history, then left for Europe in 1892 on a fellowship for study abroad. Du Bois enrolled at the University of Berlin for further training in history, economics, and sociology. In 1894 he returned home and began his teaching career at Wilberforce University in Ohio. His doctorate was awarded by Harvard upon completion of his dissertation in 1895.

His unusually thorough education and the zeal with which he delivered up his energies and intelligence to his teachers demonstrated his trust in the propriety of the educated mind and in the invulnerability of what Du Bois revered as truth. Truth for Du Bois, besides being a reflection of the nineteenth century belief in the irresistible force of science, was also a moral absolute that transcended the limitations of mere data. It liberated the mind from error and the soul from sin. For the trained Puritan conscience, the divination of this idea was the essential beauty of life. The belief in science came, however, at the expense of religious faith. The omniscient God of Du Bois' Congregational youth was slowly but surely displaced by the Unknowable of Herbert Spencer. Paradoxically, the search for truth was also the gospel of those who acknowledged this unknowable. For them, man scrutinized the universe unclouded by religious dogma: secular learning was religion enough. To those faithful to the old God, the new learning led almost inevitably to amorality and eventually to fatalism. As in his religion, so in his formal education, Du Bois would make a significant but unsteady transition between the old and new orders.

Of the three universities he attended, Du Bois later insisted that Fisk was his true alma mater: "I was at Harvard but not of it. I was a student at Berlin but still the son of Fisk."[2] The Nashville school replaced his earliest egocentricism, he noted, with "a world centering and whirling about my race in America."[3] With its dedicated faculty and lively student body, it seemed in later years to have been "a microcosm of a world and a civilization in potentiality."[4] Thirty-six years after graduation Du Bois referred to his life at Fisk as one of nearly perfect happiness, with classmates he admired and teachers who inspired him.[5]

He learned Greek from Adam Spence, "a great Greek scholar by any comparison"; in the impoverished laboratory of Frederick A. Chase he acquired a sense "not only of chemistry and physics but something of science and of life"; and under President Erastus Milo Cravath, vistas of philosophy opened.[6] The evangelical tradition at the school was epitomized by President Cravath. A Congregational minister of deeply-rooted abolitionist stock, he had dedicated his life to black education. He believed of black people that "there must be thoroughly and liberally educated [black] men and women . . . to fill the high places of influence and responsibility in school and church, in business and professional life, if the masses are to be reached and uplifted."[7] Spence, Chase, and Cravath were only three examples of the model held up for emulation in the most impressionable years of Du Bois' university career. Essentially fundamentalist in religion and aristocratic in their dedication to social service, these men confirmed in him a reverence for the profession of scholar and teacher and for the power of the educated mind. As his training broadened, he would reject many of their ideas; but as his experience of life deepened, he clung all the more tenaciously to the memory of their ideals.

Recognized at Fisk as a promising scholar, Du Bois played a

leading role among his undergraduate peers. During his three years there he served on the editorial board of the *Fisk Herald*, a monthly paper, of which in his last year he was editor-in-chief. The experience confirmed his already acquired sense of destiny as a leader of his people. Encouraged in the public life of journalist, spokesman, and social critic, he gained a taste for expressing opinion which persisted throughout his lifetime. A fiery and impassioned speaker, he also developed a reputation for excellence in oratory. Although these skills of expression were afforded less public scope at Harvard and Berlin, they were to become important instruments in his dissemination of truth when it came time for him to speak to the world.

The majority of his *Herald* articles were written during his tenure as editor-in-chief, from November 1887 to June 1888. He used his position to publish a small and very slight "novel" of his, "Tom Brown at Fisk," starting in the November number. More characteristic, however, was his year-long campaign to support the drive to build a gymnasium at the university, in which Du Bois urged the students to raise the money themselves rather than to depend on Northern white philanthropy. At one time he praised the school production of a Mozart oratorio as proof of the genius of a race only a quarter-century away from slavery. The presence of the stars and stripes over Jubilee Hall on another occasion made him wonder about the civil rights of the black students and whether the nation would protect them. The self-importance noticeable in his *Globe* and *Freeman* writings was even more fully developed in the *Herald* by Du Bois' senior year. He interpreted praise from one reader as an incentive "toward a life that shall be an honor to the Race."⁸ Elsewhere he encouraged the students to become ambitious for themselves and for black people; when he himself made his farewell to Fisk in the *Herald*, he looked "forward with renewed zeal to the great work before us."⁹

More important for the substance of his later career was Du Bois' discovery, by the end of the Nashville experience, of one version of the vocational dualism that would mark his life. On the one hand he was drawn to the certitude of history and of political and social science. On the other, he found himself fascinated by philosophy, with its capacity for moral speculation and poetic insight. In fact, to go to Harvard, he was forced to turn down the offer of a scholarship to the Hartford Theological Seminary made by his instructor in philosophy, President Cravath. Although this momentous decision was made fairly easily, according to Du Bois, he continued the study of philosophy at Harvard.

Du Bois' experience in philosophy at Fisk reflected the attempt of philosophers of conservative persuasion to deal with enduring questions concerning the nature of man and the theories and discoveries of the Darwinian age. The required texts indicate the reactionary elements of this philosophy. James McCosh's textbook on logic, *The Laws of Discursive Thought* (1870), reveals the deep conservatism of this Scots divine called to the presidency of Princeton. Hostile to the sensationalism, empiricism, and religious skepticism of the positivists, McCosh saw the methods of John Stuart Mill, Comte, and Spencer as "infected throughout" by the principles expounded in Kant's *The Critique of Pure Reason*, which he repudiated in favor of a basically Aristotelian rationalism. James Fairchild admitted in the introduction to his *Moral Philosophy* (1869), a textbook on ethics, his indebtedness to Jonathan Edwards' *The Nature of True Virtue* and to Edwards' friend and disciple Samuel Hopkins, founder of Du Bois' church in Great Barrington. John Bascom's *The Science of Mind* (1881), which tried to bring conventional theology into closer relationship with nineteenth century science, especially evolution, allowed for some empiricism and for those *a priori* principles of thought which McCosh had denied. George Frederick Wright, author of *The Logic of Christian Evidences* (1880), a book to which Du Bois particularly objected, had a similar aim. A respected physical scientist, he was determined to revitalize the appeal of Christianity, especially for the liberally educated, younger generations, by a new and more "scientific" examination of the traditional evidences of Christian belief.

History, economics, and political science must have seemed more propitious instruments for dealing with the world beyond the Fisk acres, where Cravath ruled benevolently over a moral world. What held Du Bois to the study of Puritan philosophy was its generation of idealized emotion through the force of evangelical philosophy, as well as its imperative toward an ideal world through insistence on a sense of sacred duty. Could the sum of the century's science, McCosh asked rhetorically, "satisfy the wants of the soul seeking truth, yearning for reality? . . . Does it not undermine every belief in goodness, in affection, in beauty, and in truth to which men have ever clung?"[10] But Du Bois could not for long be held by such assumptions. He quickly began to perceive that science was neither the only nor the main enemy of a morally idealistic concept of the world. Every lynching or other instance of deprivation and injustice shook his faith in the concept of an immanent God who exercises divine government over a theistic universe. Du Bois might argue with scientists, but he found it increasingly difficult to quarrel with science. At the most pressing, material level, science was to become for him what industry, its dependent, was for Booker T. Washington: a way out for the black man from the morass of slavery and serfdom. Empirical investigation, the statistical method, unbiased evaluation, these would be the basis of that social change which would justify assertions of divine intervention and predict an ideal end.

But in spite of the irresistibility of science and the collapse of the Congregational theological structure, the Puritan ethics and aesthetics held him fast, as they had generations of people far removed from the fire and ice of Puritan divines. Du Bois' concept of liberty, important in a man born in the shadow of the Emancipation, was always circumscribed in the Puritan way. Liberty was only the freedom to exercise the personal faculties toward a nobler world or, as Fairchild phrased it, "in the performance of duty, and in the pursuit of good, under the law of benevolence."[11] Nothing was so fundamental in Du Bois' personal system of moral thought as this notion of the power of duty, which he acquired directly from his early acceptance of a Puritan teleology and which was maintained by a profoundly ingrained Puritan sense of lowliness in the sight of God and in the face of the world.

But Du Bois' religious education, while it stressed the nobility of the soul and the dignity possible in man, warned him consistently against faith in that inner human power which might seek to usurp the omnipotence of God in a theistic world. Thus Du Bois would make the leap from conservative orthodoxy to liberalism without the benefit of that tradition's vital middle ground, the egocentric transcendentalism of Concord, out of which had come the most persuasive traditions of American progressive thought. His political position would rest on uncertain premises for a long time, troubled by his confusion of moral idealism and the residue of Puritan dogma, whose philosophy he had learned at Fisk and would be persuaded to discard at Harvard.

Fisk had rooted Du Bois' formal learning in Victorian soil.

Although equally Victorian in time, Harvard introduced him to concepts of history, social science, philosophy, and psychology that would prepare him for the life of the mind in the twentieth century. Harvard challenged his intellectual and spiritual resources from the outset. He was astonished by the many amicable, aimless young men who attended the school with neither an established purpose nor any sense of missing one. George Santayana, who graduated from the college two years before Du Bois' entrance, remembers its life as "an idyllic, haphazard, humoristic existence, without any familiar infusion of scholarship, without articulate religion: a flutter of intelligence in a void." At the same time, Harvard was assembling the parts of an academic machine whose educational value was sometimes obscured by its primary purpose, which was "to extend the scope of instruction, and make it more advanced."[12]

Ironically, Du Bois arrived precisely at a time when, according to the historian Hugh Hawkins, "a drastic social split" was beginning to divide the student body between its privileged, preparatory-school element and the increasing numbers admitted from poorer, more diverse backgrounds. More and more students found themselves isolated from their peers. If "loneliness could be the lot of a student who was a child of the new immigrants, poor, and hyperstudious," a black student probably faced still greater social pressures.[13] An occasional black entered aggressively into extracurricular life, but Du Bois was not prepared to make the effort. In a sense, he was doubly isolated. Having already gone the distance at Fisk, he was essentially a graduate student even as a junior, with a graduate student's typical narrowness of purpose.

He had not entered Harvard to dally under the elms: "In general, I asked nothing of Harvard but the tutelage of teachers and the freedom of the library. I was quite voluntarily and willingly outside its social life. I knew nothing of and cared nothing for fraternities and clubs."[14] The quality of the faculty then at the university served to convince Du Bois, with some justification, that the decade from 1885 to 1895 had been the most intellectually distinguished in the history of American higher education. "God was good to let me sit awhile at their feet and see the fair vision of a commonwealth of culture open to all creeds and races and colors."[15]

The Harvard faculty apparently responded to his overtures with a warmth that took Du Bois beyond the classroom. "I was repeatedly a guest in the house of William James; I sat in an upper room and read Kant's Critique with Santayana: [Nathaniel] Shaler invited a Southerner, who objected to sitting by me, out of his class; I became one of [Albert Bushnell] Hart's favorite pupils." Barrett Wendell taught him English composition and delighted him by reading to the class from one of Du Bois' papers. President Charles William Eliot and Charles Eliot Norton both invited him to their homes, although possibly on official occasions. "It was a great opportunity for a young man and a young American Negro," Du Bois later wrote of his Harvard education, "and I realized it."[16]

"My salvation," he affirmed, "was the type of teacher I met rather than the content of the courses."[17] Of all his Harvard teachers, none influenced him more, he noted, than William James. Du Bois first studied under James in Philosophy 4, a course in "recent English contributions to theistic ethics."[18] James was then emerging from his decade of devotion to psychology, which culminated in his *Principles of Psychology* in 1890. He was then comparatively unknown in America and years away from the work that would establish him as a force in popular thought. In teaching Philosophy 4, he was expediting the shift in his scholarly focus toward philosophy. He used as required texts the second volume of James Martineau's *Types of Ethical Theory* and Martineau's *Study of Religion*. Why he selected what he called "that dear old duffer Martineau's works" is not clear, but his required books were usually only convenient points of departure for his lectures.[19]

For Du Bois, the course had two immediate significances. First, he was personally captivated by James. Second, he found himself at last beyond the Congregational umbrella. Martineau was the foremost contemporary spokesman for Unitarianism in England; he differed sharply from the Cravath philosophers. He accepted the central doctrines of egoism and associationism, shared James's enthusiasm for the concept of religious experience as an intensely personal event, and saw the moral faculty as based on the recognition of a scale of relative values inherent within the individual. By the end of the year Du Bois had written a thesis for James that would have shocked Cravath. It marked both the specific declaration of his break with organized religion and his attempt to fill the resultant void.

"The Renaissance of Ethics" is by no means a mature work.[20] Du

Bois tried to be coherent and methodical, but certain passages show an unsure grasp of his material, as well as attempts to conceal his uncertainty by bold assertions and ambiguous suggestions. These passages do not invalidate the general honesty or seriousness of Du Bois' paper, which is an important document of his intellectual growth. Its thesis revealed his current approach to that aspect of philosophy which most interested him: efficacious duty. Du Bois argued that contemporary ethical study—as of Martineau, James, Royce, Palmer, and Peabody—had made little advance upon the philosophic methods of scholasticism.

With its cornerstone of faith and its insistence on deep ethical responsibility, the teleology of scholasticism had in itself been a noble event in the history of philosophy. But in it reason had played a subordinate role to dogma, at least until the age of Francis Bacon. Ethics had become an inconsistent mélange of theism, mysticism, and anthropomorphism. Turning to the search for an ethical philosophy for his own day, Du Bois boldly asserted that the fundamental question of the universe is duty. The basic determination for the individual is the exploration of the difference between the best possible world and the worst possible world. Thus, Du Bois argued, the debate over ethics was teleological in nature.

The question of duty depended on the resolution of the cause and purpose of life, an identification James applauded. Du Bois had replaced the notion of the *summum bonum*, identical with God in scholasticism, with the notion of a relatavistic prime force whose existence was arrived at by an empirical process that avoided transcendental categories. His concept was man-centered without being egotistical, moral without relying on theism, and categorical without being monistic.

The history of modern metaphysics, Du Bois continued, scarcely differed from the dictates of scholastic science. Metaphysics still insisted on blending science with teleology. Science had liberated itself from such concern in the exclusivity growing out of Francis Bacon's *Novum Organum,* arriving at an epistemological rigor that was the key to its overwhelming success in modern life. In the meantime, Christian ethics, ignored by science, had retreated from dogma to a kind of simple evangelical faith. What was needed, Du Bois observed, was the recognition of a clear distinction between science and ethics. The mixture of science, metaphysics, and ethics needed to be dissolved into the twin streams of science and teleology. The former would lead to what Du Bois called truth, the latter to ethical theory.

Mindful of metaphysics, science would nevertheless proceed to a description of all phenomena. Elevated above metaphysics, ethics would admit the discoveries of science, deriving its arguments from those descriptions furnished by science. For science is truth, which is the one path to teleology, which determines ethics. In a summation that James justifiably considered hazy, Du Bois suggested that Christian teleology was the only one yet presented which appeared to be worthy of the dignity of man. But he believed that science would bring fresh perspectives to an understanding of eternal truth. There would always be room for doubt, Du Bois warned; man would always wonder whether it were best to be St. Paul, Jeremy Bentham, or Walt Whitman.

In thus enumerating the world's choices as being basically Pauline evangelical religion, Benthamite utilitarianism, or Whitmanite aesthetic sensualism, Du Bois was engaging in a sort of self-description. As a statement of philosophy, however, the essay shows how much Du Bois had become the disciple of Herbert Spencer. His acceptance of Spencer's basic beliefs was the justification for Du Bois' faith in the power of empirical sociology, to which he devoted the first fifteen years of his career. Those beliefs provided a similar basis for the pioneer of English empirical sociology, Charles Booth, and his disciple, Beatrice Potter Webb. The conflict between the materialism and sterility of Spencer's world and the dictates of intuition, art, and the individual conscience would lead both Webb and Du Bois, as well as many other early sociologists, to a severe crisis of intellect over their chosen vocation.

William James's philosophy was not a perfect system but a constant hammering and forging. The dynamic of James's approach was based on an empiricism that insisted on morality, a cerebration that valued doubt, an optimism that recognized the force of evil in the world, and a dedication to science that pleaded the necessity and spontaneity of religion. He rejected the claims of the philosophy that had set its course by the new Darwinian stars. He refused to preach either the naturalistic gospel of evolution or positivism. He allied himself with the line of dogged British empiricists beginning with Locke and culminating with John Stuart Mill. He challenged in every philosophy those elements that were uncongenial to his basic beliefs, in a contentious process that resisted settlement into a system. Du Bois was referring to this method of intellection when, in an apparent paradox, he cited James's "pragmatism" as well as Hart's "research method" as responsible for his turn from philosophic speculation.[21]

Du Bois was probably not seen by James as an extraordinary intellect. Neither was he regarded simply as an ethnic curiosity, although William would later identify him to Henry James as a former "mulatto" student.[22] As for the attractions that James held for Du Bois, there were times, according to Santayana's memory of James, when the spirit seemed to come upon him in his lectures, and "he would let fall golden words, picturesque, fresh from the heart, full of the knowledge of good and evil . . . thoughts of simple wisdom and wistful piety, the most unfeigned and manly that anybody ever had."[23] Even as Du Bois' heart was congealing toward the white world, James appeared to transcend race by openly displaying a character that blended sentiment, intellect, and ideals into a seductive mixture. These were the passages of genius that drew students — unaccustomed then, as now, to either wisdom or candor in the classroom — under James's influence. Such revelations were the primary source of his appeal to Du Bois.

Du Bois went to Harvard as a political innocent. His farewell to Fisk had been an oration in praise of Otto von Bismarck, which he later remembered with embarrassed amusement.[24] James was the first person of any authority to articulate for Du Bois the range of views to which he eventually subscribed. James was an internationalist but a heated opponent of imperialist expansion. He resented American jingoism in Mexico and the Philippines, rejecting the license of the Monroe Doctrine. He supported the Irish and the Boers against the English, the intellectuals against the enemies of Dreyfus. James distinguished between the necessity for moral heroism and the abuses of unjustified war, so that he was regarded by the pacifist camp as essentially one of their own. He was patriotic but critical of the moral standards of government in his country. In 1884 he left the Republican party over the issue of corruption, refusing to vote for James G. Blaine. He opposed the persecution of blacks, especially the habit of lynching, which he described as an example of "the aboriginal capacity for murderous excitement" in the bosom of the average churchgoing "civilized" man.[25]

For a young man who had publicly praised Bismarck and Jefferson Davis for the force of their assertive wills, some of these opinions must have been peculiarly startling. Du Bois was an elitist who was often more than a little impatient with, and contemptuous of, the masses. James stressed the moral heroism of the common man at a time when the popular attitude among people of wealth and education was a naturalistic contempt for such people as the irredeemable, defeated species of society. James thus provided the foundations for a philosophic bridge to socialism of at least a Fabian cast. He was suspicious of those who regarded themselves as guardians of moral and aesthetic taste. He lamented in Matthew Arnold, for example, "the entirely needless priggishness of his *tone* . . . the everlasting little snickering" about vulgarities.[26] Culture manifested its greatness by the power of its sympathy for the less advantaged. By stressing the obligations of the cultured, James was humanizing Arnold's influential doctrine of the duty of the "remnant" to the masses.[27] At the same time he was providing a rationale for a link between European high culture and the masses, black and white. Most important, he was helping Du Bois define his own concept of black cultural leadership summarized in the notion of the "Talented Tenth."

"Speaking broadly," James wrote, "there are never more than two fundamental parties in a nation: the party of red blood, as it calls itself, and that of pale reflection; the party of animal instinct, jingoism, fun, excitement, bigness; and that of reason, forecast, order gained by growth, and spiritual methods—briefly put, the party of force and that of education."[28] Du Bois recognized this division as the only absolute line of demarcation within America, even after he had begun to draw another line dividing white from black. Moreover, he recognized that the two parties existed within Afro-America and that, in both instances, he belonged irrevocably to the party of education.

There were others among James's colleagues who contributed to Du Bois' broader education. His tutorials with Santayana were apparently memorable only because of the instructor's later fame, and Du Bois easily resisted the idealist monism of Josiah Royce, who in any case taught him forensics, not philosophy. Two somewhat more important figures were George Herbert Palmer and Francis Greenwood Peabody. Palmer shared common ground with Du Bois in that both were lapsed Congregationalists when they met in the

Harvard Philosophical Club. Unlike James, Palmer was a Hegelian idealist, but the outstanding characteristic of his philosophy, and its most discernible effect on Du Bois, was its emphasis on ethics. Eventually Palmer would publish in *The Nature of Goodness* (1903) a theory of self-realization through self-denial and humility, and of communal advance through individual acts of self-sacrifice, which is strikingly similar to Du Bois' words on the necessity of duty, sacrifice, and submission uttered at significant moments of his early adult years. When Du Bois told the Harvard commencement crowd in 1890, for example, that the African was the embodiment of noble submission, and that such sacrifice is superior to egotism, he was applying to the American racial situation ethical arguments clearly enunciated by Palmer; and when in a moving entry in his journal on his twenty-fifth birthday he wrote, "I am firmly convinced that my own best development is not one and the same with the best development of the world and here I am willing to sacrifice," he was dwelling personally on the dilemma between selfishness and legitimate ambition at the heart of Palmer's investigation, and he was using Palmer's very terminology.[29] Du Bois was fascinated by his arguments as he continued to refine the moral sensibility that would become his most powerful weapon in the war on racism and ignorance.

Somewhat less important but still meaningful was the example of Peabody. In his course on the ethics of social reform he stressed the application of ethics to such national "problems" as the Indians, prisons, labor, and temperance. Du Bois remembered Peabody's ideas as those of "social reform with a religious tinge," but he made that judgment as a Marxist.[30] A Unitarian minister and Plummer Professor of Christian Morals at Harvard, Peabody brought together religious orthodoxy and social concern in a manner designed, not unlike that of Cravath at Fisk, to bolster the student's appreciation of both religion and social activism. It is probable that Du Bois listened to him with respect. But by the time of his graduation, he was clearly demanding a more concrete methodological base for approaching social reform than that afforded by conventional theology.

In spite of the marked influence of Palmer on Du Bois' ethical sense, the overall impact of William James was preeminent. By his appreciation of the secular life, his political concern, and his personal flamboyance, James validated the integrity of ideas and traditions that might otherwise have been discredited by men who, with the best of intentions, could not convincingly apply them to the realities dominating the thought of a young black man like Du Bois in the America of his youth. In helping to make the "commonwealth of culture" not only accessible but also highly desirable, James confirmed in his student the basic intellectual position to which he would cling tenaciously for the greater part of his life.

Had Du Bois not traveled in Europe at the end of his Harvard experience, he later wrote, he would have encased himself from that time "in a completely colored world, self-sufficient and provincial, and ignoring just as far as possible the white world which conditioned it."[31] Largely by his own choice and design, he experienced two Harvards. On the one hand, there existed the "commonwealth of culture" to which he sought admission and into which his professors invited him; on the other, he lived in a segregated world that he coldly shared with his fellow students. Although Du Bois elected to stand apart, he had legitimate reasons to be hostile. Racial exclusiveness was probably the unwritten rule among student organizations, to which there were few exceptions. Compelled in the segregationist South to know his place, he insisted in the more liberal North on his right to keep it.

He felt subsequently that he had not been arrogant in Cambridge; he had only refused to be obsequious, and was himself ignored rather than resented by his white peers. Poor, black, and a transfer from a then obscure school, Du Bois felt the need to protect himself from potential insult; he acted "with perhaps an inferiority complex," he admitted, but also out of a defiant faith in the future of his people.[32] Some white students insisted on getting to know him, "and a few, a very few, became life-long friends."[33] In general, though, he isolated himself or associated with other blacks, who themselves, as in the case of the future radical leader William Monroe Trotter, often joined eagerly in the full college life.

Journeying into the Boston black community, Du Bois did not find perfect happiness. Determined to begin the task of bringing culture to the masses, he took a hand in church-sponsored dramatic productions, notably of Aristophanes' *The Birds,* and lectured on more than one occasion. He felt that his effort at Aristophanes, though good, was "not quite appreciated by the colored audience."[34]

Invited to lecture, he spoke of black Americans, according to Francis L. Broderick, as "a people who have contributed nothing to modern civilization, who are largely on the lowest stages of barbarism."[35] Although he may have felt himself inferior among his white schoolmates, he obviously saw himself as intellectually and morally superior to any group of black people he could thus address. Aspects of black life excusable in the racist South now outraged him in the North and left him with a sense of shame that resulted in a drift toward isolation from both black and white alike.

The white community from which he separated himself answered his disdain by awarding him not only some of the scholarships he solicited but also, on two occasions, the opportunity to speak at commencement ceremonies. Both Harvard and Du Bois were acting out parts in that often bizarre modern American melodrama of tension between liberal whites and blacks resentful of their patronage. Du Bois found himself able both to refuse to befriend his peers and to say to them, as he did in 1891, that Harvard had the responsibility to spread its ideals and traditions throughout the South in order to effect change. Desperate to show neither affection nor gratitude to a people to whom he was linked by blood and personal history, he deliberately nourished his loneliness as a reminder of the wrong his people had suffered — and still suffered — from a race that now wished to honor him. And in presuming to criticize his own people, Du Bois began to pay the grim price exacted by the grandeur of the moral prophet. A journal entry during his twenty-second year, after a day of disappointment, confirms the blend of pain and ecstasy: "Mind not, little heart, if the world were you I could love it. And so we have spent a sample day. We are disappointed. And yet I have spent the happiest hours of my life when I have come home in the twilight with a life plan in my bosom smashed — and alone — sturdy man, foresooth: laid my head on my table, and wept."[36]

Du Bois began his association with the historian Albert Bushnell Hart during his senior year at Harvard, 1889-1890. Hart's History 13 was a survey of the constitutional and political changes in the United States from 1783 to 1861. The eighth lecture, "Social Institutions and Slavery," was the first of several sessions devoted to a study of American slavery. It gave Du Bois a new academic life. Hart was pleased by Du Bois' work, awarding him an A plus at the end of the year. He supported Du Bois' application for admittance to graduate work and supervised his two years of "seminary" research between 1890 and 1892 at Harvard. Having himself been educated at Harvard, Paris, Berlin, and Freiburg, Hart encouraged Du Bois to study in Germany, where Du Bois received important academic training in sociology. Hart supervised Du Bois' doctoral dissertation and was instrumental in its publication as the first volume of the Harvard Historical Studies. Du Bois' thesis, *The Suppression of the African Slave-Trade to the United States of America, 1638-1870,* was the culmination of his interest in a topic first illuminated for him by Hart.

If History 13 had not been intended as a forum for the highest level of scholarship, the graduate seminars clearly were. Hart's standards and methods were rigorously Germanic in nature. There was a great difference between such an approach and that of the English historical tradition, best excmplified in the nineteenth century by Macaulay and Carlyle. Du Bois' first purchase for his personal library had been a five-volume set of Macaulay's *History of England,* which he read and cherished. But Hart's training moved Du Bois away from the poetry, speculations, and intuitions often characteristic of such history, in favor of the relatively new definition of historical scholarship developed by German investigators in the nineteenth century. Documentation, restraint, and what is called scholarly objectivity, together with a distaste for the influences of religion, patriotism, or the cult of personality, marked this new definition.

History, Macaulay wrote in his *Essay on Hallam,* is ideally "a compound of poetry and philosophy. It impresses great truths on the mind by a vivid representation of particular characters and incidents."[37] Macaulay detested the austere, factual approach to history, but it was this rigor which Hart stressed. When it was reinforced by the special, equally Germanic demands of the doctoral thesis, the result was doubly constraining. The influence of such standards was important for its impact on the shaping of Du Bois' thought and expression. Scholarship severely questioned what would otherwise have been considered relevant information, valid source, or admissible evidence. If Du Bois felt that he had special insight into the question of slavery or of contemporary black life by virtue of his blackness, Hart would probably have assured him that he had none. Anger and rage had no scope for expression in such history. Du Bois' only constituency was truth and all seekers after truth, and truth for the scholar was that which was manifestly verifiable.

An index to Hart's approach to historical writing in Du Bois' day is his 1890 essay on the first six translated volumes of Hermann von Holst's *Constitutional and Political History of the United States.* In this work Hart pointed out von Holst "has set the example of a scientific method; he has left a guide for later scholars; he has fearlessly made public the grounds for his conclusions." Such documentation was innovative. Hart, however, criticized von Holst's writing as being too "allusive," leaving "a disjointed and incomplete effect," and marred by a "complexity of construction and profusion of metaphor." The work was also too positive and dogmatic; von Holst should have been more cautious in dealing with this "immoral institution." Hart concluded that while von Holst "does not write judicially . . . he does write in sympathy with the spirit of the American people."[38] Hart was clearly bent on preserving the distinction between history and moral propaganda. The morality of a position did not guarantee its historical value. At the same time, the historicity of a statement placed it outside the realm of moral debate. Hart himself wrote pieces in which he gave vent to moral opinion, but he did not call them history. He was a member of the liberal camp at Harvard, anti-imperialist and antiexpansionist in American foreign policy. Once again, Du Bois was being taught by men whose views were to the left of his own as they then stood, and who were educating him into liberal thought.

What is most important, though, is the distinction insisted on by Hart between the individual as scholar and the same individual as moral force. Du Bois was never satisfied by confinement to rigorous scholarship in either history or sociology. He believed in the strict standards under which he had been trained, but the tone and style of most of his articles and addresses before his break with the university in 1910 are indicative of almost a double life. On one hand, he was the careful scholar; on the other, he betrayed his sense of the necessity for propaganda, by which means he could release the forces of poetry, intuition, and moral judgment. Viewed according to Hart's standards, Du Bois' scholarship declined. Although there is little that is illogical, untruthful, or hysterical about DuBois' polemical writing, the interplay of his two lives was not mutually helpful. Historical and sociological scholarship armed propaganda, but propaganda generally vitiated historical scholarship. By the time of his biography of John Brown in 1909, Du Bois had finished writing Germanic history. In seeking release from such restrictions, he chose as precedents the work not only of Macaulay and Carlyle but more importantly of Hippolyte Taine.

Hart recognized the significance of Du Bois' work in both scholarship and propaganda. In Hart's major work on the contemporary South, *The Southern South* (1910), he quoted Du Bois repeatedly and at length. He praised Du Bois' bibliographies on the study of black life, as well as his command of language.[39] On Du Bois' fiftieth birthday Hart acknowledged his respect for his former student: "Out of his fifty years of life I have followed a good thirty — and have counted him always among the ablest and keenest of our teacher-scholars, an American who viewed his country broadly."[40] This was the type of approval that Du Bois cherished. He had the highest regard for orthodox scholarship. Such work shaped and empowered his intellectual life, and he turned away from its demands only after a crisis of vocation and conscience.

The rein placed by Hart on the diffuse tendencies of the early Du Bois prose style came at a fortunate time. In his first year at Harvard Du Bois had suffered some unhappy moments when taking English C, a course on argumentative composition taught by the philosopher Josiah Royce. After three years on the *Fisk Herald* and academic work in forensics, Du Bois probably came to Harvard confident about his writing and public speaking. To his dismay, his first paper at Harvard was rejected by Royce (or one of his assistants) as being unworthy of a passing grade. "It was the first time in my scholastic career I had encountered such a failure," Du Bois remembered. "I was aghast."[41]

The subject of Du Bois' essay, the reason for its failure, and the response of the chastised scholar, all tell a great deal about Du Bois' attitude to writing. The essay was an attack on a miscreant Alabama senator. Du Bois himself later called it "long and blazing" and "with no holds barred." And as a result of its failure he set out to learn from those who had the authority to teach: "I realized that while style is subordinate to content . . . solid content with literary style carries a message further than poor grammar and muddled syntax."[42] He took the question of developing a command of English

composition very seriously. The following year he enrolled in the
companion course on argumentative composition, English D, again
taught by Royce. In his first year of graduate study he enrolled in
English 12, under Barrett Wendell. Du Bois obviously felt that he
had much to learn about the harnessing of power, the propriety of
syntax, and the orderly deployment of material.

The basic text of rhetorical instruction at both Fisk and Harvard
was Adams Sherman Hill's *The Principles of Rhetoric* (1878). Both
Royce and Wendell drew heavily on its theories and advice. Hill was
then Boylston Professor of Rhetoric and Oratory in Harvard
College. *The Principles of Rhetoric* attempted to set out those rules
to which "consciously or unconsciously, a good writer or speaker
must conform."[43] On the subject of oratory, Hill's work was
grounded squarely on the classical tradition of Aristotle's *Rhetoric*
and Cicero's speeches. On the writing of prose, Hill drew his
examples from British and American writers of his century, from
Samuel Taylor Coleridge to F. Marion Crawford. He passed
judgment on a variety of matters which both shaped and summarized the opinions of Du Bois' teachers on the question of composition, and through the pages of Hill's *Rhetoric* Du Bois was instructed
at both Fisk and Harvard in the *exordium* and the *narratio,* the *probatio* and the *refutatio.* Du Bois has been called a "preacher" by one
sympathetic critic, but there is really no resemblance between his
style of composition and the tradition of extemporaneous, rhythmi-
cal, and often incandescent language of the fundamentalist black
preacher.[44] Over the years Du Bois' speeches and his polemical writing became more direct and unadorned, but for the first fifty years
and more of his life he showed the mark of classical principles of
rhetoric and of other, more "modern" stylistic criteria encouraged
by Hill. *The Souls of Black Folk* is overwhelming evidence of the
influence of Hill and his disciple Wendell, just as *The Suppression
of the African Slave-Trade* and *The Philadelphia Negro* reflect the
standards of Hart. The style of Du Bois' propaganda, of all his work
away from the strictures of scholarship, found its general sanction in
Hill's *Rhetoric.*

As in the fields of history, sociology, and philosophy, Du Bois was
trained in the art of composition during a major era of transition.
"In times of intellectual ferment like ours," Hill warned, "novelties
in language are constantly coming to the surface . . . These novelties

. . . popular writers are too eager and scholars too slow to accept."[45]
The elegant, stylized syntax of the latter sentence ironically indicates that the question involved more than the use of neologisms.
The influence of classical Latin was still strong in an intellectual
community which had only recently begun to debate the status of
English literature as a proper discipline in the universities. The stylistic ideals of the literary critic of today — simplicity, directness, and
the judicious use of specialized vocabulary — were still in the future.
An essential aspect of the age of transition was a decline in the rule
of the gentleman of letters, although he still represented a powerful
cultural force. The pursuit of literary study was a gentlemanly art,
and the gentleman of letters never forgot his links to the past. Hill
was neither reactionary nor authoritarian. In presiding over a great
transitional era from the position of the most influential chair of
rhetoric and composition in the United States, Hill consciously arbi-
trated between the old and the new in language, so that his criteria
blended tradition and progressiveness into a mixture that was
neither old-fashioned nor quite modern. He made a severe
distinction between scientific and imaginative writing, but stressed
the limitations of the former.

To a large extent, Hill's standards became Du Bois'; he tended to
assume Hill's concerns, opinions, and prejudices. Not the least important influence in the area of argumentation was Hill's attitude
to his audience, which blended elementary psychology with the
manners of an educated gentleman. The way to an audience's mind
and feelings was through persuasion and indirection, not accusation
or anger. Persuasion combined with substantive argument to
capture the audience. Argument was the ordered display of evidence conforming to the rules of logic. Persuasion, in which sense,
feeling, and knowledge of human nature were essential, gave
ultimate power to cold argument.

Although almost two-thirds of his life was spent in the twentieth
century, Du Bois consistently showed that his training as a man of
letters was rooted in the Victorian age. His prose, especially in his
youth and middle age, sometimes discloses eighteenth century, even
Johnsonian echoes, as well as a fondness for certain archaic words
and expressions associated with romantic poetic diction. Yet Du
Bois retained many of the diverse strengths of nineteenth century
expression, taking them into an age and a society that has paid less

and less attention to the cultivation of prose. The older tradition, as reflected in Du Bois' writing, varied from the authoritative force of its tendency toward formalism to the desultory charm of its light-essay style, as exemplified by Hazlitt and Lamb or, in Du Bois' time, by Walter Raleigh and Arthur Quiller-Couch.

Occasionally quaint and old-fashioned, Du Bois' prose generally reflects the variety and vitality of its nineteenth century traditions, as he covered the wide ground between austere editorial journalism and poetry. His passion often reached the printed page in a restrained and at times even supplicatory manner; his coldest logic and statistical evidence, outside of explicit scholarship, were almost consistently relieved and empowered by poetic tropes. Du Bois relished the role of man of letters. It appealed to his elitism, his concern for culture, and his love of language. Hill taught him how such a man expressed himself. Wendell showed Du Bois how that man lived.

In studying under Wendell, Du Bois was exposed to a reactionary force in literary training. Wendell's theory of English composition drew heavily on Hill's *Rhetoric* for its terms and ideas; the qualities of style, for example, were clearness, force, and elegance; the principles of form were unity, mass, and coherence. Du Bois announced his intentions at the start of Wendell's course in a sentence which the professor read to the class: "I believe foolishly perhaps, but sincerely, that I have something to say to the world, and I have taken English 12 in order to say it well."[46] But again he found himself struggling to meet the highest standards of his instructor. Wendell gave his students a fair amount of freedom to choose their themes. Du Bois responded with five-finger exercises in literary reflection on subjects such as his room, his friends, vacations, excursions, and peculiarities of character.[47]

At midyear either Wendell or his assistant, a Mr. Fletcher, passed judgment on Du Bois' work: "Unthinking seems to me the word for your style. With a good deal of emotional power, you blaze away pretty much anyhow."[48] Occasionally a sentence, paragraph, or even a whole composition was excellent. More often there was "a nebulous, almost sulphurous indistinctness of outline." Du Bois appeared to hold very little power in reserve. The comment concluded that "more than most men, you need . . . an appreciation of good literature." The remarks indicate the early and basic difficulty of Du Bois' expression. His prose never lacked power. His problem was how to harness its energy. Without doubt, Wendell helped Du Bois to recognize his shortcomings and to correct them. But his influence appears to have had a distinctly corrupting potential.

Wendell had definite ideas about English composition which were then influencing the teaching of the subject throughout the United States, notably his insistence on the "daily theme." In spite of his respect for Hill, Wendell was also in some ways one of those "Anglomaniacs" of whom Hill wrote in the *Rhetoric*. Wendell was in fact an admitted and affected Anglophile, a self-conscious elitist who displayed himself ostentatiously as a man of culture in a vulgar world. Although one admirer insisted that he taught his students that "knowledge must be a part of life, that it must be used, wrought into the texture of being, and become the source of impulse," Wendell clearly belonged to that overrefined company, perceived by William James, which included Charles Eliot Norton and Matthew Arnold.[49]

Wendell's theory of literature was deeply influenced by his racial and national preferences. Literature in English was best written by those who were most English. The biased opinions of Wendell's *Literary History of America* (1900) may have set back scholarship in American literature by at least several years. With little formal reading in literature himself, Du Bois was being trained in the appreciation of letters by a charismatic figure disdainful of the problems of a struggling national literature, of the vitality of folk expression, or of the experimentation in forms and themes by which literature revitalizes itself. This reactionary approach left its mark on Du Bois. As editor of *The Crisis,* the monthly magazine of the NAACP, he played a major role in the Harlem Renaissance, but his inability to develop a taste for the progressive in art, or an appreciation of the earthier forms of expression, contributed to his failure to respond to the variety of black art. He was not deeply read in poetry, fiction, or literary criticism. His formal training was in other fields, and his informal reading was not nearly enough.

Wendell nevertheless brought a new dimension to Du Bois' intellectual experience. He helped Du Bois to appreciate the beauty of belles-lettres at precisely the time that Hart was stessing the rigor of scholarship. On the very question of historical writing Wendell differed from Hart. He favored the work of Carlyle and Macaulay over strict Germanic scholarship. Stylistically and culturally, Du Bois found himself being pulled in two different directions. While Hart was demanding specificity, documentation, and terseness, Wendell was advising a far more gentlemanly approach. At the most fundamental level, Du Bois was facing a choice between these ways. One led to science and the other to art. The life of the scholar contested the life of the poet. This was the basic vocational dualism of Du Bois' life, out of which would come three careers: historian and social scientist, poet and novelist, and propagandist. Du Bois might well have blushed to hear Wendell tell a Lowell Institute audience that "at some period in his career almost every undergraduate is seized with the idea that he can write fiction, and proceeds to submit to me a story."[50] Du Bois himself had submitted not only stories but at least one long poem. A particularly chilly reception by the instructor would not end his attempts at verse. He, too, has left a slender volume behind him.

Although Du Bois referred to Fisk rather than to Harvard or the University of Berlin as his true alma mater, Harvard was of first importance in his intellectual life. He left the school in the summer of 1892. In the fall he wrote to the *Fisk Herald* from Berlin about the significance of Harvard and Boston.[51] The university, he noted, offered the greatest opportunities for the acquisition of liberal culture among colleges in the United States. Because of its proximity to Boston, it was unequaled in high cultural standards and rich educational opportunities. The difference between Fisk and Harvard was the difference between 4,000 and 400,000 books, as well as the presence at Harvard of such figures as Oliver Wendell Holmes and Francis Peabody. Remembering the spiritual strictness of President Cravath at Fisk, Du Bois alluded ambiguously to Harvard's religious advantages, although he did not venture to say exactly what they were. Nowhere, he asserted, was so much encouragement given to talent and hard work. Du Bois condescendingly concluded that no Fisk student should miss an opportunity to spend a year attending Harvard.

DuBois was thus announcing to his old friends and professors at Fisk the "progress" he felt he had made as an individual, a scholar, and a man of religion and culture. After four years at Harvard and the attainment of his majority there, he had reason to see himself as a changed and far more able man. Whether Du Bois fully recognized the nature of the changes is open to question. With its optional religious services for undergraduates, its nondenominationalism, and its increasing secularity, Harvard had encouraged Du Bois in the surrender of his Congregational faith. Despite his remarks about Harvard's religious advantages, his years there marked the end of his participation in organized religion. The diversity of the entire experience enabled him to make the vocational transition to historical and social science with a compliant conscience and with a balance of old and new values. In place of dogma, he had acquired a new definition of religion which stressed its deeply personal nature and its justification as an emotional necessity, partly forced by the admitted existence of a supreme being and partly by man's intrinsic psychic vulnerability.

The example of William James, Royce, Santayana, Shaler, and others had stressed that the pursuit of beauty was as necessary as the search for truth, so that on his twenty-fifth birthday Du Bois could declare an ambition to succeed in both science and art. His faith in social science was also tempered by knowledge that the psychology of James and others, notably in the discovery and investigation of the subconscious as a major force, indicated a new frontier of human consciousness which resisted easy quantification and mass research. Finally, Harvard ground into Du Bois' thought a dedication to the life of the mind. He was able to see himself as part of the community of intellect even as he shifted his place into the unproved discipline of sociology. He was permitted a sense of sharing in the common sources and common goals of men of education and culture. Du Bois retained a justified intellectual self-confidence in the midst of his later vocational vacillation and ambivalence. He was stabilized always by his faith in the basic intellectual process and by the resilience of a shared intellectual tradition. The force of learning and culture purified and enriched itself, as it purified and enriched the world it served, by its allegiance to moral idealism and moral duty. This was the one faith that Du Bois would keep when all others were being assaulted by his experience of the world beyond the university gates.

There was a decided vagueness about Du Bois' academic plans for study in Germany. He was firm only about his desire to study there. Turned down in 1891 by the Slater Fund for the Education of Negroes in his application for financial aid, he sent a heated letter to its head, Rutherford B. Hayes, accusing him of insincerity in executing the plans of the fund for black education. Du Bois was encouraged to apply the following year. To the board of the organization he wrote, with some overstatement, "To properly finish my education . . . a careful training in a European university for at least a year is, in my mind, and the minds of my professors, indispensable."[52] In deciding to go to Germany, he was following the example not only of Hart but also of many other American professional scholars at the time, to whom Germany represented the summit of graduate training. With three degrees behind him and his doctorate substantially researched, though not yet finished, Du Bois felt nevertheless that he had more to learn as a formal student. With support from the Slater Fund he spent two years at the University of Berlin, where he came close to acquiring yet another degree. The importance of this European experience, however, went beyond formal university life.

Du Bois' academic work at Berlin was in the interrelated fields of economics, history, political science, and sociology, a cluster of disciplines that would only later break apart into almost autonomous academic areas. In his graduate work at Harvard he had read in each of these areas, having spent fully half of his time in historical research under Hart, with the remainder divided among economics, sociology, Roman jurisprudence, and English composition. He had studied the history of economic theory under Frank William Taussig, then an assistant professor at Harvard and later one of the most distinguished public figures in the field. Sociology at Harvard then bore little resemblance to the modern definition of the discipline. Although Peabody's course on the ethics of social reform purported to be an introduction to sociology, it was hardly the reason for Du Bois' choice of a career in the field. In graduate school, Du Bois enrolled in Edward Cummings' "The Principles of Sociology," offered under the aegis of political economy and stressing the development of the modern state and its social functions. By that time, 1891-1892, Du Bois was fully committed to history as his area of doctoral specialization, but he probably found himself interested for the first time in the potential of this new field.

Compared to Peabody's emphasis on ethical questions, Cummings' political and economic biases provided a more modern perspective on the two crucial ingredients of sociology: its insistence on empirical research as the basis for all conclusions, and its distinct tendency toward seeing itself as a remedial science. These ingredients, yet undeveloped at Harvard, were quickly becoming essential at Berlin. The implications of this mixture of empiricism and social action would seduce Du Bois away from history. The University of Berlin itself did not provide the models for rigorous empirical sociology. Such models were even then being prepared in London and Chicago, to be published as Charles Booth's seminal work, *Life and Labour of the People in London* (1891-1903), and the companion volume by Jane Addams and others, *Hull-House Maps and Papers* (1895). When Du Bois left Cambridge for Germany in 1892, therefore, he had no firmer plan than that he would continue his studies in the general areas of political theory, economics, and history.

As at Harvard, Du Bois found himself studying in Berlin under distinguished and influential men. During his first semester, for example, he was admitted to seminars supervised by Gustav von Schmoller and Adolf Wagner in history, economics, and sociology. He also studied under Heinrich Rudolf von Gneist, then professor of jurisprudence; he heard Max Weber lecture as a visiting professor during 1893. Of all these German teachers Du Bois remembered most clearly Heinrich von Treitschke, the Prussian historian and political theoretician whom Du Bois called "the German Machiavelli."[53]

There were undoubtedly far greater and more stimulating differences of opinion among the political scientists at Berlin than at Harvard. Wagner was a firm supporter of state socialism and was especially critical of the laissez-faire school of Manchester economists founded on the theories of Adam Smith. In this basic, anticapitalist position, he was joined by Schmoller, whom Du Bois identified as the leader of the younger radical German economists. Weber himself was only four years older than Du Bois, with his work on the relationship of capitalism to the spirit of Protestant ethics still in the future.

As Broderick has pointed out, Schmoller effected a major shift in Du Bois' scholarly and vocational focus in the course of his research seminar in political economy.[54] Both Schmoller and Wagner believed in inductive economic analysis based on the gathering of historical and social evidence in the form of precise, scholarly studies. Schmoller was more radical in his belief in this principle, as Du Bois himself noted at the time, but both men opposed the deductive, theoretical approach of the Manchester school. Most important, the central aim of Schmoller's analyses was to provide the basis for social justice through economic change. At the same time he insisted that analysis preceded social action and determined the nature and scope of that action. Radical change was the aim, but there were to be no radical social solutions without support from evidence gathered in rigorous, scholarly fashion. Under Schmoller's guidance, Du Bois was diverted away from Hart's history, although he obviously benefited from the academic rigor that was vital to both men.

Schmoller, however, offered Du Bois a solution to the most urgent of his vocational dilemmas: how to combine objectivity and activism. Through remedial sociology he could serve simultaneously his moral imperatives, his commitment to truth, the advancement of his people, and his love of the scholarly life. Properly applied, his training could facilitate social and moral reform for both the black community and the whites who had the power to effect change. Schmoller led Du Bois to a new career. Although there was much that was novel in Du Bois' work in black America, his general career as sociologist was founded on elements shared with his professor. As Broderick has observed, these elements were "first, accumulation of accurate information; then, social policy based on that information; the whole suffused with the ideal of justice."[55]

Heinrich von Treitschke stood on the far side of the political field from Wagner, Schmoller, and Weber. As a historian of Germany in the nineteenth century, Treitschke belonged confidently to the older tradition of scholarship that included Macaulay and Carlyle. Indeed his great work has often been compared to Macaulay's *History of England.* His Prussian viewpoint was at least as patriotic and morally complacent as Macaulay's insular perspective on England. Treitschke had little time for socialism or for liberal politics based on the sovereignty of democratic ideals. Like Carlyle, he believed that history is made by the powerful wills of great men through a process in which the masses play no significant part. While he believed, also like Carlyle, in the necessity of moral rectitude, he was fascinated at the same time by the aggrandizement and deployment of power. His concern was not for himself but for his country. He wished to see the German state thrive. Specifically, he wanted Germany to become involved in the seizure of overseas territory in order to make her, however belatedly, a major imperial power. Treitschke was thus an early proponent of the politics that would lead Germany to disaster twice in the twentieth century.

It was perfectly consistent with Du Bois' thought that he should be fascinated by this romantic authoritarianism or incipient fascism. The idea of a man such as Bismarck welding a historically disparate people like the Germans through the force of his will and personality, converting chaos into a strong political entity, intrigued Du Bois, who in his valedictory speech at Fisk had held up Bismarck as an example of what could be done for Afro-America. In spite of Hart's scholarly method, Du Bois was still inclined to see history in Carlyle's way, cherishing the power of the irresistible individual and the small band of natural leaders of intellect and vision. Treitschke, he wrote at the time, was not "a narrow man" but had the outlook of the "born aristocrat."[56]

The romantic vision of the state, with its stress on the authentic *geist,* spirit, or soul of the nation, appealed for a long time to Du Bois, as it tends to appeal to someone who is obsessed by his people's historic deprivation and disunity and who yearns for a greater national or racial future. Du Bois was able to brush aside the full meaning of the fact that Treitschke once declaimed against mulattoes in his presence. Romantic authoritarian nationalism is more than sympathetic to racism and racist oppression. The seed of Treitschke's belief that mulattoes are inferior fell from the same plant that eventually would bear the evil flower of Hitler's genocide. Although Du Bois never succumbed completely to romantic nationalist authoritarianism, strains of its ideology persisted in his thought for much of his life. In Berlin, away from the philosophic liberalism of William James and Harvard, Du Bois was susceptible once again to his almost instinctive attraction to arbitrary power, force of will, and conspicuous elitism.

Du Bois' German years introduced him to meaningful socialist thought and practice. Socialism offered a trenchant criticism of the motives of an exploitative society; it promised an end to economic and racial abuse. "Naturally," Du Bois wrote at the time, "I am attracted to the socialist movement."[57] He recognized that he had been trained at Harvard not to understand Marxism, but mainly to

refute it. Taussig had lectured on socialism in his course on economic theory, but Taussig was certainly no socialist. Although when
faced with the flamboyant and charismatic Treitschke, Du Bois
found the Christian socialism of Adolf Wagner somewhat drab, he
nevertheless attended meetings and became a member of the Socialist Club. On a trip through Eastern Europe, the sight of masses of
destitute white folk enabled him to begin sympathizing with some of
the basic tenets of Marxism: the rapacity of the propertied few, the
definition of capitalist society as the struggle of classes, the common
suffering of the world's poor, the need for solidarity among the oppressed. Here began Du Bois' engagement, at first tentatively, with
the teachings of Karl Marx.

While the plight of the European masses was leading Du Bois to
an interest in socialism, the quality of the middle- and upper-class
European way of life was also affecting him: "something of the
possible beauty and elegance of life permeated my soul; I gained a
respect for manners."[58] In an early example of the expatriate haven
that Europe was to provide for certain disaffected black thinkers,
Du Bois felt a new sense of manhood in a milieu where he was suddenly free and unusually welcome. He believed later that Europe
deeply modified the "racial provincialism" he had acquired at Fisk
and Harvard. "I became more human; learned the place in life of
'Wine, Women, and Song'; I ceased to hate or suspect people simply
because they belonged to one race or color."[59] He visited museums
and theaters, confirming in his two Berlin years a fondness for
European high culture. This was a significant stage in Du Bois'
intellectual life. The key to his acceptance of European culture was
his discovery that the white world was not monolithic. The degree of
anti-Americanism in Europe surprised and reassured him. He saw
that a distinction needed to be made between white America and
Europe. America came to represent to him in some respects a derac-
inated imitation of European culture. The only indigenous American music of any value, he early insisted, was the spirituals of black
America. Paradoxically, then, Du Bois intensified his allegiance to
white cultural values by dividing the white world. He could thereafter revile white America while bowing to European art. He remained a disciple of that art from the earliest days when, fresh from
Germany, he urged the beauty of Raphael's Sistine Madonna on a
black audience at Wilberforce.[60] He did not think, Du Bois said,

that he would ever forget the eyes of the Mother of God as she stepped from the clouds with the Christ child in her arms. A black nationalist during a great part of his life, Du Bois nevertheless remained a devotee of white cultural expression. He reported white critical admiration of ragtime and jazz, as well as the earthier blues, but to the end of his life he himself listened to Brahms, Schumann, and Handel, in addition to the black spirituals.

When Du Bois returned to America in 1894, his "Age of Miracles" had come to an end. He had been a university student for nine years. From the fall of 1894 to 1910 he would be directly associated with university life as teacher and researcher at Wilberforce University, the University of Pennsylvania, and Atlanta University. He remained throughout his life a firm believer in the value of formal education as "a glimpse of the higher life, the broader possibilities of humanity," which is granted to the man who "pauses four short years to learn what living means."[61] His life had been deeply affected by the powerful men to whom he had been exposed, by the contrasting social and intellectual milieus between which he moved, and by his own intense receptivity to new ideas and new impressions. He had left Great Barrington as a promising but innocent young scholar. Ending his formal apprenticeship in the search for truth, Du Bois confidently prepared to move toward his felt destiny as a leader of men.

His education was the rock upon which he would build the structure he so eagerly desired: a life of fame for himself in science and in art, which would help him to raise the level of his people. His confidence was not entirely misplaced. In the next seventeen years he would establish a modest but enduring reputation as an American pioneer in the field of empirical sociology. In addition, his first collection of essays would establish him as an important American essayist and prose stylist. But such success would not resolve the vocational tension of his life as Du Bois searched for an authentic voice and role. The end of his years as a student was the beginning of a generation of spiritual, artistic, and intellectual ferment which would eventually pull him out of the serene light of the college and into the glare of public activism.

CHAPTER THREE

A Divided Career

I am glad I am living, I rejoice as a strong man to run a race, and I am
strong — is it egotism is it assurance — or is it the silent call of the world
spirit that makes me feel that I am royal and that beneath my sceptre a
world of kings shall bow. The hot dark blood of that black forefather
born king of men — is beating at my heart, and I know I am either a genius or a fool . . . Be the Truth what it may I will seek it on the pure assumption that it is worth seeking — and Heaven nor Hell, God nor Devil
shall turn me from my purpose till I die. I will in this second quarter century of my life, enter the dark forest of the unknown world for which I
have so many years served my apprenticeship . . .

These are my plans: to make a name in science, to make a name in literature and thus to raise my race.   (Du Bois, 1893)

"I BUILDED GREAT castles in Spain and lived therein. I
dreamed and loved and wandered and sang; then, after two long
years in Europe, I dropped suddenly back into 'nigger'-hating
America!"[1] Du Bois returned to America in June 1894. The Age of
Miracles was over; the "Days of Disillusion," as he later called the
first years of his career, had begun.[2] They started with his anxious
search among black colleges for a teaching position, a choice forced
on him, in spite of his highly sophisticated education, by the racism
of his time. Compelled at first to teach subjects of which he knew
little, he eventually found, at Atlanta, the scholarly role for which
he had been trained and the university setting in which he was comfortable. The major result of these academic years 1894-1910 was a
body of empirical sociology, notably *The Philadelphia Negro* (1899)
and the Atlanta University Publications edited by Du Bois. The
fruit of a secondary career of cultural commentary based on history
and sociology was *The Souls of Black Folk* (1903), a work of
definitive importance to the future of black culture. The decade
between his return to America and the publication of *Souls* saw Du

Bois move from conservatism to a rejection of the most entrenched black political position, that of Booker T. Washington. The tension between his academic role and the free expression of his political and cultural views provided the main drama of his intellectual life as he moved toward maturity.

At Wilberforce University, the African Methodist Episcopal school in Ohio where Du Bois taught from 1894 to 1896, he found himself occupying the chair of classics as professor of Latin and Greek. He had accepted the position after finding no opening at Howard, Hampton, and Fisk and before receiving an offer to teach mathematics from Booker T. Washington's Tuskegee Institute. Du Bois' famed hauteur, primed in Europe and reinforced by his formal foreign clothing, his German student's cane, and his smart Vandyke beard, did not help to make him immediately popular among what seemed at times an impossibly lethargic group. He found himself "against a stone wall. Nothing stirred before my patient pounding! Or if it stirred, it soon slept again."[3] When the school did move, it was often in the direction of religious frenzy stirred up by frequent spiritual revivals and other practices repugnant to the skeptical young intellectual.[4] Wilberforce was financially poor and seemed inefficient; moreover, there was little or no chance that sociology, as Du Bois knew it, would be encouraged as a discipline. Although he believed that he had eventually gained the respect of the campus as a tireless teacher and aide, it was with eagerness that he accepted an offer from the University of Pennsylvania to carry out, between 1896 and 1897, a study of the black people of Philadelphia.

Before leaving Wilberforce in the summer of 1896 with his wife of three months, Nina Gomer Du Bois, a student from Cedar Rapids, Iowa, he had the satisfaction of seeing his doctoral dissertation published as the first volume of the Harvard Historical Studies. Although *The Suppression of the African Slave-Trade to the United States, 1638-1870* broke new ground in the scholarly study of American slavery, it marked the high point of Du Bois' attachment to a conservative methodology of history. The work observed a degree of scrupulous documentation and a denial of opinion and poetic insight never again matched by its author. In 1896, its year of publication, Du Bois could congratulate himself on complying with "the general principles laid down in German universities"; in 1954, in an

"Apologia" to a new edition, he would regret that Marx and Freud — by which he meant class analysis and his poetic and psychological intuition — had not informed the study.[5]

The crux of the book is its balance between severe evidentiary process and moral criticism. Du Bois' thesis is that moral weakness in the face of economic opportunity led to continuation of the slave trade after legal statutes forbade it; conversely, it was not moral insistence but economic and political pressures acting in concert with moral motives that ended the trade. The final message, that "it behooves nations as well as men to do things at the very moment when they ought to be done," is therefore superfluous.[6] For all his restraint, Du Bois had deliberately written a chapter of the moral history of his country, a fact that unites the sometimes dry *Suppression of the African Slave-Trade* with his later, more sensational works of history. Though he was prevented by a comparative ignorance of Marx from more sweeping historical analogy, his relentless documentation of the failure of antislave trade laws still made moral commentary of a high, graphic order, written in a restrained, clear, and often graceful prose.

At this point in his career, as the historian John Hope Franklin observed, Du Bois saw no particular conflict between history and advocacy.[7] In this work, however, his moral inference is an integral part of the argument; the evaluation of the national conscience is germane to the causes of the rise and fall of the trade. There is no special pleading, apart from the final appeal, no disposition of the evidence to create images that would have ideological consequences; there is, in other words, almost no hint of propaganda. His respect for truth was still almost fundamentalist; his ideas on how best to move a nation were still politically and psychologically naive. The exposure of injustice before the white educated classes, he believed, would steadily bring reform. The scholar, as Du Bois would warn the social statistician in his next book, "must ever tremble lest some personal bias, some moral conviction or some unconscious trend of thought due to previous training, has to a degree distorted the picture in his view."[8]

In the slums of Philadelphia, where they arrived in the fall of 1896, Du Bois and his wife lived amidst "dirt, drunkenness, poverty, and crime. Murder sat on our doorstep, police were our government, and philanthropy dropped in with periodic advice."[9] Philanthropy may have come in the person of Susan P. Wharton, a prominent member of the College Settlement House Association in the city and the person credited with taking the initiative in arranging for the study. Samuel McCune Lindsay, professor of sociology in the Wharton School of the university, was directly responsible for Du Bois' employment and was his nominal supervisor. Du Bois himself did all the door-to-door interviewing of the Seventh Ward (later claiming to have spoken to about 5000 persons), the library research on the history of the city, the mapping of demographic patterns, and the other details of sociological investigation that resulted in *The Philadelphia Negro* (1899). He spent over a year in the city, apart from the summer of 1897, when he went to Farmville, Virginia, to study one source of black migration to the northern city.[10]

The Philadelphia work, its author observed, sought to discover the geographic distribution of blacks, "their occupations and daily life, their homes, their organizations, and, above all, their relation to their million white fellow citizens" (1).[11] Concentrating first on the Seventh Ward, where perhaps one-fifth of the forty thousand blacks lived, Du Bois relied on a variety of questionnaires to uncover the basic information. He supplemented this core of facts with general surveys of other areas, especially those where differences seemed conspicuous, with previously gathered statistics and history, and with the opinion of qualified observers. The basis of his study was statistical and empirical. While he admitted the possibility of error and often allowed for it, he was finally satisfied that he had accurately represented black Philadelphia.

The excellence of *The Philadelphia Negro* has generally been admitted. Gunnar Myrdal singled it out for high praise in *An American Dilemma;* for F.L. Broderick, it represented Du Bois' only "first-class" scholarship.[12] The comparative novelty of its empirical and statistical component has tended, however, to obscure the artfulness of this book. Only slightly less austere in appearance than *Suppression of the African Slave-Trade,* the work is nevertheless a study in the art of cultural suasion through social science. At least one reviewer conceded that its author had been more severe than impartial in representing his fellow blacks.[13] Du Bois disarmed his potential critics both by his scholarly ability and by a process of manipulation, perhaps largely unconscious, that takes *The Philadelphia Negro* beyond progressive sociology.

In offering environmental rather than racial explanations of his subject, Du Bois made a remarkable distinction and choice. Ignoring for the occasion the current "genetic" approach to social theory, which was by no means repulsive to him, he refused to declare that unattractive aspects of black behavior were ingrained by race. He also meticulously refrained from ascribing attractive aspects or "gifts" of the black culture to race, although even as he was preparing the study, he was eloquently expressing ideas based on that assumption. He appeared to accept the conventional definition of race — and perhaps even to share racist views — by often deploring certain black social patterns; but without a genetic basis, his description of his race is in fact a description of a nation, which he was free to criticize without inferring its innate inferiority. Thus, *The Philadelphia Negro* is a historic document in the representation of black American cultural nationalism.

Du Bois' social criticism was harsh. The black folk of his time were "a people comparatively low in the scale of civilization" (66); the high death rate indicated "how far this race is behind the great vigorous, cultivated race about it" (163); stealing and fighting, common in the black community, "are ever the besetting sins of half-developed races" (257); and "the Negro is, to be sure, a religious creature — most primitive folk are" (201). A neo-Calvinist note creeps in when he approves a study describing a third of the black prisoners in one jail as criminal by "natural and inherent depravity" (285). Du Bois placed the blame for deplorable conditions on the social and moral depredation of slavery, on the disruptive waves of both white and black immigrants to the city (he called them "barbarians"), on inadequate black effort, and on white prejudice, which was, however, not responsible "for all, or perhaps the greater part of the Negro problem" (322). As in his first book, he made no sweeping analogies. The black man was a creature born deformed as a result of enslavement, with no meaningful prior history; and the "Negro problems" must be solved by the combined work of blacks and whites.

The national characteristics of the blacks of Philadelphia emerge clearly from the study. Above all, it portrays no faceless homogeneity but a class structure that signifies progress and must be respected as such; institutions of varying success; serious social delinquency but a capable leadership class; social fragmentation but also common bonds, indeed a common bondage; and dignity and a capacity for heroism, as exemplified by the many brief histories illustrating the section on "color prejudice" (322-55). The worst villains are not the poor and ignorant but those who abuse their talents, "shrewd and sleek politicians, gamblers and confidence men, with a class of well-dressed and partially undetected prostitutes" (61). The path to improvement is through the acquisition of skills and cultivated learning, the accumulation of property, stern moral values, and purposeful political action.

Although it often views life as through a microscope, *The Philadelphia Negro* is the natural precursor of *The Souls of Black Folk;* it is no accident that the most memorable passage of the later book — the identification of dual souls, American and African, as the constant dilemma of the black American — was first published in the middle of Du Bois' Philadelphia effort.[14] The portrait of the author that emerges from the first work is, however, different from that of the later. Both are self-consciously drawn. In *The Philadelphia Negro* his scholarly "objectivity" is so refined that it is impossible to gather from the text that its author was, as he boldly declared in the "Forethought" to *Souls,* "flesh of the flesh" of his subject. Aloofness leads at times to condescension, as when he notes the "turgid rhetoric" of a black church document, and moral grandeur comes close to prissiness when the subject is sex. A careful distinction is made between moral standards and religious feeling; the church is a social institution, its dogma is irrelevant. The trials of the upper classes are noted with stoicism, not anger. Only once does Du Bois seem to point to the pathos of his own situation, exploited by the University of Pennsylvania: "what [white] university would appoint a promising young Negro as tutor?"[15] The voice of the book coolly, sometimes coldly, presents a brief for black humanity, distrustful of the power of passion, reticent almost to the point of that glacial severity of which Du Bois would become a master.

Having completed his work in Philadelphia, Du Bois decided to accept an offer from Atlanta University to teach economics, history, and sociology there. Wilberforce had been the "Days of Disillusion"; the Atlanta years were a time of "the Discipline of Work and Play," of "great spiritual upturning, of the making and unmaking of ideals, of hard work and hard play."[16] Du Bois, the best-known scholar then at Atlanta University, enjoyed the confidence of Horace Bum-

stead and Edmund Ware, successive presidents of the school. It later
seemed to Du Bois that he had found in Atlanta his life's work and
place. He was thrilled by the vision of black youth strolling in the
groves of academe: "Not at Oxford or at Leipsic, not at Yale or
Columbia, is there an air of higher resolve or more unfettered
striving."[17]

Founded, like his alma mater Fisk, by the American Missionary
Association, Atlanta University insisted on its religious though
nondenominational character, but it was far more secular and
academically progressive than Wilberforce, as demonstrated by
Bumstead's support of sociology, a discipline still in its infancy even
at institutions as privileged as the University of Chicago and Columbia. Both the President and Trustee George Bradford of Boston,
who like Du Bois was a former student of sociologist Edward Cummings at Harvard, were anxious to move beyond the scope of the
Hampton and Tuskegee Conferences on black life, which generally
ignored scholarly rigor in favor of more informal discussion and
analysis. Du Bois developed an undergraduate sociology program
that trained students in empirical study, using only basic texts and
census reports; eventually a post graduate course in more original
research was instituted.[18]

If Du Bois "found" himself, as he claimed, at Atlanta University,
the city itself helped him further to define his racial identity; its
racially exclusive facilities and racist manners were an unending
affront. He left often to lecture throughout the United States and
beyond, visiting Europe in 1900 to attend a Pan-African Congress in
London and to represent black America at the Paris Exposition.
From Atlanta he corresponded with a variety of intellectuals, from
former professors at Harvard, such as James, Royce, Hart, Norton,
and Cummings, to other distinguished figures, such as Max Weber,
E.R.A. Seligman, Bliss Perry, Horace Traubel, and Franz Boas.
The deepest tragedy of his life, the death of his little son Burghardt,
took place in Atlanta. His extended campaign against Booker T.
Washington through his leadership of the radical Niagara Movement, his earliest attempts at magazine editorship, his rise to the top
of Afro-American leadership, all took place while he taught at the
university. He carried on, in essence, two careers: one as an academic sociologist teaching and editing the Atlanta University Publications, the other as a political and cultural commentator whose

Souls of Black Folk would establish him as the most insightful interpreter of the black experience on the American scene.

The first two Atlanta University Publications, the outgrowth of conferences on urban conditions among blacks, were completed before Du Bois took over the project. The empirical method, instituted by Bumstead and Bradford, had been diluted from the start by inspirational addresses and homiletic discussions designed to appeal to a wide audience. Du Bois swept away such contributions and insisted on higher standards of statistical and empirical work.

He conceived the idea of a hundred-year program, comprising ten-year cycles of volumes on the ten "great subjects" of black life, which would eventually provide "a body of sociological material unsurpassed in human annals."[19] The studies were to cover the areas of health, crime, the family, morals and manners, business, elementary and college education, industry, and the church, as well as to provide a bibliography of related writing. Aimed at a broad audience in theory, the Publications contained much material clearly intended for specialists only. They swelled to two hundred pages in 1903 in the series' longest work, *The Negro Church;* from 1900, bibliographies became a regular feature of each volume. Du Bois alone edited the series from 1898 until 1910, when the task was shared with Augustus G. Dill, his former student and his successor as teacher of sociology at Atlanta. They prepared three more volumes before Du Bois' withdrawal after 1914.

Produced under extremely difficult financial conditions at best, the Atlanta studies vary greatly in quality. Certain volumes, such as *The Health and Physique of the Negro American* (1906), with its photographs of black American facial types and cephalic and skeletal measurements, and *Morals and Manners among Negro Americans* (1914), now seem mementos of largely discredited intellectual approaches. Other pieces, notably those most narrowly conceived, such as *The College-Bred Negro* (1900), *The Negro Common School* (1901), and their successor studies in 1910 and 1911, are based on sound principles and present useful data. Still others, like *The Negro Church* (1903) and *The Negro American Family* (1908), while hardly flawless, are pioneering works of imagination and creativity in the field of black studies, though for thoroughness and order, according to Elliott M. Rudwick, *The Negro Artisan* volumes (1902, 1912) are probably the finest.[20]

Du Bois apologized repeatedly for the general quality of the series. Relying on unpaid researchers, graduates from Atlanta and its sister schools, and struggling for funds, he had to settle for work based on a delicate compromise, "simple enough to be pursued by voluntary effort, and valuable enough to add to our scientific knowledge."[21] Eventually a conscious policy was adopted to lower the scholarly standards to achieve a broader educational purpose. Some of the most poignant and instructive passages are the opinions and statements of nameless respondents, although as science, these pieces have little value. Du Bois increasingly saw the limitations of statistics. This "cursory sketch," he wrote in 1906 of a survey of "Negro-American" racial types, hardly justified "definite conclusions. Its object is rather to blaze the way and point out a few general truths."[22]

The Publications never became a vehicle for partisan propaganda even during the height of the Du Bois-Washington controversy. They continued to document the perceived shortcomings of black life, such as the high death rate, disease, the decline of skilled trades, and the lack of religious faith ("It is absolutely necessary for a new people to begin their careers with the religious verities").[23] But in all these areas except crime, the chief emphasis came to be on the remarkable progress that blacks had made since slavery. This confidence in the quality of the race was one of those "general truths" on which Du Bois insisted. Four other "truths" emerged clearly from the Atlanta studies and justified the work in his eyes: first, the illegal, immoral, and intolerable restraints placed on black people; second, the fact of the black race as a cohesive if varied whole, in other words, a nation; third, the continuity between Africa and Afro-America; and fourth, a profound belief in liberal culture.

In *The Philadelphia Negro,* Du Bois had concluded by warning blacks that, in spite of slavery and prejudice, "men have a right to demand that the members of a civilized community be civilized; that the fabric of human culture, so laboriously woven, be not wantonly or ignorantly destroyed."[24] By his fourth Publication he was hammering away equally at the low quality of certain black schools and at the white denial of funds for black education in the South; he wanted national aid for all Southern schools and federal intervention in funding through a powerful Bureau of Education. In *The Negro Artisan,* he exposed discrimination in union ranks, providing lists of hostile labor organizations. His language was sometimes unscientific. Discussing revenue from prisoner labor in Georgia, he noted "the sinister increase of this blood money," which encouraged criminal convictions by making profit the object of the prison system.[25] By 1909 he no longer placed responsibility for the failure of their social institutions on blacks: "so long as the race is deprived of the ballot it is impossible to make such organizations of the highest efficiency in any avenue of life, whether it be education, religion, work, or social reform; the impossibility of the Negro accomplishing the best work so long as he is kept in political serfdom is manifest even to the casual student."[26]

But the Publications also early acknowledged segregation as a unifying force in black life, a controversial position that Du Bois would stress in the 1930s. He was anxious to show in 1907 that while blacks appeared to have little business achievement, there existed among them "a co-operative arrangement of industries and services" tending to become "a closed economic circle" largely independent of whites. This fact explained "many of the anomalies" in the society puzzling to the student of black affairs; the economic response to segregation seemed to be one aspect of an enforced but real nationalism based on a distinct philosophy of Afro-American culture, which "perhaps will never surrender itself to the ideals of the surrounding group."[27] Du Bois criticized the insecurity that led some blacks to patronize white professionals rather than those of their own race. He never defended segregation; indeed, he never ceased to attack it. But each volume of the Atlanta University Publications was a kind of *de facto* separatist statement, documenting a segregated situation within which blacks were legally constrained, based on material gathered almost entirely by blacks, and edited by a black man for the clear purpose of black social advancement.

The mark of Du Bois' growing cultural nationalism in his sociology was his increasing interest in Africa. His first Publication made a vague connection between religion in Africa and America: black secret societies were termed a survival of "the primitive love of mystery."[28] *The Negro Church* provided the first significant look at the African past and at Africans in the West Indies, for which the editor relied heavily on the *Encyclopedia Britannica*. From that time, Du Bois' increasing political radicalism was matched by a deepening academic knowledge of Africa; he discovered in 1906 what he called "the new anthropology," with its comforting doctrine of cultural and anthropological relativity. At his invitation, Franz Boas gave the commencement address at Atlanta on the greatness of African culture and took part in a conference in 1906 on the "health and physique of the Negro American."[29]

Du Bois' most influential book on Africa and Africans outside the continent would come in 1915 with the publication of *The Negro*. But from 1906 he ceased separating the Afro-American experience from Pan-Africanism and the African past. In his 1907 Publication on economic cooperation, for example, the relationship is strikingly developed; similarly, volumes on social betterment, on the black artisan, and on morals and manners discussed these matters with an African reference. Almost half of the Atlanta University Publications, in fact, show the influence of incipient Pan-Africanist thought on the once inviolable ground of Du Bois' social science. Empiricism had given way to yet another "general truth."

Although his controversy with Booker T. Washington over the relative merits of "higher" and agro-industrial training left little direct impression on the Atlanta studies, Du Bois' cultural standards and ideas were clear. In 1900 he described the college graduate as "the group leader, the man who sets the ideals of the community where he lives, directs its thought and heads its social movement."[30] In a characteristic and innovative touch, he set a stanza of poetry by Paul Laurence Dunbar as an epigraph to his first volume at Atlanta, and from time to time more poetry appeared. Beyond such adornment, he seldom appeared in this scientific series as an apostle of the arts. A more political definition of culture informs the Publications, and its terms were essentially those of *The Philadelphia Negro,* with exceptions. The sometimes prim tone of the earlier book gave way to a less fastidious spirit; the distance between the scientist and the observed culture considerably lessened; scientific detachment was modified by a more democratic taste and a judiciousness that did not hesitate to express sympathy and even love. The educated and moneyed classes had a strict responsibility to guide the masses, he insisted, through their personal example of a respect for learning, whether in the arts, the sciences, or vocational skills, and through socially directed organizations such as the church. The leaders were to stress the integrity of the family, the virtues of sexual discipline, the necessity of hard work, efficiency, co-operation, and thrift. Both civil rights and a sense of civic responsibility were needed. Armed with a faith in himself and his people, the black man would prevail over the normal trials of life and the special circumstances under which he labored in America.

Scholarly work in history and sociology was only one of the two intellectual careers simultaneously maintained by Du Bois before he left university life in 1910. The second was a stream of articles and addresses that placed little emphasis on documentation, though they drew strongly on scholarship. The dimension represented by this career as advocate and cultural interpreter, poet and visionary, has in many instances proved ultimately more important than the first. Always an admirer of scholarship, Du Bois himself discouraged a proper treatment of his more imaginative writing. In his autobiographical statements he seldom mentioned such works as *The Souls of Black Folk* or his novels; in fact, the novels are not mentioned at all in his last and most comprehensive autobiography, although in 1940 he had called his second novel, *Dark Princess,* "my favorite book."[31] Yet *The Souls of Black Folk* may be the greatest work of Du Bois' imagination.

The period of Du Bois' formal education coincided with the rise of segregationist legislation across the South. The political acts of racism were supported by the science of their day. The declaration by the United States Supreme Court in the landmark case *Plessy* v. *Ferguson* (1896) that "legislation is powerless to eradicate racial instincts" took the argument over segregation out of the political hustings and into its proper setting, the intellectual cosmos of the nineteenth century. The controversy centered in that interweaving of arguments concerning genetics, heritage, and destiny called the "Linnaean Web" by Oscar Handlin.[32] Racial investigation, as Winthrop Jordan has shown, had been significant in Western thought since at least the 1500s, enjoying by the end of the nineteenth century the status of a science.[33]

The Linnaean web, spun by scholars out of the scientific work of the Swedish botanist Karl von Linné, the French natural historian Georges Buffon, and the German medical scientist Johan Blumenbach in the eighteenth century, was augmented most effectively in the nineteenth century by Arthur de Gobineau, who paved the way for a new "scholarly" method of viewing the continuum of history and the potential of both individuals and the cultures to which they belonged. By the end of the century, though, scientific rigor had become increasingly unimportant. "Many a racist," Thomas Gossett has concluded, "awaited breathlessly some scheme of race classification which would withstand the testing methods of science and was prepared — once such a method was found — to pile mountains of *ad hoc* theory concerning the character and temperament of the races onto any discoveries concerning their measurable physical differences . . . They did not really need proof for what they *knew* was there."[34]

The variations in racial "science" served generally to reinforce the concept of white supremacy over other races. Statistics such as those on cranial capacity, conspicuous in Du Bois' own *Health and Physique of the Negro American,* added to the weight of a hundred and fifty years of scientific study and supported a body of quasi-scientific books hostile to blacks. Du Bois' writings were his response to the prevailing opinion of an age that also produced, for example, Charles Carroll's *The Negro a Beast, or In the Image of God* (1900), William B. Smith's *The Color Line: A Brief in Behalf of the Unborn* (1905), and Robert W. Shufeldt's *The Negro: A Menace to American Civilization* (1907). A school of fiction complemented this intense quasi-scientific vilification of blacks as a race. In 1902 Thomas Dixon, Jr., published *The Leopard's Spots: A Romance of the White Man's Burden,* regarded by one critic as "perhaps the most bigoted of American novels."[35] Three years later came Dixon's best-known and best-selling work, *The Clansman: An Historical Romance of the Ku Klux Klan.* The appearance of *The Souls of Black Folk* between these two novels underlines the historic timeliness of the collection as a challenge to the most sustained intellectual attack on blacks in the history of American race relations.

Entangling himself deliberately in the Linnaean web, Du Bois involved himself, as a man of learning, in the complexity of racial science. While at Harvard, he had once come face to face with an emblem of the problem, "a series of skeletons arranged from a little monkey to a tall well-developed white man, with a Negro barely outranking a chimpanzee."[36] Defiantly proud of being black, he agonized over the significance of certain unflattering aspects of black life. In his oration at the Harvard commencement exercises of 1890, when he spoke on Jefferson Davis as a representative of civilization, Du Bois sought to identify the most precious qualities of the black race, with which the heroic force and egotism of Davis might be compared. These qualities he summed up in the doctrine of the submissive man. Submission was not cowardice, he insisted, but a meaningful sacrifice of personal assertion for the common good. The black man embodies the idea of personal submission.[37]

The Harvard address was a premature response to the fundamental questions answered thirteen years later by *The Souls of Black Folk*. In 1897 Du Bois made two statements that remain, with few reservations, definitive expressions of his concept of blackness and the meaning of the Afro-American experience. The first, "The Conservation of Races," was delivered in March to the American Negro Academy, recently founded by the black churchman Alexander Crummell; the second, "Strivings of the Negro People," appeared in the *Atlantic Monthly* in August and reappeared substantially unchanged as the first chapter of *The Souls of Black Folk*.

In "The Conservation of Races," Du Bois flatly declared his belief in racial theory and "the hard limits of natural law": he who "ignores or seeks to ignore the race idea in history ignores and overrides the central thought of all history." Physical differences between the races were few; Darwin and other scientists had presented evidence asserting "the whole scientific doctrine of human brotherhood." But other differences between the races did exist: "The deeper differences are spiritual, psychical differences — undoubtedly based on the physical, but infinitely transcending them." Each race has a "gift" to offer; the English had given the world constitutional liberty and commercial freedom, the Germans science and philosophy, the Romance nations literature and art. Like the Slavs, the black race had to develop and contribute their own best qualities, thereby enriching civilization.

In the most intellectually expansive argument on cultural nationalism yet made by a black American, Du Bois stated the limitations and possibilities of his philosophy. The Afro-American was both American — by citizenship, political ideals, language, and religion — and African, as a member of a "vast historic race" of separate origin from the rest of America. In spite of their citizenship, the destiny of blacks was not absorption into or "a servile imitation of Anglo-Saxon culture, but a stalwart originality which shall unswervingly follow Negro ideals." He was speaking of the fate of blacks everywhere, of a "Pan-Negroism" in which black Americans were to be the advance guard. The stress was on the separate identity of blacks; the difficulty was in trying to describe the gift of the folk in "that black tomorrow which is yet destined to soften the whiteness of the Teutonic today."[38]

In "Strivings of the Negro People," Du Bois set against the money-mad, Philistine white America the original music, folk tales, and "pathos and humor" cultivated by blacks. He declared that blacks were "the sole oasis of simple faith and reverence in a dusty desert of dollars and smartness." The major achievement of both articles was thus to state the fundamental dualism of Afro-American life and to declare the consequences of the phenomenon as a dilemma: "One ever feels his twoness — an American, a Negro; two souls, two thoughts, two unreconciled strivings."[39]

The distinctive gift of black folk was an idea Du Bois at first asserted rather than proved. An Atlanta conference in 1909 recognized that "it is difficult for the people of America to understand that the Negro is essentially an artistic being, whose emotional nature can be made to contribute much to the world's enjoyment and appreciation of beauty."[40] Du Bois' work in the periodicals was in fact largely defensive. Of a half-dozen articles in 1899, for example, two dealt with black crime, blaming the convict lease system and unequal Southern justice for a situation which whites insisted on seeing as the authentic "Negro problem."[41] In 1901, he twice wrote to refute the argument that blacks in Georgia had become progressively less thrifty with each passing decade.[42] That year and again in 1902 he wrote in defense of blacks against charges of rampant criminality.[43]

Yet there were ways in which Du Bois positively developed his assertion of the special beauty and humanity of blacks. A long illustrated article in 1901, "The Negro as He Really Is," was a journalistic adaptation of social science enlivened by deft descriptions of the sharecropper's life in Dougherty County, Georgia.[44] Moving even further from science was "A Negro Schoolmaster in the New South," appearing first in the *Atlantic Monthly,* then in the 1903 collection.[45] This account of his experiences as a young scholar among the rural folk of Tennessee and of his return ten years later provided a succession of portraits and vignettes which exemplified the pathos and humor of which he had spoken in "The Conservation of Races." It also developed a principal theme of his work: that in spite of the limitations of the black people, the hardships of their life had demanded of them and produced high standards of moral heroism.

Du Bois wrote little about the artistic gift of the blacks before *The Souls of Black Folk,* but in 1900 he published a significant essay on black religion, included later in that volume. The history of black spirituality in America, he argued, was the tale of perversion of a great natural force into cynicism and fatalism: "conscious of his impotence, and pessimistic, [the black] often becomes bitter and vindictive, and his religion, instead of a worship, is a complaint and a curse, a wail rather than a hope, a sneer rather than a faith." But the resource of spirituality persisted, with a transcendent power that stunned the outsider and which illustrated "the deep religious feeling of the real Negro heart."[46]

This confidence in the worth of his people was what led Du Bois into the political world. He persisted in seeing them as limitless in potential, given a free leadership class; and the training of that class, his experience persuaded him, could come in sufficient quantity and quality only through higher education in the arts and sciences. Opposed to his theory was that of Booker T. Washington, which emphasized the training of blacks in comparatively humble agricultural and technical skills and professed to see irreconcilable differences between the two points of view. The vital link between Washington's theory of education and his accommodationist politics, which was highly publicized and the source of a power that led him eventually to become a personal consultant to the President, made friction between the two men inevitable. Du Bois' turn in the direction of "radical" politics, though comparatively slight before 1903, significantly affected his work.

In spite of his exposure to socialism in Berlin, Du Bois had returned to America an apostle of elitism and a political conservative; his experience abroad had deepened his devotion to European high culture. In 1895, Du Bois' second year at Wilberforce, Booker T. Washington's epochal Atlanta Exposition address, in which the orator appeared to accept segregation and disfranchisement in exchange for a peaceful, gradual program of co-operation between the races, provided the scale against which all other black political and cultural positions would be measured. Du Bois enthusiastically accepted the Tuskegee philosophy as the best wisdom then available: Washington's speech was "a word fitly spoken."[47] In the following seven years, however, he grew to find it intolerable.

In *The Philadelphia Negro* the duty of the whites, as Du Bois saw it, was to recognize the wrong of prejudice and to encourage the black upper classes. Once in the South, though, his tone began to change. In 1897, while he could still speak of the "underlying principles of the great republic," he simultaneously scoffed at America's "brutal, dyspeptic blundering."[48] Lynchings, segregation, disfranchisement, the deprivation of Southern black schools, all became topics in both his sociology and his informal essays. In 1899 Du Bois played a major role in the preparation of a memorandum to the Georgia legislature opposing a bill to make disfranchisement law.[49] He began to see a grander pattern to racial prejudice. "The problem of the twentieth century," he told the Pan-African Congress of 1900 in perhaps his most memorable sentence, "is the problem of the color line."[50] He repeated this declaration in a major *Atlantic Monthly* article of 1901, and it served to introduce *The Souls of Black Folk* two years later.[51]

In going to the South in 1897, Du Bois had moved, in a sense, onto ground appropriated by Washington — or leased to him by whites — in 1895, the year of his Atlanta speech. For some time, the two men found issues on which they could co-operate.[52] In June 1901 Du Bois praised much of the work of the Tuskegee Conferences on black life.[53] The following month, though, he for the first time made clear their differences on the questions of education and politics.[54] The next year in a speech at the Atlanta Conference, Washington remarked, "the work that Dr. Du Bois is doing will stand for years as a monument to his ability, wisdom and faithfulness"; but he also warned against a parasitic tendency in university graduates and stressed that agriculture should be the "chief industry of our people."[55] The published resolutions of the conference, which Du Bois helped to formulate, restated a position by that time identifiable with the editor and in clear opposition to the Washington remark.

Du Bois would soon come to view Washington as a political boss of substantial and ruthless power, acting as a broker between the black and white worlds; he in turn would be perceived by Washington as a menace to his carefully established and exquisitely maintained influence. In 1903 Du Bois still thought of his opponent as an honorable, if limited and misguided man. He sensed, though, that the limitations were ominous in portent: they seemed to reinforce the worst suspicions of whites about the intrinsic worth of the black folk. The vision of the good life as seen from Tuskegee appeared to exclude moral and cultural ideas about which Du Bois was not prepared to compromise.

In attempting, in the essays and volumes leading up to *The Souls of Black Folk,* to serve science, art, and the need for political action, Du Bois was reflecting an important philosophical change started at Harvard under William James. The growing propagandistic element in his work documents his acceptance of pragmatism as a philosophic method, and parallels the developing insight of James himself. Later in life Du Bois would state that James had guided him to "realist pragmatism."[56] The process was probably less direct than he suggested, since James did not speak specifically of the new philosophy before 1898. But the pattern of change is clear; indeed, Du Bois' career from his college days to his resignation from Atlanta University in 1910 reads like a case study in the acceptance of pragmatism as outlined by James in his Lowell Institute lectures of 1906-1907.

Vocationally as well as temperamentally, the young Du Bois illustrated within himself the dualism James saw as central to philosophy, and which he variously described as a conflict between empiricism and rationalism, positivism and religion, practicality and idealism, and the "tough-minded" and the "tender-minded." The tough-minded empiricist stresses fact, concreteness, action, and power; the tender-minded or rationalist clings to religion or romanticism, confidence in traditional human values, and the artistic impulse, all representing dimensions of the human experience difficult or impossible to objectify but real for such a person. The pragmatic method, James argued, does not turn its back on any aspect of either side, but applies to every idea and practice the test of its demonstrated power to do good; with this end in mind, the pragmatist "turns towards concreteness and adequacy, toward facts, towards action and towards power."[57]

The absolute Spencerian faith Du Bois briefly held in social science, in his "deep sense of the sanctity of scientific truth," steadily gave way in these years to a knowledge of the limitations of pure empiricism. At the same time, he doubted that social science, in spite of its search for immutable human laws, would "eventually lead to a systematic body of knowledge deserving the name of science."[58] In 1904 he wrote that sociologists were "still only groping after a science."[59] But he also knew the dangers of trying to blend empiricism and the imagination, for in 1903 he deplored the tendency of inferior sociology to lapse into "bad metaphysics and false psychology."[60]

Du Bois recognized, nevertheless, that he was forced to brave metaphysics and psychology in order to represent experience as he knew it. In the words of another pioneering sociologist, Beatrice Potter Webb, he came to see that "science is bankrupt in deciding the destiny of man, [lending] herself indifferently to the destroyer and preserver of life, to the hater and lover of mankind," and to doubt that "the objective method, pure and undefiled," could be applied to "human mentality."[61] Du Bois was himself sure that there were "many delicate differences in race psychology" beyond the ability of "our crude social measurements" to follow, differences that would have to be described by a method other than the strictly empirical.[62]

For Du Bois, Webb, Jane Addams (who attended the Atlanta Conference of 1908), and James himself, one nineteenth century figure, Thomas Carlyle, best represented the prophetic argument against the dehumanization of science.[63] Du Bois probably discovered the appeal of Carlyle during his years at Fisk, for his first mention of the British prophet is in a *Fisk Herald* editorial of 1888.[64] Carlyle's ideas, terms, and style left a definite mark on Du Bois, although he seldom referred to the British writer and prepared only one speech on his work. Encouraged by Barrett Wendell at Harvard to admire the style of a "Titanic" artist, the young intellectual found in the often volcanic energy of Carlyle's prose a model for the expression of his own temperamental power.[65] In Carlyle's basic ideas on the dignity and purpose of life in the modern age, he found a text to which he responded enthusiastically. J. Saunders Redding had reason to judge that "only Carlyle" stands comparison with Du Bois' blend of scholarship, emotion, and poetry.[66]

The details of Carlyle's life did not interest Du Bois, he wrote, for Carlyle belonged to eternity.[67] The most valuable tenet of Carlyle, as far as black people were concerned, should be his glorification of work. "All work," Carlyle had written, "even cotton-spinning is alone noble . . . And in like manner too, all dignity is painful; a life of ease is not for any man, not for any god."[68] Du Bois' early insistence that the "Talented Tenth" must be the vanguard of black progress and the distinct strain of anti-egalitarianism in his thought reflect Carlyle's expressed faith in the power of the few over the many: "We must have more Wisdom to govern us, we must be governed by the Wisest, we must have an Aristocracy of Talent!"[69] As did Carlyle, Du Bois repeatedly puzzled over what they both called the "Riddle of the Sphinx."[70] But where the Social Darwinists had proclaimed natural selection and the doctrine of laissez faire as answers, Carlyle insisted, and Du Bois early concurred, that a moral world required a different response: "What is Justice? that, on the whole, is the question of the Sphinx to us. The law of Fact is, that Justice must and will be done."[71] Certain words — *riddle, sphinx, fact, talent, gift, soul, folk, work, wealth, truth, justice, spirit, ideal*—are at times almost as common in Du Bois' vocabulary as in Carlyle's.

But Du Bois' interest in Carlyle is finally representative only of his own lifelong respect for the accomplished moral intelligence. Du Bois' turn from rigid empirical science toward a pragmatic, political approach to racial problems was urged on him by his increased experience of white racism; but even in his most nationalist moments he believed in an aristocracy of intelligence and morality that knew neither race nor color, and in ultimate ideals beyond the distinctions of cultural relativism. He kept in constant touch with the spirit that informed the writings of Shakespeare and Balzac, Aristotle and Aurelius. He believed in the commonwealth of culture, in the leadership of men like Carlyle and James who, with material comforts open to them, still lived a life of moral advocacy. Thus he brought to the leadership of Afro-American thought and the American debate on race a moral and intellectual resource of marked assurance and complexity. The balance between empiricism and the rational, religious, and artistic spirit was nevertheless delicate, and nowhere is this balance more dramatically seen than in *The Souls of Black Folk*.

CHAPTER FOUR

The Souls of Black Folk

I am glad *glad* you wrote it — we have needed someone to voice the intricacies of the blind maze of thought and action along which the modern, educated colored man or woman struggles. It hurt you to write that book didn't it? The man of fine sensibilities has to suffer exquisitely, just simply because his feeling is so fine.   (Jessie Fauset to Du Bois, 1903)

JESSIE REDMOND FAUSET'S enthusiasm for *The Souls of Black Folk* has been matched by successive generations of readers. William James wrote to Du Bois that the work had impressed him in both substance and style and that it could count on having a recognized place in literature thereafter.[1] William sent a copy to his brother Henry, who thought that the collection was "the only Southern book of distinction published in many a year."[2] In *The Autobiography of an Ex-Colored Man* (1912), James Weldon Johnson commended "that remarkable book" as a pioneer in the exposition of the reality of Afro-American life.[3] Years later Johnson wrote that the work "had a greater effect upon and within the Negro race in America than any other single book published in this country since *Uncle Tom's Cabin*."[4] Langston Hughes singled out *Souls* in reminiscing that "my earliest memories of written words are those of Du Bois and the Bible."[5] Literary historian Benjamin Brawley felt in its cadences "the passion of a mighty heart" and considered it the most important work "in classic English" produced to that time by a black writer.[6] For the critic J. Saunders Redding, the work "is more history-making than historical," so profound has been its impact on a variety of men.[7] And the historian Herbert Aptheker has declared that the book is "one of the classics in the English language."[8]

The Souls of Black Folk sought to convert and to seduce the American people, white and black, into sharing Du Bois' optimistic view of black culture in the United States. It was apparent neither to all black people nor to all whites that the dark people living in America had a fund of spirituality which ennobled their life. Indeed, it was not even clear that "the massed millions of the black peasantry," from whom came "the confused, half-conscious mutter of men who are black and whitened," actually formed a "folk," with distinguishable traditions, aspirations, and character. "Suppose, after all," some black men undoubtedly wondered, "the World is right and we are less than men?" (89). To refute "the World's" accusations and assert the spiritual integrity of blacks, Du Bois marshaled his evidence — the history and sociology of the Afro-American from the first enslavement to the author's own era, "the time of *Sturm und Drang*" (10). From this long history he sought to extract the meaning of the years, with emphasis sometimes on individual character, on national trait, or on the vicissitudes of black fate. His prose style extended from simplicity to almost Ciceronian confabulation. He relied mainly on fact but added fiction in short-story form. He placed scholarly objectivity beside personal passion and autobiography. The result is one of the more curious books of American literature, a diverse mixture of styles and genres. *The Souls of Black Folk* is a guide not only to its author's ideas but also to his sense of style, for it represents generously the powers of a literary artist in the first years of his maturity.

Out of at least three dozen articles and addresses already written or published, Du Bois selected eight for adaptation or reprinting as nine chapters of *The Souls of Black Folk*.[9] To these he added five new or unpublished pieces. The most controversial essay and the spearhead of the work, "Of Mr. Booker T. Washington and Others," is a rigidly unpoetic attack on the policies of the most powerful black leader of the age. In contrast, the previously unpublished threnody on the death of his infant son, "Of the Passing of the First-Born," although construed along racial lines, is at once profoundly autobiographical and broadly universal in implication. *The Souls of Black Folk* was thus consciously and carefully tailored out of old and new fabric to fit a significant occasion: the first simultaneous appearance of Du Bois as poet, prophet, and scholar, appealing through a long work to the heart and mind of the American nation.

Du Bois admitted in 1904, a year after publication, that "the style and workmanship" of his book did not make its meaning "altogether clear." He believed that the collection conveyed "a clear central message," but that around this center floated "a penumbra" of vagueness and half-veiled allusions.[10] The first impression made by Du Bois' preface, "The Forethought," is indeed indefinite. He proposes to sketch, "in vague, uncertain outline," the spiritual world in which "ten thousand thousand" black Americans live. He also casually announces the central metaphor both of black existence and of the book, "the Veil." As he later elaborates, a vast veil hangs between black and white in America, with the black man perceiving himself only in murky reflections through this diaphanous barrier. But in "The Forethought" the veil appears as little more than a curtain at a fair, which Du Bois will draw aside for the curious patron. One then hears a slight rumble of approaching thunder in this peaceful scene, "for the problem of the Twentieth Century is the problem of the color line" (vii). Somewhere between servility and threat Du Bois has placed his overture. The result is disarming, even tantalizing. The method is characteristic of the entire work.

The Souls of Black Folk divides into three parts, dealing successively with the history, the sociology, and the spirituality of Afro-America. The first chapter, "Of Our Spiritual Strivings," mixes history with psychology in an extended prologue. The second chapter, "Of The Dawn of Freedom," reviews the history of black life after slavery as seen in the rise and the fall, in 1872, of the Freedman's Bureau, established by the government to ease the transition to freedom for the slaves. The third chapter, which discusses Booker T. Washington, brings the lessons of the past to bear on the present and the future. Each of these chapters reinforces the others. They try to discriminate between solid achievement and the mirages of success, pointing toward the new century and its new challenge. Although the entire book should be considered a refutation of the arguments of Washington and his admirers, Du Bois' first three chapters are the vanguard of the attack.

The second and largest section of *The Souls of Black Folk* leaves history and political theory behind. In six chapters Du Bois takes the white reader behind the veil, giving face and form to a people hitherto discussed only in general. The setting is Georgia and Tennessee, the regions of the South with which Du Bois was most familiar, from the sharecropper's lonely farm to the black university at Atlanta, "this green oasis, where hot anger cools, and the bitterness of disappointment is sweetened by the springs and breezes of Parnas-

sus" (83). Du Bois' aim was to expose the plight of the poor and
ignorant, while illuminating their potential for improvement, as
well as to defend liberal education for the black man against the
sneers of those who argued that "the picture of a lone black boy por-
ing over a French grammar amid the weeds and dirt of a neglected
home" is in many ways "the acme of absurdities" (43).

The last section of *The Souls of Black Folk* is devoted to the power
of black art and spirituality. "The Faith of the Fathers" discusses
black religion in the United States, its origins and complex social
role, its paradoxes and dilemmas. Du Bois' chapter on the death of
his son bares his own grieving soul at a time of personal tragedy. "Of
Alexander Crummell" is a biographical study of the moral black
man *agonistes*, which stresses devotion and submission as distinguishing the best black character. In "Of the Coming of John" Du
Bois leaves the essay for the short-story, describing a young man
whose attempts at education end in murder and suicide. The final
piece, "Of the Sorrow Songs," focuses on those haunting melodies
which seemed to Du Bois a reflection in art of a people's essential
capacity for grandeur in thought and expression. Thus, *The Souls
of Black Folk* ends with a firm assertion of the intent suffusing its
pages. Far from being a national liability or error, the presence of
those "ten thousand thousand" dark folk on American soil is an unrealized asset in the development of a noble national tradition.

Du Bois recognized the problem of unity in compiling his anthology. As a partial solution, he introduced each chapter with two quotations. The first, with one exception, is a piece of verse written by
an accepted author of the Western poetic heritage. The second is a
few notes of music from one of fourteen well-known sorrow songs,
the gift of black people to America. Taken together, the lines of
verse signify the strivings of the souls of white folk toward lofty
ideals; they reflect the spiritual dignity and artistic capacity of the
white world. The sorrow songs deployed beneath them remind the
reader of the community of soul which transcends race and color.
Du Bois clearly hoped that for his white reader there would be the
recognition that true genius resides not only in white civilization but
also in a transplanted people emerging from the miasma of slavery.
He believed of black people that "the rich and bitter depth of their
experience, the unknown treasures of their inner life, the strange
rendings of nature they have seen, may give the world new points of

view and make their loving, living and doing precious to all human hearts" (108).

In its variety and range *The Souls of Black Folk* indicates Du Bois' appreciation and mastery of the essay form as practiced in the nineteenth century by writers as different as Emerson and Carlyle, on the one hand, and Hazlitt and Lamb, on the other. Sensitive to the many purposes to which the form could be put, he used the essay to capture the nuances of his amorphous subject, the multiple disciplines involved in his explication, and the different and sometimes conflicting expressions of his temperament. "Of the Meaning of Progress," for example, is in part an exercise in nostalgia darkened finally by sorrow. Easily the most charming piece of the book, the essay recounts Du Bois' schoolteaching summers in a rural Tennessee village, while a student at Fisk. Its tone is romantic, sometimes even bucolic: "We read and spelled together, wrote a little, picked flowers, sang, and listened to stories of the world beyond the hill" (65). The recounting of his return after ten years is steeped in pathos. "In that little valley was a strange stillness as I rode up; for death and marriage had stolen youth and left age and childhood there" (73). "Of the Black Belt," a more somber, detailed essay, is partly in the same reflective strain. It opens: "Out of the North the train thundered, and we woke to see the crimson soil of Georgia stretching away bare and monotonous right and left . . . Yet we did not nod, nor weary of the scene; for this is historic ground" (110-111).

But Du Bois' topic was usually far too serious for the informal essay. This is best illustrated by the paradoxical fact that the most personal of the essays, "Of the Passing of the First-Born," is in many ways the most formal, with an elegiac progression and an emotional grandeur that mark its literary antecedents as clearly classical. Devices of the traditional pastoral elegy are present in modified but distinct form. There is the involvement of Nature in the infant Du Bois' illness. He falls sick while "the roses shivered, and the still stern sun quivered its awful light over the hills of Atlanta" (210). There is the traditional invective against Death: "But hearken, O Death! Is not this my life hard enough. . . ?" (211). The desire to supplant the victim is expressed: "If one must have gone, why not I?" (214). In place of the stylized procession of mourners, Du Bois notes in parody the reaction of whites to the cortege: the "pale-faced hurrying men and women . . . did not say much, — they only glanced and said,

Niggers!" (212). Traditional consolation is impossible. Although for the black infant there is hope—" 'Not dead, not dead, but escaped; not bound, but free' " (213)—the mourner himself cannot look forward to the comfort of "fresh woods and pastures new." He concludes: "Not for me, —I shall die in my bonds."

Du Bois' concern with form is constant, reflecting the influence of his training in the classical tradition of rhetoric and oratory taught to him at Fisk and Harvard. The first piece best illustrates this formalism. The *exordium* begins almost whimsically, ambles into reminiscence of Du Bois as "a little thing, away up in the hills of New England, where the dark Housatonic winds between Hoosac and Taghkanic to the sea" (2). The shadow of race falls across the idyll, and whimsy abruptly ends. The *narratio* discusses seriously the history of black spiritual striving from slavery to the present. The *probatio* is generally subsumed throughout the piece, but the start of the *refutatio* is clear and direct: "A people thus handicapped ought not to be asked to race with the world" (9). The *peroratio* of this oration lists the accomplishments and contributions of blacks to American culture. There is no windy appeal based on recrimination or undue sentimentality, but instead a blend of reason, passion, and fact, dressed out with calculation in formal periods to match the occasion.

Similarly, Du Bois sought, wherever possible, to codify or enumerate; where this was impossible, he moved to reduce apparent chaos or flux to duality, dilemma, or paradox. The very history of black people appeared as "paradox," between the shining promise during slave days of "the glory of the coming of the Lord" and the reality of the postbellum South (68). The "would-be black *savant*" encountered a "paradox," in that black people were ignorant not only of the rudiments of white education but also of the kind of knowledge which could teach the white world to respect them (5). There is also a "peculiar ethical paradox that faces the Negro of today," between the ideals encouraged by religion and the reality that these ideals avail little in dealing with the white world; thus, "the Negro faces no enviable dilemma" (202-203). The notion of duality is central to Du Bois' perception, and the habit of enumeration is crucial to his style. Major theses are always broken down to components: "there are four chief causes of these wretched homes" (140); three steps characterized the development of the sorrow song;

the black masses must rely on their talented tenth.[11]

The most important concept of the work reflects Du Bois' sense of dualism. The "souls" of the title is a play on words, referring to the "twoness" of the black American: "two souls, two thoughts, two unreconciled strivings . . . in one dark body, whose dogged strength alone keeps it from being torn asunder" (3). The black possesses "no true self-consciousness" but a "double-consciousness," seeing himself only as perceived by whites through the veil. For this insight Du Bois drew on the psychology of his time. The term "soul" was used synonymously with consciousness both by idealistic psychologists and by the religiously orthodox James McCosh, whose philosophy Du Bois had studied at Fisk.[12] His favorite professor, William James, posited in 1890 that the structure of the brain allowed "one system [to] give rise to one consciousness, and those of another system to another *simultaneously* existing consciousness."[13] The psychologist Oswald Kulpe wrote in 1893 of "the phenomenon of double consciousness or the divided self . . . characterised by the existence of a more or less complete separation of two aggregates of conscious process . . . oftentimes of entirely opposite character."[14]

Du Bois' use of the term "folk" in his title is also significant. Bernard Bell has traced the lines that linked Du Bois and other major black cultural commentators to the theories of culture which originated with Johann Gottfried von Herder, influenced Emerson, Whitman, and other nineteenth-century American artists, and directed the work in folklore of the Harvard scholars Francis James Child, Francis Barton Gummere, and George Lyman Kittredge.[15] In one central respect *The Souls of Black Folk* conforms to Herder's doctrine of the folk. By emphasizing the sublimity and originality of their music above all other accomplishments of black Americans, Du Bois accepted Herder's basic terms for evaluation of culture. But beyond his deep admiration for the religious songs, Du Bois was no champion of folk expression. The reactionary Barrett Wendell — rather than Child or the young Kittredge — had been his main literary influence at Harvard. His definition of "folk" is primarily a political one and should be understood as interchangeable with the more daring term "nation," which he had used to describe Afro-America in his "Conservation of Races" address in 1897. His definition of "folk" was less radical than that of Herder; the doctrine of the talented tenth indicates the limitations of his belief in the masses. Nevertheless, in using the term "folk" to describe the most oppressed and despised group in America, and in finding in that group striking evidence of artistic power, he was making a strong claim for the recognition of its dignity and separate identity.

"Of the Coming of John" elaborates the duality of the black soul. There are two Johns. One is "brown" and struggling; the other is the white son of Judge Jones, the main citizen of the small Georgia town where they live. The black and white worlds think only of their favorite son, "and neither world thought the other world's thought, save with a vague unrest." Playmates in childhood, the young men go away to school, and both return dissatisfied. White John is bored with "this God-forgotten town" which boasts "nothing but mud and Negroes." Black John returns a brooding figure, Du Bois' "would-be black *savant*" caught in a dilemma between two worlds. He loses his position as teacher in the black village school. Wandering in a daze, he comes upon white John playfully attempting to kiss his sister, who works as a maid for the family, and kills him. The lynch mob finds him sitting quietly on a cliff near the scene of the deed; he turns from them and leaps to his death into the sea.

The principal theme of the story is the dilemma of the educated black aspirant to culture, whose strivings are frustrated and betrayed by injustice. While black John struggles with the new world of mathematics and Greek, he discovers "the Veil that lay between him and the white world." "A tinge of sarcasm crept into his speech, and a vague bitterness into his life." His susceptibility to culture reaches its apex at a concert in New York when the music of Wagner overwhelms him; he wishes "to rise with that clear music out of the dirt and dust of that low life that held him prisoned and befouled." Ironically, it is at this concert that, snubbed by white John and mistreated by an official, he decides to return home after seven years away. His homecoming is a disaster. He offends the blacks by a blundering speech that appears to slight their religion, and provokes the whites by teaching his pupils about the French Revolution and the possibilities of change. Driven from the classroom and alienated from his race, he is psychologically and spiritually paralyzed, ready for either exile or death when he kills white John.

This tale of miscegenation, murder, and suicide is discreetly but powerfully told. It turns on the savage irony that, for the black man in a racist world, the acquisition of culture is a dangerous and often destructive process. John loses his innocence and his ignorance at the same time; his native virtue shrivels as his intellect expands. White power demands servility of him; the blacks are suspicious and deeply reactionary. The finest achievement of the story is its rendition of the emotional and spiritual paralysis that overtakes John from the beginning of his education. Neither a hypocrite nor a rebel, he stands frozen between two worlds, isolated from everything but his capacity to dream.

The tragedy of the piece is the tragedy inherent in American racism. The story is very much a tale of the South and should be read in part as a dramatization of the chapter called "Of the Sons of Master and Man," first published as "The Relation of the Negroes to the Whites in the South."[16] White John is "not a bad fellow, — just a little spoiled and self-indulgent"; his father is basically an old fool. But they represent that moribund moral leadership Du Bois deplored in the white South. Living in ignorance and fear of the blacks, they discover too late, with the death of white John, that the races have a common destiny to match their common history, and that misfortune is as blind to color as justice itself should be. The narrator of the story, an unnamed professor at "Wells Institute" where black John went to school, broods on the tragedy from afar.

In spite of the restraints of the scientific method and the discipline of classical form, a quaintness of approach runs throughout the work. Words such as "thy," "thou," "nay," "anon," "whence," "yonder," "yon," and "builded," combined with exclamations such as "Hark!" and "Ah!" might seem to point to romantic posturing on the part of Du Bois. But the narrator more often prefers a patriarchal tone to the affectations of the swooning young poet. This choice prevents archaism and romantic poetic diction from weakening the fiber of moral argument. The patriarchal tone is encouraged by Du Bois' frequent borrowing from the King James Bible. Sometimes the influence is direct, as in his quotation of the "I am dark but comely" passage from the Song of Solomon, or in such familiar terms as "house of bondage," "promised land," "wearied Israelites," or "the Valley of the Shadow of Death." Occasionally, Du Bois used Biblical phraseology with more novel effect, as in referring to the fertile black belt of Georgia as "the Egypt of the Confederacy." But it should be stressed that Du Bois did not write sermons when he intended to pen essays. He praised the black preacher for many things, but not for his preaching.

Sociology was too young a discipline for the special vocabulary of its present-day scientists to leave a mark on Du Bois' book. Even the most "scientific" prose in *The Souls of Black Folk* is free of technical language. Nor is there pedantry, although Du Bois now and then mentions familiar terms of Greek mythology. "The Quest of the Golden Fleece" sends him back to his Bulfinch to find a story to rival that of the rise and rule of King Cotton, a tale to link "the ancient and the modern quest of the Golden Fleece in the Black Sea" (136). But learning is not paraded. Of the sorrow songs Du Bois humbly writes: "What are these songs, and what do they mean? I know little of music and can say nothing in technical phrase, but I know something of men" (253). Though Du Bois sometimes reaches back for an arthritic word or phrase, he never caters to the slang of the day or relaxes into colloquialism; his language at all times avoids the usual pitfalls of indignation: carelessness and vulgarity.

The distance between poet and scientist in *The Souls of Black Folk* is variously reflected in the rhythms of Du Bois' prose. In his attack on Washington, Du Bois' urbanity chills the flow of language into mannered, Johnsonian cadences: "One hesitates, therefore, to criticize a life which, beginning with so little, has done so much. And yet the time is come when one may speak in all sincerity and utter courtesy of the mistakes and shortcomings of Mr. Washington's career, as well as of his triumphs, without being thought captious or envious, and without forgetting that it is easier to do ill than well in the world" (43-44). At the other extreme, Du Bois' syntax becomes tortured as he describes his son's race: "Why was his hair tinted with gold? An evil omen was golden hair in my life" (208). More arresting is Du Bois' ability to translate a nervous, energetic quality into prose, as in describing his first job: " 'Come in,' said the commissioner—'come in. Have a seat. Yes, that certificate will do. Stay to dinner. What do you want a month?' 'Oh,' thought I, 'this is lucky'; but even then fell the awful shadow of the Veil, for they ate first, then I—alone" (63). Or Du Bois on the death of a country girl who "worked until, on a summer's day, some one married another; then Josie crept to her mother like a hurt child, and slept—and sleeps" (70).

The death of his little son moved him to write the most majestic prose in *The Souls of Black Folk,* particularly effective in that it fol-

lows an agitated passage telling of the crisis, when "the hours trem-
bled on; the night listened; the ghastly dawn glided like a tired thing
across the lamplight": "He died at eventide, when the sun lay like a
brooding sorrow above the western hills, veiling its face; when the
winds spoke not, and trees, the great green trees he loved, stood
motionless. I saw his breath beat quicker and quicker, pause, and
then his little soul leapt like a star that travels in the night and left a
world of darkness in its train. The day changed not; the same tall
trees peeped in at the windows, the same green grass glinted in the
setting sun. Only in the chamber of death writhed the world's most
piteous thing—a childless mother" (210-211). The grand, declining
sweep of the first sentence is not typical of Du Bois. He was unusually moved.

   Always attuned to the ironies of racism, Du Bois ends his moving
reminiscence of lost youth in Tennessee with a reminder of official
insensitivity: "Thus sadly musing, I rode to Nashville in the Jim
Crow car" (74). Or the ending of "The Faith of the Fathers": "Some
day the Awakening will come, when the pent-up vigor of ten million
souls shall sweep irresistibly towards the Goal, out of the Valley of
the Shadow of Death, where all that makes life worth living—liberty,
Justice, and Right—is marked "For White People Only" (206).
There is little humor—except gentlemanly "good humor"—in *The
Souls of Black Folk*. Apart from the remarks about John's ambition
and the dialect humor of his sour arrival home after seven years,
there is perhaps only one other sally of wit in the entire book, when
Du Bois describes his hero Alexander Crummell's meeting with
Bishop Onderdonk, "corpulent, red-faced, and the author of several thrilling tracts on Apostolic Succession"; the bishop discrimini-
nates against Crummell, but in his bookcases "Fox's 'Lives of the
Martyrs' nestled happily beside 'The Whole Duty of Man' " (222-
223). Unlike Charles W. Chesnutt, Paul Laurence Dunbar, and
other black writers of the time, Du Bois did not enjoy exploiting
black dialect. His notion of the "soul" of his people went beyond the
kind of humor that some considered its major grace.

   Not radical in his creation of metaphor and simile, he nevertheless could be daring and effective. There was a church in Georgia,
"a great whitewashed barn of a thing, perched on stilts of stone,"
looking as if it were only resting a moment "and might be expected
to waddle off down the road at almost any time" (118). The general

lyric tone is less enterprising, but probably more moving, as when he speaks of the first appearance of the fugitive slaves within the lines of the Union armies: "They came at night, when the flickering camp-fires shone like vast unsteady stars along the black horizon" (14). Lyricism sometimes takes an incantatory turn: "whisperings and portents came borne upon the four winds: Lo! we are diseased and dying, cried the dark hosts; we cannot write, our voting is vain; what need of education, since we must always cook and serve? And the Nation echoed and enforced this self-criticism, saying: Be content" (10). Du Bois' prose is also capable of serenity: "Somehow that plantation ended our day's journey; for I could not shake off the influence of that silent scene. Back toward town we glided . . . A peasant girl was hoeing in the field, white-turbaned and black-limbed. All this we saw, but the spell still lay upon us" (121).

The most striking device in *The Souls of Black Folk* is Du Bois' adoption of the veil as the metaphor of black life in America. Mentioned at least once in most of the fourteen essays, as well as in "The Forethought," it means that "the Negro is a sort of seventh son, born with a veil, and gifted with second-sight in this American world — a world which yields him no true self-consciousness, but only lets him see himself through the revelation of the other world" (3). If any single idea guides the art of *The Souls of Black Folk*, it is this concept, which anticipated the noted fictional conceit, developed by Ralph Ellison, that blacks are invisible to the rest of the nation.[17]

Within the veil, blacks live; in the vaster territory outside the veil, whites enjoy power and freedom; above the veil shines the blue sky, where the eternal and ideal dwell. Black men seek "in these days that try their souls, the chance to soar in the dim blue air above the smoke" (108). Nowhere beneath God's "broad blue sky" can the dead infant find peace (212-213). The veil unites black men. They are drawn together for reasons sprung "above all, from the sight of the Veil that hung between us and Opportunity" (68). But the veil also destroys black men, as it did John. And so Du Bois' aim in *The Souls of Black Folk* is to "sweep the Veil away and cry, Lo! the soul to whose dear memory I bring this little tribute" (226).

In "Of Our Spiritual Strivings" Du Bois extends the metaphor of haze or half-sight: "The shadow of a mighty Negro past flits through the tale of Ethiopia the Shadowy and of Egypt the Sphinx." The powers of individual black men "flash here and there like falling stars" through history and "die sometimes before the world has rightly gauged their brightness." Deprived black people are "the swarthy spectre" haunting the nation's feast. Freedom is "a tantalizing will-o'-the-wisp"; "a new vision" of education began to replace "the dream" of black political power, "another pillar of fire by night after a clouded day." The blacks have "misty minds" as they toil onward in their delusion. "The horizon was ever dark . . . the vistas disclosed as yet no goal . . . In those sombre forests of his striving his own soul rose before him, and he saw himself, — darkly as through a veil" (4-9). Wherever the aspiration or history of the Afro-American is discussed in poetic terms, this image of hazy vision is dominant. From it proceed secondary images of groping, faltering, halting, and uncertainty. The world as perceived from the souls of black folk is a dark, fearsome place, inhabited by phantoms and ghosts, chimeras and mirages. The roads wind uphill all the way, though no hills are in sight. The climber, wary of precipices, cannot see the views. There is darkness at noon.

Du Bois did not want to be identified with the "car-window" sociologists who view the Negro from afar or "gleefully count his bastards and prostitutes" (9). "We often forget," he noted, "that each unit in the mass is a throbbing human soul" (143). To examine that soul, Du Bois relied on a release of his own poetic nature. The justification for this release came not only from the example of Western moral propagandists but also from the black people themselves. Du Bois believed that he shared in the common aesthetic fund of his race, whose criteria derived from a "tropical imagination" more lively and passionate than that of the West (198). The most accomplished American manifestation of black art, Du Bois thought, was the religious sorrow song, "the singular spiritual heritage of the nation and the greatest gift of the Negro people" (251). It is no wonder, then, that the criteria identified by Du Bois as elemental to the greatness of the sorrow song are also found in *The Souls of Black Folk*.

Like that book, the sorrow songs are a message to the world, and "such a message is naturally veiled and half articulate." The songs tell "of trouble and exile, of strife and hiding; they grope toward some unseen power and sigh for rest in the End . . . Mother and child are sung, but seldom father; fugitive and wary wanderer call for pity and affection, but there is little of wooing and wedding . . .

Love-songs are scarce and . . . of deep successful love there is ominous silence . . . Of death the Negro showed little fear . . . Through
all the sorrow of the Sorrow Songs there breathes a hope — a faith in
the ultimate justice of things" (257-261). All these qualities represent a major thematic and stylistic bond between *The Souls of Black
Folk* and what Du Bois regarded as the patristic literature of black
folk in America.

"Of Mr. Booker T. Washington and Others" is the key to the
book's political intent. As James Weldon Johnson has noted, this
essay proved to be a rallying-point for black radicals opposing
Washington, "thereby creating a split of the race into two contend-
ing camps."[18] Until Washington's death in 1915, he and Du Bois
were the leaders of these two camps warring over the affairs of Afro-
America. Each camp had its creed and even its Bible, for *The Souls
of Black Folk* was for the radicals what Washington's bestselling *Up
from Slavery* (1901) was for his disciples.

Du Bois and Washington had a great deal in common among
their beliefs. Both believed, for example, in work. Like Du Bois,
Washington quoted Carlyle, who called for "an original man; not a
secondhand, borrowing, or begging man."[19] They shared a basic
revulsion at the quality of black life among the masses of the people.
The opening sentence of Du Bois' "The Talented Tenth," published, like *Souls*, in 1903, illustrates his discomfort: "The Negro
race, like all races, is going to be saved by its exceptional men." Du
Bois admitted that "death, disease and crime" were the rule of black
life. "Knowledge of life and its deeper meaning, has been the point
of the Negro's deepest ignorance," he continued. The absolute need
was "to raise the Negro as quickly as possible in the scale of civilization." To this end must education address itself, striving to
"strengthen the Negro's character, increase his knowledge and teach
him to earn a living." If America does not lift blacks up, the blacks
"will pull you down."[20]

Washington's position was even more censorious of the black
masses, although it was characteristic that he seldom advertised his
views except by implication. He shared in what he called the "doubt
in many quarters as to the ability of the Negro unguided, unsup-
ported, to hew his own path and put into visible, tangible, indisput-
able form, products and signs of civilization."[21] One of his admirers,
H. T. Kealing of the African Methodist Episcopal Church, elabor-

ated on the shortcomings of black Americans. Kealing saw the Afro-
American as possessing both inborn and inbred traits. All of his
better qualities, such as cheerfulness and love of religion, were instinctive. His inbred qualities, a rogue's gallery of failings, were no
less real, although Kealing contended weakly that they could be
bred out of the black. Kealing listed the black failings as shiftlessness, incontinence, indolence, improvidence, extravagance, untidi-
ness, dishonesty, untruthfulness, unreliability, lack of initiative,
suspicion of his own race (Kealing saw no irony here), and ignorance.[22]

Du Bois had lived for years with Washington and the Tuskegee
theory of education. Although he had been finding more and more
sense in the "radical" opposition to Washington, it was probably the
latter's autobiography which made him see the deeper cultural
meanings of the Tuskegee message. His open criticism of its author
began with his July 1901 review of *Up from Slavery*. As one rising
master propagandist, Du Bois recognized the remarkable creative
power of another, a power which, yoked to an economic and political influence unmatched elsewhere in black America, made the
autobiography a kind of scriptural guide to the future of American
race relations. But although *Up from Slavery* was a holy text for
Tuskegee supporters, it was heresy for Du Bois.

In his review, Du Bois cryptically noted that Washington gave
"but glimpses of the real struggle which he has had for leadership."
He accused Washington, in fact, of telling a lie. He pointed to the
limitations of the Tuskegee philosophy, which was nothing more
than a refinement of "the old [black] attitude of adjustment to environment, emphasizing the economic phase." Even in 1901 Du Bois
saw the main weakness of Washington's leadership to be his opposition to liberal culture. Of the people named as representing the real
though unorganized opposition to the Tuskegee-Hampton idea,
three were major black artists of the day: Paul Laurence Dunbar, a
poet; Charles W. Chesnutt, a writer of fiction; and Henry O. Tanner, a painter. There could be no doubt in which camp Du Bois
stood.[23]

Earlier, in April 1901, Du Bois had showed that he was warming
to an attack on a point of view for which Washington was perhaps
the most circumspect and yet the most effective spokesman. He
wrote a crushing review of William Hannibal Thomas' *The Ameri-*

can Negro (1901), in which an educated black man bitterly criticized his people. Thomas had written, for example, that "negro nature is so craven and sensuous in every fibre of its being that a negro manhood with decent respect for chaste womanhood does not exist."[24] Du Bois saw the work as a "sinister symptom" of increasing self-doubt and self-hate among blacks, one "without faith or ideal," whose result is to satisfy the "more or less unconscious Wish for the Worst in regard to the Negro, to satisfy the logic of his arduous situation." Ominous types were appearing within the race, prominent among whom was "the better trained man who has lost faith either in the coming of the Good or in the Good itself."[25]

In December of the previous year, writing an article on black religion, Du Bois had placed himself somewhere between the radical and reactionary camps: "the danger of the one," he wrote, "lies in anarchy, that of the other in hypocrisy." Connecting the loss of spiritual sense to political and social philosophies, he criticized the complainers for being "wedded to ideals remote, whimsical, perhaps impossible of realization." His harsher words, though, were saved for the tellers of "the Lie," hypocrites who possess "another type of mind, shrewder and keener and more tortuous too, [which sees] in the very strength of the anti-Negro movement its patent weakness, and with Jesuitical casuistry is deterred by no ethical considerations in the endeavor to turn this weakness to the black man's strength . . . [forgetting] that life is more than meat and the body more than raiment."[26] Without naming Washington or Tuskegee, Du Bois had begun to fight them.

To interpret Washington in ideological terms or as "the intellectual opposite of W. E. B. Du Bois," Louis Harlan has demonstrated, is to "miss the essential character of the man . . . Power was his game, and he used ideas simply as an instrument to gain power."[27] If dissimulation was Washington's basic weapon, *Up from Slavery* was his greatest coup. Skillfully deploying the events of his life to conform to the complex, multiple desires of his audience, Washington revealed himself, from Du Bois' point of view, as finally without important principles. In his rise from the slave cabin to elegant English clubs, an honorary degree at Harvard, and gala receptions by the Southern leadership in the cities of his impoverished youth, Washington relied on a boundless faith in humanity, a beneficent Providence, the efficacy of work and thrift, and the power of humility before prevailing social conditions. What Du Bois almost alone saw, and what gifted white commentators such as William Dean Howells could not see or would not admit, were the full implications of this remarkable blackface version of the Horatio Alger myth.[28]

Du Bois did not object either to Washington's expressions of faith in work and thrift or to his belief that the "better class" of Southern whites was an ally to be cultivated by blacks; these ideas were basic to Du Bois' own thinking. He was not pleased, however, by the ambivalence of his opponent's position on civil rights. A black must be modest in making political claims, Washington wrote in *Up from Slavery*; he should not cease to vote, but must be guided by intelligent and responsible whites. Nor could Du Bois fail to be offended by Washington's ridicule of Greek and Latin education or schools that seemed to imitate New England education, by his stated disdain for poetry and fiction, or by his mention of Webster's "blue-back speller" alone among his books, as if that work were education enough for any practical man.

Du Bois could hardly be led by a man to whom, as the autobiography declared, few things were more satisfying than a Berkshire or Poland China pig, to whom Holland meant Holstein cattle and thorough agriculture, who equated the art of Henry Ossawa Tanner with the skill of growing sweet potatoes, and to whom a degree from Harvard was a testimony less to education and culture than to his own rise from obscurity. The measure of each of the many carefully documented "friendships" in *Up from Slavery* is its support of the monument of Tuskegee, behind which its master bashfully stands in the glare of his intense humility. Each unexpected gift is regarded as the work of a Providence otherwise without purpose. As secular and despiritualized as any autobiography in the language, *Up from Slavery* was, for Du Bois, the literary embodiment of the Washington "Lie."

Du Bois made clear in "Of Mr. Booker T. Washington and Others" that he was attacking not a mere theory of education but "a veritable Way of Life," for Washington had indissolubly linked policies of industrial education, conciliation of the white South, and silence concerning civil rights. The head of Tuskegee had so thoroughly learned the idiom of commercialism and material prosperity that he had lost sight of the best life as seen by Socrates or St. Francis. Uniting reactionary politics to an age of economic development and racial friction, "Mr. Washington's programme practically accepts the alleged inferiority of the Negro races" (50). While some opposition to Washington admittedly came from envy, demagoguery, and spite, there was genuine cause for regret and apprehension among thoughtful and educated blacks.

Each of Washington's basic propositions—that the South was justified in its antiblack policies because of "the Negro's degradation," that black education was misguided, and that the rise of the black man depended primarily on his own efforts—"is a dangerous half-truth." Exposing a "triple-paradox" in his opponent's program, Du Bois declared that there could be no sure economic advance without the vote, no thrift or self-respect without civic involvement and recognition, no significant "lower" education without teachers trained in black colleges or by their graduates. Washington was to be praised insofar as he preached the virtues of "Thrift, Patience, and Industrial Training" for the masses (not for the talented tenth, to be sure), but he was to be opposed as long as he "apologized for injustice . . . does not rightly value the privilege and duty of voting, belittles the emasculating effects of caste distinctions, and opposes the higher training and ambition of our brighter minds" (59).

Du Bois detested in Washington what he perceived as materialism, Philistinism, and above all, spiritual pessimism. Washington was an ardent subscriber to the doctrine of self-reliance popularly interpreted from the writings of Emerson and regenerated by the social Darwinists of the late nineteenth century in America. Although he had a place for the church in his scheme, Washington never looked for ultimate goals beyond the objective reality or materialism of this world. He did not accept the radical Spencerian Darwinist view of the poor as permanent casualties of the struggle for life, but he accepted most of the distinct limits placed by determinist philosophy upon the human experience, especially that of the lowest masses. These ideas limited Washington's vision of the rise of the black man.

Du Bois scorned institutional religion once he had attained maturity, and he certainly enjoyed material comforts. Nevertheless, he held strongly to what might be called a Platonic view of the ultimate significance of life. The true aim of work was not simply the accumulation of wealth. The pursuit of the ideals of truth, beauty, and love, of which work was prophetic, dominated his imagination. In

Washington's eyes, this pursuit was little more than vagrancy. His vision of life began and ended on earth, regardless of whatever lip service he may have paid to the Christian concept of an afterlife as the goal of earthly endeavor. Now agnostic, now atheistic, Du Bois wandered between Matthew Arnold's Hellenism and Hebraism, but he ended by adding to the Puritan God of his youth the deified ideals of Greek intellectualism. The instability of his religion does not deny its vitality or scope. The purpose of life was aspiration to the ideal. To limit life to the achievement of what is called the American dream was teleological pessimism of the most sordid kind. The dream was compatible with, indeed it was fostered by, the social Darwinist fatalism from which Du Bois recoiled.

The glitter of the American dream did not hide its pessimism about the purpose of man's presence on earth. Ornamented by the vestments of religion, it remained a delusion as far as Du Bois was concerned. For him, liberal education and culture freed the spirit to find its true, lofty level; for Washington, such ideas were almost always synonymous with loafing. In 1884, Washington had wanted the educated black man ("the proud fop" with his beaver hat, kid gloves, and walking cane) to be "brought down to something practical and useful."[29] In *Up from Slavery* a generation later, he used the same caricature of the educated black. Du Bois saw such a man as impelled by ideals, although he knew that there could be exceptions to the rule; Washington saw the same person as a confidence man, "determined to live by his wits."[30]

Du Bois pitted his own optimism against that "dark fatalism" of blacks who cannot move because of a sense of historic impotence. He insisted that "the question of the future is how to keep these millions from brooding over the wrongs of the past and the difficulties of the present" (107). A strain of malevolent pessimism was deeply rooted in the black consciousness as a result of the victory of slavery over the African, which seemed to the black's myth-making imagination to be "the dark triumph of Evil over him. All the hateful powers of the Under-world were striving against him, and a spirit of revolt and revenge filled his heart" (198). In later years of slavery, the black man's religion "became darker and more intense, and into his ethics crept a note of revenge" (200). In his own time, Du Bois felt, black hopelessness had reached a crisis. While the black church lost its members to brothels, gambling halls, and slums in the big cities, "the better classes segregate themselves from the group-life of both black and white, and form an aristocracy, cultured but pessimistic, whose bitter criticism stings while it points out no way of escape" (205).

To Du Bois' moral vision, such despair was the worst of sins. Thus in *The Souls of Black Folk* he sketched the life of Alexander Crummell, one who in his opinion had triumphed over the temptations of hate, despair, and doubt. Crummell exemplified the Afro-American spirit tempted and resisting temptation. He saw the "fatal weaknesses" of black people, "the dearth of strong moral character, of unbending righteousness" (220). Instead of giving in to pessimism, Crummell dedicated his life to changing his world. Crummell was a "hero" in the Carlylean sense. He was the apotheosis of a marvelous spirit; he was one of those "exceptional men" by whom the black man would be saved, a prophet within that talented tenth.

But in accepting the idea of salvation by aristocracy propagated in the writings of Fichte, Carlyle, Arnold, and other moral prophets of the West, Du Bois exposed a vulnerable side to his opponents. Washington's philosophy, for all its materialism, philistinism, and pessimism, reposed whatever confidence it had in the people themselves. In so doing, it was at once a native American ideology, whereas Du Bois' complainings rang of European and "bookish" exoticism out of place in the New World. There is in consequence a paradox in the reputations of these two men. Washington's name has become infamous in some quarters as being synonymous with spineless accommodationism. Du Bois has been considered a cultural nationalist, insisting on the virtues of his people and their separate destiny. These are justifiable reputations. It might be argued, though, that Du Bois was a more profound accommodationist than Washington when he wrote *The Souls of Black Folk*. If Washington was denying the power of black art and spirituality, Du Bois appeared to be adding culture to the hallucinations dancing before the eyes of men peering through the veil.

Du Bois' notion of culture was founded on the principle that cultural fertilization descended from the top down into the masses of people: "Was there ever a nation on God's fair earth civilized from the bottom upward? Never; it is, ever was and ever will be from the top downward that culture filters. The Talented Tenth rises and pulls all that are worth saving up to their vantage ground. This is

the history of human progress."[33] Du Bois was not one with Southern black people — that is, with the masses of American blacks — by
place of birth, education, or temperament, and from this fact came
both strength and weakness. His sense of apartness was effectively
counter-balanced by a dedication which amounted to a sense of personal destiny. *The Souls of Black Folk* is not a novel, but it has a
major hero: the soul of W. E. B. Du Bois, his sufferings, his virtues,
his gifts, offered as exemplary of the best achievement of the Afro-
American people. In trying to expose the souls of all black folk, Du
Bois bared his own soul. His exposition of self was aimed at those
whites unable to conceive of the black man in terms of dignity, who
suspected that "somewhere between men and cattle, God created a
tertium quid, and called it a Negro" (89). His response was to show
himself a man of learning and feeling, wishing the reader to remem-
ber, above all, that "I who speak here am bone of the bone and flesh
of the flesh of them that live within the Veil" (viii). For the author of
these essays, like the people he described, possessed two souls, two
warring ideals within his one dark body, and he epitomized the dilemma haunting the lives of all black folk. From his childhood com-
petitiveness with the white world, when he first saw the veil, he had
progressed to a sense of dedication to a greater purpose, the cultivation of learning and intelligence in order to serve not himself but the
people, and the preservation of values of the spirit in the face of
temptation and abuse. In a variety of tones the narrator of *The
Souls of Black Folk* relates the epic of his own soul-struggles, emerging finally as a man enduring but determined to prevail. Du Bois'
self-portrait stresses the necessity of moral and psychological heroism, the qualities without which, he affirms, life is meaningless. The
work ringingly affirms his faith in the strength of the African soul,
against which that other powerful soul, implanted by the white
world, wages constant war.

The greatness of *The Souls of Black Folk* as a document of black
American culture lies in its creation of profound and enduring
myths about the life of the people. Du Bois achieved with his essays
and short story an effect not unlike that which Cooper had captured
for the American people with his Leatherstocking tales, or Scott for
the Anglo-Hibernian tradition with his Waverley novels, or Yeats
for Ireland with his stories and poems steeped in the mysteries of the
Celtic twilight. Du Bois held up to Afro-America a portrait of the

people drawn by one of their own. By the force of his mythmaking imagination he thus taught them how to think of themselves and how to celebrate themselves, for the portrait was immediately recognized as an inspired reflection of the deepest level of the black American heritage. He converted the racist ascription of sensuality, emotional indulgence, and imitative artistic talent into a capacity for humanizing life, a depth of spirituality, a passion for art, especially music, and finally, an essential dualism in the black American soul. In placing the focus of his examination on the divided consciousness of the black man, Du Bois stressed the permanent potential for drama and for tragedy in each member of the Afro-American masses. There was thus an intrinsic dignity to the black experience and a destiny apart from that of the mainstream of the nation of which Afro-America had seemed for so long to be little more than an insignificant tributary. If all of a nation's literature may stem from one book, as Hemingway implied about *The Adventures of Huckleberry Finn*, then it can as accurately be said that all of Afro-American literature of a creative nature has proceeded from Du Bois' comprehensive statement on the nature of the people in *The Souls of Black Folk*. Even his choice of a basic metaphor—the dim perception by the races of each other, as through a veil—left its mark on black expression. And from his enunciation of the presence of two souls warring in one dark body has emerged the dilineation of the most acute and therefore, for the artist, the most alluring of black dilemmas, the reconciliation of his troubled presence in white America with his nostalgia for the mythic home from which he was torn. Dated though words and phrases certainly are, Du Bois' book is as alive for black America today as when it was first published in 1903.

One meaningful irony of the achievement of this work is that it is at once a tribute to black America and to the ideals of the white civilization which held black Americans in serfdom. *The Souls of Black Folk* is written out of an extraordinary spirit of generosity, evidenced not simply in the tight-lipped civility of the attack on Washington but also in Du Bois' compassion for the tragedy of the broken South, both white and black. More important, *The Souls of Black Folk* represents the refusal of one man to be alienated from those ideals of truth, beauty, and the spirituality of life cherished by a civilization which sought to make him an alien. Already in Europe

artists and writers such as Picasso, Matisse, and Gide were beginning to look toward Africa as a source of sensual inspiration and
artistic freedom unbridled by the restraints of the Judeo-Christian,
"over-civilized" Western world. But Du Bois sought those very restraints. He worked to translate the fund of emotional and spiritual
power of black America into a passion for the ideal and a dedication
to culture. The work is thus a powerful tribute to a civilization that
has largely ignored it.

CHAPTER FIVE

The Mantle of the Prophet

Now, very often it happens that the evil is there, the wrong has been done, and yet we do not hear of it — we do not know about it. Here then comes the agitator. He is the herald — he is the prophet — he is the man that says to the world: "There are evils which you do not know, but which I know and you must listen to them." (Du Bois, 1907)

The Souls of Black Folk marked both an end and a beginning in the career of Du Bois. In collecting the best of his "fugitive pieces," the book effectively summarized his thought on the subject of black America between the end of his formal education and his thirty-fifth year. His attack on Booker T. Washington, however, began a new phase of his life. While his scholarly work continued, principally on the Atlanta University Conference and its Publications, he was consciously searching for a superior solution to questions for which social science had once seemed the conclusive answer. Between 1903 and 1910, when he left his professorship at Atlanta University to join the National Association for the Advancement of Colored People and to develop its official organ, the *Crisis,* he founded and edited two magazines, the *Moon* and then the *Horizon.* During these years he wrote some of his most revealing poetry, including his major prose poem, "A Litany of Atlanta." In 1909 he published a derivative but deeply revealing biography of the most radical Abolitionist, John Brown. An equally essential part of this creative period was his first novel, *The Quest of the Silver Fleece,* which appeared in 1911.

Du Bois' more active role in black political life began formally when he called a conference of Afro-American leaders at Fort Erie, Ontario, in July 1905. Subsequently known as the Niagara Movement, the organization that resulted assumed the task of "radical" opposition to Booker T. Washington and moved its leader steadily away from a purely scholarly career. In this difficult period of his life he became finally aware of the complexity of political life. Wanting to believe still in the inviolability of truth and the benevolence and rationality of man, he discovered instead the limitations of science and the obtuseness of the world. His mind toughened.

With his 1903 collection Du Bois had shown himself the most eloquent of the anti-Washington intellectuals, but the most spirited and unequivocal opposition to Tuskegee had come from the black Boston activists William Monroe Trotter and George Forbes, especially through their newspaper, the *Guardian*. It was not modesty alone that made Du Bois admit in 1905 that he had neither founded the Niagara Movement nor planned its method of operation, and that it was Trotter who had "put the backbone into the platform."[1] Until this turning point, Du Bois had regarded his natural position, as a man of reason, to be the middle ground. He was capable of flashes of anger and of sustained criticism of white racism, but he recoiled from identification with a radicalism that would demand the slighting of scholarly and social propriety for political ends. Simply put, Du Bois did not think it appropriate that a man of his education and culture should descend to write polemical journalism, or that he should be involved in the heckling of speakers at public meetings. Trotter, in contrast, had no such reservations and represented the extremest form of opposition to Tuskegee. A man of sound academic and social credentials — he had graduated *magna cum laude* from Harvard — Trotter nevertheless plunged into the fray and went to jail for allegedly disrupting a stormy meeting in Boston on the night of July 30, 1903, at which Washington had spoken and had been severely heckled. The "Boston Riot," as the affair is called, brought Du Bois out into the open to protest the treatment of Trotter. This act of humiliation against a man of his own class and general sympathies seems to have shaken him into confronting the power of the Washington following and the limits of his own influence. His indignation "overflowed."[2]

Du Bois' reaction to the events of July 30, culminated a year of rising impatience with the Washington organization. An article earlier in the same month on the "advance guard of the race" had brought his criticism to a crucial point. He accused Washington of deliberately manipulating the political and social situation in America to serve the racist interests of whites and the selfish interests of

Tuskegee. The Atlanta scholar was obliquely accusing Washington of making reactionary politics his main occupation, for which Tuskegee Institute was a front, and of deliberately sharing in an alliance between white politicians and big business at the expense of blacks in general.[3]

Du Bois believed that Washington was a willing tool of the Republican party; the special and well-publicized relationship between President Theodore Roosevelt and the black leader helped the Republicans to secure the black vote for the nominal price of a few minor federal appointments and the illusion of concern for the black citizen in the Democratic South. In turn, Tuskegee was given the leverage to dominate the political and cultural life of black America. The link between Washington and philanthropic business — notable in the case of Andrew Carnegie, who gave Tuskegee six hundred thousand dollars in 1903 — also granted Washington the power to divert funds from "disloyal" institutions and individuals. Finally, Washington's enormous reputation as a spokesman for blacks was a wall between the radicals and the traditionally sympathetic white liberals, such as Oswald Garrison Villard, grandson of the Abolitionist Garrison and then editor of the influential New York *Evening Post* and a major force in its literary supplement, *The Nation.*

Specifically, Du Bois accused Tuskegee of bribing black-owned newspapers in order to control their political policy.[4] He believed that Washington unscrupulously used his federal and philanthropic connections to deny jobs to some opponents and to remove others from their positions. He believed that the Tuskegee machine, as he eventually called it, did not hesitate to move against universities such as Atlanta for refusing to silence intellectuals in public disagreement with Washington, or against the nonpartisan Atlanta Publications in its search for financial support, or against Du Bois himself in his efforts to find funds for an endowed national magazine to serve the interests of blacks.[5] Such Tuskegee activity was surreptitiously carried out while Washington's reputation as an impartial, principled leader grew.

Although incredible at the time to many observers, Du Bois' general charges, and most of his specific ones, were well founded. The release of the Washington papers enabled scholars to confirm later the existence of an ethos at Tuskegee somewhat more suited to a corrupt political ward than to an institute of learning.[6] For many years, though, Du Bois appeared to be in concert with the wilder voices of the black intelligentsia, especially when he sided with the outspoken and often intemperate Trotter. Few could believe that Washington would spend three thousand dollars in an attempt to control papers in New York, Chicago, Indianapolis, Washington, and Boston. Du Bois' attempts to convince the influential Villard of the soundness of his charge exemplified his frustrations and the success of the Tuskegee machine in dividing its potential enemies and preserving its power.[7]

In the aftermath of the Boston Riot, with the jailed Trotter a martyr among the radicals and Du Bois openly in support of him, Washington called for a meeting of conciliation to include all the warring factions. Du Bois' plan for the meeting—his outline of strategy and list of objectives—shows that while he was still willing to make peace with Tuskegee, he had reached a decisive stage on key issues and objectives. The civil rights of blacks and whites were to be identical, and the rights of blacks were to be fought for in the courts if necessary. Both industrial and "higher" education must be available to blacks, with elementary school training compulsory for all. There was to be a national black periodical, more intensive sociological study of black life, and an efficient union of black societies and activities. There was also to be an end to what he saw as the Washington-inspired campaign of black self-deprecation before the nation as a whole.[8]

The meeting, which took place in New York in January 1904, did little to modify this program or bring the parties together. A Committee of Twelve, designed to include a variety of opinions in hopes of presenting a common front on sensitive issues, proved unequal to the task. Du Bois resigned from it in the middle of 1904 and set about the business of leading the established opposition to Tuskegee. In March 1905 the anti-Washingtonians met in Washington, D.C., to plan the organization that would become known as the Niagara Movement. In response to a call signed by fifty-nine black leaders, the first meeting was held at Fort Erie, Ontario, July 11-13, 1905.

For a trained social scientist and academic, adoption of the rhetoric of the militant propagandist was a momentous but slow affair. In his determined respect for the sanctity of truth, Du Bois had been almost impartial in criticizing both whites and blacks in his speeches

on race and politics; he was unwilling — or unable — to separate
political considerations from those of morality. The crucial change
in the years following *The Souls of Black Folk* was in a direction
away from this uneasy combination of self-criticism with demands
for political reform. Although the shift was directly reflected in the
language of his political statements, showing up most dramatically
in their contrast between scholarship and propaganda, the change
was not simply rhetorical. Fundamentally, it marked a new understanding on his part of the nature of the political experience and a
resulting shift in the philosophic method by which Du Bois interpreted the most important social forces and issues with which he
would thereafter contend.

In 1903, when he first openly attacked Washington, Du Bois still
mixed declarations of political purpose with adverse moral judgments of black America. In "The Training of Negroes for Social
Power," a statement that anticipates the goals of the Niagara Movement, Du Bois began by demanding for blacks the power needed
for "their own social regeneration." Social power would mean "the
growth of initiative among Negroes, the spread of independent
thought, the expanding consciousness of manhood." Yet he attributed "that social disease called the Negro problem" to a deep
ignorance by black folk "of the world and its ways, of the thought
and experience of men; an ignorance of self and the possibilities of
human souls." To erase this ignorance, training was necessary.
Elementary education was needed for the youth of "that group of
people whose mental grasp is by heredity weakest, and whose knowledge of the past is for historic reasons most imperfect." And higher
learning was needed to train the leadership in the fight "to stamp
out crime, strengthen the home, eliminate degenerates," and
inspire a love of work.[9]

The crucial tension in this essay is between the stern moral and
cultural criticism of blacks and the demand for black power. Yet the
identification of independence and a full sense of black "manhood"
as the goals of that power sounded a new, aggressive note. Faced by
the intransigence of Southern racism and the Tuskegee machine,
Du Bois had begun to respond with the zeal of a combatant in an
open struggle. It was perhaps his recognition of the distorting effects
of political antagonism that led him the following year to a deliberate, measured statement of his fundamental beliefs.

In the "Credo," published in 1904, Du Bois announced a belief in

God, who is the father of all races. Races differ in "no essential particular," and all are capable of infinite development. But Du Bois declared a special faith in "the Negro Race." The black qualities prized by him are "the beauty of its genius, the sweetness of its soul, and its strength in that meekness which shall yet inherit this turbulent earth." A belief in black meekness is countered by a faith in "pride of race and lineage and self," a pride deep enough to despise injustice to others. Pride is balanced by a commitment to "Service — humble, reverent service, from the blackening of boots to the whitening of souls; for Work is Heaven, Idleness Hell." All distinction not based on deed "is devilish and not divine." He believed in "the Devil and his angels, who wantonly work to narrow the opportunity of struggling human beings, especially if they be black"; and in the Prince of Peace, for war is murder, and armies and navies "the tinsel and braggadocio of oppression and wrong." All men must have liberty to think, dream, and work in a "kingdom of God and love." Education of the young, black and white, would lead to the moral vision that assures justice and dignity for all. "Finally, I believe in Patience — patience with the weakness of the Weak and the strength of the Strong . . . patience with the tardy triumph of Joy and the chastening of Sorrow, — patience with God."[10]

In the remaining years of Du Bois' life, not one of these articles of faith would be repudiated, although most of them would be challenged in his subsequent career as outspoken agitator and propagandist. The distance between the "Credo" and his future actions would merely reflect the cost of the life of activism to a man of deep and humane conviction.

In spite of the final article of the "Credo," Du Bois' patience was at an end. "We must complain. Yes, plain, blunt complaint, ceaseless agitation, unfailing exposure of dishonesty and wrong — this is the ancient, unerring way to liberty, and we must follow it."[11] Thus he announced in 1905 the purposes of the Niagara Movement. A moment of special drama for the movement came on the first anniversary of its birth, in August 1906, when the delegates met at Harpers Ferry, West Virginia, to pay tribute to John Brown, the best-known martyr of the Abolitionist cause. Urged on by the passionate Trotter, Du Bois chose the occasion for a statement such as he had never made publicly before. "We will not be satisfied to take one jot or tittle less than our full manhood rights," he said. He did not reason with white people: "In detail, our demands are clear and un-equivocal." Confronting the issues of social equality and miscegena-tion, he demanded "the right of freemen to walk, talk, and be with them that wish to be with us." His words on black crime show the revolution in attitude from his earlier embarrassment and defensive-ness when faced with the statistics. "We are not more lawless than the white race," he now asserted; rather, "we are more often arrested, convicted and mobbed." The shift of focus is clear in his statement on the significant factors of life: nothing is worth "the surrender of a people's manhood or the loss of a man's self-respect." "We are men; we will be treated as men," Du Bois declared. "On this rock we have planted our banners."[12]

While the Niagara Movement took few important steps as an organized body, Du Bois continued to define the terms of its opposi-tion to the status quo. The following year he made an important defense of the political agitator. Since "we are gifted with human nature which does not do the right or even desire the right always," someone must be brave enough to point to evil and demand change. The agitator is "the herald—he is the prophet—he is the man that says to the world: 'There are evils which you do not know, but which I know and you must listen to them.' " Du Bois admitted that there are honest and dishonest agitators, but he urged the need to listen to the voices calling for change. All great reform movements have been preceded by agitation, he noted. The silence "in the last decade" has been "our great mistake . . . It is then high time that the Negro agitator should be in the land." Du Bois acknowledged that "it is not a pleasant role to play," but "nevertheless it is the highest optimism to bring forward the dark side of any human picture. When a man does this he says to the world: 'Things are bad but it is worthwhile to let the world know that things are bad in order that they may be-come better.' "[13] His brilliant career as an outspoken propagandist of black American, Pan-African, and eventually socialist causes was effectively launched. He was then thirty-nine years old.

Du Bois' growing political sense, the increasingly pragmatic nature of his philosophic approach to the question of race relations, had taught him that while he was free to believe whatever he wanted about the moral state of his people, open criticism of black America was a strategic blunder in the struggle for freedom. In chastising blacks while attempting to plead the case for their civil rights, he and other leaders were comforting their enemies by reinforcing their racist sentiments. In so doing, the black leadership were also undermining the confidence of their own masses and even of themselves by the contradiction between their insistence on power and privilege and their patent sense of shame at alleged black weaknesses. The major tactical foundation of the Niagara Movement was its dismissal of the racist suppositions of social Darwinism with which black thinkers had struggled since the end of slavery. In spite of its elitist tendencies, the movement thereby asserted the authority of the black masses to demand constitutional and other rights regardless of any moral, economic, or intellectual failings that might be perceived in the culture as a whole. The insight behind this historic change, to which Du Bois and his followers came only gradually, was the perception of the Afro-American experience as essentially a continuous *political* struggle with the white world, a struggle that forbids the self-incrimination which often arises from self-examination.

This revaluation of the duty of Afro-American political leadership proved to be of lasting consequence, but the movement itself never developed into a major political force. Although the organization met annually for five consecutive years — first in Canada, then at Harpers Ferry, and later in Boston, Oberlin, and New Jersey — severe financial and organizational problems made it less than cohesive from the start. Its scattered members were either unwilling or unable to pay regular dues, and the radicals received little or no financial aid from other sources, for most of whom Booker T. Washington was above suspicion. In competition with other groups, such as the interracial Constitution League or the Afro-American Council, the movement could not find the resources to back up its words of protest with sustained legal action or any other show of actual strength. Its major achievement, therefore, was in advocating a strong program of civil rights while others preached moderation, conciliation, or worse.

The tenets of the Niagara program varied little from Du Bois' position in his January 1904 meeting with Washington. It stressed the right of blacks to respect from the state equal to that accorded whites; it demanded the vote, equal economic opportunity for blacks and whites, and education for all classes of blacks; it endorsed agitation for change rather than dependence on the initia-

tive and good will of whites; it sought unity among black and interracial groups dedicated to correcting intolerable social conditions.
In the following years Du Bois preached this gospel in a variety of
ways, while the Niagara Movement itself steadily diminished in
effectiveness. Elliott M. Rudwick has suggested four major reasons
for its troubles. First, its views were too radical for the time, and the
Tuskegee machine too powerful and determined in opposition.
Second, the doctrine of the talented tenth ("actually a talented hun-
dredth," Rudwick noted) isolated its members from the masses psychologically and ideologically and encouraged "an empyrean view
of human rights," which led the movement to stress politics instead
of economic needs. Third, Du Bois' often forbidding personality
and his inexperience as an activist leader hurt a body dependent on
him for continuity and direction. Lastly, the movement was ham-
pered by the disruptive presence of Trotter, whose actions and statements more than once infuriated Du Bois and embarrassed the
organization.[14]

The movement was only nominally alive after four years when a
group of white socialists and liberals, assembling what would become in 1910 the National Association for the Advancement of
Colored People, invited it and Du Bois to join their number, assur-
ing the continuity of its program and justifying the soundness of its
underlying assumptions and principles. In extending this invitation,
the NAACP took a major step toward securing its own future.

Du Bois' professional responsibilities at Atlanta University made
him a part-time agitator at best, but by 1905 he was soliciting financial support for the one contribution he was determined to make,
production of "a high-class journal to circulate among the intelligent Negroes, tell them of the deeds of themselves and their neighbors, interpret the news of the world to them, and inspire them
toward definite ideals."[15] Although there were a few black papers,
the Atlanta professor found them inadequate in scope and sophistication. He now published only occasionally in the liberal Northern
magazines, such as the *Atlantic Monthly,* the *Dial,* the *Independent,* and the *World's Work,* which had cradled *The Souls of Black
Folk*; but the magazine he had in mind was based on such publications, with special focus on the problem of race and the future of
black America. One black magazine, *The Voice of the Negro,*
founded in Atlanta in 1904 by his friend J. Max Barber, was mili-

tantly anti-Washington in policy, and in its first four years it published several pieces by Du Bois. But he was not to be satisfied until he could publish a journal of his own. Unable to gain support from philanthropy — because of the Tuskegee influence, he later believed — Du Bois nevertheless pressed on, and in December 1905 he brought out the first issue of a weekly publication called the *Moon*.

Although only two numbers are extant, a partial relationship between the *Moon* and its successors, the *Horizon* and the *Crisis*, is clear.[16] This prototype, though clumsy and parochial in many areas, disclosed the basic patterns and concerns of a Du Bois magazine, in that it was an illustrated periodical of information, commentary, and criticism aimed at a predominantly black audience. While it attempted to serve local black communities in an expressly social function ("After a successful term in Boylen Home School, Miss Whitlock Poole is in the city again"), the *Moon* also aimed at a more important goal. It proclaimed itself "a record of the darker races," reporting on the life of nonwhite peoples in America and around the world. It reprinted news items of importance to black people from both the white and black press and reported on events in the Caribbean, Africa, and the East. Although the journal noted in March 1906 that the Niagara Movement was ending its first year of work, Du Bois did not consider his magazine as integral to the political association. Less polemical than its successors, the *Moon* seems to have been tame in its reporting of the American racial scene. It was aimed at the black middle class, and its tiny circulation — 250 to 500, according to Paul G. Partington — suggests that it may have found its mark.[17]

The periodical suffered while its editor stumbled through the difficulties of an immature journalist. Its titles often paraded the obvious, as in "The Man in the Moon" and "Whirl of the World," and the bombastic, as in "Where the Gates Lift Up Their Heads" and "By the Father of Waters" to indicate the cities of Atlanta and Memphis. The *Moon* found it impossible to remain both intellectually stimulating and a social register for the bourgeoisie scattered about America. The true scope of Du Bois' vision appeared in his "Dunbar Memorial Number," where he stressed the importance of black American literary expression. Du Bois recognized that in the death of Dunbar the race had lost its most famous artist, and he was quick to urge a realization of that loss on the people themselves.

In spite of its shortcomings, the basic aim of the *Moon* was clear: it sought to advertise in well-written prose the actions and abilities of black people in their struggle for freedom, and to place their story in the context of both world politics and a moral idealism that transcended politics. If the achievement of the magazine was modest, it trained Du Bois in a skill he would display more confidently in the years immediately following the last number of the *Moon* in July 1906.

When Du Bois began his next attempt at editing a magazine, he had a greater understanding of his goals as a journalist. In January 1907 the monthly *Horizon* appeared, coproduced by Du Bois, F. H. M. Murray, and L. M. Hershaw, associates in the Niagara Movement. Writing a section called "The Overlook," Du Bois was generally responsible for reporting national and international events, as well as for literary criticism and commentary. Compared to the *Moon*, the *Horizon* provided more extensive coverage of world events and opinions and disdained the role of social register. From the first issue Du Bois stressed the international nature of the meaning of race in the twentieth century and continued his development of the theme of the "dark races"; in addition, the journal promoted the ideas of Pan-Africanism and, to a lesser extent, of socialism. India was a "land of dark men far across the sea which is of interest to us" as either the ancestral home of dark people or a land where "in some ancestral time they wandered."[18] Relying on reports in foreign journals such as the *African Mail,* the *Horizon* informed its readers of political trends and events in Africa and kept alive the idea of a "Pan-African movement."[19] The second number (February 1907) acclaimed socialism as "the one great hope" of black Americans, and Du Bois declared himself a "Socialist-of-the-Path," in sympathy with socialist aims but uncommitted to any socialist organization.

Avoiding dogmatic socialism or party identification, the *Horizon* tried to provide readers with a pragmatic guide for making such political choices as were offered. The presidential elections of 1908 found the "Socialist-of-the-Path" looking coldly at the candidates; "as between Taft and Johnson, vote for Johnson. As between Taft and La Follette, vote for La Follette."[20] The next month the *Horizon* made its presidential choice perfectly clear: "If the Republican Party insults the black man by nominating Taft, vote for Bryan."[21]

At stake was the Republican party's traditional hold on the black electorate. In a practice that he would follow almost until the Depression, Du Bois was attempting to manipulate the black vote into a position where it would be crucial to the balance of electoral power. There is no evidence that such attempts succeeded, although in opposing the Republicans, Du Bois anticipated by decades the eventual shift of the black vote away from "the party of Lincoln" toward the Democrats.

The magazine was less than conciliatory in dealing with Booker T. Washington. It compared him unfavorably to William Lloyd Garrison in his attitude to radical opposition; he was seldom mentioned by name and praised only once, in August 1908, when he openly attacked the practice of lynching. But almost every number of the *Horizon* breathed defiance of the principles for which he was famous. Although until its last months the journal did not consider itself radical, each number exposed new examples of racial injustice in the North and South. Apparently like the *Moon,* it did not advertize its relationship to the Niagara Movement, but its pages endorsed the principles of the organization. Typical of its position was its treatment of the Brownsville Affair of 1906, in which three companies of a black regiment had been dishonorably discharged after a disturbance in Texas. The journal hammered away at the issue month after month and did not hesitate to criticize President Roosevelt when he seemed indifferent to the injustice.

Du Bois developed in the *Horizon* the type of satirical, dramatized editorial he would use so brilliantly in the *Crisis.* In one such editorial, a black leader, kicked downstairs by a white man, calls the onlookers' attention to the fact that the kick was not nearly as hard as it might have been, since the white man's boots were soft, and the fall was on dirt, not asphalt. Elsewhere, Du Bois had an "Eminent Philanthropist," upon entering a streetcar, advise the black narrator to be patient. "My friend," he says, "My dark and dear Friend, you are impatient." The black man is urged to "look up, look forward . . . Seek the greater; enjoy God's bounty in sun, air and beauty. Forget your rights, do your Duty, don't complain." A conductor rudely interrupts to demand a second fare, whereupon the incensed philanthropist storms off, sounding off about the importance of principle.[22] In yet another dramatized editorial, a white man cheats a black, then asks him to get other blacks to work for him for nothing. But won't they resist and cause trouble? The white man dismisses the question: "Don't I own the Associated Press?" The black man drops to his knees and whispers, "Here am I, send me!"[23]

An essential objective of the *Horizon* was to encourage black confidence and ambition, to raise the moral and intellectual tone of the community, and to promote racial pride based on a knowledge of the African and Afro-American past. But the journal wanted to avoid the appearance of chauvinism. It was usually adorned with inspirational quotations from a variety of sources. A text from the Bible gave way to H. G. Wells' warning that racial prejudice was the worst evil in the world. Other writers quoted included Elizabeth Barrett Browning, Horace, Milton, Pope, Emerson, James Russell Lowell, Longfellow, and Matthew Arnold. Black America was urged to read and own more books, to subscribe to magazines and even newspapers, though "of all festering abominations, away with the Sunday newspaper. It is an imp of Hell and child of the devil . . . because it is a hodge-podge of lie, gossip, twaddle and caricature."[24] Books and articles written either by or about blacks were noted (Du Bois never closed his magazines to white contributors). The journal stressed works that added to the prestige of black Africans: a two-page excerpt from a book on Egypt ends with Du Bois pronouncing that "by the harmony of this powerful triplex of proofs, I am finally compelled to pronounce in favour of the Negro origin of the Egyptians."[25]

The *Horizon* was in every way an advance over the *Moon*, but after two years Du Bois and his associates still had not succeeded in providing a solid financial foundation, and with its three editors, the journal lacked consistent standards and a clear focus. After the December 1908 issue it did not appear again until November of the following year. Instead of the triumvirate of Du Bois, Hershaw, and Murray, it was now edited by Du Bois and the "assistant editors." In July 1908 Du Bois had publicly insisted that the magazine be enlarged and broadened to meet the pressing need for a national black journal. When the new *Horizon* appeared, it announced itself as "a radical newspaper."[26] It called for universal suffrage, human equality, abolition of war, the gradual development of socialism, and an end to religiously inspired persecution. The new journal marked an increase in intellectual seriousness and political commitment, although most of its fundamental aims and methods were the same.

Du Bois' apprenticeship as an editor and journalist was now complete. The renovated *Horizon* lasted for nine issues, until in July 1910 it called upon readers to join "us" in the NAACP and announced Du Bois' resignation from the faculty of Atlanta University and his appointment to the new association. Four months later the first issue of the *Crisis* appeared.

During these difficult years of agitation and confusion, of accomplishment and failure, Du Bois published perhaps the best of his relatively few poems. Verse then served him mainly as a channel for the rage he could not express even in his liveliest essays and for the articulation of musings and fantasies alien to the logic he prized in his propaganda and scholarship. Only later, in the *Crisis*, would Du Bois develop prose pieces that gave full vent to his emotions. His poems, most of them written by 1911, extend the range of his public expression. They reveal moods of sometimes astonishing intensity, as well as a remarkable capacity for spiritual repose.

The most telling characteristic of Du Bois' poetry is that even his greatest ragings repeatedly resolve themselves into the language and forms of religion. God, Christ, Heaven, and Hell are omnipresent in his verse; the social questions that were the wellsprings of his poetry, as of his whole career, are repeatedly translated into questions of divine judgment and intention. Some titles indicate the irresistibility of religious forms and themes: "A Litany of Atlanta," "A Hymn to the People," "Christ of the Andes," "The Prayer of the Bantu," "The Prayers of God." The impenetrable meaning of human suffering matches the inscrutability of God; Christ is the incarnation of all human hope; Heaven is the world beyond the veil; and life is Hell. Only much later in life would Du Bois abandon the central metaphor of religious experience in his verse in favor of purely secular imagery.

Of the many searing experiences of his Georgia years—the period in which, as he wrote of John Brown in his own darkest days, the iron entered his soul—only the death of his son affected him more than the Atlanta Riot of September 1906. One of the most destructive outbreaks of violence by whites against blacks before World War I, the riot raged for three days as Du Bois, out of town at its start, hurried back to the city, uncertain of the fate of his wife and daughter. On the train journey he wrote "A Litany of Atlanta."[27] Couched in an ancient form, the work is a passionate address to a silent God in a time of chaos and destruction. The questions it asks are fundamental to the suffering faithful: how can divinity and evil coexist in the same universe? Why does an all-powerful God remain silent in the face of his children's suffering? Is God dead? (Thou art not dead, but flown afar, up hills of endless light"):

> We raise our shackled hands and charge thee, God,
> by the bones of our stolen fathers, by the tears
> of our dead mothers, by the very blood of Thy
> crucified Christ: What meaneth this? Tell us the
> plan; give us the sign!

In grief and confusion the black poet speaks the unspeakable: "Surely thou, too, art not white, O Lord, a pale, bloodless, heartless thing!" Recoiling from the terrible thought, he pleads forgiveness for "these wild, blasphemous words":

> Thou art still the God of our black fathers and in
> Thy Soul's Soul sit some soft darkenings, some
> shadowing of the velvet night.
> But whisper — speak — call, great God, for Thy
> silence is white terror to our heart! The way, O
> God, show us the way and point us the path!

The essential debate in "A Litany of Atlanta" is not between a man and a distant God, but within the speaker himself. Tormented by the knowledge of evil, he finds himself wavering between the rival forces of radical anger and divine reason, between human despair and sublime faith. The God of the poem, as of most of Du Bois' verse, is the potential nobility of man. In a crisis that is the psychological and moral consequence of his divided, warring soul, the black man-god struggles with himself for emotional and philosophic balance, for sanity and sense, in a mad world. The division here resembles, at one level, the psychological dualism described in *The Souls of Black Folk*. However, it is more like the tension between body and soul, spirit and flesh, that characterizes moral descriptions of man's nature, with one crucial difference: the black man suffers without hope or guilt, yet must keep the faith in a superhuman act of the spirit. All that remains to the poet at the end of his litany is a vague hope and an unnerving paradox — "O God of a godless land!" — before he lapses into silence and rest.

Other poems are less equivocal in perceiving the black man's fate.
"The Burden of Black Women," later retitled "The Riddle of the
Sphinx," expresses an intense bitterness toward the white world,
remarkable in that there is no comparable strain anywhere in his
prose.[28] The "will of the world" calls the black woman to rise, but
she is kept down by:

> The white world's vermin and filth:
> All the dirt of London,
> All the scum of New York
> Valiant spoilers of women
> . . . .
>
> Bearing the white man's burden
> Of Liquor and Lust and Lies.
>
> . . . .
> I hate them, Oh!
> I hate them well,
> I hate them, Christ!
> As I hate Hell,
> If I were God
> I'd sound their knell
> This day!

The poet hopes for the coming of a "dim, darker David" from whose
line would emerge "the Black Christ." Peace and virtue will then
come to mankind, "be it yellow or black or white." The celebration
of black womanhood is consistent with Du Bois' near-reverence of
the female sex and his belief that the hopes of the black race lie
more in the quality of its women than in its men.

Purely celebrational of the black man is "The Song of the Smoke,"
perhaps the first Afro-American poem of this kind.[29] The poem's
strength lies in its central metaphor, which relates human blackness
to a wayward column of smoke, as well as in its insistent rhythm,
invoked through verbal repetition and variation of line length.
Du Bois wrote in his "Credo" of a desirable "whitening of souls," but
here he glories in the despised color of black that billows upward
into the blue sky:

> I am the Smoke King
> I am black!
> I am swinging in the sky
> I am wringing worlds awry;
> . . . .

> I am whirling home to God;
> I am the Smoke King
> I am black.

The smoke darkens the weak white clouds; it is dominant and irresistible as it passes on toward God, "lurid lowering 'mid the blue,/ Torrid towering toward the true." The language is deliberately murky but the message is stark:

> I will be black as blackness can —
> The blacker the mantle, the mightier the man!
> For blackness was ancient ere whiteness began.

The smoke rises from the fire of the African soul; the potential of black power remains true even in the midst of social powerlessness.

"A Day in Africa" is an exercise in fantasy, as Du Bois depicted life in a continent he had not yet seen.[30] Historically important as a precursor of the vogue of poetry celebrational of Africa, the work portrays its hero as hunter, dancer, lover, and athlete reveling in the color and sensuality of African life, sleeping away "the liquid languor of the noon," rising to hunt again until "the velvet trumpet of the night" summons him to lie down with the lion in sleep, like an innocent lamb in a new Eden. The lines are impacted with images of varying success but reveal the poet's vision of the African experience. The hills smell of incense, the sun is royal, the dawn glows beneath a bridal veil of mist:

> I leaped and danced, and found
> My breakfast poised aloft,
> All served in living gold.
> In purple flowered fields I wandered
> Wreathed in crimson, blue and green.
> My noon-tide meal did fawn about my feet
> In striped sleekness.
> I kissed it ere I killed it.

Another beast, "a wild new creature," confronts the poet, who poises his spear in defiance. But when he sees fear in the eyes of the beast, he refuses to kill it. The beast is the white man, new to Africa; Du Bois' act of mercy and generosity, as well as his martial defiance, flows naturally from the African experience, heritage, and character. To the poet, the meaning of the land is a sensuous release of the body in a splendid hedonism that nonetheless knows and prizes moral discretion.

"A Hymn to the Peoples," written for the Universal Races Congress, an international gathering of scholars, scientists, and social leaders in London in 1911, provides the last important dimension of the poet's interest:[31]

> O Truce of God!
> And primal meeting of the Sons of Man,
> Foreshadowing the union of the World!
> From all the ends of earth we come!

Enraptured by the vision of the world's races united in conference, the poet turns aside from partisan debate and recrimination to behold this prospect, the dearest goal of his agitation:

> Softly in sympathy the sunlight falls,
> Rare is the radiance of the moon;
> And on the darkest midnight blaze the stars—
> The far-flown shadows of whose brilliance
> Drop like a dream on the dim shores of Time,
> Forecasting Days that are to these
> As day to night.

In an imaginative leap that imposes the future on the present and thus asserts the power of hope over the anguish of present reality, the poem acquires the serenity of a mystical experience. Du Bois seldom had the opportunity or the cause to celebrate the world in this way, but here again his poetic craft, in drawing strength from the hymnal tradition, takes as its material and style a characteristic expression of religious faith.

Other poems by Du Bois, all published first in the *Horizon,* vary in their themes, technical interests, and levels of intensity. "My Country 'Tis of Thee," appearing in November 1907, parodies an American anthem that could have only ironic meaning for the thinking black citizen; "The Song of America" and "The Prayer of the Bantu," published in February and April 1908, are more directly defiant and political. An exhibition of "donnish" wit is found in a short poem about the artistic life based on a phrase from Horace. The longest poetic effort, published November-December 1908, offers two scenes from an antiwar verse drama, *The Christ of the Andes.* In the poem "Death" of December 1907, Du Bois dealt with a subject on which he periodically brooded throughout his long life. As with the essay on his son in *The Souls of Black Folk,* the death of close friends or other admired persons often moved him to write superbly poetic eulogies revealing a deep emotional identification with the drama of death.

In the context of his life's achievement, Du Bois' poetry is an invaluable source for his private thoughts; in the context of his turn from conservatism and scholarly distance to agitation and propaganda, the poems underscore the depth of his soul-searching and the dignity of his motives. He was groping toward a full acceptance of the changes overtaking his life, as the values to which he had dedicated himself through years of systematic education as student and professor appeared to be in serious jeopardy. He was not easily converted to the role of propagandist or political agitator. His formal education, his scholarship, his reverence for reason, his elitism, his shyness, his craving for respectability, and his involuntary coldness and severity in certain social situations, all held him back from radical activism. It was one thing to fight racism with facts and scholarship from the shelter of the university. It was quite another for a man of his place and time to risk jail, to walk barefoot in protest, or to devote his hard-won education to propagandistic journalism.

Yet the gravity of moral choice challenged him, as it had challenged, in the form of slavery, the radical Abolitionists of another era. In seeking spiritual guidance and a model for his new career, Du Bois went back fifty years into American history to the example of the most radical and enigmatic of the opponents of slavery, John Brown.

The fourth book written by Du Bois, *John Brown*, was published fifty years after the historic raid at Harpers Ferry in Virginia.[32] Its appearance in 1909 marked the apex of Du Bois' interest in the meaning of the revolt. The second meeting of the Niagara Movement at Harpers Ferry in the summer of 1906 had made a "pilgrimage at dawn bare-footed to the scene of Brown's martyrdom." The resolutions of the conference ended with the invocation of Brown's memory: "We do not believe in violence . . . but we do believe in John Brown, in that incarnate spirit of justice, that hatred of a lie, that willingness to sacrifice money, reputation, and life itself on the altar of right." *John Brown* is the strangest book in the Du Bois canon, as well as the one most poorly received by the reading public. In the seven years after its publication, fewer than seven hundred copies were sold. The author depended to a great extent on passages extracted from other biographies and commentaries on Brown's life, so that whole pages of his script are often direct quotations of secondary sources. He was scrupulous in annotation, but he readily admitted that there was "little new material" in his work, only a "new emphasis" on the meaning of the subject's life. Later, he referred defensively to the biography as "one of the best written of my books."[33]

Du Bois did not set out to write a "scholarly" biography of Brown. His approach to the writing of history had changed from the institutional research taught at Harvard by Hart. He retained Hart's rule of relentless documentation, but found himself unable or unwilling to follow the related demand for thorough and original research. He was now free to express his old interest in Fichte's theory of the great man or hero as a true maker of history, an idea exemplified in histories by Carlyle and Heinrich von Treitschke. But this approach was modified by another analytical method more in keeping with Du Bois' interest in race, economics, and society. He found his ideal instrument in the historical method of Hippolyte Taine, perhaps the most influential historian of the age. Brown's martyrdom is carefully shown to be the inevitable result of forces arising from his *race, milieu,* and *moment,* together with those psychological qualities and accidents that set him apart from other men subjected to the same pressures. In addition, Du Bois takes pains to isolate and spotlight what Taine called the *pensée maîtresse* or central idea of his subject. In sum, Taine's influence on Du Bois was as strong as it was on other contemporary American writers, such as Hamlin Garland, Frank Norris, and Owen Wister.

In *John Brown* Du Bois avoided the abundance of poetic devices and images found in *The Souls of Black Folk*, but shunned the severity of his doctoral thesis. He had come to believe that the recording of history benefits from the indulgence of the poetic imagination. For him, as Herbert Aptheker has remarked, "history writing was *writing*; one who produces a book should try therefore to produce *literature*."[34] In stressing the Puritan conscience and background of the Abolitionist martyr, Du Bois was depicting a latter-day prophet acting out a vision of himself as the instrument of God. Familiar with the King James Bible, Du Bois drew on the Biblical combination of gravity, lucidity, and lyricism as a model of the language appropriate to his discussion of a prophet. His version of Taine's theories, though lacking the support of original research, is dramatically effective. He places his subject's life against a physical and historic backdrop and convinces the reader of the authenticity of the setting.

The influence of race on history, the first of Taine's insights, appears in the first sentence of the book: "The mystic spell of Africa is and ever was over all America" (15). It was Brown's response to the plight of black folk, Du Bois argues, that inspired him to greatness. His racial character was formed from a mixture of English, Celtic, and Dutch heritages, each supplying strains that would make themselves felt throughout his life. The "gifts" of these races to the New World were Puritanism ("the last white flower of the Lutheran revolt"), Dutch "vigor and thrift" dominant in the Renaissance, and the Celtic "passionate desire for personal freedom" (18). The "human embodiments" of these three forces eventually produced a descendant who combined them all in his character. Brown's ancestors included an English carpenter, a Dutch tailor, and a Welsh wanderer, all immigrants to the New World. From the blend of these racial types came the three great concerns of Brown's life: Puritanism, a sense of economic responsibility, and reverence for freedom.

The physical setting (Taine's *milieu*) of Brown's life is also stressed. Its dominant element was the Alleghenies, "that beautiful mass of hill and crag" stretching from Maine to the red foothills of Georgia. On one of these mountainsides Brown tended his herds of sheep and "dreamed his terrible dream. It was the mystic, awful voice of the mountains that lured him to liberty, death, and martyrdom within their wildest fastness and in their bosom he sleeps his last sleep" (48). Brown himself wrote that "God has given the strength of the hills to freedom; they were placed here for the emancipation of the Negro race" (106). Taine's milieu also meant the social forces surrounding a man, and the two most significant of these forces in Brown's life, according to Du Bois, were slavery and the treacherous business world of capitalist America. Brown's failure to survive as a businessman in the wool market is depicted as the inevitable failure of an idealist: "To him business was a philanthropy. We have not even today reached this idea, but, urged on by the Socialists, we are faintly perceiving it" (61). Brown refused to try to corner the wool market and watched in consternation as other men ruthlessly seized their chance to do so.

The *moment* of Brown's maturity, as defined by Taine, is also carefully set by Du Bois. Brown was born as "the shudder of Hayti" (75), the revolt of Toussaint L'Ouverture, was running through the Americas, encouraging revolution. In spite of Napoleon's failures, the social and economic doctrines of the French Revolution had also taken root. At the same time in America, the free black man was rising in the social scale. Between 1830 and 1840 the role of slavery as the basis of the cotton industry had begun to be challenged. By 1850, the underground railroad of slaves to freedom had become "systematized" through both black and white organizations. Leaders such as Martin Delany, Frederick Douglass, and Harriet Tubman, all of whom were personally known to Brown, added new power to the resistance to slavery. The attempt to make Kansas a slave state brought out the first vengeful fire in Brown, and his acts in that arena helped to polarize the nation. The lessons learned in the West pushed him to his last stand at Harpers Ferry, which in turn helped to precipitate the Civil War.

Du Bois' reliance on Taine in writing *John Brown* is most vivid in his emphasis on the *pensée maîtresse* of Brown's life: "The price of repression is greater than the cost of liberty. The degradation of men costs something both to the degraded and those who degrade" (17). The same thought, similarly expressed, tolls throughout the book. "From his earliest boyhood Brown had dimly conceived, and the conception grew with his growing, that the cost of liberty was less then the price of repression" (75-76). The lesson of Kansas was similar: "The carnival of crime and rapine that ensued was a disgrace to civilization but it was the cost of freedom, and it was less than the price of repression" (140). Repression was weakening America daily, especially in the South: "No worthy art nor literature, nor even the commerce of daily life could thrive in this atmosphere" (78). The price was the humiliation of raped and seduced black women, and the resultant demeaning of the white wives and mothers of the master caste. At the end of the work the great thought appears again: "Has John Brown no message — no legacy, then, to the twentieth century? He has and it is this great word: the cost of liberty is less than the price of repression" (383).

As an explicit essay on the power of moral imperatives and a determined conscience, *John Brown* is a study in the sociology of modern prophecy. In the case of Brown, if not of all other agitators, Du Bois' identification of the role of political agitator with that of prophet was a valid one. Du Bois wished to speak not to a sect but to the whole nation, indeed to the whole world. His fascination with the life and death of Brown tells of his apprehension of the demands on those who see themselves as God's prophets. Brown had conceived of himself as a literal instrument of the Lord and had served his master to the death. A less religiously dogmatic soul, Du Bois nevertheless saw himself as also serving ideals compatible with religious godhead. His staring into the dark well of Brown's legacy should not be dismissed, therefore, as an exercise to remind others of a dedicated Abolitionist martyr. The study was an outward, objective tracing of his inner anguish over how best to serve himself, his people, the world, and the spirituality before which he abased himself. Trapped in the gilded cage of his education and scholarship, he pondered the personal consequences of the radical life. Causing even more hesitation and indecision was his suspicion, compounded by spiritual humility and guilt, of the validity of his call to such divine service.

Du Bois' own race, milieu, and moment were not those of John Brown. But he possessed the English gift of Puritanism, not bequeathed through race but acquired through culture and education. His treatment of Puritanism in the portrait of Brown is his only explicit commentary on a spiritual and psychic process to which he himself had been exposed. Brown was raised, he pointed out, in a religious atmosphere not of "stern, intellectual Puritanism, but of a milder and more sensitive type" (24); even so, his Puritan training combined with his youthful loneliness to both exhilarate and chastise him. He learned "the depths of secret self-abasement, and heights of confident self-will"; in addition he possessed a natural skepticism which only strengthened his faith while keeping him free of institutional Christianity: "Such a nature was in its very essence religious, even mystical, but never superstitious nor blindly trustful in half-known creeds and formulas" (23). The Bible came to dominate Brown's imagination and expression. He gathered to himself "its history, poetry, philosophy, and truth." He delighted in the paradox between the "cruel grandeur" of the Old Testament and the love and sacrifice of the New, so that "both mingled to mold his soul" (25). In his manhood he became attuned to the power of "inexorable fate" and to "the mystery and promise of death" (40). With these came an abiding sense of what Du Bois called "the gloom and

horror of life" (41). Brown was led to a constant reexamination of
the self as a sinner before a jealous God. The world was "a terribly
earnest thing" in which he could never be content; he lived his life
with "a homely shrewd attention to all the little facts of daily existence," but waited for God's call to action (46).

In 1839, twenty years before the raid at Harpers Ferry, Brown
knew that he had been summoned by God to attack slavery. Du Bois
traces the pattern of Brown's decision from his earliest dislike of
slavery through the years of his observing its evils to the moment
when he suddenly realized that he must fight this "monster" (92).
He did not plan violence, because he hated war; "but he set his face
toward the goal and whithersoever the Lord led, he was ready to follow" (93). Misfortunes, including bankruptcy and the death of five
children, helped to drop "a sombre brooding veil of stern inexorable
fate over his spirit — a veil which never lifted. The dark mysterious
tragedy of life gripped him with awful intensity — the iron entered
his soul" (96). Finally Brown resolved to abandon all other concerns
and devote himself to avenging the Lord.

"This, at least it seems to me," Du Bois wrote, "is a fair interpretation of John Brown's thought and action from the evidence at
hand" (93). Clearly Du Bois was measuring his own life as scholar-
critic against that of Brown, who sacrificed all for his beliefs. Du
Bois defended Frederick Douglass' refusal to join in Brown's crusade
and commiserated with other Abolitionists who were appalled by
Brown's audacity; but he agonized over the fundamental question of
Brown's career, "the Riddle of the Sphinx." How does man know
what is right? "We are but darkened groping souls," pleaded Du
Bois, "that know not light often because of its very blinding radiance. Only in time is truth revealed" (338). He was attempting to
trace the fine distinctions beween dedication and fanaticism, between courage and recklessness, between belief and bigotry. All
men admit, he argued, that there are in this world "matters of vast
human import which are eternally right or eternally wrong" (339).
Yet men tend to search for the middle way of compromise and
safety, "a wavering path of expediency," leading possibly to the
good, but never to the best:

> And yet we all feel its temporary, tentative character; we instinc-
> tively distrust its comfortable tone, and listen almost fearfully for
> the greater voice; its better is often so far below that which we feel

is a possible best, that its present temporizing seems evil to us, and ever again after the world has complacently dodged and compromised with, and skilfully evaded a great evil, there shines, suddenly, a great white light—an unwavering, unflickering brightness, blinding by its all-seeing brilliance, making the whole world simply a light and darkness—a right and a wrong. Then men tremble and writhe and waver. (339-340)

Although Du Bois could not identify with John Brown, he was certainly measuring his own past achievement against the thunder at Harpers Ferry. Trained in Great Barrington and at Fisk, Harvard, and Berlin to appreciate the life of reason and the power of the golden mean, he now was preparing to take leave of respectability and such ease as society allowed him. His decision was hardly as momentous as Brown's, but for him it was the greatest step of his life. As had Shields Green, the fugitive slave who joined Brown's band and refused to leave when all was lost, Du Bois was finally going with "the old man" (347). His publicly stated objectives, as well as his sacrifices, were much more humble than Brown's. He sought "freedom of development and equality of opportunity," and he did not wish to pay too high a price for such liberty. In this respect Du Bois was in 1909 far from being a radical Marxist. "Revolution," he observed at the end of *John Brown,* "is not a test of capacity; it is always a loss and a lowering of ideals" (395). Revolution was part of the price of repression; inevitably destructive, it must be avoided by a full payment of the heavy cost of freedom. But with the publication of this biography Du Bois had promulgated his defense of the radical life. In the following year, 1910, he left the university to begin more than fifty years of public identification with the most forceful positions on the subject of race and the destiny of Afro-America. And as he prepared to do so, he was completing his first novel, in yet another attempt, through the power of the pen, to reach the affections of whites and blacks on the subject of the African people in the United States.

CHAPTER SIX

The Quest of the Silver Fleece

What Negro American literature needs now is careful dogged workmanship among the educated classes — and ideal of beauty and accomplishment and not of mere money.   (Du Bois, 1906)

IN SETTING OUT to write his first novel, *The Quest of the Silver
Fleece* (1911), Du Bois was attempting by far his most ambitious
effort as a story teller. His only significant publication of fiction to
that point had been the short story "Of the Coming of John" in *The
Souls of Black Folk,* which made no reference to black literature
beyond praise for the poignant words of the sorrow songs. The *Horizon* had printed a few short pieces by him, but none suggests a
major interest in the art of the novel. Nor had Du Bois written significantly on any novelist, black or white, in the years leading up to
publication of *The Quest of the Silver Fleece.* By the time his own
novel appeared in 1911 there was, in fact, little that could justifiably
be called a tradition in black fiction. Although Du Bois himself later
observed that the rise of the novelist and poet had been the "most
notable" literary event for black America in the 1890s, three men —
Charles Waddell Chesnutt, Paul Laurence Dunbar, and Sutton
Elbert Griggs — accounted between 1898 and 1911 for fully half the
number of novels and collections of stories ever published by black
Americans. There is no evidence that Du Bois learned much from
his predecessors in the field of the black novel. He regarded Dunbar
as mainly a poet in spite of his four novels, three of which have no
important black characters, and he preferred Chesnutt's novels and
short stories to the sometimes nationalistic Griggs only because the
former writer "spoke of the whole nation."[1]

Du Bois profoundly admired Harriet Beecher Stowe's *Uncle*

Tom's Cabin and liked Joel Chandler Harris' "Uncle Remus" stories, although he eventually dismissed Harris as "simply the deft and singularly successful translator" of black material for white audiences.[2] As a young man, Du Bois had responded to the best and most radical of Southern white writers, George Washington Cable, author of *The Grandissimes* and critic of the New South and racism. When Cable asked a black audience in Boston in 1888, "What Shall the Negro Do?" to combat oppression, the challenge moved Du Bois to reply in an unpublished essay, "What the Negro Will Do".[3] After an address by Cable in Boston in February 1890, Du Bois wrote to praise his "moral heroism."[4] Cable's recent work was noted in the first issue of the *Horizon* in 1907. Other writers mentioned by Du Bois in the *Moon,* the *Horizon,* and the *Crisis* before 1911 include Owen Wister, Jack London, and Gertrude Stein, whose *Three Lives,* with its story of a black woman, Melanctha, was noted. The content and style of *The Quest of the Silver Fleece* indicate that Du Bois had significant areas in common not only with Cable, Wister, and London but also with Frank Norris. Indeed, Norris' unfinished trilogy of wheat, including *The Pit* and *The Octopus,* probably suggested the basic framework for the Du Bois epic of the cotton industry, as William Stanley Braithwaite hinted in a review of Du Bois' novel.[5]

The Quest of the Silver Fleece is, first, a simple love story.[6] The lovers are Blessed Alwyn and Zora, who eventually become man and wife. The setting of the story includes a county in Alabama, the city of Washington, D.C., and Wall Street in New York. The lovers are black, and as such, in Du Bois' scheme, they are beset by problems peculiar to black people determined to lead virtuous lives in service to their race. They are both of humble origin. Like black John in "Of the Coming of John," Bles is a poor farm-boy determined to get an education. He is hard-working and intelligent. Having finished school in the South, he goes North to Washington and finds himself enmeshed in politics. Highly principled, a gifted, impulsive speaker, and yet ingenuous in dealing with the world, Bles is tempted and manipulated. In the scramble for the political crumbs dropped to black leaders by white politicians, his innocence is abused. Finally he recognizes the disgrace of political life and returns to the South to fight a more fundamental battle for his people. In so doing, he preserves his integrity and acquires new wisdom. His marriage to Zora celebrates the triumph of virtue over the powers of corruption.

Zora is of more fantastic origin. Her mother, Elspeth, is a conjurer, a remnant of African paganism living literally in a swamp. Encouraged by Elspeth, Zora consorts with the white men who come to Elspeth's cabin at night. Her life changes when she meet Bles. She falls in love first with him, then with his way of life. Quick to learn, she joins a school attended by Bles and run by an indomitable New England school teacher, Sarah Smith, who supplants Elspeth as the chief influence of Zora's life. When Bles discovers Zora's past, she pleads in vain that she had always wanted to be pure, and Bles breaks their informal engagement. Zora joins a wealthy white woman from New York, Mrs. Vanderpool, as her personal maid and, having a quick mind, educates herself through avid reading. She anonymously aids Bles in his moment of crisis in Washington, then returns with some money to help Sarah Smith keep her sinking school afloat. Zora organizes the black community to raise itself from the serfdom imposed by the powerful white landowners, and Bles joins her effort. He realizes that Zora's is a superior spirit, pure and courageous, and again offers himself to her in marriage. She accepts.

The feudal social system of Tooms County is dominated by the Creswell family, powerful but impoverished by the decline of the cotton market. Du Bois' characters are often only types. Colonel Cresswell is the old, proud, white patriarch who remembers slavery with nostalgia and retains a paternal but vicious interest in the freedmen. "No Negro starved on the Cresswell place, neither did any accumulate property. Colonel Cresswell saw to both matters" (364). His daughter is a languid Southern belle, his son Harry a decadent opportunist who draws the Cresswell money into a Wall Street plan to corner the cotton market and realize enormous profits for a small group of men. Wealth flows into the Cresswell mansion, but not happiness. Young Cresswell's first child is stillborn; presumably syphilitic, he must have no more children, "because the sins of the father are visited upon the children unto the third and fourth generation" (74). Colonel Cresswell's feudal world begins to disappear before the social and economic changes in the new South. He plays the poor whites against the blacks, but is overwhelmed when his strategy ends in the lynching of two of "his" blacks. Distracted and near death, Colonel Cresswell acknowledges a black grandchild and leaves a huge sum of money for the endowment of Miss Smith's school, an institution he had bitterly opposed during his lifetime.

The Washington section of the novel takes the reader into middle-class black society, a marginal group keeping a brave face before a world that denies its achievement and even its existence. Bles meets Caroline Wynn, a clever, talented woman made cynical and scheming by the slights of white America. He wants to marry her, but she is also courted by Sam Stillings and Tom Teerswell, petty, unscrupulous black politicians seeking patronage. Caroline almost manipulates Bles into the showcase post of Treasurer of the United States, but at the crucial moment he refuses to compromise himself and attacks the shortcomings of the party in power. She dismisses him and marries the rival with the higher position. The chief dispenser of patronage is Miss Smith's brother, a United States senator popular with blacks but rapidly deserting his ideals in favor of financial profit. His aim in handling the blacks is to keep them loyal to the Republican party in spite of its deals with the white South. He also assists the cotton cartel by opposing humanitarian legislation designed to protect Southern labor.

New York is almost synonymous with Wall Street in *The Quest of the Silver Fleece*. The financial plot to control the cotton market is hatched by the financial wizard John Taylor, whose sister Mary teaches at Miss Smith's school and eventually makes a bad marriage to Harry Cresswell. A man of little means at the start, Taylor makes his fortune through manipulating the cotton market. New York also represents the world of philanthropy, in the person of a wealthy widow who not only supplies much of the capital for the cotton enterprise but also gives away large sums for education in the South. Miss Smith has written to her for assistance in running the school. In the end, philanthropy sides with Southern conservatism.

Two major symbols perform duty in the novel: the swamp, in which Zora and Elspeth live at the beginning, and cotton, on which the fortunes of black and white depend.[7] At first glance, neither symbol appears to be in any way novel for readers accustomed to sloughs of despond or to Norris' use of wheat. But the timeworn use of the swamp as metaphor of human stagnation acquires new meaning and variety in Du Bois' treatment, for it represents a specific mirroring of what he saw as his people's historic trauma. Similarly, Du Bois' use of cotton as symbol is different from Norris' employment of wheat. For Norris, wheat is the symbol of a natural force; to the socialist-minded Du Bois, cotton is basically the labor of the people who produce it. Thus, cotton as a symbol stands closer to human representation, and Du Bois is able to explore this association to a degree impossible in Norris, who abhorred socialism.

The swamp and the cotton are opposed symbols. The swamp symbolizes all that the author finds distressing about black life; the cotton, once it has been wrested away from the exploiters, stands for black effort and achievement. The swamp stands for ignorance, sloth, superstition, paganism, and moral delinquency. It keeps the blacks wrapped in the old, miasmal mist of their pre-American past. "His religion," Du Bois had written of the captured African in *The Souls of Black Folk,* "was nature-worship, with profound belief in invisible surrounding influences, good and bad, and his worship was through incantation and sacrifice."[8] To this superstition Elspeth has added moral degeneracy. She is entirely pagan, hideous, and evil: "The old woman was short, broad, black and wrinkled, with yellow fangs, red hanging lips, and wicked eyes" (75). Not surprisingly, she terrifies even her daughter. Physically struggling through the swamp at one point, Zora "saw again the gnarled and black and clawlike fingers of Elspeth gripping and dragging her down" (93). Zora is often weary of her battle for self-redemption: "The world was against her, and again she saw the fingers of Elspeth — the long black claw-like talons that clutched and dragged her down — down" (86). Long after Elspeth dies, her daughter feels the old woman's influence trying to draw her back to the old life of sin.

The swamp is full of noises; strange music is often heard, and weird cries baffle the visitor. Spirits dwell there. Zora describes them as "little, funny dark people. They flies and creeps and crawls, slippery-like; and they cries and calls" (74). The swamp is also the place of dreams. For Du Bois, this quality is part of the evil of the place, for most dreams stand in opposition to work, wherein lies salvation. Zora has to be taught that lesson, for in the swamp, she tells Bles, "I don't work; mostly I dreams. But I can work, and I will — for the wonder things — and for you" (49). Du Bois intends the lesson for the whole race; these are those "dreams of a credulous race-childhood" of which he had written in *The Souls of Black Folk.*[9] The swamp as a stigma belongs to the whole black community. It is useful only when drained and cleared, which is Zora's project at the end. The black community joins in the labor. Du Bois thus engaged the souls of black folk in a symbolic act renouncing the sensual, indolent, pagan past for a new life of work, sacrifice, and liberal culture. Their labor is an act of atonement, matching that of Colonel Cresswell at his death. Zora's personal atonement has preceded that of the community, but both are linked. As Zora watches the people work, "amid a silence she saw . . . the cabin of Elspeth tremble, sigh, and disappear, and with it flew some spirit of evil" (375).

When the swamp has gone, cotton flourishes. Cotton is thus the symbol of virtue and self-reliance for the black people. The communal acceptance of the burden of atonement is prefigured in the labor of Bles and Zora, before their estrangement, to grow a crop of the "silver fleece." Though their magnificent cotton will eventually be stolen by the Cresswells, their intent is to use it to pay for Zora's education. This effort is Zora's introduction to work. The challenge is almost superhuman, but she is aided by the power of her love for Bles, which has led her to love work itself. The act of working together in the mud and grime of the cotton field for a noble end becomes the highest demonstration of love. To work is to pray, Du Bois believed. As he told his students at chapel in Atlanta University: "There is no God but Love and Work is his prophet — help us to realize this truth O Father which thou so often in word and deed has taught us. Let the knowledge temper our ambitions and our judgments. We would not be great but busy — not pious but sympathetic — not merely reverent, but filled with the glory of our Life-Work. God is Love & Work is His Revelation."[10] For the black worker, then, cotton is not financial profit but the visible evidence of that revelation.

To satisfy the cry of the world's naked for cotton, "the Song of Service filled the world and the poetry of Toil was in the souls of the laborers." Yet ever and always, "there were tense silent white-faced men moving in that swarm who felt no poetry and heard no song" (54-55). These are the financiers, the speculators, the capitalists, who exploit the worker and kill the beauty of work. Du Bois' socialist analysis, though not strident, is clear. It is first advanced almost playfully. Still young and wild, Zora steals a brooch from Mary

Taylor, then refuses to return it when Mary demands it back, because "folks ain't got no right to things they don't need." Picturesquely rephrasing a key Marxist slogan, Zora is adamant: "You don't own what you don't need and can't use" (79). Later on, she steals a mule from the Cresswells to help clear the land for the silver fleece; Bles does not approve of her act, but he lectures her only after the job is done. Du Bois also sympathizes with the impoverished whites, notably in a portrait of Tolliver, "one of the poor whites who had struggled up and failed" (140). Tolliver hates blacks only slightly more than he hates the Cresswells, who exploit the masses of both races by keeping them in hostile competition with each other. Although blacks and whites take a step toward unity near the end of the work, the movement is immediately subverted by those with vested interest in racial strife. Nevertheless, the socialist path out of poverty and racism, both inspired by capitalism, is clearly illuminated in the course of the book.

While socialism was a comparatively new theme as presented in the novel, a far older and more basic idea was that of the power of liberal education. Continuing the old quarrel with Booker T. Washington, Du Bois put some of Washington's words in *Up from Slavery* into the mouths of bigoted whites: "*You* are planning to put our plough-hands all to studying Greek, and at the same time to corner the cotton crop — rot!" (160). The most morally stalwart character is Sarah Smith, who has labored for thirty years to teach the blacks of Tooms County. She exemplifies the stream of teachers eulogized by Du Bois in *The Souls of Black Folk,* who brought "the gift of New England to the freed Negro: not alms, but a friend; not cash, but character."[11] As an educated woman faithful to her profession, she stands between the black community and white hostility, especially that of the Cresswells. The Cresswells oppose the school because it gives the blacks notions of independence and threatens the supply of cheap labor. Even Northern philanthropy thinks of such schools as providers of trained servants for the South. Miss Smith has other visions: "In her imagination the significance of these half dozen gleaming buildings perched aloft seemed portentous — big with the destiny not simply of a county and a State, but of a race — a nation — a world. It was God's own cause" (22). Miss Smith represents moral excellence, compassion, and a gracious acceptance of white responsibility to the children of the former slaves. Under her influence Bles discovers learning and Zora finds morality. Du Bois never divorced the two qualities, and they blend in Sarah Smith, who is culture personified in *The Quest of the Silver Fleece.*

But in giving culture to the masses, and to Bles and Zora in particular, Miss Smith brings them serious problems. They have new standards and new dissatisfactions. Du Bois applauded Bles's rigid moral idealism, but he was by this time well aware of the ironies of black Puritanism. His cynical Caroline Wynn sees them in Bles at once: "that good Miss Smith has gone and grafted a New England conscience on a tropical heart, and — dear me! — but it's a gorgeous misfit" (265). On another occasion she finds him "so delightfully primitive; you will not use the world as it is but insist on acting as if it were something else" (279). Bles personifies for Du Bois a significant variant on the theory of the divided self described in *The Souls of Black Folk.* Here, the Puritan or Calvinist conscience, only partly identifiable with the "American soul" of the black man, may be "grafted" on a tropical body and temperament, but it becomes an integral part of the identity and beauty of its possessor. The restraints of the conscience often lead to physical and psychological tension, but they are absolutely necessary to a life of dignity. Its effect, unlike that of the American soul at war with its African counterpart, is always positive and constructive as a force for moral and psychological discrimination.

To some extent, Bles comes to Miss Smith already leaning toward a life of conscience. Zora is different. Hers is an untouched, mighty, tropical heart. Her first appearance is sensational: "Amid this mighty halo, as on clouds of flame, a girl was dancing . . . Her arms twirled and flickered, and body and soul seemed quivering and whirring in the poetry of her motion" (14-15). Born of pagan, untutored Africa, Zora before her change has two outstanding and related attitudes: a scorn for whites and a disdain for books. She chides Bles for believing that white people actually rule the world through the power of books: "No, no. They don't really rule; they just thinks they rule. They just got things, — heavy, dead things. We black folks is got the *spirit.* We'se lighter and cunninger; we fly right through them; we go and come again just as we wants to. Black folks is wonderful" (46). But her anti-intellectualism is short-lived.

In *The Quest of the Silver Fleece,* hatred or cynicism concerning whites as a body is synonymous with either a primitive ignorance or a corrupted soul. The unschooled Zora exemplifies the first, and the sophisticated Caroline Wynn the latter. Du Bois criticizes white society, holding up only Miss Smith as a moral hero. But apart from the rehabilitated Zora, Bles, and some of the poor peasantry who appear in vignettes, the blacks are little better. This is especially true of those in the city, who should be providing the leadership for the black masses. Bles's reaction to his Washington acquaintances reflects Du Bois' sense of the power of urban corruption: "When he looked about him for fellowship he found himself in a strange dilemma: those black folk in whom he recognized the old sweet-tempered Negro traits, had also looser, uglier manners than he was accustomed to, from which he shrank." Nor was Du Bois insensitive to a charge commonly leveled at the professional class of which he was a conspicuous member. The "upper classes of Negroes," Bles thought, were cold and aloof; "they seemed almost at times like black white people—strangers in way and thought" (240).

Zora's problem—the problem of the precultural black—is to find "The Way." This is the most persistent theme associated with Zora, and for her it means the way out of the swamp of her past. After the double disaster of losing Bles and their marvelous crop of cotton, "a desperate resolve to find some way up toward the light, if not to it, formed itself within her. Somehow, somewhere lay The Way" (189). After Elspeth's death, she wonders in terror, "Was Death the Way—the wide, dark Way?" (210). For a long time Zora remains in spiritual limbo: "She was searching for the Way, groping for the threads of life, seeking almost wildly to understand the foundations of understanding, piteously asking for answer to the puzzle of life" (214). She turns back once in weakness to the old life, and is about to take a drink and join an "orgy" when Miss Smith steps forward and confronts her.

Sent by her teacher to work as a personal maid to Mrs. Vanderpool, Zora blossoms into a well-read, well-spoken woman, yet still searching for the way and still in love with Bles. When the news of his engagement to Caroline sends her into despair, she flees to a church where she is inspired by a sermon that summarizes both Du Bois' essential view of life and the moral of *The Quest of the Silver Fleece:*

> Life is sin, and sin is sorrow. Sorrow is born of selfishness and self-seeking—our own good, our own happiness, our own glory. . .

The good of others is our true good; work for others; not for *your* salvation, but the salvation of the world. . . Behold the Lamb of God that taketh away sin. Behold the Supreme Sacrifice that makes us clean. Give up your pleasures; give up your wants; give up all to the weak and wretched of our people. Go down to Pharoah and smite him in God's name. Go down to the South where we writhe. Strive — work — build — hew — lead — inspire! God calls. Will you hear? Come to Jesus. The harvest is waiting. Who will cry: 'Here am I, send me!' (294-295)

Zora returns to Mrs. Vanderpool: " 'I have found the Way,' she cried joyously" (296).

In returning to her people, Zora puts an end to dreams and dull vision. "Out of a nebulous cloudland she seemed to step . . . for the first time she seemed to know the real and mighty world that stood behind that old and shaken dream" (355). In other words, Zora ceases to see her own people from reflections through the veil. She is free of the "double life, with double thoughts, double duties and double social classes" described in *The Souls of Black Folk* as leading blacks to self-consciousness, morbidity, and moral hesitancy.[12] Zora and Bles, now members of the talented tenth after their humble social origins, must serve the people and help to lift them.

In contrast to Zora, Caroline Wynn exemplifies the most dangerous corruption of the talented tenth. Du Bois kept his deepest circle of Hell for those who are cynical and self-seeking in the face of communal pain. But Caroline is also the most arresting character in the book, more witty and stylish than any white: "Perhaps she wore her manners just a trifle consciously; perhaps she was a little morbid that she would fail of recognition as a lady" (253). Her schemes to seduce Bles into opportunism and dishonesty fail because Miss Smith's "gorgeous misfit" is perdurable, but she immediately settles for the next most lucrative liaison. The success of Du Bois' characterization lies in its depiction of the pathos behind her unscrupulousness. Life has cheated her of the rewards of talent and intelligence by giving her a dark skin in white America. Beyond this recognition, Du Bois' sympathy cannot go. He does not condone a vicious act because it is committed against an often vicious people. He leaves Caroline unrepentant to the end, but her marriage to Sam Stillings is punishment enough for her failure to search for the way.

Mrs. Vanderpool is the white counterpart of Caroline. She is amoral, unemotional, and scheming. She helps Zora not out of love, but out of idle interest in a new project. She is valuable to Zora in that she enables the girl to learn the skills necessary for dealing with white power. She is, as she harshly tells Zora, the world. Representing wealth and sophistication without a sense of duty to her fellow man, Mrs. Vanderpool is representative of a declining Northern and national morality. Brief episodes of cruelty startle the reader and remind him of the realities of Southern serfdom: "The Black Belt is primitive and the landlord wields the power" (183). But there is a more powerful judgment made against the North. *The Quest of the Silver Fleece* censures the new alliances between North and South forged at the close of the century, almost always at the expense of the Southern black. Du Bois laments the loss of Northern moral vigor in the observance of ideals for which men like John Brown had fought and died. This decline is particularly true of the younger New Englanders, who live only one yawning generation from Abolitionist dedication. Mary Taylor's reaction to Sarah Smith summarizes the passing of a moral era: "Miss Smith represented the older New England of her parents — honest, inscrutable, determined, with a conscience which she worshipped, and utterly unselfish. She appealed to Miss Taylor's ruddier and daintier vision but dimly and distantly as some memory of the past" (28). In a story that is national in its ambition, this loss of morality reflects, in a muted way, a larger American tragedy besides which the events in Tooms County are far less significant.

In *The Souls of Black Folk,* Du Bois had mused about the legend of Jason and the Argonauts and their journey in search of the fleece, drawing an analogy between the Greek myth and the cotton fields of the black belt. He then seized upon the grandness of this myth for his own story, casting it in the epic mold. The "silver fleece" of the title is the way of labor, love, and beauty in life. Zora is the most conspicuous pilgrim in a search that all men must make. The epic breadth is sustained in two principal ways: first, by using charged language to describe Zora's search; and second, by exploiting the physical dimensions of the cotton industry so that it provides a world-wide setting for a story that is at first provincial. Again the language is inflated, occasionally even bombastic: "The cry of the naked was sweeping the world. From the peasant toiling in Russia, the lady lolling in London, the chieftain burning in Africa, and the Esquimaux freezing in Alaska . . . went up the cry, 'Clothes,

clothes!' . . . All that dark earth heaved in mighty travail with the bursting bolls of the cotton while black attendent earth spirits swarmed above, sweating and crooning to its birth pains" (54).

This example of Du Bois' use of epic convention points up his interest in naturalism as a literary force. Of Bles's first turmoil over Zora, Du Bois notes: "He felt all this as the stirring of a mighty force, but knew not what he felt" (126). Faced with the need to hoe the fields of cotton, Bles and Zora discuss the law of the survival of the fittest and the need to sacrifice some living things so that others may thrive. Zora says that "everything ought to have a chance to be beautiful and useful," but Bles reminds her that "death and pain pay for all good things" (127). The idea of powerful internal forces wielding influence over unwitting men and women fascinated Du Bois. "I was not at the time sufficiently Freudian to understand how little human action is based on reason," Du Bois wrote in 1944, looking back on his beliefs at the start of the century.[13] But his characters do not always proceed according to the laws of reason. At Elspeth's death, Zora is overcome by strange fantasies: "Thick memories of some forgotten past came piling in upon her" (209). When Mrs. Vanderpool meets Zora, the white woman is suddenly perturbed; "her mind seemed leaping backward a thousand years; back to a simpler, primal day when she herself, white, frail, and fettered, stood before the dusky magnificence of some bejewelled barbarian queen and sought to justify herself" (223).

Du Bois' use of naturalism, however, as a force in *The Quest of the Silver Fleece* is often hesitant and contradictory. The biological argument conflicts at times with the economic explanation of the nature of society, and both forces operate in some tension with the spirit of romantic idealism that eventually triumphs. The novel suffers as a result. Naturalism stands ready to plague the moral idealist at almost every turn. It has always seemed to cooperate best with those fictional artists whose view of life is most pessimistic. In *The Quest of the Silver Fleece,* as in all of Du Bois' fiction, pessimism is the most unpardonable of sins. The novel vividly illustrates the conflict between realism and romance common in so much serious writing at the turn of the century, especially in such authors as Norris and Garland. Realism is central to Du Bois' art in depicting the lives of those middle and upper-class blacks and whites who form the majority of characters in *The Quest of the Silver Fleece.*

But romance is crucial in the presentation of the two most important figures, Bles and Zora, who rise out of the peasantry by
choosing a life of moral heroism. Du Bois was suspicious of what
Norris called "that harsh, loveless, colorless, blunt tool called Realism."[14] Now and then the result is costume romance, where lovers
speak in poetic diction or burst into operatic song. In general,
though, the romantic element is more firmly rooted. An almost
Gothic aspect develops in the acceptance of supernatural forces at
work among the black folk. Du Bois boldly asserted the existence of
such powers because he thought that the rural black masses believed
in them and that this superstition might be redirected as a spiritual
force for good.

In keeping with the American tradition of psychological
romances and reflecting his own loss of faith in social science, Du
Bois was prepared to expound the superiority of intuition over the
force of logic, the power of the heart over the power of the head. It
was an easy creed for him to accept, because it was reinforced by
two other factors in his intellectual life. First, the psychological and
philosophic teachings of William James and other writers dignified
the old romantic assertions about the power of nonreason. Second,
in asserting the power of the heart over the head, Du Bois believed
that he was showing the African mind in its best possible light. The
Transcendentalists themselves had looked eastward, beyond
Europe, for inspiration. They believed in the power of inner
promptings, although they held that these came from the better self
of man and not also from an equally innate fund of evil. Although
the subliminal and the spiritual or superstitious were by no means
the same, James himself, in asserting the power of religious belief,
had defined religion simply as "the feelings, acts and experiences of
individual men in their solitude, so far as they apprehend themselves to stand in relation to whatever they may consider divine."[15]

When Bles returns to Zora near the end of the novel, after she has
found the way, she entertains him in "a small building" set off from
the great main house which is the center of her plan for the black
community. This cottage is the symbol of her elevated moral and
mental state and of her aspirations; "the room was a unity; things
fitted together as if they belonged together" (399). Prominent
among the pictures is one of the Madonna, symbolic of Zora's new
devotion to sexual purity. This room is also Zora's study: it is filled

with books and magazines. Her reading has far outstripped that of Bles, and as he looks "curiously" at some of the titles, several works and authors catch his attention: Plato's *Republic,* Gorky's *Comrades,* an encyclopedia of agriculture, Balzac's novels, Spencer's *First Principles,* and Tennyson's *Poems.* "This is my university," Zora tells Bles.

From these deliberately named authors and works one may infer not only Du Bois' insistence on the necessity of a liberal education, but also the peculiar patterns of his cultural ideals. Plato's *Republic* provides the philosophic sanction for utopian political thought, as well as the concept that political leadership should reside with those who are morally and intellectually extraordinary. The philosopher-aristocrat rules over Du Bois' utopia as well as over that of Plato. In Du Bois' republic, however, the poet is a powerful figure. In spite of the differences in aesthetic theory and practice among Tennyson, Gorky, and Balzac, Du Bois is illustrating, by the presence of their books on Zora's shelves, his belief in the power of art as an ennobling human experience. Gorky's near-radical social perspective clarified by idealism, Balzac's realism tempered by moral judgment, and Tennyson's poetic craft provide a range of artistic freedom that should be sufficient for any responsible citizen. Spencer's *First Principles* presents the case of modern science against pagan superstition and any religion sustained by reactionary apologetics. Du Bois is not wholly endorsing either Spencer or any other writer; but the works are valuable in relation to and in reaction against each other, as they present the variety of ideas inspired by liberal education.

The presence of an encyclopedia of agriculture in Zora's "university" places Du Bois' political ideal still more accurately. The fields of the country, not the streets of the city, provide the most auspicious landscape for social regeneration. Bles and Zora recognize the especially corrupting reality of urban life; they flee its refinements as soon as they are aware that the city is almost invariably a swamp of moral enervation. Du Bois' ideal state is agrarian in its economic and social base. The tilling of the earth must be accompanied, however, by neither slavery nor serfdom. The assertion of democratic egalitarianism must be made to blend with the acknowledgment of an aristocracy of morality, intellect, and, where high morality or intellect is also present, even of birth. Du Bois indicated here, as elsewhere, a willingness to admit the claims of hereditary nobility, as long as nobility admitted both its own obligations and the valid claims of moral and intellectual excellence.

As a political statement, *The Quest of the Silver Fleece* is the earliest detailed announcement of the approach Du Bois would take to American political reality during the next three and a half decades of his life, until he began his turn toward Communism after World War II. Disdainful of capitalism, the novel sets up two competitive political constructs: the idea of socialism, and the practical world of electoral politics to which the city of Washington is central. Like his hero Bles, Du Bois was drawn to both worlds. As *Crisis* editor, he advertised the virtues of socialism while repeatedly attempting in vain to weld the black voters into a force that would be crucial to the balance of power between Democrats and Republicans. Socialism, however, has no institutional basis in the novel; the fledgling American Socialist party, to which Du Bois himself briefly belonged in 1911 and 1912, has no place in the interparty rivalry. Socialist ideas are promulgated as basic human truths, as commonplaces of the untutored but honest mind, with the primitive Zora being the principal source of such wisdom. Bles listens to these "truths" almost without comment on their validity, then discovers that to succeed in partisan politics in Washington requires a pragmatism identical with unscrupulousness. In separating his hero from involvement with either party or with the system itself, Du Bois was defining the terms of what he considered true pragmatism. At the same time, he was describing what he saw as the necessary political course for a black America faced with the same choices.

Bles and Zora accept no political party as central to their salvation; as blacks they must rely upon themselves, recognize their strengths and shortcomings, needs and aspirations, and they must work together with other blacks to bring about change. Du Bois' heroes disdain the opportunities offered by a corrupt and corrupting system, but they also decline to make socialist logic the dogmatic basis of their thought. Nor do they surrender their racial pride and identity in order to blend into white political institutions; the distinctive and wonderful quality of the black folk, as young Zora described it, must not be sacrificed for political gain. The political movement that Bles and Zora head at the end of the novel represents a unity of black folk willing to work with the white world about them but only on terms of equality and dignity. The people are

taught by common sense and painful experience the superiority of
socialist cooperation as the economic basis of society; they become
determined to live by the dictates of moral conscience and intelligence as well as by the urgings of racial pride and ambition.

Although *The Quest of the Silver Fleece* appears to prolong the
quarrel with Booker T. Washington by repeating old arguments on
the indispensability of a liberal education and the vote to black
progress, the novel goes beyond the positions of the Niagara Movement to detail and dramatize the results of a philosophic method
Du Bois described as pragmatic realism. This pragmatism had a
moral aspect Du Bois understood and accepted. In the following
years of his life, though he sometimes slipped into questionable editorial positions on topical issues, he remained faithful to a line of
thought that sought the advance of black power without the sacrifice
of moral principle and without the repudiation of the ecumenical
spirit sometimes concealed by his powerful explosions of rage or the
cold contempt which had become part of his public image. In the
world of his first novel he allowed no compromise between moral
evaluation and social evil, or between optimistic idealism and naturalistic despair. His primary use of fiction was to declare the primacy
of his moral imagination in its relationship to a variety of changing
issues involving the races of America.

The Quest of the Silver Fleece is a novel of many ideas and themes
subsidiary to and even beyond the question of race. The depiction of
the uneasy white liberal faced with the temptation of expediency is
intended to do more than criticize latter-day New England in a state
of transition from its old ideals. No revolutionary himself, Du Bois
had a keen sense of the vulnerability of the liberal conscience to the
increasing pressures of the modern world. The novel also shows an
author fascinated by the then-sensational question of miscegenation
involving black men and white women: although Mary Taylor
Cresswell is unaware of any attraction on her part toward Bles, the
work hints clearly that she is subconsciously drawn to the fine young
black hero. Yet another theme is that of the role of woman in
modern society. As an early supporter of feminist causes, Du Bois
wrote with sympathy of the attempts of women to assert the value of
their separate sensibility and experience in the affairs of the nation.
His admiration for the character and capacity of black women is
stamped on his fiction; in all his novels, the black woman is the

intellectual and spiritual superior of the male and the real hope of the race. And in presenting a dark skinned woman as his heroine, as Arthur P. Davis has pointed out, Du Bois broke the prevailing pattern of near-white female lead characters in black fiction.[16]

These themes and ideas, however, are secondary to the main purpose of the novel, which is to dramatize the moral and political consequences of the black situation in America. Writing in later years of his first novel, Du Bois described the book as simply "an economic study of some merit."[17] This prosaic characterization should not be taken too seriously. The novel was certainly the first piece of Afro-American fiction to include a serious study of economic forces among the basic factors determining the quality of black American life, but its inquiry went much further. While the principal social focus is Afro-America, the novel also addresses itself to the whole nation, dealing sympathetically with the lives of a variety of human types caught up in traditional forces too often beyond their understanding and control. Although none of his character studies is psychologically profound, Du Bois demonstrated a sure understanding of the subtle and often tragic implications of race relations in America. His portrayal of economic forces at work is not more interesting than his exposure of the psychology of racism. His treatment of individual and society is distinguished by a combination of understanding and moral candor, which enables the novel to speak sternly without being tractarian, and to sympathize without being sentimental.

The moral statement of *The Quest of the Silver Fleece* is harsh. To recognize the reality of the world is to admit its evil, in which all men are implicated and from which each must find salvation through continuous atonement. Self-denial is the start of self-fulfillment. The power of work is celebrated, but one must work with others and for others in order to give dignity to individual effort. The grandeur of love is the greatest of human emotions and sanctifies sexual passion. In spite of all success and in the face of all failure, man must bow low before the knowledge of the power of his evil; the swamp of immorality is the heart of darkness into which the American of either race must travel in order to confront the mysteries of the soul.

CHAPTER SEVEN

The Crisis and Politics

William James used to tell us that we must follow thought by action, on pain of spiritual death. Yet we hear of bankers stealing, and cabinet officers grafting, and public service corporations exploiting, and sit still and do nothing. This does not foreshadow death — it is death.   (Du Bois, 1934)

BETWEEN THE PUBLICATION of *John Brown* in 1909 and *The Quest of the Silver Fleece* in 1911, Du Bois left Atlanta University to help found the National Association for the Advancement of Colored People (NAACP) and to found and edit its monthly magazine, *The Crisis*. His conspicuous role in the new body, into which he brought the Niagara Movement, marked the full assertion of the pragmatic spirit to which he had become increasingly committed in his years of political activism following the appearance of *The Souls of Black Folk* in 1903. He gave up his academic position to join an organization as yet without either identity or financial base, and he threw his energies into a journalistic enterprise only reluctantly approved by his new colleagues because of its tenuous financial prospects. His experience with the *Crisis* and the NAACP is a record of the problems inherent in his philosophic method as well as in the man himself during his middle years. Du Bois edited the journal from 1910 to 1934. Although many significant events of his life related only obliquely to his position on the magazine, the story of his life during this time, he later acknowledged, is "chiefly the story of *The Crisis* under my editorship."[1]

The NAACP had its beginnings in the outraged response of white liberals and socialists to the Springfield, Illinois, race riots of August 1908, during which eight blacks were killed (two by lynching) and over two thousand more were driven from the city. The vicious irony of such events in the city where Lincoln had lived and where he was buried stirred the grandson of William Lloyd Garrison, Oswald Garrison Villard of the New York *Evening Post*, and socialist William English Walling in the *Independent* to attack the nationwide treatment of blacks and to insist on the need for change. Informal meetings of Villard, Walling, social workers Mary White Ovington and Henry Moscowitz, and Walling's friend and fellow socialist Charles Edward Russell, led to Villard's call for a national conference to discuss the status of blacks in American society.[2] Deliberately issued on the centennial of Lincoln's birth in 1909, the appeal was signed by an interracial body of some sixty men and women including William Dean Howells, Lincoln Steffens, John Dewey, Jane Addams, and Du Bois himself.

The National Negro Committee, formed in response, met in New York on May 31 and June 1, 1909. The consensus of the meeting was that a permanent organization should be formed, and a Committee of Forty was appointed to plan this step. In April 1910 the Executive Committee of the body heard a proposal for a permanent organization prepared by a subcommittee headed by Du Bois; on May 5, the present name of the association was adopted. On June 28, on the motion of John Milholland, treasurer of the NAACP, seconded by Ovington, Du Bois was hired as director of publicity and research, to take office on October 1. On September 6, he presented to the Executive Committee a plan for a monthly magazine devoted to the topic of race and to related news. After lengthy discussion the proposal was approved and November 1, 1910, was set as the date for the first appearance of the *Crisis*.[3]

Involvement with the NAACP came at a vital time for Du Bois. His identification as a major opponent of Booker T. Washington had placed a strain on his university and made it extremely difficult for him to find support for the Atlanta University studies, his principal scholarly involvement. In spite of the Niagara Movement, his political influence was negligible and probably dwindling. Life in segregated Atlanta was something that Du Bois endured at great cost to his sense of well-being. He patronized only the essential services rather than honor its Jim Crow laws and conventions. By 1910 he was ready to leave the South. Hired by the NAACP at the urging of the more radical whites led by Walling, he made an immediate impression on the new body: "from that time," Ovington later wrote, "no one doubted where we stood."[4] With Du Bois in their camp, the leadership of the National Negro Committee could afford to be less conciliatory to the more outspoken anti-Washingtonians, such as William Monroe Trotter, J. Milton Waldron of the National Negro Political League, and Ida Wells-Barnett of the Negro Fellowship League.[5] Indeed, Du Bois, like Washington, may have acted as a kind of broker between the white leadership and the blacks as a whole. In the middle of 1910 he wrote to Walling suggesting that they should pay less attention to adding more blacks to the National Committee of the association, and attacking one black man while urging the inclusion of a white woman.[6]

Within four years of its birth, however, Du Bois had become, according to one report, "the chief if not the only source of the disorder and lack of unity in our organization."[7] In his twenty-four years with the NAACP as *Crisis* editor he clashed at one time or another with practically everyone with whom he worked; after his departure he was referred to by Ovington as "our octopus." The major issue was usually the relationship between the journal and the association, and the place of its editor in the ranks of the leadership. To Villard, chairman of the board of directors from 1912 to 1914 and a crucial figure in making the NAACP viable, Du Bois often seemed insubordinate and near-paranoid, swift to wound those who dared to cross him and unable to place personal pride behind the welfare of the group.[8] According to Joel E. Spingarn, who replaced Villard as chairman of the board in 1914, Du Bois created needless antagonisms among both his fellow workers and "the whole colored world"; even his closest friends regarded him with "mingled affection and resentment." In many matters of dispute within the NAACP, Spingarn usually moved Du Bois to cooperation only "by wheedling and questioning, as children are." Spingarn attributed the difficulty in part to an honorable devotion to principle, but another part could not be so dignified.[9] According to Ovington, Du Bois' greatest ally in the association, Du Bois often struck at people with a harshness and directness that appalled her; but she noted that the blow was often deserved and never below the belt.[10]

In defense Du Bois argued that Villard was an intolerably autocratic administrator. Moreover, he had married a Southern woman and no black associate was ever invited to his home. Villard had also been unscrupulous, according to Du Bois, in reviewing his *John Brown* harshly while Villard's own biography was in preparation and then in denying Du Bois a rebuttal in a magazine under Villard's control.[11] Similarly, many of Du Bois' antagonists were themselves guilty of ill-will within the organization. Du Bois fell back on two major defenses of his tactics. First, he wished to see the *Crisis* "one of the great journals of the world . . . a center of enterprise and co-operation such as black folk have not themselves dreamed." Second, the magazine and his leadership of it were essential to the credibility of the NAACP, for "no organization like ours ever succeeded in America; either it became a group of white philanthropists helping the Negro like the Anti-Slavery societies; or it became a group of colored folk freezing out their white co-workers by insolence and distrust." The association, like all interracial organizations, was threatened by "the inevitable American rift of the color line." Du Bois wanted full power to run the *Crisis,* free of the prejudices of white coworkers unaccustomed to black authority. The rift of the color line should be countered "by trusting black men with power."[12]

In helping to guide the daring new enterprise of the NAACP, Du Bois became psychologically engaged with the white persons with whom he worked. He had rejoined, in a sense, the playmates of his youth—white New Englanders like Villard, or New Englandized whites like the Southern Walling and the Spingarn brothers of New York. It cut Du Bois deeply to be excluded from Villard's home, especially since Du Bois counted Villard's mother, the daughter of William Lloyd Garrison, as a friend. Nevertheless, at the height of their battles Du Bois could admit that no two persons in the NAACP were "in closer intellectual agreement on the Negro problem" than he and Villard.[13] Joel Spingarn, the only other academician among the NAACP leadership, having been a professor of comparative literature at Columbia and a pioneer of the New Criticism—made a deep impression on Du Bois, who dedicated *Dusk of Dawn* to him: "I do not think that any other white man ever touched me emotionally so closely . . . He was one of those vivid, enthusiastic but clearthinking idealists which from age to age the Jewish race has given the world."[14] Mary Dunlop Maclean, the English-born managing editor of the *Crisis* and a New York *Times* staff writer before her premature death in July 1912, provided aid and comfort. Mary White Ovington was "one of the few persons whom I call Friend."[15] His emotional eulogies in the *Crisis* on the death of John Milholland, a founder of the NAACP, and Moorfield Storey, first president of the association, reveal the depth of his emotional involvement with men and women from whom he nevertheless often kept a formal distance. He came to feel a special warmth for the group that had founded the NAACP or supported it in its brave new days — and Villard was not excluded from that regard. The presence of whites in the leadership of what soon became an overwhelmingly black organization was questioned as late as 1932, when Joel Spingarn assumed the honorary duties of the presidency. But Du Bois never publicly questioned the racial feeling of an NAACP officer until 1934, when he accused a black man, the executive secretary of the association, of insensitivity to the problems of race because of his light complexion.

Du Bois was not isolated within the NAACP, having powerful allies in persons such as Joel E. and Arthur B. Spingarn, Storey, Milholland, and Ovington. Although he was kept out of the executive secretariat, which may have been the "basic cause" of his friction with the NAACP, he was enough of an insider to help engineer the election of Ovington as chairman to succeed Joel Spingarn in 1918 and thus preserve his power on the board.[16] Villard's opposition to him probably had a strong racial element, as Du Bois believed. But when they clashed repeatedly in the first years of the body, it was the white man who in 1914 surrendered his position as chairman. And when the tension between Du Bois and the NAACP had led to the formation in 1913 of an advisory committee to oversee his editorials, Joel Spingarn and Ovington were two of the three members, a convenient arrangement for the more radical element in the NAACP.[17]

Nevertheless, the advisory committee appears to have carried out its duties responsibly, with the editor accepting its "advice." He was not always censured in favor of moderation. In 1924, for example, James Weldon Johnson, then executive secretary, decided that an editorial on segregation was too equivocal for a militant organization like the NAACP, although earlier he had peremptorily ordered an editorial deleted because it broke the confidentiality of another institution's board meeting.[18] The next year Ovington instructed Du Bois to rewrite an editorial on Fisk University so as to combine reason with emotion, and to omit a gratuitous slap at the Urban League.[19] The memoranda between Du Bois and Arthur

Spingarn show the editor to have been dependent over the years on the advice of the white lawyer in matters well beyond the legal. It was in the nature of his role as crusading editor that Du Bois should have needed some restraints, and it was consonant with his intelligence that he accepted them in principle. Joel Spingarn remarked to the board at the time of Du Bois' resignation that the editor had never once objected to the supervision of the magazine by the committee. Censorship of the *Crisis* by the NAACP was, in other words, generally salutary in its effect on a magazine that seldom lacked force or conviction.

In spite of friction within the NAACP, the *Crisis* rose like a star. Founded in 1910 without capital, it was self-supporting by 1916. The first printing was of 1,000 copies; a year later, 16,000 were sold in a month. Circulation grew steadily until the high point in June 1919, when Du Bois published his "Essay Toward a History of the Black Man in the Great War," the longest essay ever to appear in a number. Of this edition, 104,000 copies were sold. By February 1920, circulation was down to a more normal 72,000. Thereafter it went steadily downhill. A year later, 50,000 copies was the average sale; by 1924, 35,000 copies. As the Depression set in, the *Crisis* needed increasingly large subsidies from the association. In 1930 and 1931, about 18,000 copies were sold; the next year, the number had dropped to less than 14,000, or fewer than at the end of its first year.[20]

The value of the *Crisis* to the NAACP was immense. For Arthur Spingarn, the rise of the *Crisis* from its penniless start was "an unprecedented achievement in American journalism," and without its editor the NAACP could not have been "what it was and is."[21] In 1933, Joel Spingarn accounted the cost of the *Crisis* to the NAACP as no more than $2000 a year over its twenty-three years of publication; yet without it, "there would be no Association."[22] The impact of the magazine on Afro-American intellectual life was considerable. The writer Shirley Graham Du Bois doubted "if there is one American Negro who by the mid-twentieth century achieved prominence as a scholar, poet, playwright, story writer, musician, artist or athlete who was not first publicized in and encouraged in *The Crisis*."[23] J. Saunders Redding has written movingly of the almost sacred significance of the journal in his home as he was growing up.[24] And Henry Lee Moon, himself appointed editor of the *Crisis* in 1966, remembered reading the magazine "from cover to cover" as a young child: "It was, under Du Bois, a source of inspiration and a mine of information."[25]

The object of the publication, as the first number declared, was "to set forth those facts and arguments which show the danger of race prejudice, particularly as manifested today toward colored people . . . Catholicity and tolerance, reason and forbearance, can today make the world-old dream of human brotherhood approach realization . . . We strive for this broader and higher vision of Peace and Good Will." The magazine would be a newpaper first and foremost, reporting on matters concerning race, especially in the United States. Second, it would be a review of articles, books, and other pieces published on the "race problem." Third, it would publish "a few short articles." And last, its editorial pages would defend the rights of all men regardless of color, would represent no clique or party, and would assume the honesty of purpose of all men everywhere. The editor, in other words, dissociated himself and his journal from the day-to-day workings of the NAACP, and gave notice that it would resist all dogma in favor of a policy of liberal eclecticism.

The most forceful impact of the *Crisis* came from its editorial section, usually covering from two to four pages, where Du Bois spoke directly to the reader. The strength of his editorials came from the variety of their techniques as well as their themes. By April of the first year he had found his proper range and balance. First, the death of a black poet gave him the chance to appeal to young black writers for a finer, more plentiful literature. Another section deplores the tendency to stress signs of progress in the white South; he called this a "half-truth," evading the reality of oppression. A third editorial offers an emotional tribute to a Southern white man who had worked for blacks for twenty-seven years. A fourth statement assumes a completely different form in describing a recent incident:

> A curious thing happened at Harvard last fall. A boy walked from Mississippi and sought to enter the college because he wanted to learn to write.
> "Certainly. Why not?" asks the reader.
> Well — he was black.
> "Oh," says the reader, as the dean of the college said, "why didn't he go to an industrial school?"

"Because," said Smith Jones, "I want to study literature and become a poet."

"Why not become a carpenter?"

"Because I don't want to."

On arriving at Harvard with his improbable story, the boy was jailed as a vagrant, then had his poems praised by James Whitcomb Riley, and is now, the editorial reports, in the famed Boston Latin School, preparing for Harvard.

Dominating these brief commentaries is the kind of intensely poetic, symbolic tale of which Du Bois would become a master. "Easter" begins lyrically: "The land lay smiling in spring splendor, heavy with verdure, gleaming with glad sunshine." Across it falls the shadow of a chained black man: "His face was half-hopeless, half-vacant, with only a faint gleam of something dead and awakening deep in his deep-set eyes." His captors are afraid of him, of "the reproach of his dumb, low-burning eyes . . . the half-articulate sounds from his moving lips." They conspire to kill him, "lying to his ears, crucifying his soul, until he fell and lay his mighty length in stupor along the earth." The conspirators, white brothers of the North and South, are filled with guilt and confusion after the murder, so they go to the grave to confirm that the black giant is dead:

> But suddenly the World was wings and the voice of the Angel of the Resurrection beat like a mighty wind athwart their ears, crying:
>
> "He is not here—He is risen."
>
> Risen above half his ignorance; risen to more than six hundred millions of property; risen to a new literature and the faint glimmering of a new Art; risen to a dawning determination to be free; risen to a newer and greater ideal of Humanity than the world has known. RISEN!

Transparent in its symbolism—a technique Du Bois would use repeatedly over the years—this story gives mythic proportion to the struggle of blacks against racism. The note of elation on which it ends is a typical resolution of such editorials, adding dignity to the polemics.

The range of these April 1911 editorials is characteristic of the best years of the magazine and was the key to its success as propaganda, combining poetic rhetoric, tearful tribute, sober assessment, and stern rebuke. Du Bois cultivated an image of himself as both a sharp-eyed, sharp-tongued defender of his people and an incarnation of the libertarian tradition institutionalized in the association. While this image of the editor as prophet appears most distinctly in the first major autobiographical piece penned by Du Bois, "The Shadow of Years," published in February 1918, it also pervades the *Crisis*.

Under his direction the *Crisis* displayed most of the conventional devices of the artful propagandist. A piece in January 1912, entitled "A Mild Suggestion" and patterned on Swift's "Modest Proposal," proposes to whites a general massacre of all blacks, after they have been lured into white homes on a specific evening: "The next morning there would be ten million funerals, and therefore no Negro problem. Think how quietly the thing would be settled!" Another editorial, of March 1918, satirizes the muddled thinking of a newspaper: "While the editor of the New York *Times* was out the other afternoon, the office boy wrote the usual editorial about the South. He naturally slipped into some contradictions, being inexperienced, but he did about as well as the *Times* usually does on the subject." The *Crisis* helpfully provides excerpts from the offending editorial. The humor of the magazine was mainly sardonic, as best represented by a section entitled "As The Crow Flies," introduced in June 1927, where Du Bois used the style of a gossip columnist to ridicule opponents on the subject of race and politics.

While the editorial character, once established, remained constant over the years, Du Bois constantly sought ways to improve the magazine. The greatest changes came just after World War I, mainly in expansions of existing departments or emphases. In 1919, with the *Crisis* for the first time selling over 100,000 copies, Du Bois reinforced its role as a literary outlet by adding a literary editor, Jessie Redmond Fauset, to the staff of twelve. Du Bois and Augustus G. Dill founded *The Brownies' Book,* a magazine for black children, which was the outgrowth of the yearly numbers of the *Crisis* devoted to young people. Published monthly from January 1920 to December 1921, the magazine offered news and commentary from an Afro-American point of view, as well as poems and stories likely to appeal to a black child.[26] In September 1919 the *Crisis* promised a substantial increase in its size to include "more illustrations," more poetry and fiction, and "above all, one or two solid articles monthly on historical or sociological subjects affecting the Negro."[27]

In spite of expansion and change, the basic subject remained the same. In sections called "Along the Color Line" and "The Horizon" the magazine reported on events and personalities of primarily local interest. In "The Burden," Du Bois gave examples of oppression that kept the news of progress and achievement in perspective; in these reports, pathos and indignation moved the reader where statistics might have failed. In "Men of the Month" he presented photographs and biographical sketches of leaders, including women, who had consistently contributed to the solution of racial problems. Balance between optimism and resentment of injustice was probably the basic aim of each issue, but to some readers, black and white, the magazine seemed humorless and dispiriting. In answer to these critics, Du Bois argued that the *Crisis* "does not try to be funny. Not that we object to fun: our office is a cheerful place . . . But our stock in trade is not jokes. We are in earnest. This is a newspaper. It tries to tell the Truth."[28]

The few short articles promised in the first number of the magazine were soon supplemented by at least one longer article in each issue. The editor's aim was to raise the intellectual tone of the journal to as high a pitch as his audience — and his propagandistic aims — would allow. The result was that the magazine often seemed to have a scholarly air, although the scholarship was usually supportive of the editor's beliefs. Articles on history, economics, science, art, and literature as they touched on the question of race relations became a regular feature. The editor's section on "What To Read," as his review of the literature of race was first called, expanded from a generally uncritical bibliography into a steady analysis of books on race and politics, including novels, plays, and poetry; a remarkable number of reviews was written by Du Bois himself, whose reading was voluminous. "Opinion" reported the observations of a large number of journals on the topic of race. The magazine asked of its readers a serious interest in race as a subject, and was accordingly vulnerable to the charge that it was elitist and insensitive to the limitations of the masses.

In general, Du Bois tried to avoid the appearance of triviality or provincialism in the journal. He persuaded the association to develop an alternative way of communicating with branches around the country. The international flavor of the journal in reporting news from around the world was part of a policy to make the *Crisis* a counterpart of the leading American magazines of politics and culture, the kind of outlet in which its editor had formerly published some of his best essays. As an enterprise, however, the *Crisis* was limited by the very forces it was established to fight: poverty and the comparatively unsophisticated education of the blacks who were its principal support, as well as the white racism that kept the editor on the treadmill of protest. The magazine and the NAACP fostered change, which in turn encouraged journalistic competition. Thus in 1925, when Du Bois looked back on 15 years and 175 numbers of the *Crisis,* he noted that the rise of "colored weeklies" of a scope and efficiency "not dreamed of in 1910" had made a monthly newspaper for blacks obsolete; "our news therefore has transformed itself into a sort of permanent record of a few matters of widespread and historic importance."[29] The *Crisis,* once a pioneer, was by the mid-twenties only one of many journals competing for the black readership and was indispensable only to those faithful to the ideas of its editor. His ideas, because they often took a line independent of both the NAACP and rival black newspapers and magazines, and because he argued them so skillfully and passionately, gave the *Crisis* life long after other publications had altered its general role and sealed its fate as a popular paper.

The newly formed NAACP had as objectives only the attainment of civil and political rights by blacks; a concern with the economics of racism, for example, would come much later. Du Bois' announcement of the purpose of the *Crisis* in its first number did not mention the association; from the start, he imposed his own views on what was nominally only an organ of the main body. Unlike most other black and white leaders, Du Bois repeatedly argued that the separation of "the Negro problem" from other humanitarian concerns of the time was a mistake, and his goals as editor thus went far beyond those of the NAACP. The fundamental aim of the *Crisis* was to defend, praise, and instruct black people; more simply put, its goal was black power. A secondary but ultimately indispensable end was to extol certain principles that were only indirectly related to race but were irresistible in Du Bois' grand vision of man: morality, interracial harmony, socialism, and world peace. Although these two goals of black power and liberal idealism are not in theoretical conflict, in practice, conflict was almost unavoidable. With supreme confidence, Du Bois nevertheless held together the parts of his message by a force of intellect and imagination born out of faith in both the black folk and the ideals that transcend race.

Five years after the start of the *Crisis,* in concluding his important study of Africa and African peoples, *The Negro* (1915), he wrote of forces more powerful than pan-Africanism. These "coming unities," visible to farsighted black men, included "a unity of the working classes everywhere, a unity of the colored races, a new unity of men."[30] This prediction was no mere rhetorical flourish but a conscious articulation of beliefs developed steadily by him since the turn of the century and often tested in his magazine. The basic elements in his philosophy would lead to continual misjudgment of his editorial motives and actions, even by people who considered themselves his friends and allies, as well as to errors of judgment on his part. He saw the circles of unity as dependent on each other, but none was more fundamental than that which marked the welfare of the American blacks. As much as anyone, he was also aware of the necessary conflicts between his priorities and those of other men of good will, led by a different life experience to a separate sense of order. This insight produced in the *Crisis* two coexisting and vaguely defined editorial tempers, which made Du Bois appear sometimes bitter, chauvinistic, or cynical, and at other times conciliatory, optimistic, and principled. He discovered the possibilities and limitations of liberal pragmatism.

The focus of outrage in the *Crisis* was on the practice of lynching. The journal and the NAACP were at one in attacking it as a barbarism and in attempting to convince the white world — notably the Congress, where three antilynching bills were introduced without success in 1918 — of its responsibilities in the matter. The *Crisis* responded to the problem with special reports on individual atrocities and relentless documentation of the number of persons lynched, the reaction of community leaders and officers to individual cases, the alleged and probable causes of particular incidents, and the physical details of each act, along with photographs when available. In 1911 Du Bois dramatized a lynching in Pennsylvania:

> Ah, the splendour of that Sunday night dance. The flames beat and curled against the moonlit sky. The church bells chimed. The scorched and crooked thing, self-wounded and chained to his cot, crawled to the edge of the ash with a stifled groan, but the brave and sturdy farmers pricked him back with the bloody pitchforks until the deed was done.
>
> Let the eagle scream!
> Civilization is again safe.[31]

Fourteen years later lynching had declined but still persisted: the number of killings had dropped from sixty-five in 1920 to sixteen in 1924. Though there was lynching in the North, Du Bois concentrated on the issue in the South. But the power of his rage unsettled even NAACP members. In 1913 he clashed with Villard over the board chairman's astonishing suggestion that Du Bois publish reports on crimes committed by blacks, as well as on those, such as lynching, committed against them.[32]

From its start the *Crisis* endorsed militant self-defense against white mob rule: "We have crawled and pleaded for justice and we have been cheerfully spit upon and murdered and burned. We will not endure it forever. If we are to die, in God's name let us perish like men and not like bales of hay."[33] Du Bois called for vigilance committees to forestall white violence and cheered any defiance of the law in traditionally racist areas, as when a young black man in Virginia killed white policemen and then burned himself to death rather than surrender and face the likelihood of being lynched. He congratulated a black student who had refused to salute the flag during school exercises and faced official punishment. He did not except himself from the fight: "I believe in Peace. I shudder at Revolution. But when in 1906 the Atlanta mob began killing Negroes wholesale, I went and bought a repeating shot-gun and loaded it with buckshot. I have got it yet."[34]

Even more provocative from certain points of view was the *Crisis* attitude toward "social equality," the code term for a number of integrated social practices, the most controversial of which was miscegenation. Du Bois insisted on the right of the black man "to be treated as a gentleman when he acts like one, to marry any sane, grown person who wants to marry him, and to meet and eat with his friends without being accused of undue assumption or unworthy ambition."[35] Laws against intermarriage were simply "wicked devices to make the seduction of women easy and without penalty, and should be forthwith repealed," although he offered reasons why interracial marriage might be inadvisable.[36] He resented the inference that a desire for social recognition implied dissatisfaction with the company of fellow blacks: "It is race pride that fights for freedom; it is the man ashamed of his blood who weakly submits and smiles."[37]

The *Crisis* worked hard to instill race pride in its black readers.

The editor continually argued that blacks possess a superior spiritual essence, a liveliness, and a loveliness that make them incomparable as a people. His old belief in the power of black meekness was seldom expressed in the magazine. When articles recounted the African past, they stressed the heroic and inventive nature of a people who had given the first push to the wheel of progress and civilization by smelting iron, and who had developed complex social systems and institutions at least as early as their European counterparts. The poems and stories expressed the creativity of the Afro-American people. Du Bois, who had seen "the slums of Glasgow and East London and the lower New York," insisted that "we are in our higher realization beautiful and fine and splendid. We love each other and we pray that God may damn a world which systematically insults us."[38]

The *Crisis* stirred deep resentment in whites. One Texas paper wanted to put "the arrogant ebony-head, thick-lipped, kinky-haired Negro 'educator' " in his place and make him stay there. In turn, Du Bois repeatedly derided the white race in a way that must have seemed taunting to those who considered themselves "friends of the Negro." Yet he also lamented the consequences of black chauvinism. In 1913 he regretted that white "carelessness and impudence" would weld ten million blacks "into one great self-conscious and self-acting mass." It was still possible "to make Negroes essentially Americans with American ideals and instincts," but the opportunity was passing. Those who demanded an unthinking "race pride" and "self-reliance" were creating a "Frankenstein."[39] In 1920 he found danger in an extremism that led blacks "inevitably and directly to distrust and hatred of whites," who must either segregate the world and leave blacks alone or "give utter justice to all."[40] The last controversy in the *Crisis* under Du Bois' editorship involved his program of voluntary self-segregation, but to the end he counseled a rational and calculated approach to race relations, instead of overemotionalism and fantasy.

The concept of two warring souls within the one body of the black American was as meaningful for Du Bois at the end of his *Crisis* years as when he had first used the image at the start of the century. The tension between race pride and identification with the nation as a whole was nowhere more dramatic than in the most controversial editorial ever printed in the *Crisis*, "Close Ranks," which in July

1918 called upon blacks to "forget our special grievances and close our ranks" with the white people "fighting for democracy."[41] Bitterly criticized by blacks inside and outside the association, Du Bois barely modified his statement when, two months later, he set the priorities for his readers: "*first* your Country, *then* your Rights!"[42] Perhaps the editor had written more than he intended in using the word "forget," for the *Crisis* before and after the editorial showed no diminution in its criticism of racism. But he was capable of distinguishing between Allied and German ambitions, and courageous enough to declare publicly his position that defeat of the former would be disastrous for that "United States of the World" to which he was most loyal.

Du Bois nevertheless saw danger in the negation of race pride. It was dangerous when an audience of blacks could guffaw at a speaker's suggestion that a child might be as black as the night and yet be beautiful, as the *Crisis* reported in October 1920, or when the magazine received angry objections from blacks to pictures of dark-skinned women on its covers. Another kind of danger was exemplified by Du Bois' own grandfather, whose insistence on treatment as an individual had denied the reality of racial differences and caused him to collide repeatedly with the wall of white exclusiveness. The *Crisis'* responsibility was to arbitrate between the forces of "race pride and race suicide, between attempts to build up a racial ethos and attempts to escape from ourselves." The focal point of the magazine's efforts in this respect came with the rise of Marcus Garvey, the gifted Jamaican leader whose "back-to-Africa" movement, as it was popularly called, was founded on the premise, according to Du Bois, that "a black skin was in itself a sort of patent to nobility."[43] The magazine's position on race pride was further illuminated by Du Bois' leadership in the Pan-African Congress in the decade after the world war.

Garveyism, which flourished during the high point of the journal's influence and success, brought a formidable challenge to Du Bois. Garvey and his Universal Negro Improvement Association (UNIA), with its hostility to the interracial ideal and its scheme for black Americans to emigrate to Africa, threw the *Crisis* and the NAACP on the defensive by brilliantly invoking the specters of self-hate and self-doubt as characteristic of its black members. Du Bois had first met Garvey on a visit to Jamaica in 1915, and the *Crisis* announced Garvey's arrival in the United States the following year. Almost totally unknown in his new country, the West Indian invited Du Bois to preside over his first public lecture; then in 1920 he asked permission to submit Du Bois' name as a candidate in the election of a "leader" of black America at an international convention organized by the UNIA. Du Bois pleaded absence in declining the former; "under no circumstances" would he allow the latter.[44]

Du Bois had watched with interest, amazement, and finally concern the West Indian's remarkable success in persuading thousands of blacks of the probity of his scheme to launch a back-to-Africa movement and in collecting funds for the purchase of ships for his Black Star Line. By 1919, when Du Bois organized his first Pan-African Congress in Paris with the support of the NAACP, there existed two irreconcilable approaches to the "Negro problem," each supported by an institutional force. Garvey had his *Negro World* to counter the *Crisis*, and after the first Pan-African Congress he began a campaign designed to discredit Du Bois and the association by identifying it with white philanthropy, white political power, and black servility. Garvey eventually derided Du Bois as a mulatto ashamed of his black ancestry, surrounded by pale-skinned associates and close friends, harping on his European ancestry while cultivating an aristocratic manner far removed from the life of the masses. Garvey threw at integrationist blacks the accusation of the most rabid racists, that their prime concern was intimacy with whites, especially white women. Du Bois first ignored Garvey's jibes, then responded with cold questions about the finances of the UNIA — careful not to impute improper motives to his rival but openly doubting his judgment and organizational ability — and finally denounced the movement as spiritually bankrupt and futile, and its leader as "the most dangerous enemy of the Negro race in America and in the world."[45]

Near the end of his editorship and long after the collapse of the Black Star Line, the arrest of Garvey on the charges of mail fraud, his imprisonment in 1925, and his deportation in 1927, Du Bois identified the basis of Garveyism as "mere rhodomontade and fatuous propaganda."[46] As for Garvey himself, Du Bois wrote in 1923, his life exemplified the power of white racism and mulatto snobbishness to destroy the black soul. Garvey, a "little, fat black man, ugly, but with intelligent eyes and big head," had demonstrated that he was no more than "a demagogue, a blatant boaster, who with monkey-shines was deluding the people and taking their hard-earned dollars." The gaudy titles, medals, and orders that he a-warded his followers came from a disoriented mind, but Garvey "is the type of man whom the white world is making daily, molding, marring, tossing in the air. All his life whites have laughed and sneered at him and torn his soul. All his life he has hated the half-whites who, rejecting their darker blood, have gloried in their pale shame."[47] By this time no reconciliation was possible.

There were, however, superficial similarities between Garvey's and Du Bois' race consciousness and economic nationalism. Both men saw the world as comprising separate cultures, each reflecting a distinct heritage and demanding freedom of expression. By the early twenties both believed that there are no superior and inferior races in the twentieth century, only temporarily backward peoples. Both saw the speciousness of the Anglo-Saxon claim to superiority based on technological progress usually of a destructive sort. But the Jamaican's fixed belief in the idea of black racial purity, to the extent of consorting with the Ku Klux Klan, his obsession with Africa as the solution to the problems of its scattered peoples, his pessimism about any unity among racially disparate peoples, and his refusal to allow any liberal idea or ideal to modify his fixation or deflect his purpose, all these differences were of enormous consequence in the relationship of the two men. Combined with Garvey's disdain for efficiency and practicality and his fondness for spectacular gestures financed by the generosity of his supporters, these differences sealed Du Bois' opinion of a man whose success nevertheless fascinated him. Du Bois fantasized about Africa in at least one poem and wrote with romantic abandon about the continent elsewhere, but he cultivated a scholar's knowledge of the land and used that information as the basis of his discussions of Africa. Finally, Du Bois saw Garvey's failure not as one of intelligence or learning but of moral disposition. In a cryptic piece in the *Crisis* in 1922 he was surely referring to Garvey when he ominously predicted of blacks that "from now on in our new awakening, our self-criticism, our impatience and passion, we must expect the Demagog among Negroes more and more. He will come to lead, inflame, lie and steal. He will gather large followings and then burst and disappear. Loss and despair will follow his fall until new false prophets arise. This is inevitable in every growing surging group of low intelligence and poverty."[48]

Although conceived independently, the Pan-African Congress

was the counterpart in Du Bois' career to the back-to-Africa movement. The central problem facing both the Pan-African Congress and the Garvey movement was as distinct as it was emotionally charged: how to recover from European imperialism, which at the Berlin Conference of 1884 had divided Africa, the historic fatherland of the black race. At times as passionate as those of Marcus Garvey, Du Bois' essays on Africa, especially before the first congress, breathe fire at the colonialists and warn of a desperate future if exploitation is not ended. The white world must give up its habits of thought and its "plan of color serfdom" represented by its pejorative racist terms, "or trouble is written in the stars!"[49]

The Pan-African Congress organized by Du Bois met four times, in 1919, 1921, 1923, and 1927, its meetings taking place in London, Brussels, Paris, Lisbon, and New York. A fifth conference planned for December 20-28, 1929, in Tunis failed to materialize.[50] The meetings of the congress distinguished its approach to the African question from Garvey's. Interracial in character, they deliberately tried to include representatives of colonialist governments and other interested parties in metropolitan countries; almost any political or social action group that wished to attend was free to do so, although there was strong opposition to inviting Garvey. The congress looked to the League of Nations as an important medium of change in Africa. It courted the favorable opinion of the white press, and propagandizing the white imperialist nations was seen as a necessary step on the road to African freedom. These characteristics bore the stamp of Du Bois' approval and initiative; he was the central figure of the four meetings and imposed many of his ideas on the largely unformed, uninformed, or sometimes reactionary attitudes held by most of the leaders, black and white, who attended the conferences.

Only the first and second congresses proved to be of substantial importance; the third and fourth were convened with little support outside of Du Bois' circle of admirers, and were in part sponsored at Du Bois' behest by the National Association of Colored Women. The first congress convened on February 19-21, 1919, in Paris. Of the fifty-seven delegates, twenty came from the Caribbean, sixteen from the United States, and twelve from Africa. Sharing the spotlight with Du Bois was Blaise Diagne, a Senegalese member of the French Chamber of Deputies. Diagne was elected president and Du Bois secretary of the congress. In addition to fifty-seven blacks there were official representatives from France, Portugal, and Belgium and several participating visitors, such as pro-Du Bois stalwarts Russell, Walling, and Joel Spingarn from the NAACP, which spent over $2000 to subsidize the meeting.

Du Bois and his NAACP colleagues had come armed with his plan for Africa. In January 1919, at a mass meeting in New York organized by the NAACP after Du Bois' departure for Europe, details of his scheme were made public and endorsed by the association. Emphasis was placed on the postwar disposal of the colonies previously controlled by the defeated Germans. It was proposed that the territories be made the nucleus of an international but African-controlled free state which would eventually include Portuguese and Belgian possessions and total two and one-half million square miles with twenty million inhabitants. The NAACP urged the training of Africans for political power through exposure to the main forces of modern culture — science, commerce, social reform, and religious philanthropy — while retaining the efficient African institutions of government based in the family and the tribe.

The congress was not long in session before it was clear that any plan as specific as Du Bois' and aimed squarely at European colonialism would be opposed not only by Europe but also by a substantial number of black colonials, notably the four black French deputies. Diagne praised French colonial rule while holding up the ideal of black racial unity; Gratien Candace of Guadeloupe deflected criticism from France toward the United States and expressed pride at the "enlightened" policy of their European rulers. The delegate from the Republic of Liberia, while praising his country and urging that it be considered a home for the darker peoples of Africa in exile, nevertheless reminded the delegates of the need for moderation. The official representatives of France, Belgium, and Portugal spoke of the rights and concessions granted their colonies. In the face of the anti-American strategy, the NAACP members did not take to the defensive. Indeed, the most dramatically fighting speech of the congress was probably delivered by Charles Edward Russell, the veteran socialist, an ally of Du Bois, and a white man.[51]

In the end, Du Bois was compelled to set aside his plan for an African state. The resolutions of the conference had one other striking difference from the NAACP platform. Although Du Bois had declared the principle that black people must have the dominant voice in deciding the affairs of Africa, the congress reaffirmed the authority of the Allied powers there and called upon them to effect changes such as the establishment of a code of laws for their colonies. The League of Nations was also entrusted with responsibility for the future of Africa, as the ultimate guarantor of the rights of colonial peoples. The principles on which future African states should be built remained the same as in the NAACP plan, but the transference of responsibility from blacks to whites and the absence of any mention of a new African state had defeated Du Bois' aim.

Reporting in the *Crisis* on "my mission," however, Du Bois recognized some good in the final compromise reached in the resolutions of the delegates. Two paragraphs were of tremendous significance; one called upon the League of Nations to warn the world of any mistreatment of the native population in Africa; the other demanded that "wherever persons of African descent are civilized and able to meet the tests of surrounding culture, they shall be accorded the same rights as their fellow citizens; they shall not be denied on account of race or color a voice in their own Government, justice before the courts and economic and social equality according to ability and desert."[52] Du Bois later expressed the belief that out of his original plan had come the Mandates Commission of the League of Nations, which assumed authority over the former German colonies; but this is uncertain. The greatest achievement of the congress was not in specific events but in the very existence of an international meeting of peoples of African descent speaking to the white world with one voice, however muted. Du Bois was satisfied with the response of the press and with the assurances of cooperation from British, American, French, Portuguese, and Belgian officials, as well as from the League of Nations.

The second Pan-African Congress convened in London, Brussels, and Paris between August 28 and September 6, 1921. Mindful of Garvey's jeers that the first Pan-African Congress, with only twelve Africans, had been badly named, the leaders assembled forty-one Africans in their total number of one hundred and thirteen black delegates. The NAACP, which had been pushed into an active role in the first congress because of the support for Du Bois from James Weldon Johnson, Walling, Russell, Ovington, and others, had little say in shaping the line that Du Bois and his supporters pursued at the second. For the Paris leg, he received major assistance from the young scholar Rayford W. Logan, who served as secretary and interpreter of that session. In the London meeting, where Du Bois was enthusiastically received, the British-American alliance dominated, and in the resolutions adopted Du Bois was able to give full expression to his thoughts on the future course of Africa in the modern world. He discovered in Brussels and then Paris, however, how far his ideas were from those of other black leaders and their white supporters. The Brussels meeting, chaired by Diagne, offered nothing but praise for Belgian colonialism. Diagne and Candace, who had succeeded to the presidency of the congress, bitterly opposed the major new theme introduced by Du Bois in the London resolutions, that of the power of socialism. Diagne forbade a vote on the resolutions but could not prevent them from being adopted, with minor changes, in Paris. From this dissension the congress never really recovered, but Du Bois had finally brought to bear on the African question the force of ideas tested in his own career.

The manifesto of the second Pan-African Congress based on the London resolutions began by declaring the "absolute equality of races — physical, political and social," although it accepted the need to raise "backward and suppressed" groups of people to levels of "intelligence, self-knowledge and self-control." The task should be entrusted to the intellectual elite of those peoples, who must use their power not to serve colonialism but, in language reminiscent of the Niagara Movement, to "complain against monstrous wrong . . . to see and to know the source of our oppression." The end of agitation is not simply independent states but a world order based on principles of peace, democracy, and socialism. In defiance of the anti-Marxism of Candace and Diagne, the manifesto declared that the "great modern problem is to correct maladjustment in the distribution of wealth." In arguing thus, Du Bois broadened the indictment and linked white capital and white labor in the exploitation of blacks. The demands of "the Negro race" are for recognition of civilized men as civilized, local self-government leading to independence, education "undivorced from the art of beauty," freedom of religion, encouragement of internationalism, suppression of capitalism in favor of "the ancient common ownership of the land and its natural fruits," and establishment of nonpartisan organizations to supervise the study and protection of indigenous African peoples.[53]

Although it contained elements of compromise, the manifesto

summarized some of the most important positions and attitudes of its author: the equality of races, the responsibility of the intellectual elite (the talented tenth), the necessity for agitation, the power of education, the importance of art, the primacy of moral judgment, and the desirability of socialism. In view of the alternative approaches to the future of Africa — Garvey's disorganization, the complacency of Diagne and Candace, the neoslavery of the colonial powers — the manifesto is of historic significance. Actual victories were again few, although the International Labor Bureau of the League of Nations adopted a proposal for a separate section on indigenous African and other black labor. Du Bois' enthusiasm for the congress remained; although he resigned as executive secretary, his role in its affairs probably increased as support generally ebbed. He wanted to make the Pan-African Congress a permanent institution, and he was anxious that meetings be held every two years, as the first conference had recommended. The third congress met on schedule in London in 1923, but the rift between the Paris-based black leaders and the Du Bois group, which was in a clear majority, severely limited the movement. Additional support for Du Bois came from Portuguese-African colonials in Lisbon, where the conference ended, but perhaps the most important result of the third Congress was as a point of departure for Du Bois on his first visit to Africa.

Liberally published in the *Crisis,* the diary of his journey southward to Africa contains some of the most lyrical and intensely moving language in all his work. From Africa itself he wrote with almost feverish enthusiasm of the future of the land: there would be "a civilization without coal, without noise, where machinery will sing and never rush and roar," where men will "in cool dawns, in little swift hours, do all our work." "This is not a country," Du Bois concluded, "it is a world — a universe of itself and for itself, a thing Different, Immense, Menacing, Alluring. It is a great black bosom where the spirit longs to die."[54]

Back in America, however, Du Bois coldly spelled out in the *Crisis* of March 1924 his reservations concerning migration to the continent. No one of middle or old age should think of migrating, because of the climate; younger people should know that skilled and unskilled labor was already abundant. Jobs were scarce; agriculture yielded little. Africa was "full to the capacity of its present industrial development.["55] Africa was for the Africans, not for foreigners who were black. Du Bois had not lost interest in Africa or pan-Africanism, but his visit confirmed the balance between romance and reality that distinguished the *Crisis* treatment of race from the excesses of Garveyism. Even so, it was impossible to keep black American interest in pan-Africanism alive, certainly not among the class of readers who supported the *Crisis*. "American Negroes," he later wrote, "were not interested."[56] The hastily organized fourth Pan-African Congress, held in New York in 1927, ended the major phase of his involvement with pan-Africanism.

As a movement conceived by Du Bois and kept alive almost entirely by his intelligence, ingenuity, and energy, the Pan-African Congress was a remarkable personal achievement. Its successes were largely intangible, but they were real. Having identified disunity as an instrument of colonial subjugation, Du Bois brought Africa together in a symbolic but unprecedented way. The congress established as an accepted fact of political thought the eventual liberation of Africa; it transferred prime responsibility for that liberation and governance from whites to blacks; and it placed the question of Africa and the future of the continent in the context of world movements such as socialism and world organizations such as the League of Nations. Du Bois' approach was studiously antiromantic; he acknowledged the reality of political power by engaging the imperial powers and the League of Nations in essentially diplomatic relations. The degree of success enjoyed by the four congresses was limited by factors beyond his control, notably the determination of colonial powers and the self-deception of the black colonial; but the ideas generated by the Pan-African Congress had an impact on both imperialism and the colonial imagination.

In its prolonged and vituperative campaign against lynching, its sanction and encouragement of militant black self-defense, its demand for social equality, its championing of pan-Africanism, its frequent scorn for the white world, and its unceasing attempt to instill race pride in the black reader, the *Crisis* carried out one part of its self-imposed task of speaking for the rights of the black world. The other, related side of its responsibility was to preach the gospel of "catholicity and tolerance, reason and forbearance," and to defend the rights of all men "regardless of color." The magazine recognized from the start the interdependence of those many freedoms for which apparently unrelated groups were fighting. It was an early champion of the rights of women. Du Bois denounced the preference for male children as a relic of barbarism (his only surviving child was a daughter). The journal took exception both when the suffragette movement was attacked and when members of the movement failed to see that the principle behind votes for women also supported the rights of blacks. Du Bois was swift to see that the lot of Jews in America and Europe had parallels with the struggle of blacks for dignity and independence. He praised the cooperation among American Jews and identified the group as a great force for good in the nation. German anti-Semitism distressed him, and he drew comparisons in the *Crisis* between such racism and its American counterpart.

His championing of the suffragettes and his concern for the welfare of Jews came easily within Du Bois' plan. His entry into the NAACP in 1910, his part in the Universal Races Congress of 1911, and his membership in the American Socialist party in 1911-1912, together form an emblem of his dream of a new world characterized by black freedom, interracial cooperation, democratic socialism, and peace. The concerns did not suddenly strike him on leaving Atlanta; his "Credo" of 1904 is an earlier statement of the same views. The history of each ideal in Du Bois' expression shows no fixed program or foolish consistency; nevertheless, the ideals together provided the effective counterpoint in the *Crisis* to the militance and necessary provincialism of his part in the American race struggle. To many of his critics, not least of all within the NAACP, such involvements diverted energy from the main fight. It is the essence of Du Bois' genius, though, that he placed the Afro-American condition in its broadest context.

The first number of the *Crisis* remarked on a coming Universal Races Congress. In April 1911 the *Crisis* noted the meeting; the next month it carried an article on the congress chairman. Du Bois clearly had high hopes for the world meeting of scientists and political and cultural leaders on the status of racial science and the future of race relations. His reports of the congress, which took place July 26-29, 1911, in London, showed that he had been satisfied beyond expectation. Elected with Felix Adler as joint secretary of the American section of the conference, he twice addressed the body and was generally received in London as a major figure in his own right.

The Races Congress, he later declared, "would have marked an epoch in the racial history of the world if it had not been for the World War."[57] Even more certain is that the conference, organized by the Ethical Culture Society and involving more than fifty "races," marked an epoch in his personal understanding of race and of the possibilities for world cooperation. The papers delivered at the congress were extraordinary, he wrote; before their publication, the *Crisis* "would not dare to express the statements which are contained therein." Reflecting new standards of anthropology and sociology, the papers generally stressed ideas and theories he was eager to receive. They professed that no significant link could be found between physical and mental characteristics; education and general social environment were more important than race. The state of a culture at any moment was not a fixed index to the capacities of the people. There were no absolute cultural standards and no innate racial superiority or inferiority that could be scientifically proved. Physical differences were "too indefinite and elusive" to be the basis of important distinctions. Miscegenation had apparently improved rather than weakened the vitality and capacity of offspring; in any event, there was no such thing as purity of race and miscegenation was increasing with the growth of interracial and international harmony. Finally, the *Crisis* summarized, even the "lowest" groups had much to teach others and should be treated with dignity and respect unless the customs were "morally objectionable to an unprejudiced mind."[58]

Although little came of the Races Congress as an organization, its teachings gave Du Bois a scholarly basis for the liberal racial philosophy that would be accepted only gradually in a nation already fifty years behind the time, he estimated, in its attitude to race. Thereafter, his greatest task as editor and thinker was to reconcile the vision of a united world with the skepticism and hostility spawned by segregation in America. The rationalism which he brought to bear on extremist interpretations of race found its main support in the doctrine of cultural relativity that marked the modern anthropology and sociology; and his persistent moral judgment reflected the residue of that ethical concern of which scholarly disciplines were rapidly divesting themselves. But the vision of an interracial world would have had limited political significance for Du Bois had he not been led at the same time to a renewed interest in the principles of socialism, to which he had been first drawn as a student in Germany.

Influenced by the three most radical founders of the NAACP—Ovington, Russell, and Walling—Du Bois joined the Socialist party in 1911. Although he resigned after a year and later accused the party of racial discrimination, the *Crisis* remained sympathetic to socialist aims. The first number mentioned a committee formed by the Socialists to investigate conditions among blacks; succeeding references to the Socialist program identified it with opposition to color prejudice. In December 1911 the editor urged blacks to support the party, for it is "the only party which openly recognizes Negro manhood." In August 1912, however, Du Bois faced a choice between his rival loyalties to socialism and to the need for black power. He opted for the latter, in a choice he would repeatedly make until the Depression. He decided to resign from the Socialist party in order to vote for Woodrow Wilson, who seemed somewhat sympathetic to black aims and who had a chance of winning, although he advised blacks that among the contenders only the Socialist Eugene Debs stood for human rights regardless of race or color.

Du Bois consciously objected to two aspects of radical socialism: its basis in dogma and its acceptance of revolution as necessary for change. In addition, as he later admitted, his reading of the principal texts of communism was at that time inadequate to an understanding of its theories, methods, and goals. In the *Crisis* he had expressed distrust of the Menshevik revolution of 1917 and made no mention of the victory of the Bolsheviks later that year. For many years he praised the Soviet Union only obliquely, taking pleasure in the survival of the state despite capitalist predictions of doom, but suspicious of its methods as he understood them. When the black poet Claude McKay accused him in 1921 of sneering at the Soviet Union, he denied the charge but expressed an unwillingness "to dogmatize with Marx or Lenin."[59]

A visit to the USSR in 1926 led to a dramatic shift in his perception of the country: "if what I have seen with my eyes and heard with my ears in Russia is Bolshevism, I am a Bolshevik."[60] In 1927 the *Crisis* openly congratulated the state on its tenth anniversary. Still Du Bois held back, unconvinced that what was possible in the Soviet Union needed to be repeated in the United States. In 1930, comparing the program of the leftist American Negro Labor Congress to that of the NAACP, he saw little difference except, again, in the matter of revolution. What was wanted in America was "sacrifice, patience, clear thinking, determined agitation and intelligent voting."[61] Thus Du Bois held fast to the idea with which he had concluded *John Brown* twenty-one years before: revolution is always a lowering of ideals and a loss.

Nevertheless, his political ideal in the *Crisis* was usually connected to the socialist movement in the United States and abroad. But side by side with preaching the political ideal, Du Bois attempted to make the *Crisis* a guide to conventional political choices. An idea dating back to his youth was that blacks, acting in unison at the polls, could swing victories one way or another and reap the benefits of the American electoral system. In 1912 he brushed aside the Socialists as "out of the calculation" in the presidential elections and defined the choice for the black voter as between "a party which has promised and failed" (the Republicans), "a party which has failed and promised" (the Progressives), and "a party which merely promises" (the Democrats). He endorsed the last, though he soon regretted having helped give Wilson the chance to "prove once and for all if the Democratic party dares to be Democratic when it comes to black men," when the president proved to be indifferent to blacks.[62] In 1916 he toyed with the idea of a black party, but conceded that forming one would be a futile exercise. In the elections of 1920 the *Crisis* summed up the frustrations of blacks in practical politics. Blacks could not vote for Republicans or Democrats, since neither cared for them; the Farmer-Labor party and the Socialists were friendly but had no chance of winning. The answer was to support individual candidates in congressional and other local elections.

This approach persisted in 1924, although Du Bois eventually gave moderate support to Robert La Follette and the Progressives. In July he published a lively statement of his position:

Keep your eye steady, Mr. Black Voter, your powder dry. You don't really care a rap who is President. Republican Presidents are just about as bad as Democratic and Democratic Presidents are little better than nothing. *But watch your Congressmen.* Never mind the dust and yelling and large talk. Watch the candidates for Congress and the state legislature . . . Get a list of those traitors who voted against Henry Lincoln Johnson in the contest for Georgia. Nearly all of them are candidates for office. *Knife them at the polls!* Defeat your enemies even if they are Republicans. Vote for your friends even if they are Democrats. Play the political game with knowledge and brains. Watch your Congressmen![63]

In 1928 Du Bois finally endorsed a presidential candidate certain of defeat. Turning his back on Herbert Hoover and Al Smith, he urged blacks to vote for Norman Thomas as an act of moral protest. In 1932, however, he opposed Hoover but was much less critical of the Democratic challenger, Franklin Delano Roosevelt.

Du Bois played "the political game" at some cost to his credibility as a political thinker, a moralist, and a farsighted prophet of his people. Exemplifying the moral dangers of what some people saw as his tawdry eclecticism was his refusal to probe the questionable political ties of black Chicago politician Oscar De Priest, a congressman whose place in the local machine at least gave blacks some power.[64] The black Socialist magazine *Messenger,* brilliantly edited by A. Philip Randolph and Chandler Owen, between 1917 and 1923 steadily attacked Du Bois and the *Crisis* from a radical perspective and also provided an insightful critique of his political temperament. Du Bois, it stressed, was a liberal, and on his liberalism had been founded the whole New Negro movement, a term that describes the upsurge of black pride and accomplishment in the 1920s and generally dismissed by the radical socialists as illusory. In a review of *Darkwater,* the journal damned Du Bois as a political thinker by praising him as a visionary poet. The *Messenger* identified the crucial aspects of his cerebration: artistry, romanticism, sensitivity, idealism, mysticism, optimism, and morality. Together, it implied, these made him less than valuable as a political analyst and strategist.[65] Du Bois was regarded as a bridge between Booker T. Washington and the new socialist order, and his political pragmatism was dismissed as vulgar, opportunistic, and shortsighted.

The tension between the ideal and the practical was also visible in Du Bois' belief in pacifism. His "Credo" of 1904 proclaimed that "War is Murder" and that armies and navies are "the tinsel and braggadocio of oppression and wrong." His response to world socialism and the international liberal movement that fostered the Universal Races Congress reinforced this belief. The chairman of the congress, Lord Weardale (Philip Stanhope) was in fact a prominent member of the world peace movement. But Du Bois suspended his pacifism during World War I. He took pride in the deeds of black soldiers and worked with Joel Spingarn to pave the way for a segregated camp for black officers, rather than accepting the alternative of black privates being led by white men. He himself was more than ready to accept a captaincy in the armed forces, as the *Crisis* admitted after plans for his appointment had fallen through. More extraordinary, Du Bois supported the conscription of black Africans by the French government, over the objection of the Aborigines Protection Society, which he nevertheless regarded as a conservative group. As long as the terms of conscription were the same for blacks and whites, he argued, there was no violation of the Africans' rights.[66] He refused to see such service as exploitation. Yet in May 1913 the *Crisis* had attacked American peace societies for softness on colonialism. Two years later he editorialized on the same issue, this time including the European peace movement in his censure. Then and later he argued that there could be no world peace until imperialism and racism were recognized as being at the root of international warfare.

There were other reasons for his failure to maintain a pacifist position as the American socialists generally did in World War I. During the war, Henry Lee Moon has written, Du Bois was "a one-hundred-percent American, all out for victory at whatever cost to civil rights."[67] He feared the peculiarly fierce German version of the doctrine of racial supremacy; war is hell, he agreed, but "slavery is worse; German dominion is worse; the rape of Belgium and France is worse."[68] Du Bois was probably more pro-European than super-American. During the early part of the war, in fact, his daughter was in England, where Du Bois had sent her to attend "one of the world's best schools [Bedales], in one of the world's greatest modern empires."[69] And as Julius Lester has pointed out, Du Bois' identification with France was deeply personal as a result of his ancestry. As for America, his writing in support of the war effort at the temporary expense of civil rights probably came less from patriotism than from a basic position of the magazine, coexistent with the rise of its influence, namely, that there were unmistakable signs of progress in the lot of black Americans.

The idea of actual black progress, however, was anathema to many radical socialist and nationalist critics of the *Crisis,* and even in Du Bois' view Afro-American progress was limited. In November 1920 he suggested that the race's "astounding" advance in the previous five years had been principally in the rise of a "New Spirit . . . a new vigor, hopefulness, and feeling of power." Progress for him meant increasing black self-dependence and self-assertion. Yet progress did not lie in "a silly cry of self-segregation or a scream of 'Up Black and Down White!' " A balance between the positive expression of black pride and the recognition of a complex, changing world, a new "Industrial Revolution," which demanded skills not yet commanded by blacks as a group, was a requisite of further advance. Despite these reservations, Du Bois felt there had been definite progress, which must be conserved and augmented in the future.[70]

Two developments opened his eyes to the real limitations of black progress, particularly when that progress was defined in terms of militance, independence, and racial pride. The first development — written largely in the literature and life-style of the Harlem Renaissance, the mass appeal of Garvey, and the comparative failure of pan-Africanism — was the dramatic loss of moral fervor and political purpose among the younger black leaders as a result of the new freedom and confidence. The second development was the collapse of Wall Street in 1929, with its grim impact on the black population, substantiating Du Bois' belief, dating back to the Atlanta studies, that no substantial black advance could take place under unrestrained capitalism.

Throughout 1929 the *Crisis* observed with grim humor as speculation mounted at the Stock Exchange; in October, it judged that the "bursting of the Wall Street speculation bubble seems about due"; in January 1930 it denounced attempts by Herbert Hoover and the New York *Times* to make light of the catastrophe. The fall of Wall Street revealed, Du Bois wrote, "the fundamental weakness of our system." In the following years Du Bois speculated variously on the central problem facing black America: to find a practical alternative to the competitive capitalist system to which the United States seemed committed, and to incorporate into that system the primacy of ideals of racial pride and self-reliance without which black culture could not survive in white America. By 1933 Du Bois was beginning to argue a specific doctrine of increased self-segregation which reflected the reality of imposed segregation but insisted on civil rights, and which recognized the necessity of Marxist principles of cooperation without commitment to Marxist organizations such as the Communist party.

To do so, Du Bois had first to reconcile himself to his own objections to communism. The period after the crash found the *Crisis* taking its strongest positions in defense of the Soviet Union. In November 1929 the journal had paraded the announced Soviet trade surplus as evidence of the viability of a communist state; in subsequent years it kept the Soviet example alive in its pages on a variety of questions, such as disarmament, anticolonialism, and religion. In March and May 1933, Du Bois wrote two articles on Marx and the American black, which were part of a year-long introduction of his new program of voluntary segregation. Yet even as he praised the Soviet Union and Karl Marx, calling him "the greatest figure in the science of modern industry" and "a colossal genius of infinite sacrifice and monumental industry," the crux of his argument was that Marx had only limited meaning for the contemporary black American dealing with contemporary American problems.[71]

Du Bois was far more hostile to the American Communist party. He denounced the tactics of the Communists in the Scottsboro case of 1931, accusing it of being neither "broadminded" nor "farsighted" in its hostility to the NAACP's attempts to join in the defense of the "Scottsboro boys," eight of whom were under sentence of death for the alleged rape of two white girls in Alabama. In their own methods of rallying support for the Scottsboro cause the Communists were "neither wise nor intelligent." Du Bois feared the motives of the party in recruiting blacks: "American Negroes do not propose to be the shock troops of the Communist Revolution, driven out in front to death, cruelty and humiliation in order to win victories for white workers."[72] The Communists in America failed to acknowledge the power of racism as a force that made the white proletariat the persistent enemy of their black "brothers"; in fact, he argued, it was wealthy, capitalistic whites, not their proletarian counterpart, who had financed black higher education and opened up thousands of jobs to Afro-Americans.

Between 1930 and his departure from the NAACP in 1934 Du Bois developed his program of voluntary black self-segregation as the necessary answer to the condition of the black American. While it is true that elements of the scheme may be traced far back into Du

Bois' past, the program was an innovative response to circumstances peculiar to the Depression as well as to factors constant in the modern history of race relations in the United States. Du Bois' segregationist program was the result of his continuous application of the pragmatic method to forces that seemed permanent and inescapable in American life: white racism, the evils of the American capitalist system, the *de facto* (and in the South *de jure*) segregated culture of black Americans, and the technological revolution that was undermining the ability of both classical education and artisan skills to answer to the blacks' need for employment and a decent wage. In particular, Du Bois believed that the higher educational system serving blacks had broken down; technically and spiritually, the colleges and industrial schools had ceased to function in a meaningful way.

Du Bois began to develop his new segregationist program in an address of 1930 at Howard University, where he received an honorary degree. The address marked his formal acceptance of certain principles historically identified with Tuskegee. He spoke sympathetically of those "practical men" who had perceived the central importance of economics in providing technical education for the black masses. But industrial schools and colleges had both failed. The average college man is "untouched by real culture"; aping the excesses of his white counterpart, he had abandoned his ideals in favor of extravagance and dissipation; "we have in our colleges a growing mass of stupidity and indifference." In spite of the promise of technical education, black farming, artisanship, and business were floundering. The liberal arts college had failed "because with the right general method it has lacked definite objects appropriate to the age and race"; industrial schools had failed "because with a definite objective it lacked appropriate method to gain it." The rapid changes in business and technology since the turn of the century had exhausted the range of skills taught in black schools. Du Bois called for a united college and vocational system, a new rigor of training and scholarship, greater emphasis on engineering and industrial planning, and a dedication to the ideals of poverty, work, knowledge, and sacrifice.[73]

Later, he analyzed his speech as strong in criticism but "weak and vague in remedy." Immediately afterward, he began to read Marx and other communist literature seriously.[74] Still wary of American

Communists, he nevertheless denounced unethical attempts to curb their influence, especially in the state of Georgia, where old slave statutes were being revived to deal with "incitement." At the end of 1930 he made his strongest attack on capitalism, blaming the Depression on capitalism's illogical, competitive, and exploitative character. By December of the next year in a Non-Partisan Negro Conference organized in Washington by Congressman Oscar De Priest, his Marxist sympathy had become pronounced, though he offered few specifics. In March 1932 he regretted that his earlier point of view in the Atlanta University Publications and *The Philadelphia Negro* had been dominated by "religion, humanity and sentiment."[75] By May 1932 the idea of self-segregation as the basis of a new program was evident. Addressing the twenty-third annual conference of the NAACP, Du Bois outlined four charges against the association. It needed decentralization and greater emphasis on youth; more important, it needed to identify and work with "the masses," and to produce "a positive program" rather than a merely "negative attempt to avoid segregation and discrimination."[76]

In January 1933 Du Bois proposed twelve subjects, each a division of the Afro-American "problem," to be discussed in future issues of the *Crisis*; the subjects covered the areas of health, education, race, social interaction, economics, civil rights, and politics. In general, his reports were less than enthusiastic about the state of black culture. In "The Health of Black Folk" he found the old theory that blacks were dying out as a race in America totally discredited, but disease was still rampant and child mortality distressingly high. In "Color Caste in the United States" he detailed the extent of racism in the country and stressed the need for meaningful action to combat prejudice, a theme he continued in "The Right to Work," which called for an emphasis on economic organization.[77] Two pieces on the history and proper strategy of the black vote indicated that Du Bois was finally ridding himself of the opportunistic element that had marked his political philosophy almost until the Depression: the black voter must keep his eyes upon ideals "which make for the uplift of mankind" and a state dominated by the working class; in "Our Class Struggle," which showed the continuing impact of Marxist ideas on his thought, he reported a black American class struggle between the tiny but proud bourgeoisie and the lower classes despised by them, a struggle that must give way to social solidarity.[78]

Perhaps the most important pieces in the series were those on college education and race pride. At the Fisk University commencement of 1933 Du Bois had spoken on "The Field and Function of the Negro College." Reviving his memories of the University of Berlin, when the Kaiser ruled and Heinrich von Treitschke thundered the message of German national and racial superiority from the lecture platform, Du Bois demanded that "without whitewashing or translating wish into facts," the black college must begin with blacks and must be founded "on a knowledge of the history of their people in Africa and in the United States, and their present condition." Was this statement "a denial of aspiration or a change from older ideals"? Du Bois admitted only "some change of thought and modification of method" from his previous position. Was it "a program of segregation," opposed to "national unity and universal humanity"?

> It is, and it is not by choice but by force; you do not get humanity by wishing it nor do you become American citizens simply because you want to. A Negro university . . . does not advocate segregation by race, it simply accepts the bald fact that we are segregated, apart, hammered into a separate unity by spiritual intolerance and legal sanction backed by mob law, and that this separation is growing in strength and fixation; that it is worse today than a half century ago and that no character, address, culture, or desert is going to change it, in our day or for centuries to come.[79]

In "On Being Ashamed of Oneself: An Essay on Race Pride" Du Bois confronted the difference between educated, cultivated blacks and the "mass of untrained and uncultured colored folk and even of trained but ill-mannered people" with whom they were continually classed by whites. Over this latter group the socially conscious leaders had "no real control"; the black mass was influenced "only with difficulty and compromise and with every risk of defeat." But the opinion of white America, in making no distinction between the two groups in employment or social recognition, had determined the future course of blacks of both classes: "In Negro churches, Negro schools, Negro colleges, Negro business and Negro art and literature our advance has been determined and inspiring"; everywhere else, losses had been greater than gains. "*The next step, then, is certainly one on the part of the Negro and it involves group action. It involves the organization of intelligent and earnest people of Negro* descent for their preservation and advancement in America, in the West Indies and in Africa; and no sentimental distaste for racial or national unity can be allowed to hold them back from a step which sheer necessity demands." There was "no other way"; blacks would be "beaten into submission and degradation" if they merely waited unorganized for a place to be given them "in the new reconstruction of the economic world."[80] In "Pan-Africa and New Racial Philosophy" Du Bois stressed the interests that drew the black American "nearer to the dark people outside of America than to his white fellow citizens."[81]

In February 1934 Du Bois called in the *Crisis* for a discussion of his program for segregation. He declared that the NAACP had never spoken out against segregation; that is, it had supported black institutions such as the church, schools, and the all-black officers' training camp in World War I. In March he welcomed the idea of segregation in subsistence homestead colonies, proposed as a Depression measure by the federal government, as a means toward the development of racial solidarity and economic cooperation. The response to this idea and to his program in general showed him to be almost without support within the association. NAACP leaders such as its president Joel Spingarn, executive secretary Walter White, Leslie Pinckney Hill, and Francis J. Grimke almost unanimously opposed the plan, although Spingarn conceded that the psychological value of voluntary self-segregation had been defended in certain quarters, notably in the extreme wings of Jewish opinion. From Walter White, who had succeeded James Weldon Johnson as secretary, Du Bois received no sympathy: segregation was evil, and the association opposed it in every form. In his reply, the *Crisis* editor told Spingarn that if the NAACP had waged a twenty-five year campaign against segregation, as the president claimed, then the total result has been less than nothing. Legal victories had not moved and would not move the mass of white Americans to treat blacks as men. His counterattack on White was *ad hominem*, questioning White's right, as an extremely light-skinned man who seldom encountered discrimination personally, to speak about the evils of segregation.[82]

The major outcome of the *Crisis* campaign to promote the new doctrine was to bring the decades-long tension between the editor and the association to a head over questions of procedure and authority. Du Bois had been prepared, he noted, to accept a difference of opinion between himself and the leadership over segregation, but he was not prepared to be silenced by them. In May the *Crisis* carried the text of a resolution by the Board of Directors of the NAACP declaring unalterable opposition to segregation. Crucial to subsequent events was the adoption of a Walter White-inspired resolution that forbade any salaried officer to criticize the association without its prior approval. Du Bois believed that he had no alternative but to resign. After failing to persuade him to change his mind, the NAACP accepted his resignation. The text of his final letter appeared in the *Crisis* of August 1934. He was then sixty-six years old.

Du Bois had to live with the irony that his program resembled, in its materialist bias, the philosophy of Booker T. Washington. One black newspaper jeered, as the *Crisis* reported, that his Fisk speech of 1933 was a call for black colleges to give degrees in plumbing. There were other misunderstandings of his theory of voluntary self-segregation. Du Bois remained opposed to any deprivation of the civil, political, economic, or social rights of blacks, and to any segregation that included harmful discrimination. He did not wish to shut whites out of black organizations; he wanted interracial organizations such as the faculties of black colleges or the NAACP to assert the centrality of black power as a goal and to make the furthering of black pride and black economic advance their main interest. Du Bois could hardly have hoped to convince the NAACP of 1934 to adopt such a program. The white socialist corner of the association leadership had passed almost entirely from the scene, as had the more committed white liberals such as Moorfield Storey, John Milholland, and the increasingly socialist Oswald Garrison Villard, all of whom tended to defer to Du Bois' analysis of the race situation even if they found him an administrative problem. Their places had been taken by blacks exemplified by Walter White, essentially conservative except on the question of civil rights and apparently more concerned with maintaining the growing power of the association than risking innovation. Du Bois' program of voluntary self-segregation was closely prophetic, however, of the temper of black America thirty years later, when equal protection under the law, gained through a combination of NAACP-sponsored legal action and a radical activism almost contemptuous of the association's character, finally presented blacks with an honorable choice of association.

An opposition to dogmatism and radicalism of either a Marxist or a cultural nationalist extreme was the general philosophic position of Du Bois in the twenty-four years of his editorship of the *Crisis*. Occasionally in his writings this pragmatic method slipped into opportunism or casuistry, but such moments were fewer than might be expected in an undertaking so charged with emotion. To defend, instruct, and praise blacks was the basic mission of the *Crisis*, and it did so with a verve and a resourcefulness that made it the major black magazine of its age. The last fight of the *Crisis* underscores Du Bois' continuing intellectual vitality and the power of his insight into American life.

The dignity of the *Crisis* philosophy derived from its liberal and intensely moral character, as well as from its rational intellectualism and ultimately ecumenical spirit. In these essentials it was generally consistent from its tentative start to Du Bois' unhappy departure as editor; and it succeeded in its basic aims even if the magazine could control neither the events of history nor the tastes and susceptibilities of the people for whom it labored.

CHAPTER EIGHT

Darkwater

I hated to see the fine soul of a poet and literateur thus dulled and frayed
in the rough work of actual propaganda and agitation.   (Du Bois, 1940)

IF ANY SINGLE work by Du Bois is central to his career and
representative of his method as a propagandist in the years between
the rise of the Niagara Movement in 1905 and his resignation from
the NAACP in 1934, it is *Darkwater: Voices from Within the Veil*
(1920). Once again, as in *The Souls of Black Folk* almost a generation before, he gathered his "fugitive pieces" of poetry and prose,
including hitherto unpublished material, to offer yet another statement on his one great subject: the significance of race in the modern
world. Although some of its words date back to 1904, *Darkwater*
summarizes Du Bois' thought in the fifth or middle decade of his
life, years in which he brought the *Crisis* and his own influence as
interpreter of the American experience to their highest point of
popularity. By 1920, he had become well acquainted with all the
forces that thereafter would shape his thinking: pragmatism, Afro-
American nationalism, pan-Africanism, the concept of the Third
World, socialism, and the evolutionary optimism into which his
spiritual sense resolved itself as he moved away from an early faith in
empirical social science.

The importance of *Darkwater* to the whole of Du Bois' art is that
it incorporates and dramatizes the tensions between the forces shaping his thought, especially between socialism, black nationalism,
and liberal idealism — the triangulation essential to his middle years.
In one place or another, *Darkwater* appears conclusively to support
one of these approaches, only to shift to a rival argument. In captur-
ing this indecisiveness, the work reflects more accurately than any
other in his canon the agitated basis of his intellection from the time

he first became a propagandist until, much later in life, he found repose in the certitudes of Marxist-Leninist teaching.

The pattern which combined sociology, history, fiction, and poetry in *The Souls of Black Folk* had worked so well that Du Bois set about in *Darkwater* to imitate its basic lines. The counterpart to the short story "Of the Coming of John" is found in "The Comet." The epigraphs from well-known white authors that preceded each chapter of the earlier work are replaced by Du Bois' own creative work, in the shape of formal poetry, poetic prose, or parable, with the "Credo" of 1904 forming an extended epigraph to the entire book. There is, again, a thematic progression in the work from politics and history toward art and spirituality. *Darkwater*, too, begins on an autobiographical note, in "The Shadow of Years," then moves through social and political discussion to analysis of the roles of black men, women, and children in an unjust world. An essay on the meaning of beauty and death is followed by the poem "The Prayers of God," a jeremiad in which the world-sinner is confronted by the "Father Almighty." The story "The Comet" tells of the destruction of New York by poisonous gases and invites thoughts on the end of the world. The concluding poem, "A Hymn to the Peoples," demands a supplication of the world before Du Bois' concept of the divine.

"Last year I looked death in the face and found its lineaments not unkind. But it was not my time. Yet in nature some time soon . . . I shall die."[1] Du Bois was barely halfway through life when two serious abdominal operations in December 1916 and January 1917 caused him to think of an imminent death and to assess the meaning of his life. Certainly the nineteen pages comprising "The Shadow of Years" do not represent a full autobiographical statement or even a broadly emblematic one in the tradition of Frederick Douglass' *Narrative* or Booker T. Washington's *Up from Slavery*. The *Darkwater* statement is, however, significant as a self-portrait. The works of Douglass and Washington are narratives which extrapolate from the life of the autobiographer to the experience and hopes of the Afro-American people. In each case, the life of the narrator is offered as a supreme example of the lesson that the mature, successful, and reflecting public figure wishes to teach his people. Douglass and Washington encouraged the improbable but seductive myth that their rise in the face of adversity could be reduced to a formula, its

principal ingredients being hard work, courage, discipline, confidence, and faith — the virtues, in other words, of honest self-reliance. Du Bois, however, consciously described a train of events and
a combination of circumstances that tended to defy imitation. The
others saw themselves as types of Afro-American man. Du Bois
deliberately depicted himself as atypical of the masses of people
black or white, belonging to that rare community formed by those
summoned to a prophetic role. He had been called, and then chosen.

To view this self-portrait in *Darkwater* as mere egotism is to mis-
judge the nature of the prophetic conviction and to misread the style
of prophecy. One reviewer, for example, called for a more mellow,
less "bitter" Du Bois, for "a truer Christian spirit than now shines
through his writings," and for him "to walk more in the manner of
the Nazarene."² Such an accounting ignores Du Bois' deliberate
attribution of the heroic elements in his life to powerful outside
forces guiding him. Free will is subject in this narrative to a primal
force no longer explicable by the orthodox religion of Congregationalism or by the historical science of an Hippolyte Taine, as in *John
Brown*. It was no idle choice of words when Du Bois described his
life as having two "Ages of Miracles," his university years and the
present time, separated by "the Days of Disillusion" and "the Discipline of Work and Play." During the first Age of Miracles he could
deceive himself into believing that he was the cause of his success: "I
was the captain of my soul and master of fate! I *willed* to do! It was
done." Even then there was an uncanny power at work: "I *wished!*
The wish came true" (14). Out of the days of disillusion and then
discipline had eventually come a sense of himself as an instrument of
an all-powerful force, and of his main task as one of prophecy,
which launched his second Age of Miracles.

The origin of the prophet is important. Du Bois stressed two factors of his personal heritage, its racial diversity and its tradition of
defiance. His birth was timely. "I was born," he wrote, "by a golden
river and in the shadow of two great hills, five years after the Emancipation Proclamation." The dark-skinned Burghardts, his mother's
people, were "part of a great clan" traced back to "a little, black,
Bantu woman, who never became reconciled to this strange land,"
and to her husband, also African, "sullen in his slavery." (5). His
own father, Alfred, had in him "the making of a poet, an adven-

turer, or a Beloved Vagabond," but life gave him little choice (7). Like the Burghardts, the Du Bois clan was steeped in mystery and a tradition of revolt. Louis XIV had driven two Huguenot brothers, Jacques and Louis Du Bois, into the wilderness of Ulster County, New York. Alfred's father, a passionate but silent and bitter man who wrote poetry and had imperious ways, had produced children so fair of skin that one had passed over and married into the white world. Du Bois judged that in his veins there was "a flood of Negro blood, a strain of French, a bit of Dutch," but he thanked God there was no Anglo-Saxon (9). Disdainful of the notion of Anglo-Saxon supremacy among races, he was justifying his peculiar prophetic role by showing himself a child of many races and heir to a tradition of liberty.

The saga of his life, as he related it, took him from a happy childhood to his first intimation of the social stigma attached to a dark skin. With adolescence came a greater understanding of the power of racism. Du Bois summarized his reaction, as perceived from his fiftieth year: "As time flew I felt not so much disowned and rejected as rather drawn up into higher spaces and made part of a mightier mission. At times I almost pitied my pale companions, who were not of the Lord's anointed and who saw in their dreams no splendid quests of golden fleeces" (12). The combination of religious and secular, Biblical and classical reference suggests the complexity and confusion of Du Bois' prophetic sense. When finally he emerged into "full manhood" after the days of disillusion and of work and play, he went with "the ruins of some ideals about me, but with others planted above the stars" (21).

Once he had made "the great Decision" to devote his life to a crusade for social justice, his every ideal and habit was "cruelly misjudged" both by racist whites and by black people; he was accused by critics of wanting to be white — "And this to me, whose one life fanaticism had been belief in my Negro blood!" (22). And yet, whether he realized it or not, Du Bois virtually declared that he was singular and outside both races. In the dark days of disillusion, "I planned a time when I could speak freely to my people and of them, interpreting between two worlds" (23). The loneliness of the prophet he accepted, even cherished. A portion of the chapter "The Souls of White Folk" written in 1910, eight years before "The Shadow of Years," establishes the exclusiveness of his position. "High in the tower, where I sit above the loud complaining of the human sea, I know many souls that toss and whirl and pass" (29). Emphasizing his sense of place, Du Bois describes the pieces as representing merely the things "of which men think, who live . . . To this thinking I have only to add a point of view: I have been in this world, but not of it" (vii).

The combination of spiritual conviction and the desire for secular power illustrates the basic ambivalence of Du Bois' adult intellectual life. It is an attenuation of his old conflict between the role of scientist and that of poet-moralist, which he sought to resolve by the method of pragmatism, or "pragmatic realism," and the art of propaganda. The dualism is reflected in the styles of *Darkwater.* While the hero-narrator often speaks of the mighty power that has delegated its authority to him, the argument is often outlined with the cold logic of a seasoned debater. There is less reliance on historical facts and empirical research than in *The Souls of Black Folk,* but also less appeal to sentiment and sympathy; Du Bois' self-conscious depiction of himself as a man of feeling and of culture in the earlier work has become obsolete as a portrait of the artist. To the reader overly sensitive to argumentation or skeptical of prophecy, the result may seem like bitterness and bombast. To the propagandist and prophet, however, such a style is impulsive and necessary.[3]

The gospel expressed in *Darkwater* is divided into two parts: sociopolitical commentary in editorial form and a spiritual appeal lyrically expressed. In "The Souls of White Folk" Du Bois attacks the variety of white social attitudes and masks that conceal condescension and contempt. The philanthropist, the colonizer, and the opportunistic tycoon—the three major types of white humanity described in the book—hide their real intentions behind a facade of religious, educational, or socially ameliorative activity.[4] "The Hands of Ethiopia" voices the author's anger at European imperialism in Africa, a sordid story which had its start in trans-Atlantic slavery and its most bloody consequence in World War I.[5] The African colonial states, exploited by European capitalism, were a travesty of the ideals of nationhood and of civilization. The theft of land on which European settlers were building their power had reduced Africans to the status of slaves in their own fields. "The indictment of Africa against Europe," Du Bois warned, "is grave" (57). He concluded his attack on European colonialism with two demands. Deploring the role of the white missionary in Africa, he insisted that schools rather than churches should be responsible for giving Africans "the essential outlines of modern culture" (71) and he called for the establishment of "a new African World State, a Black Africa," the nucleus of which would be the million square miles of territory "owned" by the recently-defeated Germans; in a decade of tumultuous political change, he said, this idea was no "impossible dream" (65-68).

"Of Work and Wealth" is a dramatic retelling of the East St. Louis Riots of July 1917, in which several scores of blacks were killed. The rapid industrialization of the St. Louis area by the captains of industry, demanding and attracting waves of laborers, is sketched in quasi-poetic, myth-making language. The trade unions exclude blacks but at the same time expect improved conditions from the industrialists, who counter with a flood of eager black workers fleeing from Southern poverty. "Here, then," in East St. Louis, "was staged every element for human tragedy, every element of the modern economic paradox" (90). The white workers' resentment of powerful management is inevitably turned against the black scabs, who seem to be despoiling the dream of labor solidarity. A strong supporter of trade unions, Du Bois saw the solution of this modern dilemma in the exorcism of race hatred, the admission of the dignity of all labor, and the conversion of the robber baron to the creed of social responsibility. Social exclusivity must be sacrificed, and happiness, not mere profit, must be the goal of labor, for "here, in a world full of folk, men are lonely. The rich are lonely" (102).

"The Servant in the House" continues the debate on the dignity of labor, especially that of black workers allowed to be Pullman porters but not subway guards, nursemaids of white children but not their governesses. Du Bois contends that service is of "ancient high estate," and that "Personal Service," the aid of man to man, is greater than all other forms of assistance: "It is the purest and holiest of duties" (117). Again under attack is the "Theory of Exclusiveness," in which the individual equates the extent of his rise with the numbers forced to stay beneath him, while he himself proclaims the power of democracy. Du Bois looks forward to "a world of Service without Servants" (121).

"Of the Ruling of Men" examines modern theories of leadership and social responsibility in light of the suppression of blacks and all women in America. The crucial social inability of mankind is its failure to apply the theory, born during the Age of Enlightenment, of universal suffrage. The serf liberated during the Enlightenment became the lordly businessman of a later day; and blacks, women, and other groups are now suppressed by the tyranny of the white male, who expects to progress by ruthlessly excluding elements incompatible with his desires. Minorities are not consulted on their social situation; yet in the final analysis, "only the sufferer knows his sufferings" (143). The majority resists the fact that the history of the world is "the history of the discovery of the common humanity of human beings among steadily-increasing circles of men" (149). Du Bois distinguished between the tyranny of the few, which can usually be overthrown by the force of revolution, and the "spiritual losses from suppressed minorities [that] may be vast and fatal and yet all unknown and unrealized because idea and dream and ability are paralyzed by force" (155). Individual freedom, once it is identified as vital to truth, faith, and beauty, "harms no man, and, therefore, no man has the right to limit it" (156). There should be no talk of limitations on man: "Infinite is human nature" (140).

In "The Damnation of Women" Du Bois expressed his long-standing belief in the feminist movement. The future woman, he declared, must have "a life work and economic independence" (164). She must have knowledge and the right to choose or reject motherhood; it is hypocritical to be horrified by the thought of feminist freedom while allowing "the bestiality of free manhood" (165). His main concern, though, is with black womanhood. Asia is the father and Europe the precocious, self-centered, forward-striving child of civilization, "but the land of the mother is and was Africa" (166). The black woman had borne the greatest burden during slavery; the one unforgivable sin of the South was not slavery, which is a "world-old habit," but its abuse of the black woman. The idea that black is not beautiful in womankind comes from "the defective eyesight of the white world" (183). But unlike her white counterpart, the black woman is not relegated to the status of adornment. Indeed, matriarchy may be natural to African peoples, Du Bois reasoned; "despite the noisier and more spectacular advance of my brothers, I instinctively feel and know that it is the five million women of my race who really count" (179).

"The Immortal Child" moves ostensibly to the issue of education but also deals with two other themes. One is the character of the emblematic black hero, represented in *Darkwater* by Samuel Coleridge-Taylor (1875-1912), the British musician of Anglo-African descent. The other theme is Du Bois' evolving concept of the divine, which he identified as the potential of mankind for good. Children are the future, and "immortality is the present child" (212). As a treatise on education, "The Immortal Child" reveals Du Bois' continuing intransigence about the importance of the liberal arts. When should "culture training" give place to technical education? "Never," he replies (215). But the rigidity of his earlier claims for the talented tenth is gone, having succumbed to the impact of socialist thought. "Without wider, deeper intelligence among the masses Democracy cannot accomplish its greater ends"; the learning of a craft or trade is irrelevant to true education: "We must seek not to make men carpenters but to make carpenters men" (209-210).

Addressing himself to the special needs of the psyche of the black child, Du Bois advised against either shielding it completely from a knowledge of the color line or leaving the young mind to discover, usually in brutal fashion, the realities of racism. In *The Souls of Black Folk*, Alexander Crummell's life exemplified spiritual endurance. Here, the success of Coleridge-Taylor represents the fulfillment of black potential, once granted the opportunity to develop in relative freedom. The black psyche, in the absence of racism, flowers into unlimited achievement. That the musician's mother and wife were white and educated bespoke the potential of interracial harmony, given an enlightened culture. The accomplishments of Coleridge-Taylor repudiate notions of innate black or mulatto inferiority; his productive career in British music was an augury of the future of the black man and of race relations in general. Free to live as he liked and to do the work he loved, subject only to the vicissitudes common to all humanity, this man had left his mark on the world.

The essay "Of Beauty and Death" is the most philosophically reflective of all the pieces in *Darkwater,* and best seen when read with "The Comet." In the short story, poisonous gas from a great comet kills all the people in New York except for a black worker caught underground and a wealthy white woman engaged in her photographic darkroom. Believing themselves to be the only survivors in the world, the two are forced to confront the meaning of life and death. Distinctions of race and wealth now mean nothing. Humanity must start anew. The man comes to view his companion, whose life he has saved, as "primal woman; mighty mother of all men to come and Bride of Life." In turn, she sees him as the essence of manhood in his strength, "his sorrow and sacrifice. He was . . . her Brother Humanity incarnate, Son of God and great All-Father of the race to be." The once humble black man knows now what it is to be king. Between them, "it was not lust; it was not love—it was some vaster, mightier thing . . . a thought divine, splendid" (269-270). But the moment of truth is shattered by the sound of an automobile. People living outside the city, who have not been affected, arrive to view the disaster. The woman is reunited with her father, who is grateful—after a fashion—to her protector. The black man hears the jibes of the white crowd and even some angry words about lynching the "nigger" for daring to help a white woman, before he is met and embraced by his wife. Life continues.

The principal theme of this melodramatic story is the power of death to illuminate the meaning of life. This theme underscores a pattern of thought, apparent throughout *Darkwater,* which had come to dominate Du Bois' mind as he passed through middle age and began to dwell on the idea of mortality. In the essay "Of Beauty and Death," the author again reflects on death: "This Death—is this Life? And is its beauty real or false? . . . Of this heart questioning I am writing" (221). In the process of outlining twenty-one ways of looking at life and death, Du Bois composed not only the most complex piece of the book but perhaps his most involved statement on the significance of race in the context of human experience.

In his questioning of life, Du Bois surveyed the ground between racist indignity and the unmistakable beauty of the world. Too reticent to speak like Plato of "the beauty of Love and Friend," he spoke first of the loveliness of physical nature, the "least of beauties," yet "divine" (225). Interspersed with reflections on the mean actions of mankind are lyric descriptions of Bar Harbor, Maine, evenings at Montego Bay, Jamaica, and above all, the Grand Canyon. Du Bois was searching in the natural landscape for any reflection of the quality of evil that comes so easily to mankind. In the Grand Canyon, with its combination of beauty and terror, he finally discovered an approximation of the human condition. "It is awful," he wrote of the scene. "It is the earth and sky gone stark and raving mad. The mountains up-twirled, disbodied and inverted, stand on their peaks and throw their bowels to the sky." There nature imitates—or parodies—the human capacity for mixing loveliness and evil: "It is a grim thing, unholy, terrible! It is human—some mighty drama unseen, unheard, is playing there its tragedies or mocking comedy." The kaleidoscopic colors at dawn transfix the searcher as he gazes into the heart of its radiance. "I have seen what eye of man was never meant to see. I have profaned the sanctuary. I have looked down upon the dread disrobing of the Night, and yet I live" (238-239).

The combination of beauty and terror found in the Grand Canyon is the earth's counterpart to the basic human mixture of squalor and wealth, malice and kindness, oppression and freedom. Evil and good are everywhere—in the shameful treatment of black soldiers by their government, in the beauty of French hospitality to their dark-skinned liberators. As he had stared into the Grand Canyon, so the poet peers through the city's haze at the canyons of New York. He sees the mysteries of the metropolis at day and night. In contrast to the culture of Europe, the American city is an emporium obsessed by power. It is also a setting for the passage of humanity of all classes, races, and ages. In the dark world of Harlem, where "the street is crowd and leisure and laughter," humanity of a special kind parades, but the texture of humanity does not change: "all is good and human and beautiful and ugly and evil, even as Life is elsewhere." Du Bois sees the tragedy of life in the fact that the "Doer" seldom if ever "sees the Deed and the Victim knows not the Victor and Each hates All in wild and bitter ignorance" (246).

The author arbitrates between the rival powers of beauty and ugliness. The latter is inevitable, repetitive, and eternal. But it is also incomplete, and "its eternal unfulfillment is a cause of joy." The essence of beauty is in its completion, which is guaranteed by the power of death, "the sweet silence of perfection, the calm and balance of utter music" (247). There is no basis for the superficial optimism that declares everything to be beautiful. However, pessimism is cowardice. The man who cannot acknowledge racism and yet "live and hope is simply afraid either of himself or of the world" (230). Beauty, like ugliness, though finite in its earthly representations, is also immortal, if its ideals are renewed in successive generations. The eternity of beauty is implicit in the Immortal Child, who offers a renewal of hope with the renewal of life, for "children are the future" and "immortality is the present child" (212). The central fear of mankind is death, but Du Bois welcomes it: "If we were not dead we would lie and listen to the flowers grow . . . But we know that being dead, our Happiness is a fine and finished thing" and that death is final (248). In embracing the meaning of death, rational man pledges allegiance to the pursuit of beauty and truth, and demonstrates this faith through a life of service.

Du Bois was fascinated by the potential value of using religious forms for propagandistic ends. The idea of the immortal child is one example of such usage. More significant is his cultivation over many years of the idea of a deity compatible with the black experience. As was appropriate to a prophet who saw himself crying in the wilderness, he settled upon the idea of a black Christ. As his style of propaganda began to take shape after 1910, the images of a black Messiah, a black God, became increasingly evident, especially so in many of the poems and parables that separate the *Darkwater* essays. In the poem "The Riddle of the Sphinx" the seer awaits the time when:

> some dim, darker David, a-hoeing of his corn,
> And married maiden, mother of God,
> Bid the black Christ be born! (55)[6]

The parable "The Second Coming" tells of the birth of a black babe, the illegitimate grandson of a Georgia governor, under Messianic circumstances. "Jesus Christ in Texas" relates the mysterious passage of a dark stranger through the lives of a variety of moral delinquents, a story published previously by Du Bois as "Jesus Christ in Georgia" in the December 1911 issue of the *Crisis*. "Why," remarks a black convict visited by this Christ in Texas, "you are a nigger, too" (129). In "The Call," the mighty King who sends a lowly black woman into battle on his behalf reveals his face, which is black, to convince her of her power to act for him. The persona of the poem "Children of the Moon," who is already dead, strives upward "to the blazing blackness/Of one veiléd face" (191). When God is personified in *Darkwater*, He is inevitably black.

The foundation for this depiction of a black Christ rests on the fact that Jesus Christ was a Jew and that Jews, like blacks, are despised by racists who nevertheless profess Christianity; the Semites are among those "darker races" for whom Du Bois wrote. He was not bent, however, on making an historical argument about the origins of Christ. With his stress on the immortal child as man's link with eternity and as the guarantor of a finer world, he had come to believe in some form of evolutionary optimism, which should not be confused with his former faith, encouraged by Spencerian Darwinism, in the inevitable progress of the world. Du Bois knew that neither he nor anyone would see the end of social injustice. Yet he insisted that the good deeds of individual men accumulate power and slowly but surely make for human advance. The modern yardstick for the moral state of the white race and of civilization becomes the treatment accorded the darker peoples. The black Christ presents a figure to be revered or crucified, according to the moral state of those challenged by Christ's life and suffering. Du Bois was among the earliest modern writers to use suffering blacks as figures of Christ-like redemption, not merely as examples of Christian piety, in a manner successfully employed in this century by writers from William Faulkner to Flannery O'Connor.

Du Bois' faith in the immortal child and his portraits of a black Christ did not make him meek and mild. Parts of *Darkwater* are among the most militant in all his writing. In his essay "The Souls of White Folk" he made perhaps his most severe condemnation of the white spirit. Looking on the carnage of the war, "we darker men said: This is not Europe gone mad; this is not aberration nor insanity; this *is* Europe; this seeming Terrible is the real soul of white culture—back of all culture,—stripped and visible today. This is where the world has arrived,—these dark and awful depths and not the shining and ineffable heights of which it boasted. Here is whither the might and energy of modern humanity has really gone" (39). At the end of *The Quest of the Silver Fleece* the author had daringly depicted armed black men and women preparing to fight for their rights; in *Darkwater* he went further. Du Bois promised that the carnage of the war was *"nothing to compare with that fight for freedom which black and brown and yellow men must and will make unless their oppression and humiliation and insult at the hands of the White World cease. The Dark World is going to submit to its present treatment just as long as it must and not one moment longer"* (49). Such treatment must end, he warned elsewhere, "or trouble is written in the stars!" (60).

In starkly representing the "White World" as opposed in battle by the "Dark World," Du Bois was prophetic of the spirit later exemplified in the Bandung Conference of 1955, which recognized an informal but distinct sense of community among nonwhite peoples, a sense that has increased rather than diminished over the years. But while *Darkwater* is vehemently against racism and imperialism, the central political message of the work is conciliatory rather than divisive. In view of the romantic potential of the African question, Du Bois' proposals for an enlightened colonialism in "The Hands of Ethiopia" are extremely restrained; given the destruction of World War I and the historic treatment of the black folk in America, his criticism of the white soul is hardly excessive.

Darkwater represents not only the triangulation among socialism, black nationalism, and liberal idealism characteristic of Du Bois' thought in his middle age but also their emerging order of importance. In his political analysis, the main tool is socialism, not race. Essays such as "Of Work and Wealth," "The Servant in the House," "Of the Ruling of Men," and "The Damnation of Women" develop out of a socialist analysis of the effect of capitalist traditions in American society. Although this analysis falls far short of the positions taken by radical socialists or communists, the influence of Marx is clear. Socialism mitigated Du Bois' racial feeling, but without escaping the scrutiny of this self-appointed guardian of Afro-America and the "darker races." Drawing on notions of both socialism and black nationalism, and becoming probably more influential than either, is Du Bois' love of liberal idealism. The interdependence of these concepts, which he attempted to unify in his version of the pragmatic method, should not obscure their tendency toward separation into competing forces.

In praising socialism in "Of the Ruling of Men," Du Bois wrote that its finest contribution lies in "neither its light nor its dogma, but the idea back of its one mighty word — Comrade!" Beyond all political and social strategy "must come the Spirit — the Will to Human Brotherhood of all Colors, Races, and Creeds; the Wanting of the Wants of All" (159). The final message of *Darkwater* is not Marxism or black power but the need for a redirection of civilized man in the aftermath of a war that epitomized the disastrous contradictions of Western culture. On this point the work concludes in the poem "A Hymn to the Peoples," published four years before the start of the world war. *Darkwater*, with its icon of the black Christ and its faith symbolized in the concept of the immortal child, appeals to the ancient Indo-Christian community of the spirit, which had been obscured by the materialism of the industrial age that had spawned slavery and the excesses of capitalism.

Asia is the world father, Du Bois had written in praising the black woman. In "A Hymn to the Peoples," "the Buddha walks with Christ! / And Al-Koran and Bible both be holy!" (275).[7] In *Darkwater* there is no proselytizing for any specific Eastern doctrine; there is only the search for greener fields of faith, away from the mercantile wasteland of America, the carnage of European war, the helplessness of a black America trapped by the consequences of centuries of slavery. Consolation comes with faith in the future, which is prepared for by a life of sacrifice and restraint moderated by an appreciation of beauty, with humility dignified by pride, and with service that rejects servility.

Powerful as Du Bois' attacks are on the white world, his deepest concern in *Darkwater* is ecumenical, interracial, and international in scope. The totality of the work supports the lines of verse from "A Hymn to the Peoples" with which the writer ends:

> We see the nakedness of Toil, the poverty of Wealth,
> We know the Anarchy of Empire, and doleful Death of Life!
> And hearing, seeing, knowing all, we cry:

> Save us, World-Spirit, from our lesser selves!
> Grant us that war and hatred cease,
> Reveal our souls in every race and hue!
> Help us, O Human God, in this Thy Truce,
> To make Humanity divine! (276)

CHAPTER NINE

The Crisis and Literature

Negro art is today ploughing a difficult row, chiefly because we shrink at the portrayal of the truth about ourselves . . . We want everything that is said about us to tell of the best and highest and noblest in us. We insist that our Art and Propaganda be one.
  That is wrong and in the end it is harmful.   (Du Bois, 1921)

All Art is propaganda . . . I do not care a damn for any art that is not used for propaganda.   (Du Bois, 1926)

WHEN DU BOIS FORMALLY announced the intentions of the *Crisis*, he did not propose that the magazine should serve as a vehicle for literary art and criticism. Nevertheless, the journal soon became the most significant outlet for poems and stories written by black Americans, a position not seriously challenged by any other black magazine until the appearance in 1923 of *Opportunity: A Journal of Negro Life,* edited by Charles Spurgeon Johnson for the National Urban League. Together with the radical socialist *Messenger,* founded in 1917 by A. Philip Randolph and Chandler Owen, these two magazines and their editors were the principal journalistic forces in the postwar blossoming of Afro-American arts and letters known as the Harlem Renaissance. Although it is probable that Johnson contributed more to the younger black writers and artists in the mid-twenties than did Du Bois and the *Crisis*, in the decade preceding the Renaissance Du Bois' journal was preeminent among black publications in its encouragement of art, and seminal in its relationship to the phenomenon itself.

By 1934, however, when Du Bois relinquished the editorship, he had divided feelings about the literature he had helped to foster. Proud to have been a major force in the growth of black American art, he had yet become identified with a point of view that estranged him from many of the gifted younger writers whose earliest work had appeared in his magazine. Scornful of some of the most acclaimed and successful pieces of the era, he was almost alone in his vigorous questioning of the assumptions and achievements of the black writer in those exhilarating years when, as Langston Hughes remembered it, "the Negro was in vogue."

The first verse of the *Crisis* appeared in its second number with the black poet Leslie Pinckney Hill's "Jim Crow": "By what dread logic, by what grand neglect,/Wise as our nation, does this relic last . . ."[1] In 1911, the importance of literature was stressed by Du Bois in his remarks on the death of the poet Frances Ellen Watkins Harper: "She was not a great singer, but she had some sense of song; she was not a great writer, but she wrote much worth reading. She was, above all, sincere." The editor had no illusions about the state of Afro-American letters: "We have among ten millions today one poet, one novelist [surely W. S. Braithwaite and Charles W. Chesnutt] and two or three recognized writers of articles and essays. That is all." The lesson of Harper's life was clear: black literature had to be systematically encouraged. If the *Crisis* flourished, "we hope to have ready for the beginning of our second year's work a matured plan for encouraging young writers" to emulate her example.[2]

In April 1912 the *Crisis* published its first significant fiction, "The Doll," a story commissioned from Charles Chesnutt. In August, Du Bois announced the results of a short-story competition organized by the magazine. The entries were of three types: didactic stories, rejected for their preaching; "old-time 'darky' stories," well-written but too stereotyped in the plantation tradition; and character sketches, one of which was chosen for publication. With this modest beginning the *Crisis* launched itself as a literary journal and also announced its basic artistic criteria: a literature set in black life but not so directly propagandistic that it ignored the principles of art.

Until he added a literary editor to his staff in 1919, Du Bois appears to have maintained as strong an influence on the literary role of the *Crisis* as he did on its editorial policy. Other figures were associated in important ways with the magazine. The *Crisis* aesthetic reflects the range of their tastes and interests. The first was William Stanley Braithwaite, the Boston poet and editor later noted for his yearly collections of magazine verse between 1913 and 1929. The second was Jessie Redmond Fauset, daughter of a prominent black Philadelphia family, and eventually the author of four novels

published between 1924 and 1934. In March 1912, the *Crisis* identified her as director of its "What To Read" department. Fauset
became literary editor of the *Crisis* in 1919 when at the high point of
its circulation the magazine expanded its staff. She was the only
person to hold this position formally, and when she resigned it in
1926, the task reverted to the principal literary spirit of the journal,
Du Bois himself.

It is difficult to document the exact influence of Braithwaite on
the *Crisis*, but he was a member of its first editorial board, established in 1910, and remained for many years as a kind of contribut-
ing editor. Following the death of Paul Laurence Dunbar, Du Bois'
Horizon had referred to Braithwaite as the poet laureate of black
America. The *Crisis* underscored his importance by devoting an
article to him in 1911. Braithwaite refused to write political propaganda and generally avoided the theme of race. "Art is the embodiment of spiritual ideals," he wrote in the *Crisis* in 1915; "there is no
human progress without a previsioning of the aspiration through
one of the symbolic languages of art."[3] But he had some sense of the
historical implications of black literature as part of a rising culture,
as he remarked in 1919: "While we have no traditions in the art, we
have a rich and precious tradition in the substance of poetry; vision,
intense emotionalism, spiritual and mystical affinities, with both
abstract and concrete experience, and a subtle natural sense of
rhythmic values." He was confident that "the poets of the race with
compelling artistry can lift the Negro into the only full and complete nationalism he knows — that of the American democracy."[4]

His comparison of James Weldon Johnson and Claude McKay in
1924 illustrates the point of view he brought to the *Crisis*, and which
Du Bois for some time appeared to tolerate, if not share. Johnson's
work was the greater, Braithwaite wrote, because it was "based
upon a broader contemplation of life, life that was not wholly con-
fined within any racial experience, but through the racial he made
articulate that universality of the emotions felt by all mankind."
Braithwaite discriminated between McKay as pure dreamer, contemplating life and nature, and "the violent and angry propagandist, using his natural poetic gifts to clothe arrogant and defiant
thoughts." The art that produced the militant sonnet "If We Must
Die" must give way to "those magnificent Psalms against which all
the assaults of time dissolve, and whose music and whose vision wash
clean with the radiance of beauty."[5]

In Fauset's works there is an even greater tension between her acknowledgment of the separate and special experience of blacks and her desire to assert the universality of human emotion. Eager to write of the injustice of racism, she still insisted on the essential similarity of blacks and whites, by which she meant the similarity between educated, cultured blacks, like herself, and their white counterparts. She preferred to write "of the colored American who is not being pressed too hard by the Furies of Prejudice, Ignorance, and Economic Injustice. And behold he is not so vastly different from any other American, just distinctive."[6] Hughes gave her an important place in the Harlem Renaissance, noting that with Charles S. Johnson and Alain Locke, she "midwifed the so-called New Negro literature into being. Kind and critical — but not too critical for the young — they nursed us along until our books were born."[7] Observers of the scene generally distinguished between the immediate, personal importance of Fauset and the more removed significance of Du Bois. But she was both loyal and intellectually indebted to the man whom she publicly called in 1924 her "best friend and severest critic."[8]

Fauset was responsible for the appearance in the *Crisis* of the first published poems by Hughes and by Arna Bontemps. Fauset's letters to Jean Toomer are instructive. An admirer of Walter Pater, she deplored the modern tendency of poets toward obscurity; she urged Toomer to read the classics, which would give him a sense of the universality of poetic experience. In Bontemps' opinion, she was a very good editor, making the most of the free hand Du Bois gave her and full of encouragement to younger writers, who genuinely liked her.[9] Fauset was the *Crisis* link between Braithwaite's conservative idealism and Du Bois' bent toward propagandistic art, as well as between the aloof Du Bois and the younger writers who respected, even revered his accomplishment but feared his manner.

On the question of appropriate themes and techniques, Du Bois was generally vague. Poetry, he wrote in March 1915, is the most difficult of all forms of writing; "it must have ideas. It must above all be beautiful, alluring, delicate, fine." As reading, he suggested Palgrave's *Golden Treasury* and a recent anthology edited by Max Eastman. Upon Joseph Conrad's death, he urged young writers to study his craft. In the main, though, the *Crisis* favored traditional renditions of themes centered on race, with such fare as detective stories, impressions, and nature poetry added for relief. It is probably true of Du Bois as a literary editor working with fledgling writers that, as Bontemps remarked, "he leaned toward the tidy, the well-mannered, the Victorian — literary works in which the Negro put his best foot forward, so to speak."[10]

Although Du Bois favored a franker treatment of sex, the *Crisis* in effect observed strict standards of restraint in this respect. Perhaps more important, it hardly concealed its disdain for jazz, the blues, and the popular gospel song. While it now and then praised black popular entertainers, especially the celebrated comedian Bert Williams, it seldom questioned the artistic criteria of the white world except on matters such as patronage and publishing. Du Bois' idea of a notable musical event, of which he recorded hundreds in the *Crisis*, was a black performer interpreting serious Western music, or a white composer or musician introducing African or Afro-American themes into his work. As late as 1940 Du Bois could write slightingly of a major indigenous black form: "Most whites want Negroes to amuse them; they demand caricature; they demand jazz."[11]

Although it encouraged black artists, the *Crisis* asserted the universality of genius over the demands of nationalism. Verses were published from traditional British authors such as Thomas Campbell, Edward Young, George Eliot, and Tennyson. Their lines not infrequently appeared on the cover of the journal, as did a selection from Thoreau, but they generally appeared in epigraphs to sections, as was often the case with Emerson, Longfellow, or Whittier as well. Contemporary British writers such as Shaw, H. G. Wells, and Chesterton were often quoted. H. L. Mencken's jibes at Georgia and the South were noted with satisfaction by the former resident of Atlanta. Braithwaite, through his association with contemporary white poets, notably with Harriet Monroe's *Poetry* circle, was almost certainly responsible for the occasional appearance of poets such as Monroe herself, Carl Sandburg, or the young Vachel Lindsay. At the height of the Harlem Renaissance, Du Bois could rely on the help — in judging *Crisis* competitions, for example — of many people then prominent in American letters, such as Mencken, Eugene O'Neill, Sinclair Lewis, Dorothy Canfield, Alfred Knopf, and Edward Bok.

Since the *Crisis* aspired to report on all the darker races, it developed an international flavor in its literary offerings. The magazine at one time or another published essays on Japanese "hokkus,"

Brazilian writing, and Pushkin; it presented poems by Rabindra-nath Tagore, then in vogue, and reported on the nascent literature in the Caribbean. The major emphasis, however, was on Afro-Americans and their culture. Always keenly interested in promising young blacks, Du Bois made mention of Paul Robeson, Marian Anderson, and Shirley Graham (later the second Mrs. Du Bois) while each was still a student. The editor seldom overestimated the quality of work being produced by the contributors to his maga-zine. In 1916 the *Crisis* remarked that "interesting developments in Negro literature" were taking place, even though the attempts to write poetry were variously "good, bad and indifferent."[12] Noting the latest muddled trends in New York drama involving blacks, Du Bois later in 1916 predicted "the slow growth of a new folk drama built around the actual experience of Negro American life."[13] In the twenties he himself would organize the Krigwa Players Little Negro Theatre, which performed successfully as part of the New York little-theater movement.

Du Bois' sense of a rising black literature was accurate. In 1919, the appearance of some lines by McKay introduced the *Crisis* read-ers to the first of the seminal artists of the Renaissance to publish there. Hughes' first published poem, "The Negro Speaks of Rivers," appeared in June 1921, dedicated to Du Bois. And in April 1922, a year before the poem appeared in *Cane,* perhaps the greatest single work of the Renaissance, the *Crisis* published Toomer's "Song of the Sun."

As the major phase of the Harlem Renaissance opened between 1922 and 1923, there was no doubt that the *Crisis,* with a circulation far superior to that of its competitors and in apparently good finan-cial shape, was the most important black magazine interested in the arts. Even its most spirited rival, the radical socialist *Messenger,* which hounded Du Bois almost from its inception in 1917, admitted that he was "the leading literateur" of the race, pointing out that music, art, and literature dominated his journal's monthly survey of events.[14] The *Messenger* also admitted that Du Bois had been the chief force behind the new radical pride discernible by 1920.[15] From a literary point of view, in fact, there was little to choose between the two magazines, the writers in both journals coming generally from the same small pool of talent. And the political radicalism of the *Messenger* made it no more receptive to popular culture: it openly declared its preference, for example, for "classical" melodies played by an accomplished black pianist over such fare as the black musical *Shuffle Along* and its imitators.[16]

Between the quality of these two magazines and that of the black newspapers as journals of literature there was an enormous gap; none of the papers had a coherent policy in the arts or systematically published the work of important young writers. More than once Du Bois used the *Crisis* to attack the quality of black newspapers for both inaccuracies of substance and infelicities of style. Little work by black writers appeared in white magazines. Although McKay was supported in his early efforts by Frank Harris of *Pearson's* and Max Eastman of the *Liberator,* most of his peers were entirely dependent at first on the black journals. Most white journals had become apathetic to the concerns of blacks, and at least one, the *Outlook*, was regarded by Du Bois as hostile. By 1929 the situation was somewhat different. The *Nation,* the *New Republic,* and H. L. Mencken's *American Mercury* had published stimulating though not necessarily sympathetic assessments of the Renaissance, and the *Survey Graphic* had in March 1925 published a "Harlem Number," the most successful issue in its history to that date and an historic document in defining the spirit of the age.[17]

In short, from its own beginnings to the first days of the Harlem Renaissance, the *Crisis* was among all publications the prime mover in black American literature. By the end of the era, though, the journal would seem to many a reactionary and divisive force, and Du Bois a capricious and destructive critic as he entered yet another controversial passage in his voluntary supervision of the intellectual life of black America.

When an angry McKay wrote in 1928 to denounce the editor for his review of McKay's first novel, he remarked that the life of propaganda had precluded Du Bois from contact with real life and that there should be no surprise "when you mistake the art of life for nonsense and try to pass off propaganda as life in art!" Previously McKay had expressed the opinion to Du Bois that "nowhere in your writings do you reveal any comprehension of esthetics and therefore you are not competent nor qualified to pass judgment upon any work of art."[18] McKay had correctly identified the two points on which Du Bois was most vulnerable in his connection with the Harlem Renaissance. First, he had written so ambivalently and confusedly about the relation of art to propaganda that misinterpretation of the *Crisis* position on this subject was inevitable. Second, although he insisted on reviewing new fiction and poetry, he was not very well qualified to do so. The review of belles-lettres was never the primary literary focus of the magazine, which tended to stress social and historical studies of race and politics, and reviewed comparatively few novels, plays, and poems related to those fields. Du Bois' one-paragraph review of E. M. Forster's *A Passage to India* ("a little dull and affected" at first, then "a tremendous epic of racial clash") typifies the extent to which the *Crisis* noticed current fiction, plays, and poetry.[19]

His distinction between art and propaganda must be inferred from his criticism and fiction. In 1921 he used a defense of O'Neill's *The Emperor Jones* to vindicate the right of an artist to depict evil traits in black characters. Afro-American art was suffering because "we shrink at the portrayal of the truth about ourselves . . . We want everything that is said about us to tell of the best and highest and noblest in us. We insist that our Art and Propaganda be one. This is wrong and in the end it is harmful." The black writer must treat the full range of life within his community in spite of criticism from those who "fail to see the Eternal Beauty that shines through all Truth, and try to portray a world of stilted artificial black folk such as never were on land or sea."[20]

More encouraging to those younger writers eager to depict the more sporty aspects of Harlem life was a *Crisis* warning in 1922: The aesthetic life of blacks was likely to be choked by "the over-emphasis of ethics to meet the Puritans round about who conceal their little joys and deny them with crass utilitarianism . . . Our love of life, the wild and beautiful desire of our women and men for each other — all, all this sinks to being 'good' and being 'useful' and being 'white.' " This trend must be resisted, for "the great mission of the Negro to America and the modern world is the development of Art and the appreciation of the Beautiful."[21]

Du Bois' remark about the "over-emphasis of ethics" is one of the most curious passages in all his writings. He did not realize that the liberty on which he insisted for the black artist could turn to license. He failed to sense that, whereas morality was central to his vision of America, this view might not be shared by younger writers less disciplined in their moral education and more contemporary in their resistance to moral arguments.

Du Bois' inadequate reading of the ethical temper of the new generation was matched by his limited understanding of the stylistic trends of the new age. His review of *Cane* exemplifies this problem. Toomer's art, Du Bois wrote, "carries much that is difficult or even impossible to understand. The artist, of course, has a right to make his art a puzzle to the interpreter (the whole world is a puzzle) but on the other hand I am myself unduly irritated by this sort of thing." Toomer's writings had "their strange flashes of power, their numerous messages and numberless reasons for being. But still for me they are partially spoiled." Toomer was described as an impressionist but also as "a conscious artist who offends often by his apparently undue striving for effect." *Cane* was nevertheless one of the two books that "would mark an epoch." Du Bois predicted that the black world would one day point to Toomer "as a writer who dared to emancipate the colored world from the conventions of sex."[22] This is perhaps the only positive point in the review. Faced with a writer who was at once black and aware of the stylistic experimentation in the age of Joyce, Gertrude Stein, and Sherwood Anderson, and who was ready to explore techniques of interior monologue and word association, Du Bois was so puzzled that he praised him for what the reviewer himself would later censure in others.

There was some truth, too, in the charge of elitism leveled against the *Crisis* circle in its cultural leadership. Alain Locke's review in the *Crisis* of Fauset's first novel, *There Is Confusion* (1924), was indicative of attitudes that would prove divisive. Locke noted that the novel was one that "the Negro intelligentsia have been clamoring for." Yet the work betrayed inner conflicts not simply of the Harlem Renaissance but also of the whole black intellectual class. Something more than simply the artist's search for fresh material was involved in choosing to write "of the educated and aspiring classes," of what Locke called "our better circles." One barely disguised motive was to show the white world that blacks had produced sophisticated people with all the graces of civilization. Locke himself revealed this intent in his italicized summary of the complications of character in the novel: "the *primary confusions are those more universal ones of human nature and its type-psychologies.*"[23] The subtle argument here, however unintentional, was that only by lifting the setting of the black novel out of the slum could the novelist attain universality in presentation.

Although his review appeared in the *Crisis*, Locke was a key figure in the first serious challenge to the position of the *Crisis* as the major black literary journal. While Du Bois was away on a four-month trip to Europe and Africa in 1923-1924 on business such as the third Pan-African Congress, Charles S. Johnson in effect wrested away from the *Crisis* its leadership of the cultural movement by his brilliant development of *Opportunity: A Journal of Negro Life*, the official publication of the National Urban League. On his return, Du Bois' role at a meeting of important young writers dramatized the change. It was Johnson who opened the meeting and introduced the "virtual dean of the movement" — Alain Locke. The *Crisis* editor was welcomed "as a representative of the 'older school,' " and he spoke defensively of the limited opportunities of earlier generations of black writers.[24]

By making culture rather than politics the principal focus of *Opportunity*, and links between young writers and the major white publishers, patrons, artists, and critics its immediate goal, Johnson, assisted by Locke, removed Du Bois and the *Crisis* from center stage in spite of the far greater circulation of the NAACP magazine and the fame of its editor. By means of three well-publicized and brilliantly orchestrated literary competitions and awards dinners involving the best black writers and the cream of the available white literati and patrons, the "chief entrepreneur" of the Harlem Renaissance — as Johnson has been called — was instrumental in bringing publishers directly to writers such as Langston Hughes and Countee Cullen and in compelling recognition of the cultural life of black America from white anthologists and newspapers.[25]

The first *Opportunity* competition was announced in September 1924, and prizes were awarded, with much fanfare, in May of the following year. In October 1925 the *Crisis* responded with its own Amy Spingarn competition, but the initiative had been lost. Spurred on by the rivalry, no doubt, the black writer felt a new confidence in his relationship to editors and publishers. Countee Cullen published his first volume of verse, *Color*, in 1925; the next year brought Langston Hughes's *The Weary Blues*. In June 1926, Hughes spoke in *The Nation* for the majority of writers: "We younger Negro artists intend to express our individual dark skinned selves without fear or shame. If white people are pleased we are glad. If they are not, it doesn't matter . . . If colored people are pleased we are glad. If they are not, their displeasure doesn't matter either . . . We stand on top of the mountain free from within ourselves."[26] The artists who had thus proclaimed their independence of blacks and whites in a white magazine went a step further in November when they brought out their own periodical, *Fire!!* The seven writers (including Hughes) behind the journal showed further independence in explaining its title: "FIRE . . . weaving vivid, hot design upon an ebon bordered loom and satisfying pagan thirst for beauty unadorned . . . the flesh is sweet and real."[27] Organizationally and philosophically, the Harlem Renaissance had outgrown the *Crisis*.

Perhaps the first sign that Du Bois was becoming apprehensive about the course of the Harlem Renaissance was his firm censure of Locke, the Oxford and Harvard man-of-letters and professor of philosophy at Howard University whose personality and expertise had made him an important resource for new writers. Du Bois called Locke's *The New Negro* an extraordinary book marking an epoch in Afro-American culture; in it, he himself had published an article. But he then struck the first blow in what would be a five-year action to regain control of the movement he had helped start: "Mr. Locke has newly been seized with the idea that Beauty rather than Propaganda should be the object of Negro literature and art." Du Bois continued that *The New Negro* proved Locke wrong, for it was both beautiful and propagandistic; "it is a grave question if ever in this world in any renaissance there can be a search for disembodied beauty which is not really a passionate effort to do something tangible, accompanied and illumined and made holy by the vision of eternal beauty." Du Bois threw out a warning: "if Mr. Locke's thesis is insisted on too much, it is going to turn the Negro renaissance into decadence." The fight for life and liberty was "giving birth to Negro literature and art today and when, turning from this fight or ignoring it, the young Negro tries to do pretty things that catch the passing fancy of the really unimportant critics and publishers about him, he will find that he has killed the soul of Beauty in his Art."[28]

The next month, February 1926, Du Bois fired his second shot. The *Crisis* organized a symposium, "The Negro in Art," designed to secure replies to seven questions from an impressive array of names. But the range of the questions was not wide. They centered on the matter of class and character representation in fiction by and about blacks, in Du Bois' belief that publishers were conspiring to prevent the representation of "Negroes of education and accomplishment." The questions worried about the "image" of the black man projected in the literature of the decade, "the continual portrayal of the sordid, foolish and criminal among Negroes." They suggested that this trend was destroying any chance of a broader representation to match the reality of Afro-American life: "Is there not a real danger that young colored writers will be tempted to follow the popular trend in portraying Negro character in the underworld rather than seeking to paint the truth about themselves and their own social class?"[29]

In response, the loyal Fauset accepted the spirit of the inquiry and took all seven questions seriously. There was, she wrote, a "grave danger making for a literary insincerity both insidious and abominable." [30] Sinclair Lewis called for a conference to discuss the whole matter; Vachel Lindsay was for complete freedom for the black artist; Sherwood Anderson thought it "a great mistake for Negroes to become too sensitive."[31] Alfred Knopf expended few words in reply, finding one question about publishers and the depiction of the black middle class "senseless."[32] H. L. Mencken did not see what all the fuss was about. If white authors portrayed blacks as ridiculous, the "remedy is to make works of art that pay off the white man in his own coin. The white man, it seems to me, is extremely ridiculous. He looks ridiculous even to me, a white man myself."[33]

But white authors and publishers could not feel nearly as threatened by the thrust of the symposium questions as did the black authors who had to live within the community and respond to its needs. Langston Hughes did not bother to answer: "What's the use of saying anything? — the true literary artist is going to write about what he chooses regardless of outside opinions." The novelist and NAACP official Walter White concluded similarly that "sycophants and weaklings will follow whatever trend is mapped out for them; genuine artists will write or paint or sing or sculpt whatever they please."[34] Countee Cullen saw no real danger in the young black writer finding inspiration in the slums. If the slums were congenial to him, he should depict them, but "not pander to the popular trend of seeing no cleanliness in their squalor, nor nobleness in their meanness and no commonsense in their ignorance."[35] The evidence showed that apart from Du Bois and Fauset, few active writers saw a problem in the class interests of black and white authors and white publishers. James Weldon Johnson categorically denied that there was any evidence that the publishing houses were suppressing Afro-American letters by restrictive policies.[36]

This could not have been the response for which Du Bois had hoped. Before 1926 was ended, he took the offensive. He spoke in October to an important NAACP conference and made his clearest declaration on the criteria of Afro-American art. He stressed that art for the black man was an important part of a greater struggle, the larger purpose of which was not to replace white vulgarity with its black counterpart, but to change the texture of American society. Black folk were crucial to a return of the beautiful to national life. Within them were "stirrings of the beginning of a new appreciation of joy, of a new desire to create, of a new will to be." The artists might claim that beauty had nothing or little to do with truth and goodness; Du Bois was there to insist that the two were "unseparated and inseparable." The material for the artist of the beautiful lay in the history and aspiration of the black people. The reinterpretation of the Afro-American past by black historians pointed to themes of romance hitherto denied in that past. Heroism in the face of enslavement was truth and beauty at the same time, and the artist served both ideals simultaneously in recording the acts of courage. "Thus it is the bounden duty of black America to begin this great work of the creation of Beauty, of the preservation of Beauty, of the realization of Beauty . . . The apostle of Beauty thus becomes the apostle of Truth and Right not by choice but by inner and outer compulsion. Free he is but his freedom is ever bounded by Truth and Justice." All art is propaganda, "and ever must be, despite the wailing of the purists."[37]

Du Bois blamed white publishers, patrons, and artists (though by no means all of them) for the unsatisfactory state of black letters and the inaccurate depiction of black life in current literature: "white Americans," he wrote in 1927, "are willing to read about Negroes, but they prefer to read about Negroes who are fools, clowns, prostitutes, or at any rate, in despair and contemplating suicide. Other sorts of Negroes do not interest them because, as they say, 'they are just like white folks.' But their interest in white folks, we notice, continues."[38] The previous year, after the appearance of Carl Van Vechten's unfortunately titled *Nigger Heaven*, Du Bois had delivered the most crushing review in the history of the *Crisis*. In this sensational novel of the wealthier Harlem set, Van Vechten delighted in the flamboyant world of the cabarets and contrasted their energy and style with satirized elements of the black bourgeoisie. Du Bois denounced the book as "a blow in the face . . . an affront to the hospitality of black folk and to the intelligence of white." He found the novel "neither truthful nor artistic." He urged readers to burn the book and read the *Police Gazette*.[39] In spite of Du Bois' attack, *Nigger Heaven* sold well. But Du Bois had just begun to fight.

Julia Peterkin's *Black April* (1927), he thundered, was for the most part "a veritable cesspool of incest, adultery, fighting and poverty."[40] Nor did Du Bois restrict his invective to white authors. He saw the urban novel of the lower class as part of a Van Vechten school, in which Claude McKay was the star black pupil. Ironically, Du Bois was becoming increasingly aware of the reality of Harlem decadence side by side with its vitality. He wrote at about the same time that it was becoming more difficult for blacks to steer between "the Scylla of prudery and the Charybdis of unbounded license." Harlem was simultaneously "crime, gambling, sexual depravity, waste, luxury, self-assertion, science and art."[41] But he crushed McKay's *Home to Harlem* (1928) as if there were no such contradiction in black America: "He has used every art and emphasis to paint drunkenness, fighting, lascivious sexual promiscuity and utter absence of restraint in as bold and as bright colors as he can." He suggested that McKay had set out "to cater for that prurient demand on the part of white folk for a portrayal in Negroes of that utter licentiousness which conventional civilization holds white folk back from enjoying — if enjoyment it can be called."[42] Ironically, Du Bois three years later called McKay's *Banjo* superior to *Home to Harlem*, although it is far less restrained by conventional moral standards. By 1931 Du Bois had so thoroughly categorized a large part of the Harlem Renaissance that he could damn a book as being "of the School of 'Nigger Heaven' and 'Home to Harlem.' " Nearly all of Arna Bontemps' *God Sends Sunday*, he wrote, apart from the depiction of the pathetic hero, "is sordid crime, drinking, gambling, whore-mongering, and murder."[43] Langston Hughes himself although he had probably published more verse in the *Crisis* than any other poet, did not pass untouched. Du Bois' campaign undoubtedly influenced Allison Davis' remark in the *Crisis* of August 1928 that Van Vechten had misdirected Hughes as a poet and thus harmed black literature. In the September number, however, Hughes demolished the charge by revealing that many of the offending poems had been written before his first meeting with Van Vechten.

Du Bois found little support among blacks outside of the *Crisis* office, although at least one black writer, the journalist George S. Schuyler, found many assumptions of the new movement to be so much "Negro-Art Hokum."[44] *Opportunity* and the *Messenger* certainly did not share the *Crisis* view of Van Vechten and McKay. To Wallace Thurman, the black novelist who reviewed *Nigger Heaven* for the *Messenger*, the white writer had been "most fair, and most sympathetic in his treatment of a long mistreated group of subjects."[45] The same magazine endorsed *Home to Harlem* as an accurate depiction of "a slice of Harlem life."[46] *Opportunity* found much to praise in both works and saw no dangerous tendencies in such writing. Alain Locke defended the course of the movement. The urbane and intelligent James Weldon Johnson remained outside the fray but continued to admire Van Vechten as a perceptive interpreter of culture, the first man, according to Johnson, to write of blues singers as artists.[47]

In any event, the days of the Harlem Renaissance were numbered. With the collapse of Wall Street and the deepening of the Depression, the cultural activity of the movement ground nearly to a halt. Charles S. Johnson had left *Opportunity* to join the faculty at Fisk. Du Bois and a shrunken *Crisis* continued to fight, but there was less to fight for or about. He alternated between conciliation and censure, and in 1931 offered a compromise. Fiction, in addition to being "clear, realistic and frank," should show "the possible if not the actual triumph of good and true and beautiful things"; but, he added, "we are quite fed up with filth and defeatism."[48]

Nevertheless, he had come to identify the welfare of the journal with its role as a literary magazine. An editorial council to read and criticize the failing *Crisis* was proposed with his approval in 1932, the members to include Langston Hughes, Nella Larsen, Countee Cullen, Zora Neale Hurston, Arna Bontemps, Rudolf Fisher, and James Weldon Johnson; the next year Du Bois suggested that, if available, Claude McKay should write a book column for the *Crisis*.[49] Neither of these changes was made. When in 1933 Du Bois proposed to discuss in the *Crisis* the twelve major problems of Afro-

America, he indicated that each part would also be treated fictionally, to "illustrate the problem humanly."[50] He may well have been referring to a project he had outlined to his publisher Alfred Harcourt of Harcourt, Brace in 1928, not long after the publication of *Dark Princess*, in which he proposed "a series of novels on the Negro race; a sort of short black Comedie Humaine. 'Dark Princess' was the first and I am working on the second, 'Bethesda, A.M.E.,' which is the 100 years' history of a Negro church. I have others more or less definitely in mind."[51] Nothing came of this project, however, and the result of the *Crisis* plan was some of the most wooden stories in its history. In a real sense, they marked the end of the road both for the magazine as a vehicle of literature and for Du Bois as its editor.

Looking back on the best years of the movement, Du Bois saw the experience as a major disappointment and a lesson for black Americans. He believed that little had been accomplished in spite of the unprecedented opportunity. In 1927 he had declared, in response to H. L. Mencken's charge that black literature was second-rate, that "we Negroes are quite well satisfied with our Renaissance."[52] But by 1933 he was talking of the cultural phenomenon as a thing of the past and a failure: "Why was it that the Renaissance of literature which began among Negroes ten years ago has never taken real and lasting root? It was because it was a transplanted and exotic thing. It was a literature written for the benefit of white people and at the behest of white readers, and starting out privately from the white point of view. It never had a real Negro constituency and it did not grow out of the inmost heart and frank experience of Negroes; on such an artificial basis no real literature can grow."[53]

His judgment of the age was fundamentally correct, although he was not well equipped by education or temperament to lead a youthful cultural movement that was an integral part of the Jazz Age and subject to many of the stresses that simultaneously produced the Lost Generation. In too often sacrificing psychological subtlety for propagandistic force, his statements on the cultural implications of the age failed to convince a group eager to learn but sensitive to the manner of instruction. But it is not true that Du Bois wanted "a literature of uplift in the genteel tradition," and it is a gross error to categorize him as a Philistine.[54] The Harlem Renaissance, in spite of the genius of Hughes and Toomer, produced little first-rate work. Du Bois judged accurately if unpopularly that sudden and intense white patronage, unless judiciously received, would distort the self-perception of writers and their depiction of race. For many whites the literature of blacks could only be another beguiling aspect of show business, like the cakewalk or the "coon" song. Nothing in Du Bois' life prepared him to accept this definition of art, which he resisted with passion.

Although Du Bois was not immune to the deflective power of middle-class values nor an accomplished novelist and poet, he almost always saw the function of the black artist in comprehensive moral and political terms, informed by a broad though not faultless intellectual range. In varying degrees, cultural interpreters such as Locke, Cullen, Fauset, Braithwaite, and Hurston prided themselves on their ability to transcend rather than confront the horror of life under white racism. Portions of their literature grew not out of "the inmost heart and frank experience of Negroes," in Du Bois' phrase, but from a desire — like that of American writers and critics of another age — to reflect what William Dean Howells called the "smiling aspects" of the culture at the expense of truth.

In his sometimes erratic but necessary criticism of the period Du Bois expended the anger of the frustrated moralist. In demanding moral evaluation, he remained faithful to the ethical sense in which he had been schooled, and which had given his political propaganda its persuasiveness. Undoubtedly, though, his standards were those of another age and, some would say, another people. To find an appropriate precedent for what he was trying to achieve, one must look to the man who invented the term "genteel tradition" to ridicule the contradictions in the most revered literature of America in the nineteenth century. For George Santayana, literature must reflect "visions of beauty, order, and perfection." Compared to that standard, he wrote in "The Poetry of Barbarism," "this age of material elaboration has no sense for those things. Its fancy is retrospective, whimsical and flickering; its ideals, when it has any, are negative and partial; its moral strength is a blind and miscellaneous vehemence. Its poetry, in a word, is the poetry of barbarism." Santayana's definition of the barbarian would have appealed to the *Crisis* editor: "For the barbarian is the man who regards his passions as their own excuse for being . . . He is the man who does not know his derivations nor perceive his tendencies, but who merely feels and acts, valuing in his life its force and its filling, but being careless of its purpose and its form."[55] Du Bois may not have remembered the opinions of his one-time tutor, but his moral view of literature is much the same. For the *Crisis* editor, the age of decadence was upon civilization.

Dark Princess (1928) was Du Bois' major contribution to the creative life of the Harlem Renaissance. In this novel, he attempted to assert the link between the ideal and the frankly political that he saw repudiated in much of the literature of the period. The pragmatic compromises that led him to urge blacks during World War I to "close ranks" with white Americans and forget their grievances, or later to barter their votes eclectically for political gain, was one side of the delicate balance he maintained between "visions of beauty, order, and perfection" and the cold reality of American power. Politics was only one part of his philosophic pragmatism and only one goal of his imagination. He lived politically but also spiritually in a dualism of mind and act forced on him by the pressure of American reality. His politics was consciously ephemeral; his spirituality was constant. In *Dark Princess* he resorted to the traditional refuge of the visionary, the work of art, to impose his dreams on the recalcitrant social situation.

The *Crisis* and its rival magazines serving black America had limited success in influencing the national conscience. As Nathan Huggins has asserted, the sense of importance that their "tone and self-assurance" instilled in the blacks who read them, and their role as "the Negro's voice against the insult America gave him," were their chief contemporary contributions.[56] But as chronicles of one of the most difficult ages in black American history and vehicles for the necessarily confused expression of the creative artists of the time, they performed an indispensable function. In this respect, no magazine was more important than Du Bois' *Crisis*.

CHAPTER TEN

Dark Princess

"I saw Zion and the new Jerusalem and came into the ancient valley of the Nile and into the narrow winding streets of Cairo."
"You have seen the world, Kautilya, the real and darker world. The world that was and is to be."   (Du Bois, 1928)

LATER IN LIFE Du Bois affirmed that *Dark Princess* (1928) was "my favorite book."[1] In spite of a predictably enthusiastic review in the *Crisis*, however, the critical reception was not encouraging. Neither did the work find much favor with the general public. Yet it is clear that Du Bois expended much energy and affection in constructing his second novel. It was written when the Harlem Renaissance was at a critical stage of development, and new black novelists were emerging in response to unprecedented encouragement. *Dark Princess* is a far more ambitious effort than *The Quest of the Silver Fleece*. Both novels reflect common themes and values which Du Bois continued to cherish as he moved toward old age. But compared to *Dark Princess*, Du Bois' epic of cotton seems an almost provincial exercise. In his second novel, characters come from and represent all continents and many nations of the world. Culture is pitted against culture, and the lines between racial communities are starkly drawn. Side by side with its political commentary, the novel asserts the depth of Du Bois' commitment to the ideal. Although *Dark Princess* is not thoroughly successful in its objectives, the work, because of its scope and seriousness, defines some of Du Bois' most ambitious thoughts during the middle passage of his life.

Like *The Quest of the Silver Fleece, Dark Princess* is first a story of love. Virginia-born and trained at Hampton Institute, Matthew Towns is a black medical student denied a place in a New York medical school because of his color. Having fled in disgust to Germany, Matthew finds himself without place and purpose in the world, but with a mighty resentment against the power of white prejudice in his native land. In Berlin he rescues Kautilya, an Indian princess, from an importuning white American by knocking the man down. He discovers that she is part of an organization, the "Great Council of the Darker Peoples," conspiring to end the domination of white nations over the entire globe. Within this organization, however, there is grave doubt about the ability of people of African descent to free themselves or to make a worthwhile contribution to the struggle. Unlike the other leaders of the council, though, Kautilya is drawn to radical socialism. In Moscow she has heard a story of a planned uprising of American blacks against their white rulers. Matthew undertakes to return home at once to investigate this report; Kautilya decides to go to America separately, to find out for herself more about democracy and the proletariat, from which she has been shielded all her life.

Back in New York, Matthew meets Miguel Perigua, leader of the most radical nationalist group among black Americans. Perigua gravely disappoints Matthew, who finds him disorganized, demagogic, and untrustworthy. Examining conditions among black workers, Matthew takes a job as a Pullman porter. When one of his fellow workers is lynched after being mistaken for Matthew and accused of making advances to a white woman, the distraught Towns joins forces with Perigua in a scheme to dynamite a train carrying a delegation of Ku Klux Klansmen to a convention in Chicago. Before the two can act, Kautilya suddenly appears and dissuades Matthew from the act of violence. Perigua is killed. The plot is discovered, and Matthew is tried and convicted for his part in it. He is sentenced to ten years in the Illinois state prison.

His pardon is arranged almost immediately by a black Chicago ward politician and businessman, Sammy Scott, who intends to exploit Matthew's reputation as a fighter for his people. The grand strategist behind Scott is his ambitious and clever secretary, Sara Andrews. Very successful as Sammy's lieutenant, Matthew is soon elected to the Illinois state legislature, where he becomes a tool of wealthy interests, manipulated by Sara. They marry. Confused and unhappy but unable to resolve his problems, he is about to be nominated for the United States Congress through his wife's wiles, when Kautilya reappears. She has worked hard at humble jobs, organizing the people, and is now a high-ranking union official. Disrupting a fancy dinner party planned by Sara, she and Matthew confess their love for each other, and he turns his back on the life of corruption.

After a brief but passionate affair, the lovers part again, for Matthew must atone for his disaffection and rediscover the beauty of work and the honest life. Having lost his political influence, he becomes an object of scorn in his Chicago constituency, where once he was honored and respected. His attempt at reconciliation with his wife, Sara, made out of loyalty to the marriage ideal and urged by Kautilya herself, is rejected with contempt. The marriage is dissolved. Kautilya in the meantime lives in Virginia with Matthew's mother, who is a source of strength to the dark princess, teaching her lessons in endurance and faith. Matthew and Kautilya exchange many letters in which they debate on work, truth, beauty, and life. Finally, Matthew receives a call from Kautilya. He hurries to her side to find himself received as father of Kautilya's new-born son, Madhu, an infant hailed by her Indian subjects as the new Maharajah of Bwodpur. He learns, too, that the council of darker races is meeting and planning, and that black America is now represented. The lovers are married in a ceremony that takes place on May 1, 1927, and blends elements of Judaic ritual with Moslem, Hindu, and Buddhist traditions, performed on Virginia soil in the New World. Matthew's quest is complete.

This queer combination of outright propaganda and Arabian tale, of social realism and quaint romance, is a challenge to the casual reader. Du Bois' creative faculty, straining to accommodate the variety of his interests, could find satisfaction only in an arrangement of fluted arguments and multiple themes. He turned to the epic as the appropriate form for his ambitious novel, whose language often swells to keep pace with its concepts. Nevertheless, Du Bois' revelation of a plot among the darker peoples of the world, although melodramatic, is not historically unfounded.[2] Moreover, his analysis of Afro-American culture and its leadership avoids the fanciful and provides the sinews for a major personal achievement. The professional propagandist had produced a novel of serious, even grim purpose. Its aims and effects do not always succeed, and occasionally a failure is ludicrous. But it was Du Bois' favorite book because it said much of what he regarded to be essential and true, at a time when his effectiveness as a political and cultural leader of black America first appeared to be under serious threat.

The idea of a revolt among the darker races of the world against the power of Europe and America had long intrigued Du Bois. In 1915 he expressed a belief in the necessity of such a conflict: "There is slowly arising not only a curiously strong brotherhood of Negro blood throughout the world, but the common cause of the darker races against the intolerable assumptions and insults of Europeans has already found expression. Most men in this world are colored. The future world will, in all reasonable probability, be what colored men make it."[3] Five years later, in *Darkwater*, he gave militant expression to the same thought. In editing the *Moon*, the *Horizon*, and the *Crisis*, Du Bois always regarded these journals as vehicles for news not only of Afro-America but also of nonwhite people everywhere. Each magazine tried to be "a record of the darker races," and the *Crisis* preserved a definite international flavor in its pages. In addition, Du Bois had shown an active interest in organizations that attempted to unite races for the purpose of ending exploitation and colonialism, having both served at the Races Congress in London in 1911 and spearheaded the four Pan-African Congresses between 1919 and 1927. Although these meetings were too public to be considered conspiratorial, they provided an unusual forum for nonwhite peoples to speak to the world and air racial grievances. Paradoxically, the pan-African movement probably gave Du Bois the model for the "Great Council of the Darker Peoples" posited in *Dark Princess* as a force poised to strike against the white world.[4] The difference was that the "Great Council" in the novel did not at first include representatives of black or sub-Saharan Africa and of Afro-America. Perhaps Du Bois' experience in organizing the pan-African conferences and in trying to keep the movement alive was too chastening for any other arrangement.

The novel ascribes the omission of black Africa and Afro-America to the shortsightedness of leaders of other darker races: "How the Egyptian rolled off his tongue his contempt for the 'r-r-rabble'! How contemptuous was the young Indian of inferior races! But how humorous it was to Matthew to see the tables turned; the rabble now was the white workers of Europe; the inferior races were the ruling whites of Europe and America" (24). Matthew recognizes that an attack on the white lower classes as uneducable "rabble" is an oblique blow at Afro-American ambition. He bursts into a Sorrow Song when someone questions whether art had ever come from the canaille. The American experience has taught him differently: "America is teaching the world one thing and only one thing of real value, and that is, that ability and capacity for culture is not the hereditary monopoly of a few, but the widespread possibility for the majority of mankind if they only have a decent chance in life" (26).

In defending the canaille of the world, Matthew appears also to be speaking up for the masses of his people. Yet the masses remain a hazy, unknown quantity in *Dark Princess*. His defense is really of the old talented tenth, of whom Matthew himself—educated, idealistic, brown-skinned—is the prime example. The basic question raised at the start of the book is "that of the ability, qualifications, and real possibilities of the black race in Africa or elsewhere" (21). The princess herself had conceived of the black world as the shock troops for a frontal assault, cannon fodder in a war with whites. The important lessons in democracy learned by the princess during her long stay in America are taught by the country as a whole, not by the black section in particular, although Matthew's old, black mother clearly symbolizes the ancient spirit of her race. Thus, the Bandung spirit of the novel does little to dignify the black masses or to reveal the value which Du Bois claimed to be inherent in them. When the novel descends from the dizzy heights of its international political theme to become a more personal affair, Du Bois and the reader are more comfortable.

Matthew Towns exemplifies the tradition of black male heroism begun by Du Bois with the creation of John in *The Souls of Black Folk* and continued in the figure of Blessed Alwyn in his first novel. With each new story the character and intelligence of the hero has broadened. All three men share common characteristics of the Du Bois black hero. They all display a vagueness and hesitation in dealing with the world, a susceptibility to manipulation because of this lack of confidence, and in the case of Bles and Matthew, a powerlessness in the face of the ill-chosen black women preying on their idealism and indecisiveness. They all feel deeply; they worship purity and beauty. John, Bles, and Matthew gaze upward to the stars of moral and aesthetic perfection, groping out of the darkness of insufficient education and tawdry origins. Because their vision is focused above the world, they lose sight of enemies whose ambitions are more vulgar. Such a hero stumbles until resolution is pressed upon him by life, as in the case of John, or until he can finally identify his enemy through the gloom and confront the evil seeking to destroy him, as in the case of Bles. Until that time, his destiny seems to him to be governed by caprice. It is Matthew's belief that, almost always, only the unexpected happens in this world, a thought that appalls him.

A medical student, Matthew is the most educated of Du Bois' heroes, but he knows that his sense of culture is lamentably narrow. He is a product of both the limited Afro-American tradition and the blighted white American heritage. The culture that he wishes to make more his own is European culture. When Matthew meets the conspirators for the first time in the princess's Berlin home, all the talk is of European art, literature, music, and sculpture, of Picasso, Matisse, Croce, and Proust. But Matthew's prime concern is his anger at the white world for its injustices against him. In this respect he is a different Du Bois hero, curiously "modern" in his rage and determination. He enters the work as "a man whose heart was hate"; confronted by an example of American racism, "his heart began again to glow and burn. Action, action, it screamed—no running and skulking now—action. There was murder in his mind—murder, riot, and arson" (9). Side by side with black anger is black helplessness. His involvement with Kautilya and the plot of the darker peoples gives him his opportunity, which Matthew perceives clearly: "He was groping toward a career. He wanted to get his hand into the tangles of this world. He wanted to understand . . . His sudden love for a woman far above his station was more than romance—it was a longing for action, breadth, helpfulness, great constructive deeds" (42). Again in Du Bois' fictional world, it is the woman who points the way to a better world.

The Du Bois black hero has the mark of saintliness in him, a nostalgia for asceticism, a yearning for Puritan self-control, against which the passionate black body steadily rebels. Matthew's life is a struggle between poles of passion and self-denial, between barely furnished rooms and sumptuous appointments, between the rigor of truth and the lure of beauty. His life reflects that gorgeous hybrid of instinct and training ascribed to Bles Alwyn: a Puritan mind at war with a tropical body. In its more political aspect, the struggle is between cynical materialism and social responsibility. But Du Bois was anxious to show that there is no substitute for a moral perception of the world. A cultivated aestheticism is no substitute. After Matthew has joined Sammy's political machine, his aesthetic perception rather than his moral sense first causes him to revolt against the life of corruption: "It was not moral revolt. It was aesthetic disquiet . . . His revolt was against things unsuitable, ill adjusted, and in bad taste; the illogical lack of fundamental harmony; the unnecessary dirt and waste — the ugliness of it all — that revolted him" (147). But by the same token, beauty in itself is not enough to replace the moral vision. For Matthew uses his love of order and taste to justify to himself a larger corruption, one that will remove him from petty dishonesty and confusions. A seat in Congress will put him, he thinks, above the grime of ward politics: "He had sold his soul to the Devil, but this time he had sold it for something. Power? Money? Nonsense! He had sold it for beauty; for ideal beauty, fitness and curve and line; harmony and the words of the wise spoken long ago" (207).

Du Bois' black heroes are dreamers bound for rude awakenings, but their instinct toward idealism is strong. "Liquor gave him pleasant sensations," Du Bois wrote of Matthew, "but not more pleasant and not as permanent as green fields or babies" (145). Even in his deepest depression, Matthew has to suppress and deny "that old boundless silly self that once believed and hoped and dreamed" (141). Such heroes are aspiring souls caught in what their creator called "the iron of circumstance" (192). Matthew's mistake in marrying a woman like Sara results from his inability to read the mystery of the common world, which baffles those who perpetually look beyond for inspiration. Recognition that he is living a lonely, loveless existence sends Matthew into the arms of a woman who appears to represent order, taste, and discipline. Too late he discovers that he has embraced only an illusion in his search for the ideal.

Far from being the apologist for the black middle class that he so often appeared, Du Bois was capable of being its hostile critic. The point is that his hostility did not come from egalitarian zeal but from a more rigorous spirit of moral aristocracy. Nor is there anything conventionally prudish about his novel's attutude to sex. Matthew's liaison with a brown cabaret-girl, a prostitute, is treated about as freely as is the same subject in Claude McKay's *Home to Harlem*. Matthew and Kautilya consummate their love while Matthew is still married, and Du Bois describes their "honeymoon" in terms of sensual lushness. Their child is born out of wedlock. Here the senses are indulged as a necessary complement to spiritual striving. Sexual passion is the natural outpouring of a nobility of mind. The very elements conspire to celebrate the union of Kautilya and Matthew, as floods of rain soak into the earth after they have pledged their love to each other. When the lovers again part and Matthew begins his period of atonement, he is paying not for the breaking of his marriage vows but for the despair into which his spirit had sunk, a despair that had moved him to dishonesty and deceit. The sexual act has consecrated Matthew's rededication to a life of the ideal: "The cause that was dead is alive again; the love that I lost is found" (210).

The woman who first stirs Matthew's imagination, then rescues him from degradation, and finally marries him, reveals Du Bois' criteria for the ideal consort for the black male hero. In contrast to Matthew's dark brown skin, Kautilya's is golden brown: "It was darker than sunlight and gold, it was lighter and livelier than brown. It was a living, glowing crimson, veiled beneath brown flesh. It called for no light and suffered no shadow, but glowed softly of its own inner radiance" (8). Kautilya is beautiful, regal in bearing, gracious in manner, and utterly accomplished. Her manner reveals a trace of haughtiness, however, and she is "ever slightly remote" (14). She must undergo change before she becomes Matthew's wife, just as he must atone before his final reward. Du Bois prized the diamond as much for its hardness as for its brilliance. Kautilya returns to Matthew with calloused hands and broken nails; work and suffering have marked her face; a new humility softens the old hauteur of the born aristocrat. Her experience among the common folk of America, black and white, has qualified her to sit by Matthew and begin the task of political liberation on which her mind is set. Du Bois does not strip her of her titles, however, or ask her to abdicate her position. His democratic zeal went only so far. Du Bois had nothing against kings and princesses, provided some were black. Indeed, he seemed to prefer royalty and saw no contradiction between it and his propaganda for the masses.

Of the four main characters of the novel, however, Kautilya is the least successfully drawn. She represents the central fantasy of the novel, the union "of Yellow, Brown and Black" to change the racial course of the world (296). In fact, the existence of a committee organized to this end is mostly her idea. Melodrama dogs her heels. Her own career incognito in the United States, where she mysteriously emerges as an influence in a large trade union, is incredible. Her return to Matthew elicits the most affected writing of the novel. Her marriage ceremony ends the novel with a masquelike effect, unsettling in a novel which is for the most part relentlessly realistic in style.

Kautilya bears the unwieldy burden of romance in *Dark Princess*. Moreover, her presence points to a strain between the novel's propaganda for the black people of America and its heady enthusiasm for the solidarity of darker peoples everywhere. Where once Du Bois had seen the civilizing of Afro-America as a moral responsibility of the white world, he was now transferring the burden to darker but still foreign backs. He turned to those nations sharing in the common disaster of European domination, especially to India. For India appeared to possess the long and varied spiritual tradition needed for the task, and to be experiencing the beginnings of an upsurge of greatness among its young leaders. Names like Mohandas Gandhi and Rabindranath Tagore were familiar to *Crisis* readers. But the creation of a character such as Her Royal Highness the Princess Kautilya of Bwodpur may seem to some readers an act of self-indulgence. The parading of her pedigree and wealth suggests a materialistic tinge that seems strange set beside the novel's indictment of materialism.

But *Dark Princess* is not a vulgar fantasy of the rich; the stress on Kautilya's wealth and breeding has philosophic implications. Du Bois must have taken the name of his heroine from Kautilya, the male author of the *Artha-śāstra* (321-296 B.C.), an Indian treatise on government noted for its combination of idealism and realism.[5] The distinguishing feature of Kautilya's work is his emphasis on the economic roots of life, on which depend artistic and spiritual concerns. Its view of society is basically utilitarian rather than moral or religious. Du Bois' dark princess shares with Kautilya a sense of the importance of political power. She is determined not to surrender her kingdom to either the British or rival Indian princes; she remains to the end an enthusiastic member of the Council of Darker Peoples, and while she prefers peace, she is prepared to fight for her rights and her freedom. Her politics coexist with the doctrine of love she finally urges on Matthew; the practical is not subservient to the ideal. Her philosophy of life is dualistic and her method distinctly pragmatic. In spite of the romantic elements in her depiction, she speaks for an approach to truth readily observable in Du Bois' career.

In contrast to Kautilya, the character of Sara Andrews is more realistically drawn. It is perhaps the most accomplished portrait in all of Du Bois' fiction. Sara is basically similar to Caroline Wynn of *The Quest of the Silver Fleece*. They are both intelligent, pretty, and light-skinned, with a cynicism and materialism that make them peculiarly well-equipped to deal with the fate forced on the black American. They possess more confidence, determination, and style than the black men about them. They take the initiative, where the black male surrenders to self-pity or abnegation. A long-time supporter of the rights of women, Du Bois believed in the special quality of black women, of whom Caroline and Sara represent talented if delinquent examples. In contrast, he revered the kind of woman represented by Matthew's mother. She is old, black in color, gnarled by work and the experience of life, deeply religious, close to the land, and profoundly kind. It is the mother who helps the dark princess to a new knowledge of the world's truth. To Kautilya, she becomes an embodiment of almost supernatural power generated by her uncanny relationship to the earth. Kautilya speaks of her to Matthew: "Have you seen her hands? Have you seen the gnarled and knotted glory of her hands? . . . Your mother is Kali, the Black One; wife of Siva, Mother of the World!" (220).

Sara, on the contrary, is nobody's wife, although she contracts marriage with Matthew and, after their divorce, is about to join Sammy Scott in wedlock as the story ends. She is as far removed from the natural black mother as possible. She is, indeed, pale enough to pass for white, a fact that she trades on in her maneuvers. The idea of motherhood and a quiet family life bores her. Her home is a showcase to stun black Chicago and impress the whites who dispense power and patronage. She was "neither a prude nor a flirt. She simply had a good intellect without moral scruples and a clear idea of the communal and social value of virginity, respectability, and good clothes" (114). Sara is "in no sense evil"; she merely scorns anyone who shows too much sensitivity or an excess of emotion: "she herself was furious if sympathy or sorrow seeped through her armor" (200). She breaks down only once, when Matthew throws over her plans to send him to Congress and runs off with Kautilya, but she quickly recovers. Matthew begins to understand her only when he recognizes that she has no virtuous use for human sympathy. Beneath her cold exterior is a heart of stone.

The Honorable Sammy Scott, big, brown, and handsome, intelligent, patient, and funny, completes the quartet of major characters. He is a ward boss raised to new heights of venality by Sara. Yet there is little of evil or menace about this man who controls gambling, prostitution, and graft in his half-acre of Chicago. Du Bois' portrait lacks serious indictment. It is almost indulgent of Sammy, who is merely the instrument by which the intelligence of Sara operates. Sammy is a man of the people and from the people. His vices are the people's vices magnified by opportunity. Du Bois' portrait of Sara and Sammy is the most detailed commentary on the contradiction between his moral fervor and the fact that, as he admitted in 1928, "I have supported corrupt machines by my vote in many cases." [6] He had done so because he had judged their corruption to be more tolerable than that of apparently honest leaders either implacable in their opposition to black progress or indifferent to it. *Dark Princess* shows its author to have been totally aware of the limitations of such political pragmatism.

Du Bois was also opposed to certain forms of black nationalism. The character of Perigua, a West Indian, was undoubtedly patterned on Marcus Garvey, although there are specific differences between Du Bois' nationalist and the UNIA leader. Matthew admits that the man is brilliant, dedicated, and sincere; but he is also a demagogue driven by delusions of grandeur. Perigua's movement is inefficient to the point of recklessness. Its members are unable to meet on time, to avoid clashes of personality, or above all, to purge themselves of self-hatred. Few in the group believe for a moment that the black masses are willing to make any real sacrifice for liberty. After attending one meeting of Perigua's people, "Matthew felt bruised and bewildered" (53).

When Matthew finally joins Perigua in his suicidal scheme, he surrenders to a feeling of exultation in anticipating the act: "Vengeance was his. With one great blow he was striking at the Heart of Hell" (88). His response to the invitation to violence exemplifies a larger plight within the Afro-American community. As a black man, Matthew is tempted to fill the void of his identity with a symbolic act of violence. As a cool political observer, though, Du Bois

Neither Kautilya nor Du Bois specifically explains the extent of this doctrine of deified love. Does it mean primarily the love between persons? Is Du Bois preaching a Christlike submission to political adversity, a turning of the other cheek? Certainly Kautilya opposes Matthew when his old temper flares briefly in a cry that justice must be won with fire and sword, to "beat the world into submission and a real civilization" (285). But her council has set a date for the freedom of the darker races "—whether in Peace and fostering Friendship with all men, or in Blood and Storm—it is for Them— the Pale Masters of today—to say" (297). Yet love for each other is what has brought Matthew and Kautilya to their new life. Love for ideals has made Matthew worthy of Kautilya's love. Love of the world's depressed peoples has given meaning to Kautilya's princely life. The circles of significance move outward from the lovers' mutual affection. Du Bois is echoing Plato as well as Buddha. Hate is indulgence in self-destruction, and love is a necessity for growth and harmony. A love for the world's beauty and a commitment to work for the ends of love will be the religion of the new order, the hope of the new world.

In a quaint postscript to *Dark Princess*, Du Bois called on the sprites who had helped him weave his story to "lift with deft delicacy from out the crevice where it lines my heavy flesh of fact, that rich and colored gossamer of dream which the Queen of Faërie lent to me for a season" (312). This whimsical note points to the principal dualism in the construction of *Dark Princess*. The flesh of fact and the gossamer of dream do not always combine in a perfect fit. The title page proclamation that *Dark Princess* is "a romance" does not help the reader to perceive a unified construction. *The Quest of the Silver Fleece* is every bit as romantic but was published as "a novel." Again Du Bois seems to have equated romance with permissiveness, for the idea of a wealthy, beautiful Indian princess involved in a plot to change the balance of power in the world is a direct invocation of the license of romance. It evades some of the technical responsibilities demanded by the "heavy flesh of fact." Du Bois was bewildered by the problems of rendering in propagandistic fashion his notions about the ideal life. Admirably suited by his journalistic career to write works of social realism, he desired a greater freedom. In the end, the novel resolves itself into two basic areas served by two separate styles. Du Bois was left with the technical problem of providing an illusion of unity.

As a novelist, Du Bois was at his depictive best in the drawing room. In *Dark Princess,* as in *Quest of the Silver Fleece,* his dialogue shines in a formal social setting. He had no comparable skill in dealing with the life of the urban masses or the rural poor, where his exchanges betray an untuned ear. Du Bois' life had been a preparation not for the soil but for the settee and the study. Only Jessie Fauset of the Harlem Renaissance writers moved with such confidence in the parlors of the talented tenth. Indeed, there is so much comfort in Du Bois' exposition of mannered black society that Matthew's strictures on the need for work, for physical labor, and his extolling of the virtues of the soil seem at odds with the best style of the novel. The sophistication that Du Bois was eager to reveal not only in his pen but in the lives of the aristocracy of the darker world is often at war with the central thoughts of the book as moral and political propaganda.

This striving after effect sometimes leads the novel into absurdity. The cloak-and-dagger melodrama surrounding the plot of the Council of the Darker Peoples reaches its lowest point with the disappearance and recovery of a bag containing the crown jewels of Bwodpur, which Kautilya had misplaced when she rescued Matthew from Sara and the United States Congress. A flaw more serious is the language used in at least one exchange between the two lovers. When Kautilya returns to claim Matthew, the lovers speak in utterly stilted terms: "We are going down the King's highway to Beauty and Freedom and Love . . . Listen, God's darling, to the singing of the rain; hear the dawn coming afar and see the white wings of the mist, how they beat about us" (218). Such extravagance of language returns at the end of the novel, when little Madhu is enthroned as Maharajah and his parents are married. It is the language of masques and pageants, in which Du Bois delighted. But the formal phrases also represent his determination to stress the spirituality that dignifies the sexual experience. Such flights suggest his uneasy relationship with an eroticism after which he seemed nevertheless to hunger. His abiding problem was to establish a moral situation in which eroticism would develop out of nobility of thought and deed. The physical urge to sex betwen them, Matthew says to Kautilya, "rises from the ecstacy of our bodies to the communion of saints, the resurrection of the spirit, and the exquisite crucifixion of God. It is the greatest thing in our world" (260). By itself, such language is strained and inappropriate. Within *Dark Princess,* it adds to the instability of tone and expression, leaving the novel weaker for its presence.

The essential theme in *Dark Princess* is summed up in the lesson taught to Matthew: Love is God, God is Love, and Work is His Prophet. The central problem involves the tension between the spiritual emphasis proper to this idea and the undeniably secular and political concerns that the novelist also brought to his work. Here the story falters. The author seeks to be both geopolitician of the darker races and prophet lifting his eyes to the truths beyond. In the final analysis, though, the novel is a utopian exercise and must be judged as such, for it attempts to reflect in fiction Du Bois' vision of the ideal political, moral, and social world. The most notable casualty among his day-to-day concerns is his interest in socialism, which had been increasing since his visit to the Soviet Union in 1926. Although the collapse of Wall Street and the onset of the Depression would soon set him firmly on the socialist road, *Dark Princess* epitomizes the blend of convictions, in which socialism had only secondary importance, which he held at this point in his life.

The *Crisis* propagandist, forced to attend to the petty details of racial strife, yearned for the power to exercise his larger vision of leadership. The theme of might, the hurly-burly of preparation for racial war, and the bitterness of invective against white domination are gradually transcended in *Dark Princess,* although they are never repudiated. Matthew and Kautilya surrender up the main struggle to a new-born babe and his messianic hope. Rage gives way to love and work. For Du Bois had no taste for war, although he hated the unjust peace that locked the darker races in slavery.

His vision may be called grandiose, but his promotion of an agricultural future for Afro-America and Matthew's search for an aristocracy of merit point to the Jeffersonian affinities of Du Bois' political thought, even as he was expressing elsewhere a growing belief in more orthodox socialist principles. For Du Bois too presided intellectually over an embryonic American state. The young nation of Du Bois' mind was that gathering unity of the scattered Afro-American peoples. It was perhaps wishful thinking to conceive of precise leadership for a body so imprecise, but Du Bois was surely at liberty —especially in his fiction—to think of himself as the guiding mind of a new nation and to resuscitate the basic debate of the Revolu-

tionary age. The Platonic insistence on the identification of philosophy with government, and of philosophers with governors, still
contrasts with the practices of Machiavellian expediency to which
generations of politicians are drawn by the temptations of their profession. The tension of *Dark Princess,* even in its style, is a reflection
of this dualism. Du Bois' debate may seem unbalanced or even
unreal, but the reason probably lies more in the pathos of his situation than in the pitfalls of romance. Unlike Jefferson, Du Bois had
no national constituency except in his imagination. The influence
he exerted over the intellectual life of black America was dissipated
in fighting the petty, indecent injustices that stunted the growth of
solidarity and blocked the realization of grander visions. For the
black philosopher who sought to govern, dreams were the only reality, and romance was the most compelling mode of expression.

When the mists of romance are blown away from *Dark Princess*
and the trappings of melodrama are forgotten, Du Bois' aspirations
appear quite humble, and his solutions sane. Politically, there is at
the heart of the book an affection for the simplicity of classical re-
publicanism. Spiritually, the religion of Du Bois' state regrets insti-
tutionalism, but is tolerant of all beliefs: it yearns after Hindu and
Buddhist transcendentalism, but admires the simplicity and com-
munality of early Christianity. It is clearly hesitant about endorsing
radical socialism, but it is intransigently against European colonialism among the darker peoples. Finally, Du Bois' deification of love,
to which the Puritan work ethic is subservient, points to the paradox
of his public career as agitator for Afro-American rights and his private reputation for arrogance and hostility. A rage for personal and
social order is at the center of *Dark Princess.* In fashioning the work,
Du Bois resisted the vogues and trends of the decade — the cabaret
school of Harlem, the new amorality in American life and letters. If
Dark Princess as a result seems old-fashioned or clumsily tailored,
the novel's failings are only partly owing to the limitations of Du
Bois' fictive gift and his lack of creative practice. Du Bois persisted
in depicting the American experience and the meaning of his life in
the largest way possible to a black man. The day-by-day polemicist
refused to deny the historic view; the angry man did not forget that
the ultimate goal of his passion was tranquillity.

CHAPTER ELEVEN

The Coming Unities

But the difficulty was to know how, without revolution, violence, and dislocation of human civilization, the wrong could be righted and human culture started again upon its upward path. One thing, at any rate, was clear to me . . . and that was that a continued agitation which had for its object simply free entrance into the present economy of the world, that looked at political rights as an end in itself rather than as a method of reorganizing the state; and that expected through civil rights and legal judgments to reestablish freedom on a broader and firmer basis, was not so much wrong as short-sighted; that the democracy which we had been asking for in political life must sooner or later replace the tyranny which now dominated industrial life.   (Du Bois, 1940)

WHEN THE BOARD of Directors of the NAACP accepted Du Bois' resignation in 1934, the members paid tribute to his contribution to black life: "He created, what never existed before, a Negro intelligentsia, and many who have never read a word of his writings are his spiritual disciples and descendants."[1] Privately the board also recorded the fact that the editor of the *Crisis* had attended only two meetings of the directors since January of the previous year, and none since September 1933.[2] In effect, Du Bois had already moved on to a new position. In 1933 he delivered a series of lectures at Atlanta University, and in 1934 he finally accepted a long-standing invitation from his close friend John Hope, president of the university, to return permanently and develop a department of sociology, an essential need of the school, which had become the graduate division of an affiliated system of black colleges in the area.

Du Bois later recalled three goals in his resumption of an academic career. He wanted to continue his work on the history of the African peoples around the world; he wished to establish a scholarly journal on the race problem as an international phenomenon; and he planned to seek ways of restoring the work that had brought distinction to Atlanta University at the turn of the century—"the sys-

219

tematic study of the Negro problem." [3] While he succeeded eventually in founding a journal of race study and in reviving sociology as a discipline at Atlanta, his major contribution during these academic years was in his continued attention to the history of black people in Africa and the Americas, which formed the basis of his credibility as a teacher of black intellectuals and as a crusading propagandist.

Faithful to his pragmatic spirit, but redefining liberal pragmatism to stress the economic and socialist arguments he now saw as indispensable to the future development of world order, Du Bois' work during this period recorded his continuing desire for a compromise short of a doctrine of revolution. While at the start of his second academic career he taught Marxism in the classroom, using the *Manifesto* as his basic text, and in his first book published during the period made Marxist rhetoric and logic a major feature, other volumes show a moderation of that initial enthusiasm. To black Americans he continued to preach the controversial doctrine of voluntary self-segregation and internal cooperation developed by him in his last years with the *Crisis*. In newspaper columns on international events, however, he remained at once a champion of the USSR, a partisan of the darker races (notably India, China, and Japan), an enemy of European colonialism, and a supporter of the Allied cause against Germany. He refused to be silent on three issues: the virtue of socialism, the evil of colonialism, and the necessity of agitation in the face of entrenched reaction.

Upon returning to Atlanta University at the age of sixty-six, Du Bois' initial aim, shared by President John Hope, was to revive the yearly conferences in sociology begun in 1895 and guided by him between 1897 and 1914. Du Bois and Hope found financial support as elusive in the thirties as in the former years of the program, and Hope's death in 1936 further limited efforts in this direction. Not until 1940 was Du Bois at last able to move on two fronts toward the basic objective. The first volume of the quarterly *Phylon: The Atlanta University Journal of Race and Culture* appeared, with Du Bois as editor-in-chief. In the same year, with modest support from the Carnegie Foundation, Du Bois applied his doctrine of cooperation and voluntary self-segregation among blacks to the problem of academic sociology in an ambitious program of integrated research involving more than a score of black colleges and universities.

Although Du Bois claimed that *Phylon* in a sense revived the old

Atlanta University Publications, under his editorship it generally resembled the more scholarly side of the *Crisis*. Its discussions of race and culture (terms that were interchangeable for the magazine) were to be from the point of view of black Americans. The editor made clear that he would uphold neither scientific nor political orthodoxy. With a "new view" of the social sciences, he foresaw in *Phylon* "a re-interpretation of history, education, and sociology; a re-writing of history from the ideological and economic point of view."[4] The volumes under his editorship (1940-1944) stressed the problems and accomplishments of blacks. Out of twenty biographical essays comprising more than a quarter of its articles, only one recorded the life of a white person. Du Bois later admitted that only articles on philosophy, physical science, the Soviet Union, and Asia did not refer to blacks specifically. He believed that because of this emphasis, which he defended as natural to a journal edited by black scholars in a largely segregated country, *Phylon* had come to be regarded by some critics as an instrument more of propaganda than of science. While he guarded the magazine against the chauvinistic view that black problems were "the content of all American life," he stressed that his editorial policy assumed both the intrinsic dignity of the black experience and the belief that the four-hundred-year passage of Africans to the Americas, with its impact on modern capitalism and democracy, had been "the greatest social event of modern history."[5] Du Bois had defended this belief in a variety of ways from the start of the century, and an impartial reading of *Phylon* under his control reveals no other propagandistic "bias" than this sense of the profound impact of European slavery on modern civilization.

The second major institution-based attempt to further the study of black Americans was launched officially in 1941 with the First Phylon Conference on the problems of black higher education. In addressing the meeting, Du Bois insisted on the need for gathering facts through the latest scientific techniques in order to prepare black Americans for the realities of economic life during and after World War II. He deplored the fact that the important work on the sociology of Afro-America had passed from black schools like Atlanta into white institutions. Later that year he proposed that black land-grant, state-supported colleges join a cooperative venture in social studies whereby each Southern state would be closely studied by at least one black institution, with the resulting data pooled and interpreted for practical application to the needs and objectives of black life. As part of the project, instruction by black colleges in history, anthropology, sociology, economics, and psychology would be upgraded. Finally, the schools would be given the political and cultural orientation which he had repeatedly called for, notably in addresses at Howard and Fisk in 1930, 1933, and 1938.

The presidents of twenty land-grant colleges, in addition to those of Fisk, Howard, and Atlanta, agreed to the program; perhaps only a figure as formidable and revered as Du Bois could have moved them to such cooperation. In 1942 he was designated official coordinator of the proposed studies. The following year he convened the Twenty-Sixth Atlanta University Conference, choosing as its theme this plan for intensive social study and assembling distinguished black and white sociologists, such as E. Franklin Frazier of Howard University and Howard W. Odum of the University of North Carolina, to provide technical instruction in the gathering and interpreting of data and to set the tone of the future work. A further conference was planned for 1944, when the accent was to have been on the economic life of black Americans in light of the war. Du Bois had not only returned the leadership of black sociology to a base at Atlanta, but had in effect gained a fair degree of influence in the affairs of a considerable number of black colleges. What he might have accomplished in the twenty years left of his life is a matter of conjecture, for in 1944 he was removed without warning or ceremony from his position as professor and head of the department of sociology. The project was moved from Atlanta to Howard and administered by E. Franklin Frazier. Without adequate funding, it soon died.

For Du Bois, the defeat of his attempt to reinvolve himself in scientific study marked both a personal humiliation and a setback for blacks and for science. Trained by the first generation of modern sociologists, he had watched what he considered the decline of the discipline from a science rivaling psychology, physics, chemistry, and biology into an instrument of social work. He had planned, he remembered, "to plot out beside the world of physical law, a science of sociology which measured 'the limits of chance in human action.' If this field proved narrow or non-existent, world law was proven. If not, the resultant 'chance' was what men had always regarded as 'free will.' "[6] His defeat probably had at least one other consequence. Rebuffed in his attempt to rekindle his youthful enthusiasm for scientific truth, in absolute laws and the power of empirical evidence, Du Bois perhaps felt more urgently than ever the need to embrace precisely such an absolute, and to do so in a context outside of the limitations of race. Leaving university life for the second and final time to assume the duties of a propagandist, he was psychologically better prepared to express confidence in and solidarity with that radical socialism which he had resisted in the name of academic sociology, liberal pragmatism, and moderation.

While Du Bois attributed much of the cause of his dismissal both from Atlanta University in 1944 and from the NAACP in 1948 to the jealousy and egotism of his superiors, his newspaper columns between 1936 and 1948 contained a great deal that might have offended those responsible for financially dependent institutions such as Atlanta and the NAACP. Between February 1936 and January 1938 he wrote each week "A Forum of Facts and Opinion" for the Pittsburgh *Courier*. From October 1939 to October 1944, his column "As the Crow Flies" (bearing only slight resemblance to the pieces by that name in the *Brownies' Book* and the *Crisis*) appeared weekly in the New York *Amsterdam News*. His "Winds of Time" was published in the Chicago *Defender* between January 1945 and May 1948. In addition, during this period he published for some time a column entitled "Pan-Africa" in the New York *People's Voice*, controlled by Adam Clayton Powell. Du Bois' writing in these black newspapers may be broken down into two categories: his views on Afro-America and other internal matters of the United States, and his interpretation of world political events.

He had comparatively little to say about black America in his newspaper columns; in spite of his involvement with the land-grant college scheme, he had begun a slow but steady turn away from a primary interest in Afro-American affairs to a deepening concern with the fate of international socialism and the rise of the colonial peoples. His willingness to criticize fellow blacks, especially the black leadership in business and education, returned. In his Fisk commencement address of 1938, "The Revelation of St. Orgne the Damned," called by Rayford W. Logan "probably the most significant" of its author's many addresses, Du Bois inveighed against the appallingly low standards often accepted by blacks in their manners and morals, and in their concept of family, education, business,

labor, politics, religion, and art. He made clear that self-segregation as he interpreted it was to be a culturally remedial exercise for
blacks rather than a hate-inspired isolation from whites.[7] "We have
to do something about race," he insisted; "absorption into the nation" could come when it was decided "whether such racial integration has to do with poverty-stricken and half-starved criminals" or
with "intelligent self-guided, independently acting men, who know
what they want and propose at any civilized cost to get it."[8]

The basis of Du Bois' growing estrangement from what he used to
call the talented tenth was the unpopularity among such people of
his doctrine of voluntary self-segregation and his espousal of socialism as a political philosophy; most educated and affluent or prog-
ress-oriented blacks clearly favored integration and increased capitalistic opportunity. In 1939 he believed that trade union and other
activities were showing signs of enlightened self-segregation, but in
general he found little to encourage him. Although in 1937 he
mildly defended blacks against a charge in the *Nation* that they
were given to praising mediocrity out of misguided racial feeling,
over the years his own attacks on the talented tenth became the
norm.[9] In 1942, for example, he attacked the "economic morality"
of black businessmen who shamelessly exploited their own people.[10]
In the same year he devoted at least three columns in the *Amsterdam News* to the phenomenon of black crime, especially crimes
against fellow blacks. Previously, he had criticized the presence of
anti-Semitism among Afro-Americans. He was exasperated to find
self-segregation misunderstood: at one time he had to denounce a
proposal to form an all-black political party, which conformed to
neither political reality nor common sense. A poignant column in
the *Amsterdam News* in January 1941, in which Du Bois answered a
query as to whether he genuinely loved black people and "ever
cursed the fate" that made him black, summed up his twin positions
of love for the folk or masses, and increasing impatience with the
class of black Americans whose duty he believed it was to lead
them.[11]

Du Bois' growing estrangement from a major part of the black
leadership class was paralleled by a rise in his estimate of white
American intentions and achievement. Specifically, he found himself drawn with millions of other blacks toward the charismatic figures of Franklin and Eleanor Roosevelt. Although, as the *Crisis* edi-

tor, he had withheld support from Roosevelt in 1932, Du Bois endorsed his candidacy with increasing confidence in the three following presidential elections. At first the President was praised as a leader who did little but at least was trying; as the New Deal rolled on, Du Bois found it easier to support a man who, born a wealthy aristocrat, had turned to socialist measures to remedy the failures of capitalism. Du Bois campaigned vigorously for the Tennessee Valley Authority, and defended the President's right, in a time of emergency such as the Depression, to consolidate power at the expense of the democratic process. Du Bois was not uncritical, however. The New Deal, he once charged, was doing little or nothing for farmers; he was also angered by the deliberate inequities of pay among the races in the South. But far more often he wrote of Roosevelt as a man of vision and courage in bringing socialist measures to bear on the depressed economy of the United States and in joining with the USSR in a common fight against Hitler's Germany. Roosevelt's unprecedented involvement of blacks at high levels in the administration of federal programs sealed his popularity with Du Bois. Eleanor Roosevelt was repeatedly praised as a woman of conspicuous honesty and determination. When Roosevelt died in 1944, Du Bois made two assessments of his career as president. In the black Chicago *Defender*, he forthrightly praised the former President for his stand on the New Deal, on racial matters, and on the war; in the leftist *New Masses*, he identified the Roosevelt years with new hope for blacks and poor whites in the United States.[12]

Two concerns dominated his analyses of international events in the 1930s and 1940s: the success of socialism, objectified in the fate of the USSR, and the rise of the darker races out of colonialism or, in the case of Japan, to the height of international power. His championing of the Soviet state continued unabated. He was not entirely unaware or uncritical of the cost of totalitarianism, professing in 1940 to "love the victim [K. B.] Radek more than the tyrant Stalin," but Russia remained for him the great hope of modern industrial democracy.[13] The nonaggression pact signed by Germany and the USSR in 1939 confused Du Bois, as it shook the faith of many prosocialist thinkers, but he defended both Soviet neutrality and its seizure of Finland as strategically sound, on the one hand, and justified by history on the other. Nevertheless, he was relieved when the pact was broken and the Allied effort finally included the Soviets.

Russia remained a crucial symbol for him, not simply as the stan-
dard-bearer of socialism but as a nation which demonstrated that to
be white was not necessarily to be racist and imperialist. Thus Russia offered hope of eventual interracial world peace.

Toward the Western Allies, notably the United States, Britain,
and France, Du Bois was more ambivalent. He wanted victory for
them during World War II, but the reaction of the major powers to
the Italian invasion of Ethiopia in 1935 had deepened his cynicism
about the intentions of major powers fighting for "democracy." He
valued Charles De Gaulle as a man who had defied Hitler and would
defy attempts by the British and Americans to compromise the integrity of a free France, to which Du Bois was as partisan as ever.
Roosevelt, on the other hand, was repeatedly criticized by him for an
incoherent colonial policy. And Du Bois was immune to the spell
cast by Winston Churchill over the American people. He deplored
the "iron curtain" speech at Fulton, Missouri, in 1946 as typical of a
man who had opposed the feminist movement, attacked the Russian
Revolution, and upheld British colonialism in the face of independence movements around the world.[14] Japanese involvement in
China appeared to some observers to be an imperialism as indefensi-
ble as that of the white powers, but Du Bois distinguished between
the hold of Europe and the United States on the darker races and
the effect of Japanese militarism, which kept white racism out of the
world's largest community and increased the chances of economic
and social reform. He insisted that Roosevelt was led by his advisers
into a deliberately bellicose position against Japan, making the
Pacific war inevitable.

Du Bois was at one time accused of being rabidly pro-Nazi.[15] This
misinterpretation stemmed from his sense of wonder at the economic revolution wrought by Hitler, encouraged by his visit to Germany (as well as other European countries, the USSR, China, and
Hawaii) in 1936. But he simultaneously made clear that a nation
which practiced anti-Semitism on the scale of the Germans and
which opposed Russia with such passion was no example for the rest
of the world. "There has been no tragedy in modern times," he
wrote in 1936, equal to the persecution of the Jews in Hitler's Germany; "it is an attack on civilization, comparable only to such hor-
rors as the Spanish Inquisition and the African slave trade."[16] He
was undoubtedly confused by the superficial similarities between the

totalitarianism of fascism and that of communism. Both seemed to succeed through the forceful cooperation of a diversity of interests united through loyalty to an idea; the old man who had thrilled as a boy to the exploits of Bismarck found much that was intriguing in Hitlerite Germany. In no sense, however, was Du Bois pro-Nazi in comparing the Third Reich to either the Soviet Union or the United States.

In September 1945 Du Bois summed up the meaning of the war for black people and for the future of the world. Although the defeat of Japan was a defeat for the darker races, and the use of atomic weapons was a chilling testimony to the new destructive power of science, it was also clear that colonialism could not long survive the end of hostilities. The Soviet Union had emerged as a power of increasing might, China had resumed its central role in history, and Africa was on the road to self-determination and independence from Britain.[17] Du Bois' participation in the Fifth Pan-African Congress in Manchester in 1945 confirmed his belief that Africa was on the move; his sense that the battle against colonialism had advanced to a new and vital stage was encouraged by his experience as a consultant to the United States delegation to the San Francisco conference of 1945, at which the United Nations was founded. Between 1944 and 1948, or during his second period with the NAACP, Du Bois clarified his sense of the part he was to play in the coming years. In the summer of 1944, between his enforced retirement from Atlanta University and his return to the association as director of special research, the question of the coming elections seemed to be whether the United States would become "a new realm of private profit and exploitation or a new land of socialized wealth, medicine and opportunity." But for him, the greater question concerned the end of colonialism: "This is the problem to which I propose to devote the remaining years of my life."[18]

Although Du Bois remained clear of the most radical socialist and anticolonialist positions between 1934 and the end of World War II, he increased his writings on the history and culture of the African peoples. In 1935 he published his longest single work, *Black Reconstruction in America*. In 1934 he was appointed editor-in-chief of the "Encyclopedia of the Negro" project organized by the Phelps-Stokes Fund, having independently started to plan such an undertaking in 1909, and he produced two preparatory volumes in 1945

and 1946. His *Black Folk Then and Now* (1938) included much
material from his 1915 volume *The Negro* but updated the history
of blacks in Africa and the Americas. In addition, Du Bois published in 1940 the first of two major autobiographies, *Dusk of Dawn*.
Together with his *Phylon* writings and newspaper columns, these
were the means by which he continued to educate the black intelligentsia that the NAACP had credited him with creating.

The publication of *The Negro* in 1915 was a major event in Du
Bois' career as historian and cultural interpreter. As George Shepperson has pointed out, it was the original attempt to draw together
"into one succinct but comprehensive whole" the diverse histories of
the scattered African peoples.[19] It was also the first book-length
manuscript of nonfiction published by Du Bois after his acceptance
in 1910 of the role of propagandist. While his increasing political
consciousness had been evident in every volume published since his
doctoral thesis in 1896, his 1915 volume was the first extended example of what had become his forte in essays and articles: the revaluation and restoration of black history.

No one was more aware than the author himself of the shortcomings in his historiography after the completion of his doctoral thesis.
He apologized in *John Brown* for his departure from the standards
of research in which he had been trained. In prefacing *The Negro*
he admitted that the time had not come for a complete history of
the African peoples, that archeology in Africa was barely established, and that he did not command sources of information available in certain languages. When some twenty-three years later he
spliced great portions of the work into *Black Folk Then and Now*,
he demurred that the new book was not "a work of exact scholarship," and that although it contained "a body of fairly well-ascer-
tained truth," there were areas of "conjecture and even of guess
work which under other circumstances I should have hesitated to
publish."[20] He admitted the risk in his attempts to write history
without adequate scholarly preparation: "in fine," he wrote in *The
World and Africa* in 1947, "I have done in this book the sort of
thing at which every scholar shudders."[21]

In addition, he was reticent about defending his determination to
bring poetic imagination to bear on works of scholarship or polemics, as when he apologized in the preface to *Darkwater* for including
his poems, "tributes to Beauty, unworthy to stand alone." More

important still was his later judgment that his earlier works, namely those written without socialist logic, had been vitiated by a blend of religious piety and moralizing.[22] In other words, he regretted the tenaciousness with which he had clung to a liberal philosophy in defiance — or ignorance — of Marxism. But the truth about his career is that in none of his major works between 1915 and the end of his life did Du Bois hold dogmatically to any one of the three contesting positions out of which he fashioned his general historical method. That method is best seen as a triangulation among a soulful, impassioned liberalism, the discipline of Marxism, and the power of racial partisanship. If any one of the three dominates, it is the last. Lions have no historians, Du Bois liked to muse, but they surely have a history. He labored to apprise the world of the piecemeal discoveries of researchers who had usually felt neither the urgency nor the authority to write comprehensively and sympathetically of the African heritage. Without ever palming off the scholarship of others as his own, he worked in the tradition of interpretive, confluential historiography that has produced some of the most popular and powerful of histories. He persisted in his belief that there could be no serious historical writing without the application of moral standards and mythopoeic imagination to accumulated data.

"Africa," Du Bois declared in beginning *The Negro*, "is at once the most romantic and the most tragic" of lands. He had a twofold purpose in approaching this romance and tragedy. First, he wished to replace rumor and impression with fact. His purpose was also, however, to deepen the sense of Africa as romance and to dramatize the tragedy of her fall from greatness. His first goal sprang from his reading in the aftermath of Franz Boas' electrifying speech on the greatness of Africa at Atlanta University in 1906; his second goal came from Du Bois' certainty that it was absolutely necessary for blacks to have a proper appreciation of, even reverence for, the African past. His participation in the Races Congress of 1911, with its emphasis on the doctrine of cultural relativity, was also significant.

In this first comprehensive telling of the African story Du Bois revised his earlier theories of race. While in 1897, in "The Conservation of Races," he had stressed the distinct differences between the eight races and their "gifts," he now propounded the idea of racial relativity. Africa is primarily "the land of the mulatto"; the European is the lightened, as the African is the darkened version of this mixture of races. Both blacks and whites were "slowly differentiated from a common ancestry and continually remingled their blood while the differentiating was progressing."[23] The theory of a common origin of all men was the basis for his vision of a world culture, with Africa as the determining force in the rise of civilization. The major influence of black Africans on the culture of Egypt, an idea resisted by most white historians but propounded by others, became the basis for the final assertion that Arabian, Jewish, Egyptian, Greek, and Roman influences were disseminated from a black foundation. In his theory of racial relativity Du Bois delighted in the sense of cultural flow between Europe, Asia, and Africa. As charted in *The Negro*, however, the flow tends to be in one direction; in mixed cultures, it is the Negro "blood" infused in peoples which gives them their special distinctions. Such logic was the result of the author's desire to generate out of a combination of fact, intuition, faith, and hope a mythos of Africa that would guide the modern black in directing himself.

The components of this mythos were determined by the prejudices among blacks and whites concerning the African peoples. Du Bois would show that blacks had contributed to the rise of world civilization, that their influence had continued to assist progress throughout the Western world, and that they had a capacity for cultural regeneration even where they seemed to be in permanent social disarray. He would show that there was an African tradition of complex social integration; far from being leeches on European intelligence, blacks had shown an inventiveness from which the world had profited. Generally derided as an artless, imitative people, Africans had, in fact, a vigorous, influential tradition in music, sculpture, and drawing. Often denounced as improvident, they had in many places demonstrated a talent for commerce. Above all, black people had a deep sense of their dignity and destiny, shown by a history of heroic resistance to oppression, a love of liberty which augured well for the future. These are the central ideas of Du Bois' propagandistic history of the African peoples, appearing tentatively at first in the late Atlanta Publications, dominating *The Negro* in 1915, and revitalized as late as 1947 with the appearance of *The World and Africa*.

African culture, Du Bois stressed in *The Negro*, was built by the triumph not only of character but also of intelligence over an often hostile environment. Many tribes of the Guinea and Congo regions "developed intelligence of a high order," he noted, quoting one commentator who called "the Ba Luba 'a nation of thinkers.'" Intelligence was reflected in a capacity for invention. The smelting of iron, crucial in world history, was an African discovery. The technical achievements of the Yorubas and Ashantis in the terra cotta industry, in the working of precious metals, and in weaving, often ascribed by white historians to foreign inspiration, were signs of native mental ability. A people who exhibited unmistakable evidence of indigenous civilization was the west-coast Africans. Commerce was a well-developed science in Africa: "The Negro is a born trader."[24] A remarkable system of agriculture provided the stable basis of the economy; together with large-scale raising of livestock, it was the basis of industry for the African artisan, trader, and manufacturer.

Du Bois showed the existence of a complex, stable society centered in the family and characterized by either the loose village system or the more highly organized tribal towns. Social solidarity was evident in some groups through forms of benevolent association, and in others through a discipline sometimes totalitarian and even ruthless. The matrilineal system in the family contrasted with European custom but was no less effective. The idea of African society as being lawless is repudiated. Efficient systems of justice existed, from the arbitrary but responsible power of the village headman to the more sophisticated tribunal arrangement in which precedent was as important as in English law. African religion was not mere fetish and superstition; there were distinct tendencies toward monotheism, as well as beliefs common to both Europe and Africa, as in the Yoruba myth of a dying divinity and the concept of an over-god.

Africa was in temporary disarray because of the effects of the slave trade and the continuing European presence, Du Bois argued. In the long term, slavery and colonialism would prove to be only episodes, albeit important ones, in the history of the people. The slave trade was the only cause of African decline. The tragedy of the continent lay in its combination of greatness and vulnerability. The tropical climate had spawned an environment so hostile that the struggle to survive surpassed that of any other continent. The crucially important Congo valley, home of the influential Bantu, was especially vulnerable to outside forces. In the fifteenth century, when European and African civilizations were, according to Du Bois, at comparable stages of development, nature played a major role in their futures. Physical barriers protected Europe, while African centers of culture were easily assaulted by barbarians from both within and without. The European thirst for cheap labor turned ancient internal African slavery, characterized as comparatively mild in nature and a by-product of war, into the object of war itself. Thus was African culture devastated by factors largely beyond its control.

Du Bois placed his confidence in the future of the African heritage on two solid planks: the moral and intellectual temper of the people, and their history of resistance to oppression. As in *The Souls of Black Folk*, he stressed the beauty and humility of their demeanor, expressed in personal attitude and in a love of art which, especially in America, marked the triumph of humanity over degradation. Within Africa itself he found important characteristics which had been sometimes lost in the diaspora. "In disposition," he asserted, "the Negro is among the most lovable of men."[25] Marked by ceremony and courtesy, African life possessed a dignity second to none among peoples of the world. Reverence for beauty had produced great art both of primitive expression and in the more sophisticated foreign genres incalculably enriched by African influence. Even among tribes capable of savagery, such as the cannibalistic Bassonga, there was extraordinary artistic and social development.

Black Africa and blacks elsewhere could be proud of their historic love of liberty. Few intruders had progressed with impunity through the continent. The Ashanti, Zulus, Sudanese, and Ethiopians had each supported long campaigns against European aggressors. In Jamaica and Haiti in the Caribbean, blacks had defied slave owners and resisted white domination after Emancipation. The black soldiers under Robert Gould Shaw exemplified the valor of black warriors in the American Civil War. In Latin America, men of African descent had aided in the overthrow of slavery and in the nationalist campaigns of heroes such as Simón Bolívar. This historic pride in their freedom would find expression again as the darker races in the twentieth century revolted against the offensive assumptions and insults of Europe and white America.

Du Bois gave no credit to the idea that another, less sympathetic conclusion might be drawn from the available evidence on Africa: that the slave trade, in which black men were certainly complicitous, was mainly the result — and not the cause — of weaknesses in a flawed culture. By 1915, Du Bois would no longer admit such speculation. The resulting portrait of the continent mirrors his aggressively liberal politics. His Africa is a basically agrarian society comprising a loose arrangement of rural tribes and city-states. There are the people and there are barbarians. With an ingrained sense of aristocracy and style, the people cherish art and blend creativeness into their daily lives. Religion too is vital to them. Although some persist in superstitious ways, most aspire to a more ordered concept of the spiritual forces ruling over their world. Commerce is developed, but not massive industry. The African is fundamentally ethical in his dealings, and some are thoroughly honest. Law is honored and justice is administered in satisfactory, if varied, ways. There is a distinctly socialist basis in the tradition of communal ownership of property: land is never owned by a private party, but belongs to the community, if to anyone at all. Women might be sold into marriage, but they are generally respected, often revered, and sometimes become rulers of their people. In spite of tribal and other types of warfare, the basic disposition of the people is toward peace and friendship. Certainly the inhabitants are human; but in bearing they are not unlike gods, and godlike, they provided the prime force in the motion of the world toward civilization. In temporary eclipse because of the cruel and rapacious white folk from abroad, Africa will rise again.

The Negro stands as the foundation of Du Bois' writing on Africa and the African peoples of the world, of his development of what has been called "Ethiopianism." The glorification and dramatization of the African past by black leaders had become a racial tradition expressed in various ways in the preceding centuries; its most spectacular moment would come with the rise of Garveyism in the decade after the publication of *The Negro*. With the confirmation of his role as a political activist through the Niagara Movement and the NAACP, Du Bois became, as Wilson J. Moses has called him, "a poet of Ethiopianism, dedicated to embodying his view of history in mythical form."[26] In this respect, his best and characteristic poetic achievement was not in verse but in celebrational epic historiography, in which he blended the accumulation of facts, often recounted in scholarly language, with passages of evocative power that converted scholastic detail into mythopoeic legend. *The Negro* is seldom more powerful, for example, than when it chants the dirge of African slavery: "Such is the story of the Rape of Ethiopia—a sordid, pitiful, cruel tale. Raphael painted, Luther preached, Corneille wrote, and Milton sung; and through it all for four hundred years, the dark captives wound to the sea amid the bleaching bones of the dead; for four hundred years the sharks followed the scurrying ships; for four hundred years America was strewn with the living and dying millions of a transplanted race; for four hundred years Ethiopia stretched forth her hands unto God."[27]

In writing *The Negro*, Du Bois had fashioned the Bible of pan-Africanism. Building on the work of black men such as Edward Wilmot Blyden and J. E. Casely-Hayford, as well as of sympathetic white scholars, he fulfilled one of the greatest needs of black political and intellectual life in the first years of the century. Immediately after the war he would begin to preach the gospel of pan-Africanism in ways that would contribute meaningfully to the African sense of self and to the eventual liberation of Africa and Africans abroad.

Du Bois' work on the *Crisis* consumed most of his time as a writer during that period; apart from the collection *Darkwater* in 1920, he produced no book-length work until *The Gift of Black Folk* in 1924. Among the least motivated of Du Bois' volumes on Afro-American culture and history, the study was commissioned by the Knights of Columbus as part of a series on the contribution of various races to America, probably intended to counter the rising and anti-Catholic influence of the Ku Klux Klan. He later regretted that his book had been "too hurriedly done, with several unpardonable errors."[28] More fleshed out with statistic and fact than *The Souls of Black Folk*, with which it shares the same cultural breadth, *The Gift of Black Folk* is not nearly so powerful a work as the 1903 volume. Little was added to the basic idea of the earlier piece—that blacks had played an integral part in the making of America, that their music had no superior among native art forms, and that their soul was singular in its exhibition of humility and spiritual fervor. The black folk stood in metaphorical relationship to American society, in that the history of their treatment as a minority group served as a proper index to the sincerity of American democracy.

The Gift of Black Folk, however, marks an important stage in the evolution of its author's thought on the Reconstruction years. Du Bois saw the post-Civil War era as a paradigm of modern American racial history; he slowly moved toward discovery of the argument that would refute the traditional claim that the age had been a burlesque of democracy in which the freedman had disgraced himself and proven his unfitness for equality in the American political system. In the essay "Of the Dawn of Freedom" in *The Souls of Black Folk*, Du Bois had examined Reconstruction from the perspective not of the black folk but of the white Northerners who had inspired and run the Freedmen's Bureau and its member societies, and who in particular had moved into the South to educate the former slaves. The blacks in this essay, first published in slightly different form in the *Atlantic Monthly* of March 1901, crouch "bewildered between friend and foe," stumbling toward freedom after years of being "emasculated by a peculiarly complete system of slavery, centuries old." Not surprisingly, they make grave errors in the first days of freedom. The brave white men and women of the North are the heroes; or more accurately, duty is the hero.[29]

By 1909, though, a more radicalized author looked again at the Reconstruction period in one of his most brilliant historical articles, "Reconstruction and Its Benefits," first delivered to a meeting of the American Historical Association in December 1909. Two black agencies, the church and the school, shared the task of raising the freedman with the federal government's bureau. The record of the black legislators is stoutly defended; the common accusations of widespread graft and corruption are either denied or placed in the perspective of the American political system, the uncertainty of the times, the slander and hostility of the white South and their Northern supporters, and the natural but by no means excessive corruptibility of black men who had matured under the ethics of slavery. Du Bois' thesis was that blacks in power had acted with general honesty, good will, and foresight in their legislative duties. His trump card was the fact that the legislative decisions taken by black men had endured beyond their disfranchisement: "Practically the whole new growth of the South has been accomplished under laws which black men helped to frame thirty years ago. I know," he concluded, "of no greater compliment to Negro suffrage."[30]

By 1924, when Du Bois published "The Reconstruction of Free-

dom" in *The Gift of Black Folk*, his understanding of the period had
changed further. The black man had been freed not "by edict of
sentiment" but by Abolitionists "backed by the persistent action of
the slave himself as fugitive, soldier and voter." The impact of
Marxist logic on the historian is clear in his analysis of the causes of
the nation's vacillation between defense of the freedman and his
abandonment. These "contradictions" were forced by the black
man himself. His motives were "primarily economic. He was trying
to achieve economic emancipation. And it is this fact that makes
Reconstruction one of the greatest attempts to spread democracy
which the modern world has seen." The intransigence of the white
South even in defeat compelled the full enfranchisement of the
black upon the federal government; the black was allowed to make
an attempt at freeing himself, and this attempt, Du Bois argued,
was both successful and the Afro-American's "greatest gift to this
nation." While "every effort" of historical and social science and
propaganda had supported the view that the granting of suffrage to
the freedmen was a catastrophe, the facts showed otherwise. In attacking property, these men had gone to the root of the problem
that had kept them as chattel to white power for centuries. Their
efforts to redistribute land among the former slaves, the poor whites,
and the master class through appropriation and taxation were justified by the exigencies of their situation and by the lessons of history.
As a group, the blacks made no more mistakes than any other of the
factions involved. With the memory of the collapse of the Freedmen's Bank, controlled by prominent whites but involving the loss of
considerable savings by blacks, "America should utter no sound as
to Negro dishonesty during reconstruction."[31]

The pathos of the defeated white South and of the confused ex-
slaves, personified in Du Bois' 1901 essay by "a gray-haired gentleman, whose fathers had quit themselves like men, whose sons lay in
nameless graves," and an old mammy, "her awful face black with
the mist of centuries," had disappeared as a theme in Du Bois' historiography of the Reconstruction. The white Northerners are replaced by black leaders as the heroes of the era; in many instances,
these men were honest, generous, and gifted. Economic determin-
ism displaces duty as the crucial idea behind heroic action, and the
battle between reactionary capitalism and instinctive socialist philosophy is seen as a prophetic struggle that made of the age a turning
point in the history of American democracy.

After the Wall Street crash and the onset of the Depression, Du Bois became increasingly conscious of the need further to explicate this lesson. In 1931 he asked the Board of Directors of the NAACP for assistance in an attempt to write a history of the Reconstruction in order to complete and offset recent studies.[32] The suggestion for the book had come from James Weldon Johnson, and he had secured a year's support from the Rosenwald Fund to begin it. The result of his efforts was *Black Reconstruction in America: An Essay Toward a History of the Part Which Black Folk Played in the Attempt To Reconstruct Democracy in America, 1860-1880,* published in 1935.

In both his 1903 and 1924 depictions of the Reconstruction Du Bois had made little of the role of the black masses as a force in history. In *Black Reconstruction*, however, he attributed to the people considerable initiative toward historic change. The roots of his new analysis lay not in the theory of American democracy which, he had written in 1924, encouraged "the power of the common, ordinary, unlovely man" rather than the idea of "exceptional genius" surrounded by masses of "hereditary idiots."[33] Rather, as the titles of some of the chapters ("The Black Worker," "The White Worker," "The General Strike") proclaim, Du Bois' analysis was based on his version of dialectical materialism. The black worker is the hero in this canvas, as he is the hero of the struggle of workers everywhere against capitalist exploitation. He is so because he had been "the ultimate exploited," lacking either the wish or the power to join the exploiters of humanity. Exploited by capital, poorer whites drove the occasional black entrepreneur back into the proletariat, thus welding it into a mass steeled against capitalism, its organizations and traditions. So motivated, the black slave had revolted and "brought civil war in America. He was its underlying cause, in spite of every effort to base the strife upon union and national power."[34]

Written at a time when Du Bois first began a serious reading of Marx, *Black Reconstruction* illuminates the difficulty he had in accommodating radical socialist theories to his historical method. As a result, there have been widely different views of the extent of Marxist influence on his argument. As Herbert Aptheker pointed out, in this work Du Bois has been called variously "a confirmed Marxist, a plain Marxist, a quasi-Marxist, and not a Marxist."[35] Yet the limitations of his knowledge of Marxist theory are clear. Only an ignorance of Lenin, as well as an insecure grasp of Marx, could have

led the historian to persist, for example, in his Procrustean use of
the term "dictatorship of the proletariat." To label as a "general
strike" the drift of large numbers of black folk from the slave farms
to the Union armies is also eccentric. But Du Bois employed such
inappropriate terms less in their scientific than in their tropological
sense. Although he ventured the opinion that "the record of the
Negro worker during Reconstruction presents an opportunity to
study inductively the Marxian theory of the state," it would be a
misrepresentation of the book, though one fostered by the author
himself, to interpret it as a consistent expansion of this idea.[36] Du
Bois wrote of the "dictatorship of the proletariat" to stress the power
of moneyed interests, although he tried to defend his use of the term
on stricter grounds.[37] The sensational title "The General Strike"
reflects little of the content of the chapter, which makes only modest
claims for the concerted force of the blacks. The activity of Marxist
organizations in the mid-nineteenth century, including those led by
Karl Marx himself, are reported with almost no comment and, in at
least one case, unflatteringly. But the radical socialist terminology
appearing in *Black Reconstruction in America* is not merely a cos-
metic; it is also used to explicate as well as dramatize the historically
ignored features of black participation in the events of the period.

In 1943 Du Bois summarized the "propositions" he had made in
the work: the black was both the cause of the Civil War and "a
prime factor" in the victory of the North; he was "the only effective
tool" in restoring the federal union after the war; enfranchisement
was one of the greatest steps taken toward democracy in the century;
and disfranchisement and segregation in the post-Reconstruction
era had made of the South "the nation's social problem Number
One."[38] These "propositions" should be distinguished from the predispositions and determinations that were at least as important in
shaping his argument, and which sometimes operated in tension to
one another. For example, Du Bois was writing to defend and en-
hance the reputation of black people. He was also convinced of the
authenticity of dialectical materialism as sociopolitical theory. And
he was passionately bent on refuting the racist and elitist nature of
the mainstream of white historians. But whatever his desires and
biases, he wanted to be fair and truthful. He believed the mere as-
semblage of facts to be insufficient; history must be subject to moral
scrutiny. Finally, the whole must be recounted according to the

highest standards of literary art accessible to the academic historian.

Of the author's predispositions, perhaps the most crucial in its impact on the study was his war on racist historians, documented in the final chapter, "The Propaganda of History." Determined to write forcefully, Du Bois employed colorful devices and styles no longer in vogue in American academic historiography. Although not all his dramatic effects are successful, they were conceived as supplementary to the scholarly argument, and are therefore divorceable from it. A nervous shifting between fact and fancy, prose and poetic flight, reason and invective, serenity and anger, is indeed the stylistic dynamic of *Black Reconstruction*. At times, the influencing art form seems to be the pageant, that festival of color and rhetoric, light and sound, in which the author delighted.[39] Du Bois certainly made a spectacle of himself and his arguments, but he felt it was necessary to do so in order to upstage and overshadow, as far as he could, the mass of biased scholarship which had stressed the unfortunate aspects of Reconstruction and analyzed the era at the expense of both the reputation of the black man and the truth of history.

Of this work, as of *The Negro* and many other volumes, Du Bois was apologetic about his dependence on secondary sources. In this case, however, he utilized a mass of monographic material "formerly ignored," as one writer put it, "that every future historian must reckon with."[40] Du Bois himself marveled that he should have this opportunity to be original; he could not believe that "any unbiased mind . . . can read the plain, authentic facts of our history . . . and come to conclusions essentially different from mine; and yet I stand virtually alone in this interpretation."[41] Once asserted so forcefully, however, his revaluations of the behavior of the freedmen and the poorer whites, the nature of the constituent assemblies, the machinations of industrial capitalists preying on black and white alike, and the federal government's failure to give land to the former slaves, could not thereafter be ignored. Based on premises of social and political activity which either were being stated for the first time or had been timidly urged previously, *Black Reconstruction* inaugurated, if not influenced, a line of histories of the Reconstruction and of the South written by blacks and whites alike, attesting to the probity of Du Bois' assumptions and insights, though wary of the excesses of his style. However little they were guided by him, studies such as John Hope Franklin's *Reconstruction after the Civil War* (1961) and C. Vann Woodward's *Origins of the New South* (1951) reinforce Du Bois' depiction of the history of the Southern people. From this point of view, it may be true that, as Aptheker has claimed, "with this book he revolutionized the historical profession in the United States."[42]

With the publication of *Black Reconstruction* Du Bois completed the best part of his historical writing on the black man in Africa, the United States, and elsewhere. But he did not lose interest in the subject, and he continued to bring his commentary on Africa up to date. Not only was there recent scholarship to be synthesized and made popular, but in the aftermath of the second world war, Africa itself began to move steadily out of colonialism toward the political freedom which promised to bring about the renaissance of the continent.

In 1939, however, when *Black Folk Then and Now* appeared, the march toward independence was hardly evident in a world dominated by a Hitlerite Germany, an imperialist Great Britain, a depressed United States, and a neutral USSR. Du Bois suggested that no matter what the visitor from Altruria might expect of the future of the African peoples, those who believed in the modern philosophy of white superiority seemed determined to hold sway. *Black Folk Then and Now* reproduces large portions of *The Negro,* adding the fruits of Du Bois' further reading in African history and of his knowledge of changes in black America. The book documents the further decline of his belief in the reality of racial differences. It asserts that it is generally recognized that no scientific definition of race is possible. Although there are three basic stocks of man, it is impossible to separate them absolutely. The lack of Marxist influence on this book, the first full-length effort after *Black Reconstruction*, is notable. The indiscreet use of communist terminology found in the earlier work is not repeated. Although tribute is paid to Marx and the communists, the analytical method is not particularly indebted to them. In fact, the repetition in the last sentence of Du Bois' warning at the start of the century that "the problem of the twentieth century is the problem of the color line" contradicts the socialist position, accepted by him in recent years, that the crucial issue is the redistribution of wealth. Writing on the black folk had pushed him to think once again of racism as a force greater than the capitalism with which it was inevitably intertwined.

It was therefore in probably the most uncertain period of his life that Du Bois published his first full-length autobiography, *Dusk of Dawn: An Essay Toward an Autobiography of a Race Concept* (1940). The odd subtitle of the work suggests that his approach is unorthodox. As personal history, the book is both modest and ambitious. It includes enough facts to provide a reasonably clear self-portrait. At the same time, it studiously avoids the revelation of intimate details of its author's life. In addition, the sense of prophetic importance developed in the *Darkwater* self-portrait is absent, in spite of the identification of Du Bois' life with the evolution of racial theory and the major modern events related to race. "My life," the author wrote, "had its significance and its only deep significance because it was part of a Problem." But the problem happened to be "the Problem of the future world." He would attempt to elucidate the "inner meaning and significance" of the dilemma of race by reference to the human life he knew best; beyond that point, his autobiography would not go.[43]

Dusk of Dawn divides into three parts. The first comprises four chapters of direct autobiography forming less than one-third of the work. The book then treats the history of the concept of race and its impact on whites and blacks in American society. The last two chapters return to a recounting of "personal annals" but reflect the controversial, public nature of Du Bois' life between his founding of the *Crisis* and his resignation from the NAACP and elucidate more recent developments of a national and international nature.

Dusk of Dawn illuminates three aspects of Du Bois' current beliefs. First, the work defends minutely, even repetitively, his theory that voluntary self-segregation would serve as the best means of progress for blacks. Second, it makes clear his current position on communism. "I was not and am not a communist," he stressed; "I do not believe in the dogma of inevitable revolution in order to right economic wrong. I think war is worse than hell, and that it seldom or never forwards the advance of the world." Nevertheless, Marxism was correct in emphasizing the economic foundations of culture, "and this conviction I had to express or spiritually die" (302-303). Lastly, Du Bois began to voice publicly his growing fascination with the idea that uncharted, irrational forces were at work in the world.

Only partly psychological in origin, this power was "influencing folkways, habits, customs and subconscious deeds. Here perhaps is a realm of physical and cosmic law which science does not yet control" (222). Like his interest in the relationship between chance and free will, which he hoped to investigate as part of his land-grant social studies scheme, this theme would again surface near the end of the *Black Flame* trilogy in 1961.

In spite of the integral political aims of *Dusk of Dawn,* the central theme of this autobiography is its author's search for community in a world that insists on distinctions. It is the story of a man seeking harmony in the midst of social chaos, beauty amidst encroaching squalor, repose in an era of hostility, spiritual solace in a wasteland. On the one hand, Du Bois maintained that "the goal of all consciousness" is inevitably the "anarchy of the spirit," the capacity of the mind to indulge its natural desire for freedom from outside constraints (134). But such license can exist perfectly only in a socially responsive human environment where freedom will be the dividend of the individual's democratic responsibility. In a world of radical social inequity, such a balance is impossible. The sorrow expressed by Du Bois was twofold. He deplored the crippling effects of racism and other social abuses on the oppressed in their struggle to be free. In addition, he noted the tragic irony that "the great and oppressing world outside is also real and human and in its essence honest." Yet oppression leads to "unreasoning resentment and even hatred" of this outside world; idealism is exhausted by bitterness and paranoia in a process that is "something to drive a man mad" (137).

In spite of his accomplishments and his claims of having lived a life that included laughter, wine, women, and song, the central character of *Dusk of Dawn* is a troubled hero, victimized by history and by man's fears and delusions. Fashioning his own parable of the cave in this work, Du Bois depicted the black world as entombed in a dark mountain recess, calling to the passer-by with words of logic and courtesy. Slowly it becomes clear to the blacks that they are not being heard, "that some thick sheet of invisible but horribly tangible plate glass is between them and the world." The veil of *The Souls of Black Folk* has here solidified. Hysteria within the cave seems bizarre and ridiculous to those outside. Smashing through the glass, bloody and disfigured, the occasional escapees find themselves, in a grotesque paradox, faced by "a horrified, implacable, and quite overwhelming mob of people frightened for their own existence" (131).

In two long debates with fictitious white friends on the question of racial superiority, Du Bois built on his early conviction, supported by his later experience, that in all things general, "white people were just the same as I: their physical possibilities, their mental processes were no different from mine" (136). The shared values, sympathies, and ideals of the three men—Du Bois and the whites—far exceed their racial differences; yet the latter persist in the absurdity of a social philosophy based on distinctions. Du Bois admits of the whites that he himself shares in "their sins; in fine, I am related to them . . . By Blood" (152). In defense of members of his own race, he argues their physical beauty, the depth of their spirituality, the authenticity of their intelligence, the liveliness of their art, and their capacity for the enjoyment—and not mere endurance—of life. He attacks white culture as fearful of the truth, believing in "the efficacy of lies as a method of human uplift" (151). As a system, that culture is "idiotic, addle-brained, unreasoning, topsy-turvy, and without precision" (143). But however obtuse the minds of the whites or waspish the words of their black opponent, Du Bois is finally pleading the cause of unity.

Spiritual power is seen in black Americans as the triumph of their humanity over centuries of oppression, which had fortified their soul against materialism and utilitarianism, taught them to treasure the consolation of religion and art, to revere democracy, to be skeptical of divisive social theories, and to be perceptive of injustice under its many masks. Du Bois then countered this lofty view of Afro-American character by a cold assessment of its failings. There were unmistakable signs that the force which had diverted the worst aspects of white culture away from blacks had begun to erode both the better influences and those positive African values which had survived slavery. Well-to-do blacks in a city apartment near midnight lament their dilemma; they are caught between the goad of white racism and their despair at the moral and physical squalor in much of the black world. The average standard of black culture is low both "in itself" and by comparison with the rest of the land: "this is still an ignorant people" (180). The educated man is "jammed beside the careless, ignorant and criminal" (185). Progress is hindered by "unwashed and unshaven black demagogues" who intimidate their betters; even the best class of blacks are corrupted by "crime, gambling and prostitution" when they seek jobs for their people through the political machinery (217).

Except for his 1938 address "The Revelation of St. Orgne the Damned" at Fisk University, one would have to return to the period before the Niagara Movement to find similar public admissions from Du Bois about the general state of black culture. His open censure, offered as part of the rationale for black self-segregation, is balanced by his continuing faith in the masses of people. His hope is that the "communalism of the African clan" can be revived among black Americans, "implemented by higher ideals of human accomplishment" learned through contact with the modern world (219).

From his perspective as a man prevented because of race from fulfilling his deepest desires for the ideal life in communion with other men, Du Bois looked down on a Western civilization, of which Afro-America was a captive but integral part, trapped in that maze of moral contradiction, anxiety, and despair which many in the contemporary world were coming to accept as the modern condition of man. "Hitler," Du Bois wrote before the start of the Nazi war, was merely the latest "crude but logical exponent of white world race philosophy" to emerge since the imperialist Berlin Conference of 1884, when Africa was carved up by Europe (169-170). Just as race was only the most tragic facet in the ideology of the German leader, so racism was only the most modern expression of man's tendency toward spiritual suicide.

Secular in its acceptance of Marx's materialist principles of society, *Dusk of Dawn* yet stresses the distinction between the machinery of society and the spirit of individual man. Though discreet as personal history, this self-portrait is distinguished by its author's compassion, founded on his own admission of complicity as a human being in the human criminality against which he took a stand. Du Bois occasionally exaggerated his impact on this or that area of Afro-American life. But he was a sober judge of his achievement. He was justly proud to have been "a main factor in revolutionizing the attitude of the American Negro toward caste" (303). He was as judiciously humble in admitting that he had done "little to create my day or greatly change it"; but he added, "I did exemplify it and thus for all time my life is significant for all lives of men" (4).

CHAPTER TWELVE

The Wisdom of Age

Youth is more courageous than age because it knows less. Age is wiser than youth because it knows more . . . I would have been hailed with approval if I had died at 50. At 75 my death was practically requested. If living does not give value, wisdom, and meaning to life, then there is no sense in living at all.   (Du Bois, c. 1960)

AFTER RETIREMENT FROM his professorship of sociology at Atlanta University in the spring of 1944, Du Bois returned to New York and embarked on the last stage of his life and career. In the next four years he served as director of special research for the NAACP. In 1948 he was fired by the association. Immediately invited by the leftist Council on African Affairs to join its leadership as chairman, Du Bois used that tiny organization by mutual consent as the base for launching the final major campaign of his life, in support of anticolonialist movements and the spread of international socialism. He became involved in a highly publicized but essentially subsidiary and tactical aspect of the socialist goal, the international peace movement. By 1950 he had so identified himself with the American left that he became a candidate for the United States Senate from the state of New York on the American Labor party ticket. His challenge to the prevailing anticommunist spirit of the nation was answered in 1951 by his indictment with four colleagues in a peace organization on the charge of being unregistered agents of a foreign "principal." Acquitted by the presiding judge at his trial, Du Bois countered by deepening his commitment to the left. On October 1, 1961, he applied for membership in the Communist party of the United States. Later that month he left for Africa, from which he was never to return.

The end of World War II began an era of unprecedented change in international affairs. The use of atomic weapons by the United

States against Japan united science to destruction in a way that had profound repercussions on political and social reality. The war established Russia as a major power; it also began the decline of the European imperialist countries. The independence of India in 1947 was the prelude to self-determination for all the darker races; the triumph of the Chinese Communists in 1949 expanded the meaning of this fundamental change beyond the limits of race. The Marshall Plan aided in the restoration of Europe to commercial and cultural eminence, but in a changed world. In the United States, anticommunism found focus in the Korean War; and the last days of the McCarthy era coincided with the first stirrings of a movement that would radically alter the status of the black citizen and, in so doing, affect the character of the American republic.

Du Bois would die before the major victories of the civil rights struggle and before the first wave of _coups d'état_ confirmed that pan-Africa remained a dream. With a still vigorous intelligence, however, he watched the changes and participated actively in some of them. Within the United States his audience shrank, but the volume of his commentary was not diminished. The major works of this period include _Color and Democracy: Colonies and Peace_ (1945), _The World and Africa_ (1947), _In Battle for Peace: The Story of My 83rd Birthday_ (1952), and the fictional trilogy _The Black Flame: The Ordeal of Mansart_ (1957), _Mansart Builds a School_ (1959), and _Worlds of Color_ (1961). In addition, he continued to publish articles in such magazines and newspapers as would print his increasingly socialist and controversial message. Apparently indefatigable, he undertook two years before his death the preparation of a multivolume _Encyclopedia Africana_, a task that he knew he would never see to its completion.

Whoever was responsible for Du Bois' return to the NAACP—his association friends Arthur Spingarn and Louis Wright, as he supposed, or Executive Secretary Walter White—drastically underestimated Du Bois' commitment to socialism, his spirit of personal independence, and his energy. He himself thought that he had returned to develop the NAACP's African policy, especially through revival of the Pan-African Congress. Walter White, Du Bois later believed, saw him as a potential ghostwriter and a personal representative acting entirely at the executive's discretion. Spingarn and Wright, on the contrary, wanted to give the seventy-six-year-old warrior a place to spend his last days in peace. Without an alternative offer of employment, he had no choice but to return to the association. He was never to feel comfortable there; he thought his office space so inadequate as to be deliberately confining, and friction with White pitted Du Bois against the principal force in an organization that had changed drastically from its earlier days. The power of the Board of Directors had declined sharply, and that of the executive had correspondingly grown, so that in opposing White, Du Bois risked instant dismissal.[1]

Within a few months of his arrival in New York, Du Bois published perhaps his most underrated volume, *Color and Democracy: Colonies and Peace* (1945). In leaving Atlanta the previous year, he had declared his intention to devote the rest of his life to anticolonialism and, by inference, socialism.[2] *Color and Democracy* is the manifesto of his last period, attesting to his determination to link the problems of Africa with those of the rest of the world, and to align African nationalism with international socialist thought. The crucial term in the work is "colony." Du Bois joined the fate of Africa to that of the whole world by expanding his definition of colonial status to include all nations dominated by foreign powers, whether through constitutional acts, coercive treaties, or economic domination. Thus, countries such as China, the dominion states of the British Commonwealth, South Africa, the republics of South and Central America, and the Balkan states, for example, could not be free while they belonged to greater powers through coercive treaties and financial indebtedness. With the end of the war in sight, the crucial question would be "the riddle of Russia," for the restoration of European imperialism and colonialism was impossible without the complicity of the Soviet Union. But "come what may, it is to the glory of God and the exaltation of man that the Soviet Union, first of modern nations, has dared to face front-forward the problem of poverty, and to place on the uncurbed power of concentrated wealth the blame of widespread and piteous penury."[3]

With *Color and Democracy* Du Bois declared himself to be far beyond the NAACP in the scope of his world view and his radicalism. Nevertheless, he tried to work within its organization. In 1945 he attended the founding conference of the United Nations in San Francisco in the capacity of consultant to the United States government delegation and representing, with Walter White and Mary

McLeod Bethune, the position of the NAACP. In *Color and De-mocracy* he had criticized the Dumbarton Oaks Conference of 1944, at which the framework of the United Nations, including the Security Council, had been worked out, for its tacit condoning of colonialism and its patently racist distribution of power. But with Russia and China among its ranks, there was at least the potential for change. In 1946 Du Bois organized an appeal to the United Nations Commission on Human Rights on behalf of black Americans, in the form of a pamphlet edited and introduced by him, comprising pieces written by legal and other experts within the association and sponsored by the NAACP.[4] First declined by the world body for publication or debate, the "Appeal to the World" was finally accepted in October 1947. Embarrassed by its criticism of their country, the United States delegation, including Eleanor Roosevelt, prevented its scheduled discussion at a meeting of the commission in Geneva that year. As with the League of Nations after the first world war, Du Bois was respectful of an organization apparently designed to further world unity, and was willing to appeal to its judgment, but he soon came to consider the United Nations as progressing too slowly against colonialism and as being dominated by the more powerful white nations.

Yet the world itself was changing in an unmistakable way. The presence at the Fifth Pan-African Congress, held at Manchester, England in 1945, of a number of talented nationalist leaders such as its organizer George Padmore, Kwame Nkrumah, Jomo Kenyatta, and Nnamdi Azikiwe was an indication that Africa was on the move. At the congress Du Bois was ceremoniously hailed as the "father" of pan-Africanism and was declared international president of the congress. More epochal for him was the achievement of independence by India on August 15, 1947, advanced by Du Bois as the greatest historical date of the nineteenth and twentieth centuries.[5] And he considered Mahatma Gandhi the greatest figure of his time.[6] The twentieth century, Du Bois declared, would see the end of the color line through the collapse of imperialism and the assertion of international socialism. Nevertheless, he was sensitive to the dangers facing government and democracy in the emerging states. Both in *Color and Democracy* and elsewhere he anticipated the neocolonialist role of industrial corporations and their control of nominally independent poorer nations. The Marshall Plan was the archinstrument of a new colonialism in the postwar period, as the United

States strove to resuscitate European capitalism and to destroy the opportunity for world political change presented by the defeat of fascism and the decline of imperialist and expansionist power.[7]

The World and Africa (1947) documents the fact that Du Bois continued less than confident at this time about the shape of things to come. Russia was still a "riddle," Africa little more than a vague hope. Europe had finally paid the price for the historic contradictions of her culture. Individually blameless men and women had been complicitous in the enslavement and exploitation of others in "the modern paradox before which the Puritan stands open mouthed and mute." Du Bois did not gloat at the sight of Europe in ruins at the end of the war; he was far more disturbed by the "illogic in modern thought and the collapse of human culture" that the war had epitomized. The price of slavery and imperialist competition had been paid in the moral and artistic decline of European culture: "Art, in building, painting, and literature, became cynical and decadent. Literature became realistic and therefore pessimistic."[8] Religion had declined into hypocrisy, morality into a charade of manners.

The desperate need for world spiritual and cultural rejuvenation became the focus of Du Bois' concern. It led to a shift in his perception of the Afro-American future. He who had once encouraged blacks to go North now urged the opposite. "The future of American Negroes is in the South," he declared in 1948 at a meeting in Columbia, South Carolina, of the Southern Youth Legislature, an interracial effort sponsored by the leftist Southern Negro Youth Congress. "Here is the magnificent climate; here is the fruitful earth under the beauty of the southern sun; and here, if anywhere on earth, is the need of the thinker, the worker, and the dreamer." The South was the "firing line" for the emancipation of blacks in America, Africa, and elsewhere, for all colored races, and "for the emancipation of the white slaves of modern capitalistic monopoly." The accent was on youth—young blacks and whites in a culture "led by black folk" and joined by peoples of all races.[9] As he had done at least twice elsewhere, in addresses on education at Fisk and Howard in 1930 and 1933, he quoted the poem that represented for him the articulation of the triumph of hope, from a black perspective, over twentieth-century existential despair, Arna Bontemps' "Nocturne at Bethesda": "I thought I saw an angel flying low . . ."[10]

With the death of Franklin Delano Roosevelt and his replacement as President by a man of "apparent good-will but narrow training and small vision," Du Bois no longer had reason to discriminate between the two main American parties.[11] In 1946 he outlined the major problems facing the American people: labor unions, colonialism, the relationship of the United States with Russia, rotten boroughs in the South, lynching, and job discrimination. Neither party would speak to these issues, and neither deserved support for its silence.[12] In 1948 he precipitated his departure from the NAACP by touting his "fifty years as a political independent" and coming out boldly for Henry Wallace and the Progressive party. Although traditionally skeptical of the chances of a third party, Du Bois called on blacks and the association in particular to rally to the Progressives because of the "unusual liberalness" with which Wallace had faced the problems of race, peace, and relations with the Soviet Union.[13] Du Bois' support of the Progressive party leader brought him in conflict with Walter White, who was quietly swinging the power of the association behind President Truman. When the executive secretary accepted an invitation to join the United States delegation to the United Nations, then meeting in Paris, Du Bois demanded that some censure of American colonial policy be made lest the NAACP be linked in the public mind with "the reactionary, war-mongering colonial imperialism of the present Administration." The memorandum was leaked to the New York *Times* and published on September 9, 1948; less than a week later the *Times* carried the notice of Du Bois' dismissal by the board of the NAACP, effective the last day of the year.[14]

Du Bois had sacrificed his position for the left, and the left responded to his plight. In the final stage of his stay with the NAACP, he had begun an open association with the radical socialist movement by publishing in such journals as the *National Guardian, Soviet Russia Today,* the *People's Voice, New Masses,* and *Masses & Mainstream.* His personal link to this section of American political and cultural life, with which he had often quarreled over the years, was undoubtedly Shirley Graham, an intellectual and activist in her own right and the daughter of a Methodist minister long known and respected by Du Bois. In 1951, on the eve of his trial as an unregistered agent of a foreign principal and subsequent to the death of his first wife, Nina Gomer Du Bois, Du Bois and Graham were married. In her memoir of their relationship to the end of his life, Shirley Graham Du Bois candidly related her deliberate attempts to introduce Du Bois into the circles to which she was politically and emotionally committed—the interracial and international alliance of intellectuals and activists of radical socialist persuasion—and for whom Du Bois had long shown strong philosophic affinities. The predominantly white left, she believed, needed Du Bois, and he himself would benefit from such a companionship in the pursuit of what was essentially a common objective.[15] Typical of her dual roles as friend and independent propagandist was her article "Why Was Du Bois Fired" in *Masses & Mainstream,* November 1948, which traced her understanding of the conflicts between Du Bois and Walter White, who had been hired by the NAACP as a young man with Du Bois' active support. White had steadily resisted all attempts, especially those by the former *Crisis* editor, "to bring the framework of the N.A.A.C.P. in accord with its needs as a mass organization."[16] Du Bois had been sacrificed to the secretary's egotism and reactionary political instincts.

Late in 1948 Du Bois made two moves of crucial importance to his later life. He accepted the offer of office facilities and secretarial assistance—but no salary—from the left-wing and anticolonialist Council on African Affairs. The organization was in some disarray after the Attorney General's designation of the group as "subversive," which had led to the resignation of one of its founders, Max Yergan, and litigation by Yergan against the other leaders of the council. Du Bois joined Paul Robeson and Alphaeus Hunton on the council, financed largely by Frederick V. Field, a socialist member of the wealthy Chicago family. In 1951 Du Bois gave two reasons for this decision: he believed in the work that the organization "should do" for Africa; and he was determined that "no man or organization" should be denied a voice "because of political or religious beliefs."[17] Du Bois remained with the council until it was suddenly closed down in November 1956. By mutual consent, it became his base for the pursuit of his interests in anticolonialism and radical socialism.

In 1948 Du Bois also responded to the efforts of Harlow Shapley, the Harvard astronomer and chairman of the leftist National Council of the Arts, Sciences, and Professions, to mount a Cultural and Scientific Conference for World Peace. A belief in "the Prince of Peace" and an expressed hatred of war had been prominent in Du

Bois' "Credo" of 1904, and though he had been a less than radical pacifist over the years, he now enthusiastically supported the international and socialist-inspired movement encouraged by the fear of atomic weaponry. The conference met in New York between March 25 and 27, 1949, the participants including Alexander A. Fadeyev, secretary-general of the Soviet Writers' Union, Dimitri Shostakovich, and Lillian Hellman; Du Bois himself chaired a panel on literature with Fadeyev, Louis Untermeyer, Norman Mailer, and F. O. Matthiessen. Meeting under intense pressure from the government, the press, and the public, the conference concluded in a mass rally at Madison Square Garden, where Du Bois was one of the speakers. He told the assembly that "the dark world is on the move," and that it wanted not revenge but a decent world free of racism: "All this depends first on world peace. Peace is not an end. It is the gateway to full and abundant life."[18]

This speech marked his debut as an international socialist propagandist for peace; the evident unpopularity of the conference with mainstream America only intensified his involvement. At the end of April he went to Paris as the head of an American delegation to the World Congress of the Defenders of Peace. It was at this conference that Paul Robeson remarked that American blacks would not fight in a war against the Soviet Union and thus ended his public acceptance in the United States. Du Bois brought word that socialism was spreading everywhere, with only one real enemy—colonialism, led by the United States: "Drunk with power, we are leading the world to hell . . . and to a Third World War."[19] When twenty-five American intellectuals were invited to an All-Soviet Peace Conference in August 1949 for the Moscow stage of the international campaign, only Du Bois attended, in what was his third visit to the USSR. Bringing greetings, he said, from American peace organizations such as the Progressive party, the Council of Arts, Sciences, and Professions, and the Quakers, Du Bois denounced American capitalism, racism, and suppression of dissent. But socialism had made changes in the country and would make many more, were the people not swayed "by almost hysterical propaganda that the freedoms which they have and such individual initiative as remains are being threatened and that a third world war is the only remedy."[20]

Early in 1950 O. John Rogge, a former assistant attorney general of the United States and an associate of Du Bois in activities such as the recent American Continental Congress for World Peace, began to organize a Peace Information Center to publicize a petition against the use and proliferation of nuclear weapons. Adopted as a resolution by a conference of pacifists in Sweden, the Stockholm Peace Appeal was circulated internationally by the Paris-based World Council of the Defenders of Peace. Du Bois was elected the chairman of the American center. When Dean Acheson attacked the petition as a communist device on July 12, 1950, Du Bois spiritedly replied that its articles—to ban atomic warfare, to place the ban under international supervision, and to censure the first nation to use atomic arms as a criminal against humanity—enjoyed genuine and widespread support in the United States and around the world from men of unimpeachable integrity. The Peace Appeal was "a true, fair statement of what we ourselves and many countless other Americans believed."[21] With that exchange, the Peace Information Center and the United States government were set on a collision course.

In 1950, Du Bois also participated in one of the more extraordinary events of his life, when he ran for the United States Senate from the state of New York on the Labor party ticket. Although he claimed that he was persuaded to do so by the wish to help the Labor candidacy of Vito Marcantonio, running for Congress, the act was further evidence of the ability of the leftist movement to challenge and rejuvenate his energies while simultaneously honoring him as a leader. He was undoubtedly perceived at this time as a crucial factor in the attempts by American socialism to heal its most persistent sore, its inability to deal effectively with the conflict between a desire for mass membership and the demands of American racism. Du Bois ran spiritedly but in vain. He was gratified to receive almost a quarter of a million votes, but that number was less than his Labor co-candidates received. In Harlem he received fewer than fifteen percent of the votes cast, as he ironically fell victim to the very eclecticism he had preached over the decades to the black voter. Marcantonio himself was not elected. For Du Bois, the election was another important stage in his growth as a radical socialist leader carrying simultaneously the message of Marxism, antiracism, and anticolonialism. He seldom failed, before any audience, to stress the point that the progress of blacks and the other darker peoples was closely related to world peace and world socialism.

While Du Bois was on the hustings, another more serious drama was developing. The Peace Information Center, with Du Bois as chairman, had been resisting all attempts by the Attorney General's office to compel it to register in accordance with the Foreign Agents Registration Act of 1938. Between August 1950 and February 1951 the Center debated Washington officials on the question of its ties to overseas interests. On October 12, 1950, the governing body of the center voted to disband as an organization, hoping to nullify the issue of its legality, but on February 8, 1951, a grand jury in Washington, D.C. returned an indictment against five members of the body: Du Bois, Abbott Simon, Elizabeth Moos, Kyrle Elkin, and a secretary, Sylvia Soloff. On February 16 Du Bois and his co-defendants were arraigned in Washington and released on bail; during the proceedings Du Bois was handcuffed briefly. Facing a maximum sentence of five years in prison and a fine of five thousand dollars, the defendants and their supporters began the public campaign for support that they regarded as essential to their relief.

The United States and international socialist communities, accustomed to fighting such battles, responded with an overwhelming and, to Du Bois, gratifying show of loyalty; but a comparatively mild appeal for support addressed to the black leadership class was so poorly answered that it was abandoned. Du Bois was "deeply disappointed. I recognized the fear in the Negro group, especially among the educated and well-to-do."[22] Nevertheless, support began to grow among blacks; the black press was sympathetic from the first, although Du Bois reasoned that pressure from the black masses was responsible for whatever assistance he received. He took this split among blacks as a sign of emergent class differences that were to be expected with the decline of discrimination. He was particularly disappointed that only one of over thirty chapters of a black graduate fraternity to which he had belonged for over forty years, and whose convention he had addressed as recently as August 1948, expressed sympathy for him. Whether or not he was justified in doing so, he saw the indifference or fear shown by so many of his social and professional peers as sealing his relationship with the predominantly white left.

"I have faced during my life many unpleasant experiences; the growl of a mob; the personal threat of murder; the scowling distaste of an audience. But nothing so cowed me as that day, November 8, 1951, when I took my seat in a Washington courtroom as an indicted criminal."[23] The chief defense lawyer was Vito Marcantonio; the chief prosecution witness was O. John Rogge, who named the Soviet Union as the ultimate foreign "principal" to which the Peace Information Center, which he had helped to found, was agent. The prosecution, however, made the Paris-based World Council of the Defenders of Peace, admittedly central to peace activities, principal in its case. The defense strategy was built around Du Bois, who was to be its only witness from among the indictees, with Albert Einstein prepared to give testimony to his good character. The trial was both dramatic and, finally, anticlimactic. The drama was provided by the testimony of Rogge against his former friends, and by Marcantonio's lively cross-examination. The anticlimax came on November 21 with the granting of a motion by the defense for a directed acquittal; the presiding judge ruled that while the existence had been established of the Peace Information Center and of the World Council of the Defenders of Peace, no evidence had been presented of a relationship of principal to agent between the latter and the former. Therefore the case against Du Bois and his former colleagues in the center was dismissed.

"Blessed are the Peacemakers," Du Bois wrote not long after, "for they shall be called Communists."[24] He thus openly accepted the imputation of American critics of the peace movement that its goals were essentially those of the Communists. In April 1951 he had boldly declared his "stand" for peace in the face of "this hysteria, this crazy foolishness." Perhaps the United States really wanted war, but the Soviet Union certainly did not seem willing to fight, although "we have publicly and privately insulted it."[25] In spite of the outcome of the trial, Du Bois was now a marked man during the era when the McCarran and Smith Acts, as well as the power of the Departments of State and Justice, were used to curtail the influence and travel of socialist critics of the American system, as well as to imprison and otherwise penalize such people. In the aftermath of the trial, for example, Du Bois was prevented by the Passport Division of the State Department from traveling to Rio de Janeiro for yet another peace conference. But if the aim was to intimidate him, it did not succeed. He publicly defended the innocence of Julius and

Ethel Rosenberg, executed in 1953 for allegedly passing atomic secrets to the Soviet Union.[26] At the funeral service of the couple, he recited the Twenty-Third Psalm; at midyear he published a commemorative poem on their death: "Crucify us, Vengeance of God/As we crucify two more Jews..."[27] The following Christmas the Du Boises hosted a party for the Rosenberg children. When several Communists were jailed for allegedly conspiring to overthrow the government of the United States, Du Bois joined the protest against their imprisonment, notably in the case of Benjamin J. Davis, Jr., the lawyer who had defended Angelo Herndon in a celebrated civil rights case some twenty years previously, and Ben Gold, the labor leader.[28]

More than ever now, Du Bois depended for publication on the left-wing press. From 1948, but especially after his trial, he was grateful for the outlet provided by the *National Guardian* of New York. His columns on the passing of Harry Truman from the presidency and the death of Joseph Stalin shortly afterward illustrate how much he contrasted American political leadership with that of the Soviets. Truman was a blend of homely affability and "human insensibility and stubbornness which has no regard for the truth." Although he had fought the reactionaries McCarran and McCarthy, "he ranks with Adolph Hitler as one of the greatest killers of our day" for his unapologetic use of atomic weaponry in Japan; even President-elect Dwight Eisenhower was preferable.[29] Stalin, on the contrary, was "a great man," hardly rivaled in this century. "Simple, calm and courageous," he rose to greatness through his identification with the common man. A keen judge of men, he had seen through the "flamboyance and exhibitionism" of Trotsky, who had fooled America and the world. His major accomplishments had been his approach to the Russian peasant question, when he had risked a second revolution in order to destroy kulak capitalism; his preservation of the state in the face of West European attempts to destroy it, with Hitlerism being the most recent major challenge; and his compromise with the other victors in the second world war in order to keep the peace. "Such was the man who lies dead, still the butt of noisy jackals and of the ill-bred men of some parts of the distempered West."[30] Du Bois' denunciation of Leon Trotsky is especially valuable in determining the nature of his socialist beliefs at this time.

His dismissal from the NAACP, his indictment, and his socialist writings combined to cut Du Bois off from most of his traditional opportunities to be heard in the black community. He could not appear under the auspices of the association; he believed that black papers had been warned not to carry his writings or even mention his name. Neither as a commencement speaker nor as a general lecturer was he welcome at black colleges. While he was glad to live in the wider world forced on him, he found it, he said, a bitter experience to be shunned by members of his own race. He reasoned that he was being sacrificed for the undoubted advantages that were accruing to black Americans, such as the legal victories of the NAACP and the cracks in the color line: "Was not the sacrifice of one man, small payment for this? Even those who disagreed with this judgment at least kept quiet. The colored children ceased to hear my name."[31]

Campaigning in Harlem in 1950 he had asked blacks to stand up "for Peace and Civil Rights," but few had answered by voting for him.[32] His continual warning was against the appearance of class divisions among blacks as a result of racial "progress." This was the "choice" facing blacks, either to divide between successful capitalists and the exploited, or to maintain solidarity among themselves and with oppressed people of all races.[33] In 1955, he found the ties between black Americans and Africa to be breaking, which he attributed to the harsh anticommunist climate in the United States. The Council on African Affairs, which had once had over two thousand members, now barely subsisted. The silence of most blacks on the issue of socialism was ominous; they did not fully realize that they were "being bribed to trade equal status in the United States for the slavery of the majority of men."[34] In 1956, in a five-part series in the *National Guardian* on "The Negro in America Today," Du Bois again pointed to class division as a major problem facing blacks. He stressed, too, the unavailability of reliable sociological data on the black population of the United States, whose study the government discouraged because of fear of what it would show. There had been advances in many areas, but the masses were generally untouched; greater freedom had come, but not as much freedom as the common man enjoyed in socialist countries. Racism in the South and capitalism everywhere had to be fought; "the Negro intelligentsia must assert its influence on the masses of Negro labor" and align it with the world labor movement, especially in Asia and Africa; "of which today Black America dare not talk."[35]

Du Bois looked with interest and favor on the rise of civil rights activism by blacks in the South, starting in 1956 with the Montgomery, Alabama, bus boycott. He compared the nonviolence of Martin Luther King to that of the late Mahatma Gandhi and was particularly pleased that the masses of ordinary people had apparently committed themselves to the struggle.[36] The epochal Supreme Court decision of 1954 in *Brown* v. *The Board of Education,* with its tantalizing phrase "all deliberate speed," was obviously not going to be implemented with zeal, he felt, and he blamed the leadership of Eisenhower for the failure of enforcement in a recalcitrant South. A leader stigmatized as a Communist had no role to play in that struggle, but it came as no surprise to Du Bois either that leadership had come from the South or that the civil rights movement had met with such violence.

Unable either to publish freely or to travel, Du Bois continued to write. Between 1955 and the spring of 1957 he wrote the first draft of the *Black Flame* historical trilogy, comprising some eleven hundred printed pages. By 1960, he had completed his final autobiography, subsequently recovered in 1966 and edited for publication by Herbert Aptheker. According to Shirley Graham Du Bois, the author had been unable to find a publisher in the United States and had sent the manuscript to Moscow for publication.[37] Refused permission in 1956 to travel to the People's Republic of China to participate in the celebration of the two hundred and fiftieth anniversary of Benjamin Franklin's birth, Du Bois wrote a small book on Franklin to mark the occasion.[38] But as a veteran traveler and a man honored more outside his country than within, Du Bois was elated when the Supreme Court ruled that the affidavit concerning Communist party membership required by the Passport Division exceeded the authority granted to the Department of State by the Congress of the United States.

Almost immediately, on August 8, 1958, Du Bois set out on a tour that took him to Britain, France, Czechoslovakia, the German Democratic Republic, the USSR (a three-month stay), and the People's Republic of China (in February and April, 1959). In Prague and Berlin he received honorary doctorates, which he was never to receive from a white American university. In Moscow Du Bois had a

long interview with Nikita Krushchev, in which he suggested to the
Soviet leader the establishment of the Institute of African Studies in
Moscow. In Moscow on May Day 1959, Du Bois received the Lenin
Peace Prize. For Du Bois, the Soviet Union was not perfect: there
was "power rivalry and personal jealousy," inefficiency in some respects, and unanswered questions about social roles and expecta-
tions. But there were also studied attempts to encourage progress.
The success exemplified by Sputnik, the pioneer man-made
satellite, "was more than triumph in physics; it was the growth of a
nation's soul, the confidence of a great people in its plan and future."[39]

Du Bois entered China in the dark ages of its relationship with the
United States. His passport specifically forbade him to visit there,
but he openly advertised his presence in a country whose warmth of
welcome apparently surpassed that of any other country. He had
visited China previously in 1936 en route from Russia to Japan, but
since then he had had little contact with a nation still officially at
war with the United States after the Korean hostilities. He wanted to
visit the country "because it is a land of colored people," and
because, he said, of the hostility of the State Department. His
interview with Mao Tse-tung lasted four hours, Du Bois recalled,
and he dined twice with Chou En-lai. His ninety-first birthday was
observed with a radio broadcast from Peking. With Shirley Graham
Du Bois he traveled thousands of miles to visit the major cities of the
People's Republic, meeting "universal goodwill and love, such as we
never expected." The "secret" of China, as he saw it, was that its
people were convinced "that human nature in some of its darkest re-
cesses can be changed, if change is necessary." Chinese history,
much more so than the history of American slavery, epitomized
man's inhumanity to man; yet the soul of the nation had been
cleansed by the struggles of Sun Yat-sen and of the Communists led
by Mao Tse-tung: "Oh beautiful, patient, self-sacrificing China,
despised and unforgettable, victorious and forgiving, crucified and
risen from the dead."[40]

Du Bois returned to the United States on July 1, 1959; three
months later his passport was confiscated. The following year,
however, when he was refused permission to travel to Ghana for the
inauguration of its first President, Kwame Nkrumah, the State Department was forced to reconsider its decision, almost certainly be-

cause of protest from Africa. On this visit in 1960 Du Bois received the invitation that was to shape his last days: he was urged by Nkrumah to return to Ghana and begin preparation of an *Encyclopedia Africana,* an undertaking he had twice attempted, in 1909 and again in 1934. He recognized that at ninety-three he could barely hope to sketch the planning stages of the project, which he conceived as including scholars from all over the world, white and black. But before leaving Ghana to go on to Nigeria for the inauguration of Nnamdi Azikiwe as Governor-General of the Federation of Nigeria, and thence home to the States, Du Bois sent Nkrumah a copy of the poem "Ghana Calls," signifying his acceptance of the project.

In the last stage of his life, from the end of World War II to his death, Du Bois was as much directed by history as he was master of his fate. Events overtook him, and at no time more so than in his final return to Africa in response to Nkrumah's invitation. In the *Autobiography,* completed only recently, he had written that he wanted to be buried in New Haven beside his grandfather. His love of Berkshire County in Massachusetts, where he had been born, was considerable. When his daughter Yolande died in Baltimore during his visit to Nigeria in 1960, he buried her beside her mother and her infant brother in Great Barrington. But he would be buried elsewhere, in part no doubt because of loyalty to his second wife. In any event, he wished to spend his last days in America. The rise of independent Africa and the chance of a last and crowning work of scholarship altered his perception of the proper end of his life. In "Ghana Calls," he lamented, "I became old; old, worn and gray/ . . . I walked with Death," and he wondered "Were all dreams true?/And what in truth was Africa?" A seer had appeared to send him on his great journey to Russia, China, and—at last—to Africa:

> Here at last, I looked back on my Dream;
> I heard the Voice that loosed
> The Long-locked dungeons of my soul
> I sensed that Africa had come
> Not up from Hell, but from the sum of Heaven's glory.

Every good man must turn his face "from reeking West whose day is done"; dark America must come "with us" to the newest world, "And Africa leads on/Pan Africa!"[41]

The greatest aspect of the challenge for him was probably not so much the chance to contribute to African glory and cultural identity as to continue his discipleship to the power of work. Failing health in his old age often made him depressed and discontented. Willing to accept death, he nevertheless submitted to life-preserving abdominal operations and to a process of treatment for physical rejuvenation in Rumania in 1961 and 1962. Du Bois understood that he would probably never see his native land again. Before leaving America on October 5, 1961, he underscored the finality of his departure by disposing of a good part of his large library, selling his house, and consigning his considerable collection of personal papers to the guardianship of the scholar Herbert Aptheker in New York. The most momentous step, however, was to apply for membership in the Communist party of the United States.

He had been long in making the decision, he wrote on October 1, 1961, to Gus Hall, chairman of the party, "but at last my mind is settled." He traced the development of socialist influence on him from his days as a student in Berlin to the present time, including the friendship of Mary White Ovington, William English Walling, and Charles Edward Russell of the young NAACP, his brief membership in the Socialist party in 1911 and 1912, his initial difficulty in understanding the Russian Revolution, and his visits to communist countries over the preceding thirty-five years. "Today I have reached a firm conclusion," he wrote; "Capitalism cannot reform itself; it is doomed to self-destruction. No universal selfishness can bring social good to all. Communism . . . is the only way of human life." Listing the ten general aims of the American Communists, Du Bois concluded that "no nation can call itself free which does not allow its citizens to work for these ends."[42]

He was admitted to the party on October 13, 1961, eight days after he had left New York for Ghana. The New York *Times* noted that he had reached his decision at a time when the Communist party faced a fine of ten thousand dollars a day if it refused to register as a subversive group under the 1950 Internal Security Act.[43] On October 9, 1961, the Supreme Court, in *Communist Party of the United States* v. *Subversive Activities Control Board,* upheld the government's right to compel registration of the party by refusing to reconsider such a ruling of the previous June. Du Bois had fled the country in anticipation of this decision, afraid of being forbidden to leave the United States in its aftermath, and his decision to join the party was made with the Supreme Court ruling specifically in mind.

Although the decision was unpopular with a large number of people and confusing to others, Du Bois' entry into the Communist party epitomized the changes that had overtaken him in the last two decades. For the historian Rayford W. Logan, friend and associate of Du Bois since 1921, his " 'two-ness,' the conviction that he could not be both a Negro and an American may well be one explanation" of this act and of his later renunciation of his citizenship in Ghana in 1963.[44] For David Du Bois, stepson of the author, his decision to join the party was more a political act than it was an ideological or philosophical act. It had been designed as a gesture of defiance against the most powerful interests in the United States.[45] Aptheker's opinion of Du Bois' motive is similar: "He saw it as embodying the best in the radical and liberating tradition of this country and the best in the egalitarian and militant traditions of all humanity."[46]

The wonder is not that Du Bois joined the party in 1961, but that he had not done so before. His support of the USSR was as old as the nation itself, although his understanding of the aims of communism changed over the years. He admitted in 1959 that "with New England conservatism" he had favored the Mensheviks over the Bolsheviks in 1917 "until Kerensky began to play the fool for capitalism."[47] Independent of any knowledge of Lenin's interpretation of the role of European colonialism in Africa and its effect on international power, as George Shepperson has remarked, Du Bois had arrived at similar conclusions by May 1915, when he published his "African Roots of the War" in the *Atlantic Monthly*.[48] After his visit to Russia in 1926, an enthusiastic defense of the Soviet Union became a fixed part of his teachings. Perhaps his last published expression of a desire for social and political change without revolution, which he had decried in 1909 in the last line of *John Brown* as being "always a loss and a lowering of ideals," appeared in *The World and Africa* in 1947. Marxism, he wrote then, is no panacea; achieve the ideal goals by other means, "and Communism need not be feared."[49] By 1957 he was making an important distinction: "The violence that accompanies the revolution is not the revolution."[50] In 1960, Du Bois declared in Ghana that socialism is the "panacea of the evils of the world in the 21st century."[51]

Du Bois' commitment to Marxism grew steadily during the early

years of the Soviet Union; his study of Leninist thought began with
the onset of the Depression; and his acceptance of the communist
milieu in the United States dated from the late forties. From this
time, and certainly after his trial, Du Bois was philosophically a
Marxist-Leninist. There is a sameness about almost every speech
and article produced in this period, with only the autobiographical
elements of *In Battle for Peace* and aspects of the trilogy *The Black
Flame* adding significantly to the recurring themes of socialism and
anticolonialism. The sameness came not from a desire to be an ideological parrot, but from a deeply felt sense of rededication to the
philosophical quest that he had consciously abandoned when he
embraced the role of liberal propagandist. Late in 1948 J. Saunders
Redding traced accurately and prophetically the basic patterns of
Du Bois' life. The first phase was a search for truth, trusting in the
power of its revelation to affect change. The second phase was a
move to propagandize and popularize that truth. The third phase
emphasized the security and survival of the race during the
Depression. In the last and present phase, Du Bois "has gone back to
the first path now, and it is likely that he will remain in it until his
journey's done."[52]

In the end, Du Bois did indeed return to a search for truth—not
the truth of social science that he had left in 1910 and from which
he was further disbarred in 1944, but the science of socialist logic,
over which he had vacillated since at least 1911. The sameness in
much of his last writing was the mark of a new discipline and a new
spirit of sacrifice. He divested himself of the accoutrements of
liberal pragmatism that had served him well, if inadequately, for a
quarter of a century as editor of the *Crisis*. He almost completely
abandoned the last remnants of that combination of liberal idealism
and piety which had given *The Souls of Black Folk* its remarkable
flavor. And he strove to erase from his writing the confabulation of
the self, the deliberate design of the ego as hero, which had been a
principal source of dramatic power in his propagandistic literature
from the dawn of the century.

A major indicator of Du Bois' sense of intellectual integrity, and a
mark of his clear sense of purpose in life, was his refusal to indulge
himself in theoretical and philosophical writing. A would-be philosopher at Harvard, he had accepted with finality William James's
advice to him to steer clear of the vocation in spite of Du Bois' inter-

est and abilities. Du Bois was no Marxist theoretician, but his acceptance of Marxism-Leninism had philosophical implications. The authentic American buffer between moral idealism and the abuses of materialistic logic, the pragmatic method had served Du Bois personally as a link between his intense moral fervor and the soulless empiricism of the social sciences, providing the shaky philosophic base for his career as liberal propagandist. In his last years, indeed, starting with his return in 1934 to Atlanta and a career of academic sociologist, he revived his faith in the empirical sciences but began to transfer his philosophic allegiance from pragmatism to dialectical materialism. Most of the dialectical issues did not interest him enough to be reflected in his polemical or fictional work, but the absolutes of Marxist-Leninist thought led him to repudiate the relativism of the pragmatic method and to accept once again the existence of that objective truth of which both natural and social science are necessary parts, and which Lenin argued most successfully in his *Materialism and Empirio-Criticism.*

Finding a more secure philosophic base and discovering truth in radical socialist logic did not bring Du Bois emotional security. Truth exacted payment, and the price was his estrangement from the majority of the black leadership and consequently from the masses whose opinions they helped to mold. The journalist H. L. Moon summed up the reaction of one section of that class: "His generation was during the thirties and early forties. He truly inspired us and nurtured all that had intellectual aspirations. He held our banner aloft. Most of us still have great reverence for him. But we feel that he in recent years has departed from his original position, and is pursuing a path that we of the NAACP do not choose to follow. Very, very few of us go along with him today." Less than a decade after Du Bois' death, Julius Lester took issue with "many young black radicals today" who, out of antipathy to the Communist party, "find Du Bois' membership a fact they would rather forget. They want to blame it on his age."[53] The irony of his last years was that Du Bois moved toward communism at the very moment that black America turned to a revival of extreme nationalism and activism to recover and assert the rights for which he had long toiled; his path to liberation and theirs radically diverged. By the middle of the fifties Du Bois was aware of this isolation, and deeply moved by it. His response was in one respect the same as that in 1910, when he had left Atlanta University, and in 1926, when he had split the Harlem Renaissance with his attacks on the new freedom of the younger writers. In such times of crisis, he turned to the writing of fiction. In *The Black Flame,* published in 1957, 1959, and 1961, he looked back on the history of black Americans from the end of Reconstruction to the present, a period through which he had lived and in which he had been an unsurpassed force in the interpretation of his people's experience. Through the novels' blend of fact and fiction, he confided his hopes, dreams, and intuitions as he neared the end of his long life.

CHAPTER THIRTEEN

The Black Flame

When we live through a great series of human events, we do not necessarily see them, nor can we arrange them to fit logically into the world we already know. Perhaps (and this complicates understanding even more) current events clearly show us that our interpretation of the past has been wrong, that only through the present can we see the past. Time, in other words, shifts—future is partly the past and the past is future.   (Du Bois, 1961)

TWENTY-NINE YEARS AFTER the publication of *Dark Princess,* Du Bois produced the first book of a trilogy designed to follow the history of the black man in the United States from 1876 to 1954. *The Black Flame* includes *The Ordeal of Mansart, Mansart Builds a School,* and *Worlds of Color.*[1] The period described in *The Black Flame* fell entirely within Du Bois' own life-span. As scholar and journalist, he had examined and commented on most of the personalities and events important to black Americans as a group during this time. The attempt to compose a trilogy near his ninetieth birthday testifies to the confidence Du Bois felt in his intellectual powers in the twilight of his life. To the end, he believed he had something more to say to the world about the black folk behind the veil, adding to the thousands of pages he had already written in their defense and for their celebration. It is tempting to think of *The Black Flame* trilogy as a summary of Du Bois' previously expressed wisdom on Afro-America. In fact, the work attempts something more than this. It is a final revaluation of his perception of a nation and its history, of his own attitudes and philosophy, in the light of new experiences which were stimulating a still active intelligence.

The Black Flame relates the story of the birth, life, and death of Manuel Mansart, and of the growth of his family unto a fourth generation. Mansart is born in the year 1876, on the night when his

266

father is killed by a white mob. Mansart moves from South Carolina to Georgia during his youth, attends college in Atlanta, and becomes a schoolteacher in a small Georgia town. He begins a life devoted to the education of black youth. His career takes him back to the fast-rising Atlanta, where he eventually becomes head of the impoverished black school system, then moves to the leadership of the state agricultural and mechanical school for blacks. He is first principal, then president, of the institution. Such positions of influence bring Mansart repeatedly into conflict with the white men whose power over black lives is almost total. Mansart is intelligent but not brilliant. He wrestles constantly with the meaning of the world about him. Puzzled by the distribution of power, he is disturbed by what appears to be the destiny of his race to be little more than hewers of wood and drawers of water. The world of finance fascinates him. Similarly, he wishes to understand the world outside of Georgia, indeed outside of the United States. The wars and conquests of the great European nations distress and confuse him. To the end of his life, Mansart ponders the questions of race, power, and the individual conscience. The trilogy attempts to provide the answers.

Mansart marries a young girl from a background as humble as his own. They struggle through a marriage that is strained by relative poverty, sexual inhibition, and differences in temperament and intelligence. Children are born, grow up, and meet their several destinies. One is hanged. Another finds joy in music and in her husband. A third becomes a wealthy but corrupt politician in Chicago. A fourth climbs his way, at times unethically, to a judgeship in New York. None appreciates or understands the mind and spirit of Mansart. They do not break with him, but neither do they feel for him any profound attachment. They misunderstand or refuse to accept his role as a link between white power and black ambition. Only his daughter Sojourner, a plain, neglected creature, shares with him a common bond in their love of music. His grandchildren are mostly Northerners and know little of him. One commits suicide. Another grows to hate his mother and exiles himself from America. A third surrenders to the materialism that Mansart daily repudiated in his life and work. Mansart's family is therefore ordinary as earth, bearing a tall tree here and there, but common and human in its strength and weakness.

Parallel to the growth of the Mansart clan, Du Bois traces the fortunes of several white families who represent business, aristocracy, education, and labor in Southern life. One character, John Breckenridge Du Bignon Baldwin, represents the alliance by marriage of three dominant families: the South Carolina Breckenridges of the old plantation aristocracy; the Du Bignons of New Orleans, with ancestors at the French Court; and the Baldwins, poor whites distinguished by one intellectually and morally gifted member, Dr. Sophocles Thrasymachus Baldwin. The poor whites are best represented by the Scroggs family. They struggle no less intensely than the blacks for economic security in the face of rapacious business and conniving aristocracy. Their hatred of blacks makes them easy pawns in the efforts of business to control labor. Untutored and graceless, the Scroggses can only move upward in the world. A Scroggs marries a daughter of Arnold Coypel, a saintlike educator from North Carolina, who has quietly championed the rise to power of Manuel Mansart. Another white family, that of President Sheldon of black Atlanta University, has a less fortunate history. John Sheldon, the son, rises with the fortunes of the Pierce family in Atlanta and then kills himself in 1929. His sister marries John Pierce III and suffers physically and emotionally during their self-imposed exile in France, where their radical but ineffectual son is reared. These intricate genealogical lines and ties are charted carefully, through not flawlessly, by Du Bois.[2] Together, the white families represent that part of the white world which most powerfully affects the fate of black Americans living in the South. Unlike *Dark Princess, The Black Flame* is not satisfied with a muted reference to whites. The white characters are in no sense secondary to the action. The trilogy is concerned with the nature of power in the world, and power rests with the whites.

The relationship between the black and white families of *The Black Flame* appears tenuous at first but is deeper in reality. Mansart's father is killed trying to help the Du Bignon Breckenridges. Mansart's greatest support in his career comes from Jean Du Bignon, a white woman of slight African ancestry, who chooses public membership in the black world against the wishes of the Du Bignon family head. The daughter of Arnold Coypel, Zoe, who marries Abe Scroggs, sets Bruce Mansart on the way to the gallows when she inadvertently causes him to be mauled by the town police after the

black man refuses to yield a sidewalk to her party. The wealthy John
Baldwin, son of Dr. Sophocles Thrasymachus Baldwin, is a trustee
of Mansart's college and both a help and a hindrance to the black
man in running the school. Beyond the personal ties, there is the
powerful yoke of financial and political control. John Pierce and
John Baldwin, leaders of business, dominate politics and finance in
Georgia. Their decisions affect not only the running of Mansart's
college but also the daily lives of the black masses in their search for
employment and a decent wage. The whites and blacks of *The
Black Flame* are always intensely aware of each other. Divisions
within these two basic groups intensify the awareness, as they
maneuver for influence in the rising Southland.

But Du Bois' fictional gallery is only half the story. History is the
foundation of the trilogy. Historic figures pass swiftly through the
pages of *The Black Flame,* often in close touch with its fictional
characters. Tom Watson, Huey Long, Henry W. Grady, Booker T.
Washington, Theodore Roosevelt, Woodrow Wilson, Harry Hopkins, Franklin Roosevelt, Hitler, Stalin, and Du Bois himself,
scarcely disguised as one James Burghardt, are among the actors.
Their position is not simply to provide rubrics for the fictional world
but to participate directly in the passage of the history they make.
Du Bois also brings forward lost names of black history, minor
figures like Heman Perry, H. S. Doyle, or Madame Walker, whose
efforts in finance or politics or fashion, against great odds, were
remarkable. He telescopes repeatedly between the more minute
figures of his fictional world, especially those in the Mansart family,
and the epic sweep of historical continuity. Along with the famous
personalities go famous events, coming to the forefront of the story
like characters themselves: the Atlanta riot of 1906, the first world
war, the Harlem Renaissance, the collapse of the American financial world in 1929, the New Deal, the second world war, the Korean
conflict, and the Supreme Court desegregation decision of 1954.
Each character and each event has to be related to the total ambition of *The Black Flame.* Each reflects in its presentation Du Bois'
brooding on that riddle of the sphinx to the solution of which he
devoted his lifework: the mystery of the world and its injustices, the
lowly position of his own people in the hierarchy of race, and the
fate of the man of principle in a world hostile to ideal.

Manuel Mansart stands at the center of the book yet paradoxically is almost peripheral to its historical action. There are few triumphant heroes in *The Black Flame*. Indeed, only Franklin Delano Roosevelt rises to such stature, through Du Bois' depiction of his physical, intellectual, and spiritual ordeals and triumphs. Other men, such as Mansart and Coypel, cling just as tenaciously to virtue, but end their lives as figures of pathos. For such men can do little in the face of all-powerful history. Du Bois' inability to place Mansart in an overtly heroic light points to the changes that had overtaken his view of the black world since the days in which Matthew Towns struggled and triumphed in *Dark Princess. The Black Flame* reflects a less sanguine estimation of black—and human—potential than that described in Du Bois' earlier fiction. The heady scheme of a plot of darker peoples against white dominion is replaced by a tortured questioning about the future of the race and a more varied rendition of the white world. Du Bois' primary emphasis on black affairs, the near chauvinism of his middle age, has given ground to a more universal concern. He who had appeared to threaten racial war was now preaching the imperative of peace. The white world was no longer the specific enemy of the black man. Though *The Black Flame* is vague in its heroes, it is clear in its villain. Capitalism, hydra-headed, is the ultimate evil. Injustices flow from the fangs of ravenous business; even racial prejudice is subordinate to its economics. In this respect, what Henry Steele Commager has written of John Dos Passos' trilogy is even more true of *The Black Flame:* "It is a kind of Domesday Book, a Calendar of Sin, an Index Expurgatorius of economic malpractices."[3]

The historical novel is one of the more torpid genres, and *The Black Flame* does appear sluggish at times. Du Bois did not submit his manuscript to the process of intense revision that had marked the preparation of *Black Reconstruction in America.* "Time," he wrote in 1957, "is running out." In writing the trilogy, he hoped to "rescue" from his long experience "something of what I have learned and conjectured and thus I am trying by the method of historical fiction to complete the cycle of history which has for a half century engaged my thought, research and action." As a trained historian, he had gathered as many of the available facts as possible; as a creative artist he had "added the fiction of interpretation so as to make a reasonable story. I may have blundered in places; I may have widely misinterpreted what seemed truth to me. But I have tried and I believe the effort was worth while. Here lies, then, I hope, more history than fiction, more fact than assumption, much truth and no falsehood" (I, 315-316).

Du Bois, in starting his story in 1876, was picking up the thread of history where he had left it in closing *Black Reconstruction,* which charts the years between 1860 and 1880. The trilogy opens with the drama of the return to power of property. Three basic forces meet and press for influence. The old planter class, soon to be reinforced by Northern conservative business, is represented by Colonel Breckenridge. Labor comes to him to seek an alliance and direction. But labor is divided between the poor whites, led in Breckenridge's territory by members of the Scroggs clan, and the dispossessed blacks, whose spokesman is Mansart's father, Tom. Both Scroggs and Mansart recognize that their groups have been used as tools of the planter class. The poor whites have stocked the Klan and subdued the blacks in spite of the loss of the Civil War. The blacks, on the contrary, represent a plentiful supply of cheap labor. They threaten the economic hopes of the poor whites, preventing unionization and better working conditions. As long as the whites refuse to work side-by-side with blacks, the planters control both groups. It is therefore in the interests of the Breckenridges to keep the races apart. Racial bigotry and all its results — poverty, crime, lynching, ignorance — stem from the power of property, which is a force above race. Du Bois' history is divided between sympathy and praise for those men, black and white, who seek to change the temper of life by weakening the grip of capitalism, and censure for those who are capitalism's willing tools.

Manuel Mansart is privileged to be close to some important events of post-Reconstruction history. He is a sophomore in high school when Tom Watson leads the Populist movement against capital. The portrait of Watson is one of the most detailed among the historical figures of the book, especially in his relationship to Sebastian Doyle, the black minister who becomes one of his guides and friends. In their unity, these men are attacking the roots of the racial and economic problems of the South. The young Mansart is thus educated into seeing "that more often than not what he called the 'problems' of his race were in essence problems of all men in similar positions" (I, 126). Mansart is present at the Atlanta Cotton States Exposition on September 18, 1895, when a new black leader speaks to an important gathering of blacks and whites. Booker T. Washington's speech signals a new force in Afro-American affairs; his praise of a racial division of labor and social separateness adds new strength to the forces of property. While Washington plays no great role in *The Black Flame,* the impact of his philosophy helps to shape the history of the South. With the blatantly racist politicians James K. Vardaman of Mississippi and Ben Tillman of South Carolina and Thomas Dixon the novelist, the rise of Washington brings the counteraction of the Niagara Movement and the foundation of the NAACP. The growth of industrial trusts and monopolies marks the further triumph of property. The price of Southern white labor is the disfranchisement of the black man, his removal from traditional areas of employment, and his humiliation through segregationist practices. The abuse of the black man is the foundation for the rise of the New South.

The disfranchisement of the black voter through unscrupulous and often brutal means was, in Du Bois' view, the key to all other deprivations. Washington's 1895 speech had practically assented to disfranchisement as a voluntary concession to the reality of power. In place of the vote, the black man depended on the good will of the white electorate. The results were disastrous. The Atlanta riot of September 1906 is a focal point of the first book of *The Black Flame.* Rendered as a cataclysmic force by which the hand of an avenging God shakes the world, the riot is seen as the natural result of the racial hatred preached by white demagogues in order to keep the races apart under an economic order prescribed by capitalism. The consciences awakened by the riot can do little to change the fundamental order of life in the South, but there is at least a beginning. Black businesses arise in spite of limited opportunity, so that the black community, "in its search for wealth, with its ups and downs — on the whole was pressing forward" (I, 297).

"The Corporation was the Frankenstein of the 20th Century, contrived by the lawyers of the 19th. By 1950 in America it would be the Robot ruler of Man. It had 'neither Body to be kicked nor Soul to be damned'; but in the present century, it owned the Earth and enslaved Mankind" (I, 261). Du Bois identified the year 1900 as the beginning of the "Age of Big Business." A natural result of the triumph of business was the development of the United States as a colonial power. But racism, as well as profit, dictated the imposing of power on Africa and India. The novel stresses the conspiratorial nature of modern colonialism. Representatives of the white race meet on a sumptuous yacht that takes them to a castle on a Caribbean isle. There they talk and listen to speeches analyzing the world chaos of which the Civil War, recently ended, was only one example. The meeting elects Cecil Rhodes as "Grand Commander" of a movement to ensure the supremacy of the white race through the execution of a fourfold program. The aim is to expose the truth of the world to the American North, misled by fanatics into war; to "beat the Negroes back to their kennels"; to control "and cajole" white labor; and to "consolidate capital into imperial control of the world; guide world trade and monopolize gold and credit" (I, 89).

No significant event of the twentieth century is unrelated to these twin strains of race and capital, although the trilogy never again alludes to the organization of which Rhodes was allegedly the head. The bitter American antiblack riots of 1919, the year that Du Bois regarded as the worst for the freedman, are the bloody result of theories of race. The collapse of Wall Street puts a temporary halt to the career of business in the United States and the world, but sets the stage for the most heroic American figure of the century and of *The Black Flame,* Franklin Roosevelt. For Du Bois, Roosevelt's greatness lay in his conversion to socialist thought as represented in the New Deal, showing his ability to move past his aristocratic bias when faced by the distress of the American poor: "He believed in private wealth, hereditary property and investment. But he was honest; he could look at facts. He could do right even if it clashed with inherited predilections" (II, 335). During Roosevelt's presidency, black America was represented as it had never been before. Du Bois stressed also the physical suffering that was a part of Roosevelt's daily life; years before, the *Crisis* had jeered at that suffering.[4] In Du Bois' analysis, the second world war and Harry Truman interrupted what might have been the socialization of America and the world: "None can say how far Franklin Roosevelt would have gone in reorganizing the economy of the nation if the work of the first eight years of his reign had continued and expanded. We might now live in a different world. But war intervened and once again, as so often in the past, ruined the future of mankind" (III, 175). With the passing of Roosevelt, capitalism reasserted its sovereignty in the United States.

The long historical review of *The Black Flame* ends in optimistic
confusion. The Soviet Union is the hope of the world, preventing the
apocalypse of racial war by splitting the European camp and siding
with the darker peoples. Jean Du Bignon sees it all clearly: socialism
is succeeding and will include the whole civilized world before long.
This success drives big business in the United States toward fascism,
using repressive forces to control thought and expression. "This is
succeeding today. But tomorrow it will fail. Americans are not complete fools not will they remain perpetual cowards" (III, 326). The
Supreme Court decision of 1954 excites some of the characters, but
the narrator of *The Black Flame* reacts little. The trilogy ends with
a summary of the state of the Union and the world. In his old age
Mansart rages against the futility of war: "Down with war! Never
again war! War is the bottomless depth to which human beings have
fallen in this 20th century of the miscalled Prince of Peace!" (III,
327).

Dismissing many of the representatives of the black leadership in
America and Africa as spineless and venal, Du Bois dramatized
what he felt to be the spiritual sickness of a corrupt class. In a
masquelike scene around Mansart's deathbed, members of his family take turns in listing the ills of Afro-American life: "Oh, I am
ashamed, ashamed of my people. We have lost all clarity of vision,
of purpose. We have forgotten our purple history, of endless resistance to white terror, of suffering which made us strong, of struggle
which made us wise." The past work of the NAACP is acknowledged, but there is gloom about its present and future role. "Our
Congressmen are for the most part nonentities. Our dozen or so
legislators champion no great causes. Our judges almost all hew to
the standard line: it's safe that way." A dirge at the close mourns the
decaying quality of Afro-American life, the passing of an age of serious effort and racial pride, of love of culture and a search for order:
"Where is the outburst of literature which we began a generation
ago—the poetry and music, the dance and drama? In the last
decade we have not produced a poem or a novel, a history or play of
stature—nothing but gamblers, prizefighters and jazz . . . Once we
could hear Shakespeare in Harlem" (III, 345-346).

Although this masque involves members of the Mansart family,
its political criticism belongs to the historical, or nonfictional, half
of *The Black Flame*. Du Bois' bitter words about Afro-America in

the mid-fifties should not obscure, however, the racial bias that is integral to his historiography. Du Bois attacks capital, but he attempts to make heroes out of fumbling black capitalists. His praise for Roosevelt is almost total, yet he advances racism as the main reason for the war with Japan over which Roosevelt presided. He gloats over Japanese victories against the forces commanded by Roosevelt; yet he recognizes that the "colored" Japanese were thoroughly devoted to capitalism, whereas Roosevelt was at least inclined toward Marxism. His closing tirade against war does not conceal the pride which he felt in writing about the deeds of black warriors. In addition, Du Bois sometimes makes questionable accusations and insinuations. One sympathetic critic has noted "a literary tendency on Du Bois' part which took the form of rather exaggerated assertions" as well as, at other times, an imprecise symbolism.[5]

Du Bois clearly would have been less unhappy under capitalism if more blacks had been successful capitalists. He would have railed less against war, if black victories were in the offing. The result in *The Black Flame* is that history is seen from the dark underside of America. Though this view is sometimes distorted, it is still vital to the general perspective. *The Black Flame* is also written by a man who has suffered at the hands of history. Du Bois' depiction of individual historical personages is not always vivid, although there are exceptions, as in the case of Tom Watson. But he was writing essentially two stories: one is based on historical fact; the other is that of the life of Manuel Mansart and his family. The Mansart story appears at first only to facilitate the telling of history; in the end, it both complements and modifies what Du Bois has advanced as plain facts. Du Bois did not intend to confound the reader for the sake of confusion. It was his hope that somewhere between both ways, between academic analysis and the intuitions of the fictive artist, the truth would be found by those who sought it. The "eternal paradox of history," Du Bois wrote at the end of *The Ordeal of Mansart,* is the discovery of truth in the absence of personal involvement or completely reliable witness. "After action and feeling and reflection are long past, then from writing and memory we may secure some picture of the total truth, but it will be sorely imperfect, with much omitted, much forgotten, much distorted . . . There is but one way to meet this clouding of the facts and that is by the use of imagination where documented and personal experience are lacking" (I, 315-316).

Who is Manuel Mansart? Born in the midst of bloodshed on the night of his father's murder in 1876, Mansart (man's art?) is intended to link the history of his race in America from the end of Reconstruction to the year 1954. He is anointed with his father's blood by his sybil-like grandmother, who presents him to the world in a pagan ritual: "Curse God! Ride, Devils of Hell, with the blood-bought baby! Burn! Kill! Burn! Crawl with the Snake! Creep and Crawl! Behold the Black Flame!" (I, 72). But Mansart's life from the outset is a repudiation of this call to vengeance. He is a dutiful and good-tempered child, attentive in school and open with people. Eventually the problems of race enter his young world. He retaliates stealthily against a white bully and his conscience bothers him thereafter: "Just where did white folk fit into this world? Were they all essentially evil? Or were some fairly good?" Manuel comes to dislike blanket condemnations of a people; "he wanted more unity in his world" (I, 119-120). He decides to avoid white people as much as possible but to treat them cordially and without prejudice when in their company. He settles down into a pragmatic approach to life, sensing that he is part of a vast social revolution which he cannot hope to understand fully.

Unconsciously Manuel Mansart is imposing his own definition on the terms used at his baptism: "I burn, I almost consume myself, I burn slow and dark but always, always . . . I am that Black Flame in which my grandmother believed and on whose blood-stained body she swore. I am the Black Flame, but I burn for cleaning, not destroying. Therefore I burn slow." Others burn with brighter flames; James Burghardt (named after one of Du Bois' cousins) is "crimson flame disciplined by his thought" (I, 313). The black flame of Mansart wavers in doubt and casts only a little light. But Mansart recognizes that it is his personal flame, which must be kept alive. He assumes the burden of his people. He will work slowly and steadily for their well-being, turning his back on promises of wealth and freedom. Faith, optimism, and hard work are the fuel for the black flame. Mansart often does not understand, but always he endures. He stands up for the virtuous life and resists corruption, but he seeks only quiet victories which leave him and his people free from enmity or pride. Often misunderstood, he suffers without complaint. His end is obscure; the tributes are mild, even critical. But he burns to the last with the black flame, faithful to his ideals and his loving perception of the world and his people. In his spirit, Mansart contains the best soul of the black folk, as Du Bois saw it.

Like John of *The Souls of Black Folk* and both Blessed Alwyn and Matthew Towns of the first two novels, Manuel represents more than the most common of black folk. He has the intelligence of a potential leader, a member of the talented tenth. The question is whether or not he will rise to his responsibilities. Mansart meets his duty in a way which makes him the most specifically committed of all Du Bois' characters. His significance, though, lies in the special nature of his character and opinions. Only late in life does Mansart begin to see the world in a way even remotely radical. Mansart's distaste for revolt arises out of his faith in the intentions of others. When his fellow students are hostile to Washington's accommodating speech of 1895, Mansart sympathizes with Tuskegee: "It was a shrewd speech, it was an answer to some counter-proposal not fully revealed; it was an offer to make great sacrifices which would be followed on the part of the best whites" (I, 129). Faced with the choice offered by the Populists, Mansart instictively reposes trust in the landed aristocracy, "the heirs, spiritual and temporal of the planters" (I, 127). His faith is in the Breckenridges and Baldwins of the Southern world, until he is slowly converted to a belief in radical socialism.

In addition, Mansart possesses the generosity to empathize with those who, mistakenly, consider him their enemy. He sees the poor white Scroggs as a man who has suffered under a poverty greater than his own, "fighting his way up and trying to drag up with him his family, friends and race." Mansart is willing, therefore, to endure the man's racist snubs. The result is the scorn of Mansart by those who cannot understand humility. His son Douglass calls him "a coward and a lick-spittle, an Uncle Tom and a white folks' 'nigger' " (II, 185). Years later, a black stranger in France repeats the slur: "You're a white folk's 'nigger,' Mansart. You've been kicked and walked on so much that you're used to it, and you wouldn't know what to do if you had the chance to do a little kicking yourself" (III, 45). His sons flee Georgia as soon as they can; Mansart is left to do the job of educating the masses.

Besides a general faith in human nature, Manuel is convinced to the end about the essential goodness of the American character. "This nation has been cruel to us—cruel and unfeeling. Yet at bottom, its heart is right. It will yet do us justly, love mercy and walk humbly with its God" (III, 274). To the end, also, he preserves his faith in certain aspects of segregation, especially the black school. Most of his attitudes are anathema to a younger generation. One member passes judgment on him as he dies: "We're here to watch the ending of a life. It was a good life but it was ineffective. It's up to us to carry it on and make it work for the future—the future of our colored people here in America; yes, and the future of mankind, too" (III, 344). But between Mansart's first maturity and his death at the age of seventy-eight, there are vital changes in the simple philosophy which has enabled him to rise and keep his position at his Georgia school. The radicalization of Manuel is a slow process that draws him surely away from the habits of a lifetime and the timidities of a gentle temperament. Radicalization means little to Mansart's fundamental dilemma; it represents instead a different response to his oldest question: "how shall integrity face Opposition? What shall Honesty do in the face of Deception, Decency in the face of Insult, Self-Defense before Blows? How shall Desert and Accomplishment meet Despising, Detraction and Lies? What shall Virtue do to meet Brute Force?" (I, 275). Fifty years before, Du Bois knew, he himself had examined John Brown's thundering reply, approved its radicalism, but fallen short of fully emulating it.

Mansart's drift away from racial provincialism and simplistic analysis of the world's problems begins in school. He meets Northern whites, notably a Miss Freiburg from Wellesley, whose ideas and example force him to think. The greater influence comes from Jean Du Bignon of Radcliffe College and the University of Chicago, who devotes her life to assisting Mansart run his college. But Du Bignon does not openly impose her views on her employer. Although a world trip organized by Du Bignon opens Mansart's eyes, he arrives at important transitional conclusions long before such a trip is planned. The constant frustration in running his black college is an education in itself. Mansart comes to see that his old view of Afro-Americans as "a chosen people, a group dedicated to the emancipation of the dark and tortured people of the world," is wrong. "Negroes were not exceptional in soul and sacrifice. They were just human. They had all human frailties, with some of the lower and meaner emphasized by what they had suffered. They were still a cramped and degraded people" (II, 160). Du Bignon sends Mansart away to see "a world divorced from the essentially trivial and temporary question of skin color" (III, 19).

Mansart goes to England, Europe, and Asia, where he meets people of ability and renown, reads and questions, and returns a changed man. He begins to have "a conception of the world as one unified dwelling place," and of himself "as part of humanity and not simply as an American Negro over against a white world" (III, 85). From this point near Mansart's sixtieth birthday, the road winds to the left. He sees the potential tragedy of his new universalism. He knows that his black students and "the seething dark millions back of them were melting away from his touch . . . Once they were all his people. He had had his arms about them and was protecting and guiding them. This was no longer true." The greater cause of peace and socialism, "the meaning of all life," has taken him from them. Mansart wishes to return to the old embrace. "And yet, if he and his folk were part of this wider world, how could he or they ever be really separate?" (III, 249). Faced with the "human ganglion" of modern Harlem, grinding out its "fatal vintage," Manuel stands speechless and bewildered (III, 328).

The dramatic material of Manuel Mansart's life, then, lies not in the changes in his beliefs but in the implications of those changes. Along with his discovery of the wider world comes a sudden awareness of art and culture, of which Mansart has known little or nothing. He is staggered by the museums of Europe, moved by the genius of Beyreuth. He returns home determined to plant lawns and hang paintings and display pieces of sculpture, dissatisfied with a campus which he sees for the first time as "ugly." There can be no escaping that this triumph of culture is at the expense of Manuel's old embrace of his people. The tirade against the people at the end of the trilogy may be traced to the Louvre in Paris or the temples of Japan. Manuel is surrendering to an irresistible alienation from his own society. He can no longer keep the faith. And it is clear that the Marxism which he imperfectly understands cannot replace the feeling of suffusion in a common past of suffering and joy, on which Mansart could draw while lost in his provincialism. With his loss of faith comes, too, the brooding suspicion of a life's work wasted toiling in the wrong fields.

On his deathbed Mansart succumbs to two hallucinations about the world's future. One is a journey into hell, with death by fire raining on the world's great cities; the other is a vision of the world at peace with itself, birds singing in the blue air. Thus, to the very end, Mansart moves in a haze of confusion. Old and new loves, visions, desires, and faiths are at war in his dying imagination. The conflicts of Mansart are the conflicts of his entire race; his confusion is their confusion. Only the rigidity of his moral beliefs prevents confusion from becoming delinquency, or self-doubt from becoming self-hate. Mansart steers a more perilous course than either Bles or Matthew before him. But like them, Mansart prevails over temptation and change by reliance on the fixed stars of truth and beauty, by loyalty to ethical and aesthetic absolutes. The questions posed as the dilemma of Mansart's life are thus answered. In the face of opposition, the individual of integrity must remain honest. Desert and accomplishment must bend to the task of life and counter despising, detraction, and lies. Not a modern political ideology but an age-old faith in moral absolutes is Du Bois' answer to the tragedy of history. From this response comes his final verdict on Mansart's life: "Over his dead body lay a pall of crimson roses, such as few kings have ever slept beneath" (III, 349).

In depicting Manuel Mansart, Du Bois was to some extent writing vicarious autobiography. But a complete accounting of Du Bois' personal investment in *The Black Flame* must go beyond the limitations of Manuel's intelligence and pacific spirit to another character who shares with Mansart the task of speaking — and living — for Du Bois within the pages of his trilogy.

Like Blessed Alwyn and Matthew Towns, Manuel Mansart relies heavily on a woman for guidance. Unlike the others, Mansart is himself never tempted from his ideals by any conniving black female such as Caroline Wynn or Sara Andrews. But his debt to Jean Du Bignon is profound. Du Bignon is black only according to the racist theory and practice of her country: she looks white, although there is no doubt about her partially African ancestry. Her decision to live the life of a black woman is a deliberate act, one against the wishes of her family. Both blacks and whites are hostile to her, but Du Bignon accepts the burden of their criticism out of a sense of loyalty and service to black people: "Acceptance would come. She would make it and it was the natural thing, for race was not color; it was inborn oneness of spirit and aim and wish; and this made this school her home; her very own" (II, 128).

Du Bignon represents the highest level of membership within Du Bois' talented tenth. A sociologist, she is thoroughly trained academically and socially for a position of leadership. To Mansart's gifts of the spirit, she adds the force of learning and intellect. Nor does Du Bois minimize the importance of style in his aristocracy. Etiquette, deportment, and eloquence are more than visible signs of superiority. They are instruments of leadership to be stimulated by constant practice. Du Bignon's function in Mansart's basically crude environment is to provide the knowledge of the larger world of refinement and discipline. This is not to say that Mansart lacks natural dignity, only that natural dignity is insufficient in a world where greed and ignorance thrive on every failing of the unsophisticated mind. Du Bignon schools Manuel in the full use of the power that comes with his position. She enables him to consolidate his authority until he is virtually above the control of the forces inimical to black development.

Du Bois introduced details of his life and temperament into three characters of *The Black Flame:* the intense radical intellectual and sociologist James Burghardt, who comes to Atlanta to teach at the turn of the century, plans a hundred-year study of blacks, writes a book attacking Booker T. Washington, and forms The Niagara Movement for radical reform in 1905; Mansart, especially in the last fifteen or twenty years of his life; and Jean Du Bignon. Like Du Bois, Du Bignon is trained in sociology and has a deep faith in the possibilities of a scientific analysis of human action. Although she is diverted from scholarship into service to President Mansart, she cherishes the hope of launching a broad study of racial relations in the South, using thinkers from both black and white colleges. The date and nature of her attempts closely parallel Du Bois' own revival in the forties of his early interest in empirical sociology. Du Bignon's determination is based on more than a nostalgia for the scholarly life. She sees a necessary and hopeless clash between Mansart's newly found desire for the expression of beauty about him and the poverty that starves all appreciation of the beautiful: "What was to be done about this? . . . Her idea, firmly fixed at first, was to achieve a scientific knowledge of the truth, even in sociology, a discovery of its rhythms, a realization of the possibility of prophecy. To this she still held" (III, 85). She faces within herself one dilemma which Du Bois himself never resolved, that between scholarship and the world of activism based on a knowledge of scholarship, between "pure" science and politics. She admits to herself that "despite her own purely scientific goal, she was really more interested in the uses of information than just in obtaining it" (III, 95). Like Du Bois, she surrenders to the activist call, though in a mainly clandestine way. The result is a process of radicalization that ends in her dismissal from Mansart's school and the end of her plans for a large-scale study.

There is a further paradox in the importance of scientific investigation to Jean Du Bignon, a paradox which troubled Du Bois deeply in his attempts to resolve the meaning of intelligence in a world of chaos. Du Bignon prizes sociological study not for its attempts at certitude, which she characterizes as a nineteenth century obsession, but for its increasing admittance of the elements of probability and prophecy: "We have come down from our high horse of measured certainty to the business of collecting with infinite pain the fact, and coming to possibilities and probabilities as to the real conclusions of science. In fact . . . we have opened the doors to our old friends, Chance and Free Will" (III, 314). Jean believes in the aggregate force of superior minds and in a brand of intuition that to the rest of the world often appears as the height of insanity. In the throes of a nervous breakdown, she babbles of a coming universe "with no assumptions of Space nor hypotheses of Time," of a black flame glowing "between the pillars of the universe, looming from Heaven to lowest Hell," of the black spirit reigning triumphant in a new world (III, 314-315). Although Du Bignon speaks these words in a moment of illness, her prophecy is part of a larger prophetic and visionary strain in the book. Mansart's deathbed visions of a world in flames and a world at peace have antecedents throughout the trilogy. The pagan prophesying at his birth is only the first example. Later, on a long train ride at the start of World War II, Mansart muses as the landscape flows by: "Then, suddenly, with startling clearness, out there in the night he seemed to see a great green Spider nesting in Hell, weaving an impenetrable Web. It sat in a pool of blood." Mansart is beset by a hallucination about the world's evil: "It was too horrible. It seemed to divide the Darkness from the Light and the White World fought the Dark World and both faced Death" (III, 163-164).

The Atlanta riot of 1906 is argued by one character to be the cause of the San Francisco earthquake, although the riot occurred five months after the earthquake: "Time is but our habit of thought. Reason is more than Time, and Deed embodies Reason . . . That murder and flame came from the hate and horror of Atlanta" (I, 250). The most sustained prophetic figure in the trilogy is old Dr. Baldwin, to whom radical wisdom has come in old age. Becoming more and more eccentric, he is restrained by his family but escapes to preach and prophesy to the people of Atlanta. An incredible figure with long white hair and black gown, he foretells the coming of a war, to begin in 1914 and last a century, with "interludes of Starvation and Insanity" (II, 29). Baldwin has escaped both the provincial prejudice of Georgia and the isolation of the scholar's study. He preaches against war, capitalism, and imperialism; he cries out for justice for the black man and colored peoples everywhere. He is soon committed to an asylum, but escapes. According to Du Bois, he and a band of followers set fire to Atlanta on May 21, 1917, the day when an entire square mile of the city was destroyed.

Thus the wisest people, like the fools in Shakespearean drama, appear as madmen to the rest of the world. The purpose of these concessions to the irrational in *The Black Flame* is, on one level, to defend the apocalyptic tone of impassioned radicalism, whose constant message promises the fire next time. Du Bois is defending, too, the vision behind his own dramatic historical analysis, behind his insistence on an almost religious division of the world into a new Manichaeism of capitalist power and irresistible socialism. More than this simple defense, though, is Du Bois' obvious belief in inspiration, the source of which is more elusive than mere learning or empirical effort. The man of social science and the poet had suppressed, except for relatively oblique manifestations in his fiction, his life-long impulse toward prophecy. Many of his essays threaten to become jeremiads, though necessarily reflecting the restraints imposed by Du Bois' education and experience: his love of order, of logic, of the classical middle way; his passion for respectability in spite of his rage; his desire to be understood and applauded and loved.

The flights of romantic imagination offered under the license of fiction reflect the tensions in Du Bois' apprehension of truth, but give scant notice of the explosions of moral indignation that empower them. Such are the drastic limitations of propaganda. The hero and heroine walking into the sunset at the close of a novel, as in *Dark Princess,* are the obverse rendition of Du Bois' rage for revenge at their enemies. On behalf of what he considered to be the eternal verities, Du Bois had not faith but fanaticism. Like many others, he felt profoundly the wrongs inflicted by evil in the world. It is given to far fewer to simmer through life with hatred for those wrongs, but Du Bois was certainly one of these. In his eyes, the change in Dr. Baldwin from scholar to apparent lunatic, then to arsonist, was a promotion and not a decline. As with the prophets of old, it was a sign of election to the highest office on earth. Only in the few scattered pieces of Du Bois' poetry does the volcanic anger begin to appear. He knew early that he had to endure the harness of practical restraint.

He was restrained throughout his life from giving expression to prophetic rage by more than the practical or the political. The unattractive aspect of Du Bois' personality — his lack of tact, his arrogance, and his coldness — concealed what was perhaps the most significant single force of his complex mind, shaping the basic choices of his life, influencing the quality and style of his vocation. That quality was Du Bois' deeply rooted sense of his humbleness in relation to the universe. In spite of his musings about descent from kings and his search for black power, Du Bois was fundamentally humble. He saw himself — and all men — as lowly in the face of the world. His gospel of work and his passion for service were both outward signs of the most fixed of his inner graces. This sense of lowness had nothing whatever to do with the pressure of white notions of black inferiority. From his sense of lowness came his nearly fanatic devotion to the absolute, his desire to submit to the imperatives of conscience. His own sense of humiliation made him rage at pride in others and act in ways that appeared to be both proud and sometimes malicious. To be sure, his sense of humility did not extend to preaching submission to the injustices that kept him and Afro-America in suppression. He made abundantly clear the difference between the absolute power of the ideal and the abuses of power common in the temporal world. He would bow before the force of infinite beauty, truth, and love, but never before the might of those who repudiated conscience and the ideal for their own selfish ends.

The doctrine of submission was an early and permanent part of Du Bois' expressed thought. In his tribute to Bismarck, paid at the

Fisk commencement of 1888, Du Bois warned of the difference between various types of achievement under explicitly moral terms. Bismarck's life illustrated the power of purpose, the force of an idea, he said. But black folk must beware the moral cost of Bismarck's life and not sacrifice a love of virtue, truth, and liberty simply for racial advancement.[6] Two years later, at the Harvard commencement, Du Bois was more precise. He adjudged the character of Jefferson Davis to be noble according to the standards of Teutonic civilization, but less than noble when judged by the standards of justice. Du Bois contrasted the Teutonic or white doctrine of force with what he believed to be the African doctrine of submission. Neither attitude was sufficient in itself. But however successful the white doctrine of the strong man in gaining its ends, in accumulating wealth and power, it could not serve the realities of the spiritual world without a recognition of the need for the black virtues of patience and humility.[7] This identification of humility as an African or black virtue persists in *The Souls of Black Folk.* On this theme Du Bois builds his case for the special humanity of a despised portion of the American people: "Around us the history of the land has centered for thrice a hundred years; out of the nation's heart we have called all that was best to throttle and subdue all that was worst; fire and blood, prayer and sacrifice, have billowed over this people, and they have found peace only in the God of Right." Elsewhere the voice of Time speaks a single message, from Goethe's *Faust: "Entbehren sollst du, sollst entbehren."* The same message warns Du Bois in the tragedy of his son's death: "But now there wails, on that dark shore within the Veil, the same deep voice, *Thou shalt forgo!* And all have I forgone at that command, and with small complaint."[8]

In spite of the "racial provincialism" which, Du Bois admitted, clouded his life during the following years, there is no mistaking the insistence on the same message in Du Bois' fictional world. He identified humility as the basis of John Brown's spirituality, even to Brown's surrender of life itself in becoming an instrument of the Lord's vengeance. The message of humility is embedded in the fictive setting of *The Quest of the Silver Fleece* and years later in *Dark Princess.* Zora, Bles, and Matthew rise to greatness by bowing down in submission to the laws of duty and right. They endure. And humility is the essence of Manuel Mansart, a humility that goes further into servility than in any other Du Bois hero, but which flows from the same vision of moral lowliness in the face of the ideal. And at the end of his life, Du Bois had not forgotten the text of the message. He quoted the same lines from Goethe to the African peoples in 1958, imploring them to recognize the need for sacrifice and for the surrender of freedom to the larger goal. Mansart's drift into radical thought derives as much from his humility as does his silence in the face of racist convention. Always there are goals larger than the personal victory, a cause greater than the saving of face. It is for this recognition that Du Bois sends Mansart into death with a tribute proper to a king. The meek shall inherit the earth.

For both Mansart and Du Bois, the essential warring of their lives ended not in resolution but with an inconclusive peace. "God is no playwright," Mansart remarks; "His lives end dimly, and without drama; they pile no climax on tragedy nor triumph on defeat. They end quietly or helplessly—they just end" (III, 343). Du Bois was surely musing through Mansart's words on the ending of his own life. A strong sense of approaching death had brought Du Bois to the point of whispering words "to the Almighty Dead, into whose pale approaching faces, I stand and stare; you whose thoughts, deeds and dreams have made men wise with all wisdom and stupid with utter evil." In the last thirty of his ninety years, he confessed, "the wraith of Death has followed me, slept with me and awakened and accompanied my day."[9]

Both Mansart and Du Bois went to their deaths uncertain of the worth of their lives. They could be certain, indeed, only of the indifference of the masses for whom they had made every sacrifice. For both men had elected to expend the energy of their years grappling, as on a darkling plain, with the dilemma of their blackness. Best described by Du Bois more than fifty years before *The Black Flame,* the dilemma of being black in America hovered over their lives and their every meaningful action like the force of Nemesis in another age. Life was a struggle, in which the final enemy was not poverty or injustice, but self-doubt and self-contempt. The field of battle was the psyche; the forces were—and are—the essential dualism of the black American, "an American, a Negro; two souls, two thoughts, two unreconciled strivings; two warring ideals in one dark body, whose dogged strength alone keeps it from being torn asunder." The history of the black American, Du Bois had noted in *The Souls of Black Folk,* "is the history of this strife,—this longing to attain self-conscious manhood, to merge his double self into a better and truer self."[10] The dutiful, humble, and courageous, such as Mansart or Du Bois, leave the field of battle on their shields. There is no higher honor, nor can anyone hope for a happier end. Nothing happened in the seventy-five years of Du Bois' adult life to change the basic struggle. Each act of his public life — the novels, the propaganda, the controversies — had its first and final justification in Du Bois' compulsion to resolve the mystery of being black in the world where he lived. It was the foundation and substance of his career; everything else was a variation on that theme.

The making of Manuel Mansart's story was the last creative act of Du Bois' life. He sought to enshrine, in what would be his last major statement, a reiteration of what once was best in his people and crucial to his own life. Though Mansart believes generally in Marxist theory by the end of his life, he has already demonstrated a moral magnificence beside which all political theory pales. His history is the history of the best human spirit facing the complex forces that swirl about man in his passage through life, clouding his perception of the events of which he is a part until, when all else is lost, old age brings clarity and wisdom. To pass through the haze of history with dignity calls for reliance on faith, humility, and courage. It is these qualities which Mansart possesses and exemplifies in his lifetime. They are prominent above the ideological rigidities, the sometimes wild accusations, the limitations of technique in what is an unfulfilled work of art. Faith, humility, and courage were Du Bois' constant religion and the last message of his eloquent career. For this world, he wrote near the end of his life, "is a beautiful world; this is a wonderful America, which the founding fathers dreamed until their sons drowned it in the blood of slavery and devoured it in greed. Our children must rebuild it. Let then the Dreams of the Dead rebuke the Blind who think that what is will be forever and teach them that what was worth living for must live again and that which merited death must stay dead. Teach us, Forever Dead, there is no Dream but Deed, there is no Deed but Memory."[11]

CHAPTER FOURTEEN

Africa Calls

Awake, awake, O sleeping world
Honor the sun,
Worship the stars, those vaster suns
Who rule the night
Where black is bright.   (Du Bois, 1960)

WHEN DU BOIS WAS prevented in 1957 from attending the ceremonies marking Ghana's attainment of dominion status within the British Commonwealth, only one step short of becoming a totally independent republic, he wrote to Kwame Nkrumah to outline his hopes for an emerging Africa. Ghana must lead the continent, just as it was the first black African state to shed colonialism. A new series of pan-African congresses would stress Africa's common goals, including those of economic cooperation, universal education, and freedom from religious dogma. A new African economy would replace the colonial system geared to European industrialism. Standing between Europe and Asia, Africa would draw culturally on both heritages and give to them the wisdom of its people. The new states must be socialist in organization and outlook. The father of pan-Africanism ended his greetings to Nkrumah with a flourish: "I hereby put into your hands, Mr. Prime Minister, my empty but still significant title of 'President of the Pan-African Congress,' " to be passed on as the African leader saw fit.[1]

Du Bois' gesture was gracious but unnecessary. The mantle of pan-African leadership would soon be openly repossessed by black Africa in 1958 at the First All-African Peoples' Conference in Accra. To the American writer, "the rise of an educated group of Africans" made it "natural" that they should lead the movement toward unity.[2] Du Bois nevertheless remained a revered figure among African intellectuals. Arriving in Ghana in October 1961 to begin planning the Encyclopedia Africana, he and Shirley Graham Du Bois received generous assistance and consideration from the Ghanaian government and enjoyed the friendship of Nkrumah, who liked to call Du Bois "my father." In his work on the Encyclopedia Du Bois was aided by W. Alphaeus Hunton, who had served with him on the Council on African Affairs in New York.

Dogged by a recurring illness that took him to Rumania early in 1962 and at midyear to London for a dangerous abdominal operation, Du Bois still managed to oversee the secretariat planning the project. Six Information Reports were published, and a statement on his concept of the undertaking was given wide circulation. He wanted a work of some dozen volumes prepared in about ten years, "not on the vague subject of race, but on the peoples inhabiting the continent of Africa." He was "anxious that it be a scientific production and not a matter of propaganda." Edited mainly by African scholars and "from the African point of view," the work would nevertheless draw on the knowledge of all the best students of African life and would also involve countries other than its immediate sponsor, the Republic of Ghana.[3]

Du Bois made the most of his enforced visits to Rumania and London. Returning from the former, he visited Cairo for the first time; after a convalescence in Switzerland later in the year, he journeyed to the People's Republic of China and joined Mao Tse-tung and Chou En-lai at festivities marking the thirteenth anniversary of the founding of the state. In Moscow he addressed the members of the Institute of African Studies, founded at his suggestion in 1958. He returned to Ghana to begin an important phase of the Encyclopedia project, arranging a series of conferences throughout Africa to advertise the work and stress its international scope.

In February 1963, Du Bois became a citizen of Ghana. His great-grandfather, he wrote, had been carried away from Guinea as a slave: "I have returned that my dust shall mingle with the dust of my forefathers." Though near its end, "my life will flow on in the vigorous young stream of Ghanaian life which lifts the African Personality to its proper place among men."[4] This step gave a symmetry to the life of one who, in the subtitle to *Dusk of Dawn* (1940), had identified himself with the history of a "race concept." Like his membership in the Communist party of the United States, his acceptance of a new citizenship was more a symbolic than a substantive act. Not long before, he had written of the United States as "my country and the land of my fathers . . . a land of magnificent possibilities . . . the home of noble souls and generous people," although he lamented that America was selling its soul for the sake of power and wealth.[5] Honored in Ghana, shunned by his own government (the United States Embassy had only token representation at his funeral), and aware of approaching death, Du Bois asserted his confidence in the new nation — and his gratitude for its attention — by pledging allegiance to it.

Like his membership in the Communist party after decades of sometimes troubled relations with it, Du Bois' new citizenship symbolized a heightened level of political involvement. It has been argued that Du Bois' ties to Africa "remained pure racial romance, whether he related to it as an individual, as a propagandist . . . or as a geopolitician of race."[6] But while Du Bois entertained romantic notions of race for most of his life, his sense of the potential of sub-Saharan Africa was often more conservative in scope and soberly expressed, especially after his first visit to the continent in 1923. Indeed, in *Dark Princess* (1928) Africa is almost entirely omitted from the comity of darker peoples engaged in planning a new world. Only the North African countries, especially Egypt, receive passing attention. In *The Black Flame* Manuel Mansart travels around the world in search of an education, but not to Africa. Although Du Bois had enjoyed his first visit to Africa, he returned more than ever convinced of the folly of back-to-Africa movements; he was too much a cosmopolite and sophisticate, and too much an intellectual and lover of freedom, to thrust himself into the African experience as an immigrant among black colonials and their white masters.

But Du Bois' service to Africa was great. His reputation as an anticolonialist was immense, as was his effectiveness as a historian of the continent. William Leo Hansberry has judged that, whatever their limitations, Du Bois' Africa writings were, "in terms of the African story as a whole, the most inclusive and influential publications" up to the time they appeared, along with the work of the popular historian J. A. Rogers.[7] Prized by Nkrumah as a guest who brought credit to the government, then as a distinguished citizen of the republic, he passed his last months in as much comfort and security as his deteriorating health would allow, and certainly far more than would have been accorded him in his native land.

In spite of his Ghanaian citizenship, however, Du Bois died an American in exile. He was unmistakably a child of America, although he reached for the whole world. As W. Alphaeus Hunton noted, in becoming a citizen of Ghana, Du Bois "simply formalized the fact that he was also a son of Africa."[8] To the end, the attempted reconciliation of his divided souls, African and American, tested his greatest strength. His place in Ghana was in fact far more tenuous than he might have imagined. Had he lived three more years, he would have witnessed the military coup that routed Nkrumah and his government, suppressed socialism and the doctrine of pan-Africanism, and aborted the scheme for the Encyclopedia Africana. He was spared this last disillusionment by his death on August 27, 1963. His passing was peaceful, with his wife at his side.

His final message to the world was read at his funeral. His death was a privilege, Du Bois wrote:

> I have loved my work, I have loved people and my play, but always I have been uplifted by the thought that what I have done well will live long and justify my life. That what I have done ill or never finished can now be handed on to others for endless days to be finished perhaps better than I could have done. And that peace will be my applause.
>
> One thing alone I charge you as you live and believe in life. Always human beings will live and progress to greater, broader and fuller life. The only possible death is to lose belief in this truth simply because the great end comes slowly: because time is long.
>
> Goodbye.[9]

In the years since Du Bois' death in 1963, the memory of his gifts as a poet, scholar, and fighter has stayed alive among the majority of thinking black Americans. For others, though, his contribution has sunk to the status of a footnote in the long history of race relations in the United States. This decline has come in spite of the decades of brilliant political crusading, the beauty and cultural significance of *The Souls of Black Folk,* the power of historical imagination represented by works such as *The Suppression of the African*

Slave-Trade, The Negro, and *Black Reconstruction in America,* and the innovative and thorough social science of *The Philadelphia Negro.*

But in a way both modest and extraordinary, Du Bois was a maker of history. Although he sometimes raged, he achieved success through his long, slow influence on the thinkers of black America and their white sympathizers and allies. If the history of ideas in Afro-America is ever written, Du Bois should occupy the most conspicuous place. If—even more unlikely—the full history of the impact of blacks on the American mind is ever charted, his education of the whole nation will be seen as significant indeed.

His works have not received the study they deserve, and his modest reputation now rests on grounds that he would not wholly appreciate. He is remembered for his strategy in controversies not always properly understood, and for slogans and concepts that inadequately represent the range of his mind. His words appear to support a variety of contradictory causes and, in common with great bodies of art and literature, are susceptible to such a large number of interpretations that the casual reader is sometimes bewildered.

These inexact views of the man occur because Du Bois' vision was filtered through a variety of experiences possible only in America. He was a product of black and white, poverty and privilege, love and hate. He was of New England and the South, an alien and an American, a provincial and a cosmopolite, nationalist and communist, Victorian and modern. With the soul of a poet and the intellect of a scientist, he lived at least a double life, continually compelled to respond to the challenge of reconciling opposites.

The essential rhythm of his mind was not so much a steady transition from one set of beliefs to another as a vibrant oscillation between extremes. No matter how distant in time, each of his autobiographical statements is authentic because it represents an expression of mood rather than a definitive, final statement. His politics swung between saturnine conservatism and radical optimism, his body between sensuousness and moral asceticism, his psyche between elation and gloom. To calm the terror inherent in this instability, he relied on a powerful reason that dominated his mind without always fully controlling it.

Of equal importance in his struggle for balance and order was the force of moral idealism. Belief in the necessity of ethical culture gave perspective to the chaos in which he sometimes recklessly embroiled himself. In few ways was Du Bois more typically American than in this moralism, although his alliance with, and peculiar application of, the mainly nineteenth century New England prophetic tradition would often seem old-fashioned, even reactionary, to generations maturing in a later age. But he did not shirk his moral responsibilities. On the question of race, he was the conscience of America.

His final achievement was in his service to his folk, his nation, and to all those who could comprehend the fuller human significance of the lessons of his life. More than any other individual, he was responsible for the conversion of the facts and episodes of Afro-American history into that coherent, though necessarily diffuse, mythology on which collective self-respect and self-love must inevitably be founded. And far more powerfully than any other American intellectual, he explicated the mysteries of race in a nation which, proud of its racial pluralism,has just begun to show remorse for crimes inspired by racism.

While it is possible to dispute Du Bois' opinion that the problem of the twentieth century is the problem of the color line, the analogous questions of justice and accommodation, of tolerance and benevolence, persist at the center of a civilization still deeply divided by race. Du Bois' works form an index to these matters, just as his life exemplified their effect on humanity. Until such problems disappear from the list of man's concerns, his life is, as he himself saw it, "significant for all lives of men."

NOTES

INDEX

Notes

1. The Making of the Man

1. *The Autobiography of W.E.B. Du Bois: A Soliloquy on Viewing My Life from the Last Decade of Its First Century,* ed. Herbert Aptheker (New York: International Publishers, 1968), p. 423. For Du Bois' life, see also Du Bois, *Dusk of Dawn: An Essay Toward an Autobiography of a Race Concept* (New York: Harcourt, Brace, 1940); Du Bois, *The Souls of Black Folk* (Chicago: A.C. McClurg, 1903); Du Bois, *Darkwater: Voices from Within the Veil* (New York: Harcourt, Brace & Howe, 1920); Du Bois, *A Pageant in Seven Decades, 1868-1938,* pamphlet, n.d., reprinted in Philip S. Foner, ed., *W. E. B. Du Bois Speaks: Speeches and Addresses, 1890-1919* (New York: Pathfinder Press, 1970), pp. 21-72; Du Bois, "My Evolving Program for Negro Freedom," in Rayford W. Logan, ed., *What the Negro Wants* (Chapel Hill: University of North Carolina Press, 1944), pp. 31-70; Du Bois, "From McKinley to Wallace: My Fifty Years as a Political Independent," *Masses & Mainstream* 1 (August 1948): 3-13; Herbert Aptheker, ed., *The Correspondence of W. E. B. Du Bois, vol. I. Selections, 1877-1934* (Amherst: University of Massachusetts Press, 1973).

2. *Autobiography,* p. 80.

3. *Darkwater,* pp. 10-11.

4. *Autobiography,* p. 93.

5. *Autobiography,* pp. 92-95.

6. *Autobiography,* p. 89.

7. *Autobiography,* p. 75.

8. *Autobiography,* p. 71.

9. Not 1884 or Fall 1884, as in *Darkwater,* p. 12; *Dusk of Dawn,* p. 20; *Autobiography,* p. 102.

10. *What the Negro Wants,* p. 38.

11. Howard J. Conn, *The First Congregational Church of Great Barrington, 1743-1943: A History* (Great Barrington, Mass., 1943), p. 38.

12. William Henry Hudson in Thomas Carlyle, *On Heroes and Hero Worship* (London: J. M. Dent, 1908), p. xv.

13. George Santayana, "The Genteel Tradition in American Philosophy," in Douglas L. Wilson, ed., *The Genteel Tradition: Nine Essays by George Santayana* (Cambridge: Harvard University Press, 1967), pp. 37-64.

14. Du Bois, *The Quest of the Silver Fleece* (Chicago: A. C. McClurg, 1911), p. 265.

15. *Dusk of Dawn,* p. 134.

16. Ralph Barton Perry, *Puritanism and Democracy* (New York: Vanguard Press, 1944), p. 357.

17. *Annual Report of the Town of Great Barrington for the School Year 1876-1877* (Great Barrington, Mass., 1877), p. 7

18. *What the Negro Wants,* p. 35.

19. *Dusk of Dawn,* p. 23.

20. *The Souls of Black Folk,* p. 2.

21. *Autobiography,* p. 98.

22. *Darkwater,* p. 8.

23. *Autobiography,* p. 67.

24. See *Dusk of Dawn,* pp. 100-103.

25. New York *Globe,* Apr. 14, 1883.

26. *Globe,* May 5, 1883.

27. *(Globe) Freeman,* Dec. 6, 1884.

28. *Globe,* May 17, 1884.

29. *Globe,* Sept. 29, 1883.

30. *Autobiography,* p. 121.

31. *Autobiography,* pp. 107-108.

32. Du Bois, "How I Taught School," *Fisk Herald* 4 (November 1886): 10.

33. James Weldon Johnson, *Along This Way* (New York: Viking, 1968), pp. 119-120.

34. Du Bois, "The Religion of the American Negro," *New World* 9 (December 1900): pp. 614-615.

35. C. Vann Woodward, *Origins of the New South, 1877-1913* (Baton Rouge: Louisiana State University Press, 1951), p. 212.

36. Eleanor Hoysradt, "To Dr. W. E. B. D.," *Crisis* 36 (May 1929): p. 160.

37. *Dusk of Dawn,* p. 136.

38. *Negro World,* Jan. 8, 1921.

39. *Autobiography,* p. 211.

40. Sinclair Lewis, "N.A.A.C.P. Battle Front," *Crisis* 36 (July 1929): p. 247.

41. Claude McKay, *A Long Way from Home* (New York: Harcourt, Brace, 1970), p. 110.

42. Johnson, *Along This Way,* p. 203.

43. *Autobiography,* p. 284.

44. Francis L. Broderick, *W. E. B. Du Bois: Negro Leader in a Time of Crisis* (Stanford: Stanford University Press, 1959), p. 18.

45. *The Souls of Black Folk,* p. 109.

2. The Age of Miracles

1. W. E. B. Du Bois, *Darkwater: Voices from Within the Veil* (New York: Harcourt, Brace & Howe, 1920), p. 14.

2. Du Bois, "Diuturni Silenti," in Herbert Aptheker, ed., *The Education of Black People: Ten Critiques 1906-1960 by W. E. B. Du Bois* (Amherst: University of Massachusetts Press, 1973), pp. 42-43.

3. Du Bois, "My Evolving Program for Negro Freedom," in Rayford W. Logan, ed., *What the Negro Wants* (Chapel Hill: University of North Carolina Press, 1944), p. 37.

4. *The Autobiography of W. E. B. Du Bois: A Soliloquy on Viewing My Life from the Last Decade of Its First Century,* ed. Herbert Aptheker (New York: International Publishers, 1968), p. 108.

5. "Diuturni Silenti," pp. 42-43.

6. *Autobiography,* p. 112.

7. *Fisk Herald* 2 (December 1884): 4.

8. *Fisk Herald* 5 (February 1888): 9.

9. *Fisk Herald* 5 (June 1888): 8.

10. James McCosh, *Christianity and Positivism: A Series of Lectures to the*

Times on Natural Theology and Apologetics (New York, 1871), pp. 177-178.

11. James H. Fairchild, *Moral Philosophy or, The Science of Obligation* (Oberlin, 1869), p. 228.

12. George Santayana, *Character and Opinion in the United States* (New York: W. W. Norton, 1967), pp. 51-52, 55.

13. Hugh Hawkins, *Between Harvard and America: The Educational Leadership of Charles W. Eliot* (New York: Oxford University Press, 1972), pp. 108-109.

14. Du Bois, *Dusk of Dawn: An Essay Toward an Autobiography of a Race Concept* (New York: Harcourt, Brace, 1940), p. 35.

15. Du Bois, "Harvard and Democracy," ms., n.d., Du Bois Papers, quoted in Francis L. Broderick, *W. E. B. Du Bois: Negro Leader in a Time of Crisis* (Stanford: Stanford University Press, 1959), p. 24.

16. *Dusk of Dawn,* p. 38.

17. *Autobiography,* p. 133.

18. For course descriptions and texts, see issues of the *Harvard University Catalogue,* 1888-1892, Harvard University Archives.

19. William James to G. Croom Robertson, Oct. 7, 1888, in *The Letters of William James,* ed. Henry James (Boston: Atlantic Monthly Press, 1920), II, 196.

20. W. E. B. Du Bois, "The Renaissance of Ethics: A Critical Comparison of Scholastic and Modern Ethics," ms., 1889, James Weldon Johnson Collection, Yale University Library.

21. *What the Negro Wants,* p. 39.

22. *The Letters of William James,* II, 196.

23. Santayana, *Character and Opinion in the United States,* p. 96.

24. *Autobiography,* p. 126.

25. *Springfield Republican,* July 23, 1903.

26. William James to Henry James, Apr. 19, 1888, quoted in Ralph Barton Perry, *The Thought and Character of William James* (Boston: Little, Brown, 1935), I, 407.

27. See esp. Matthew Arnold, *Discourses in America* (London, 1885).

28. William James to the Harvard Graduate School, Jan. 9, 1902, quoted in *Thought and Character of William James,* I, 405.

29. See Du Bois, "Jefferson Davis as a Representative of Civilization," ms., 1890, Harvard University Archives; Du Bois, Diary, Feb. 23, 1893, Du Bois Papers, in Herbert Aptheker, ed., *A Documentary History of the Negro People in the United States* (New York: Citadel Press, 1951), II, 753.

30. *Autobiography,* p. 133.

31. *What the Negro Wants,* p. 40.

32. *What the Negro Wants,* p. 40.

33. *Autobiography,* p. 139.

34. *Autobiography,* p. 137.

35. Du Bois, "Does Education Pay?" ms., 1891, Du Bois Papers; Broderick, *Du Bois,* p. 19.

36. Broderick, *Du Bois,* p. 23.

37. Thomas Babington Macaulay, *Critical Historical Essays* (London: J. M. Dent, 1907), I, 1.

38. Albert Bushnell Hart, "Hermann Von Holst," *Political Science Quarterly* 5 (December 1890): 677-687.

39. Albert Bushnell Hart, *The Southern South* (New York: D. Appleton, 1910), pp. 16-17.

40. *Autobiography,* p. 269.

41. *Autobiography,* p. 144.

42. *Autobiography,* p. 144.

43. Adams Sherman Hill, *The Principles of Rhetoric* (New York, 1897), p. iii.

44. Vincent Harding, "A Black Messianic Visionary," in Rayford W. Logan, ed., *W. E. B. Du Bois: A Profile* (New York: Hill and Wang, 1971), p. 282.

45. Hill, *Principles of Rhetoric,* p. 27.

46. *Dusk of Dawn,* p. 39.

47. Several of these manuscripts are in the Du Bois collection, Fisk University Library.

48. Broderick, *Du Bois,* p. 21.

49. M. A. DeWolfe Howe, *Barrett Wendell and His Letters* (Boston: Atlantic Monthly Press, 1924), p. 86.

50. Barrett Wendell, *English Composition: Eight Lectures Given at the Lowell Institute* (New York, 1891), p. 217.

51. W. E. B. Du Bois, "Harvard," *Fisk Herald* 10 (December 1892): 1.

52. Herbert Aptheker, ed. *The Correspondence of W. E. B. Du Bois, vol. I. Selections, 1877-1934* (Amherst: University of Massachusetts Press, 1973), p. 17.

53. *Autobiography,* p. 164.

54. Francis L. Broderick, "German Influence on the Scholarship of W. E. B. Du Bois," *Phylon* 19 (Winter 1958): 367-371.

55. Broderick, "German Influence," p. 370.

56. *Autobiography,* p. 165.

57. *Autobiography,* p. 168.

58. *Dusk of Dawn,* p. 45.

59. *What the Negro Wants,* p. 42.

60. Du Bois, "The Art and Art Galleries of Modern Europe," ms., c. 1894-1896, F. L. Broderick transcripts, Schomburg Collection, New York Public Library.

61. Du Bois, "Careers Open to College-Bred Negroes," in *Two Addresses Delivered by Alumni of Fisk University* (Nashville, 1898), p. 2.

3. A Divided Career

1. *The Autobiography of W.E.B. Du Bois: A Soliloquy on Viewing My Life from the Last Decade of Its First Century,* ed. Herbert Aptheker (New York: International Publishers, 1968), p. 183.

2. W. E. B. Du Bois, *Darkwater: Voices from Within the Veil* (New York: Harcourt, Brace & Howe, 1920), p. 14.

3. *Darkwater,* p. 18.

4. See Frederick A. McGinnis, *A History and an Interpretation of Wilberforce University* (Wilberforce, Ohio: Wilberforce University, 1941), pp. 162-164.

5. Du Bois, *The Suppression of the African Slave-Trade to the United States of America, 1638-1870* (New York, 1896), p. vi; Du Bois, *The Suppression of the African Slave-Trade to the United States of America, 1638-1870* (New York: Social Science Press, 1954), pp. 327-329.

6. *Suppression of the African Slave Trade,* p. 199.

7. John Hope Franklin, "Foreword: W. E. Burghardt Du Bois: Pioneer Historian of the Slave Trade," in Du Bois, *The Suppression of the African Slave-Trade to the United States of America, 1638-1870* (Baton Rouge: Louisiana State University, 1969), p. x.

8. Du Bois, *The Philadelphia Negro: A Social Study* (Philadelphia, 1899), p. 3.

9. *Autobiography,* p. 195.

10. Du Bois, "The Negroes of Farmville, Virginia: A Social Study," U. S. Labor Dept., *Bulletin* 3 (January 1898): 1-38.

11. Du Bois, *The Philadelphia Negro* (New York: Schocken, 1967), p. 1. All parenthetical references in the text are to this edition.

12. Gunnar Myrdal, *An American Dilemma: The Negro Problem and Modern Democracy* (New York: Harper, 1944), p. 1132; Francis L. Broderick, *W. E. B. Du Bois: Negro Leader in a Time of Crisis* (Stanford: Stanford University Press, 1959), p. 228.

13. See "The Philadelphia Negro," *Outlook* 63 (Nov. 11, 1899): 647-648.

14. Du Bois, "Strivings of the Negro People," *Atlantic Monthly* 80 (August 1897): 194-198.

15. *The Philadelphia Negro,* p. 327.

16. *Darkwater,* p. 14; *Autobiography,* p. 213.

17. Du Bois, *The Souls of Black Folk* (Chicago: A. C. McClurg, 1903), p. 82.

18. Du Bois, "The Laboratory in Sociology at Atlanta University," *Annals of the American Academy of Social and Political Science* 21 (May 1903): 160-163.

19. Du Bois, "The Atlanta Conferences," *Voice of the Negro* 1 (March 1904): 88.

20. Elliott M. Rudwick, "W. E. B. Du Bois as Sociologist," in James E. Blackwell and Morris Janowitz, eds., *Black Sociologists: Historical and Contemporary Perspectives* (Chicago: University of Chicago Press, 1974), p. 45.

21. Du Bois, *The Negro in Business* (Atlanta, 1899), p. 4.

22. Du Bois, *Health and Physique of the Negro American* (Atlanta: Atlanta University Press, 1906), p. 36.

23. Du Bois, *The Negro Church* (Atlanta: Atlanta University Press, 1903), p. 208.

24. *The Philadelphia Negro,* p. 389.

25. Du Bois, *Notes on Negro Crime Particularly in Georgia* (Atlanta: Atlanta University Press, 1904), p. 61.

26. Du Bois, *Efforts for Social Betterment among Negro Americans* (Atlanta: Atlanta University Press, 1909), p. 133.

27. Du Bois, *Economic Co-operation among Negro Americans* (Atlanta: Atlanta University Press, 1907), p. 179.

28. Du Bois, *Some Efforts of American Negroes for Their Own Social Betterment* (Atlanta, 1898), p. 5.

29. See Franz Boas, "The Outlook of the American Negro," *The Shaping of American Anthropology, 1883-1911: A Franz Boas Reader,* ed. George W. Stocking, Jr. (New York: Basic Books, 1974), pp. 310-316.

30. Du Bois, *The College-Bred Negro* (Atlanta: Atlanta University Press, 1900), p. 62.

31. Du Bois, *Dusk of Dawn: An Essay Toward an Autobiography of a Race Concept* (New York: Harcourt, Brace, 1940), p. 270.

32. Oscar Handlin, *Race and Nationality in American Life* (Garden City, N.Y.: Doubleday, 1957), pp. 57-73.

33. Winthrop Jordan, *White over Black: American Attitudes Toward the Negro, 1550-1812* (Chapel Hill: University of North Carolina Press, 1968).

34. Thomas F. Gossett, *Race: The History of an Idea in America* (Dallas: Southern Methodist University Press, 1963), pp. 82-83.

35. Hugh M. Gloster, *Negro Voices in American Fiction* (Chapel Hill: University of North Carolina Press, 1948), p. 11.

36. *Dusk of Dawn,* p. 98.

37. Du Bois, "Jefferson Davis as a Representative of Civilization," ms., 1890, Harvard University Archives.

38. Du Bois, "The Conservation of Races," *American Negro Academy Occasional Papers* no. 2 (Washington, D.C., 1897).

39. "Strivings of the Negro People," p. 194.

40. *Efforts for Social Betterment*, p. 133.

41. Du Bois, "The Negro and Crime," *Independent* 51 (May 18, 1899): 1355-1357.

42. Du Bois, "The Savings of Black Georgia," *Outlook* 69 (Sept. 14, 1901): 128-130; Du Bois, "The Freedmen and Their Sons," *Independent* 52 (Nov. 14, 1901): 2709.

43. Du Bois, "The Spawn of Slavery: The Convict Lease System in the South," *Missionary Review of the World* 14 (October 1901): 737-745; Du Bois, "Crime and Our Colored Population," *Nation* 75 (Dec. 25, 1902): 499.

44. Du Bois, "The Negro as He Really Is," *World's Work* 2 (June 1901): 848-866.

45. Du Bois, "A Negro Schoolmaster in the New South," *Atlantic Monthly* 83 (January 1899): 99-104.

46. Du Bois, "The Religion of the American Negro," *New World* 9 (December 1900): 614-625.

47. Herbert Aptheker, ed., *The Correspondence of W.E.B. Du Bois, vol. I. Selections, 1877-1934* (Amherst: University of Massachusetts Press, 1973), p. 39.

48. "Strivings of the Negro People," p. 197.

49. See Du Bois, "The Suffrage Fight in Georgia," *Independent* 51 (Nov. 30, 1899): 3226-3229; Du Bois, "A Memorial to the Legislature of Georgia on the Hardwick Bill," in Herbert Aptheker, ed., *A Documentary History of the Negro People in the United States* (New York: Citadel Press, 1951), II, 784-786.

50. Du Bois, "Address to the Nations of the World," in Alexander Walters, *My Life and Work* (Westwood, N.J.: Fleming H. Revell, 1917), pp. 257-260.

51. Du Bois, "The Freedmen's Bureau," *Atlantic Monthly* 87 (March 1901): 354-365.

52. See Elliott M. Rudwick, *W. E. B. Du Bois: Propagandist of the Negro Protest* (New York: Atheneum, 1969), pp. 57-58; Louis R. Harlan, *Booker T. Washington: The Making of a Black Leader, 1856-1901* (New York: Oxford University Press, 1972), pp. 265-268.

53. Du Bois, "Results of the Ten Tuskegee Conferences," *Harper's Weekly* 45 (June 22, 1901): 641.

54. Du Bois, "The Evolution of Negro Leadership," *Dial* 31 (July 1, 1901): 53-55.

55. Du Bois, *The Negro Artisan: A Social Study* (Atlanta: University of Atlanta Press, 1902), pp. 5-7.

56. *Autobiography*, p. 133.

57. William James, *Pragmatism: A New Name for Some Old Ways of Thinking* (New York: Longmans, Green, 1907), p. 51.

58. Du Bois, "The Study of the Negro Problems," *Annals of the American Academy of Political and Social Science* 11 (January 1898): 1-23.

59. "Atlanta Conferences," p. 89.

60. "Laboratory in Sociology," p. 160.

61. Beatrice Potter, *My Apprenticeship* (New York: Longmans, Green, 1926), p. 135.

62. Du Bois, "The Relationship of the Negroes to the Whites in the South,"

Annals of the American Academy of Social and Political Science 18 (July 1901): 121-122.

63. See Jane Addams, *Democracy and Social Ethics,* ed. Anne Firor Scott (Cambridge: Harvard University Press, 1964) pp. xii, lxxii; Josiah Royce, *William James, and Other Essays on the Philosophy of Life* (New York: Macmillan, 1911), pp. 39-40.

64. *Fisk Herald* 5 (January 1888): 8.

65. Barrett Wendell, *English Composition: Eight Lectures Given at the Lowell Institute* (New York, 1891), p. 158.

66. J. Saunders Redding, *To Make a Poet Black* (Chapel Hill: University of North Carolina Press, 1939), p. 80.

67. Du Bois, "Carlyle," ms., c. 1895, Du Bois Papers, cited in Broderick, *W. E. B. Du Bois,* p. 51.

68. Thomas Carlyle, *Past and Present* (London: J. M. Dent, 1908), p. 148.

69. Carlyle, *Past and Present,* p. 29.

70. See e.g. Du Bois, "The Riddle of the Sphinx," *Selected Poems* (Accra: Ghana University Press, 1965), pp. 14-15.

71. Carlyle, "The Sphinx," *Past and Present,* p. 13.

4. The Souls of Black Folk

1. Du Bois to F. G. Browne, June 1903, Du Bois Papers, F. L. Broderick transcripts, Schomburg Collection, New York Public Library.

2. Henry James, *The American Scene* (Bloomington: University of Indiana Press, 1960), p. 418.

3. James Weldon Johnson, *The Autobiography of an Ex-Colored Man* (New York: Knopf, 1961), p. 169.

4. James Weldon Johnson, *Along This Way* (New York: Viking, 1968), p. 203.

5. *Black Titan: W. E. B. Du Bois: An Anthology by the Editors of Freedomways,* ed. John Hendrik Clarke, Esther Jackson, Ernest Kaiser, and J. H. O'Dell (Boston: Beacon, 1970), p. 8.

6. Benjamin Brawley, *The Negro in Literature and Art* (New York: Duffield, 1918), p. 18.

7. Du Bois, *The Souls of Black Folk,* ed. J. Saunders Redding (New York: Fawcett, 1961), p. ix. All references in the text are to Du Bois, *The Souls of Black Folk* (Chicago: A. C. McClurg, 1903).

8. Herbert Aptheker, *Annotated Bibliography of the Published Writings of W. E. B. Du Bois* (Millwood, N. Y.: Kraus-Thomson, 1973), p. 551.

9. In *The Souls of Black Folk,* for ch. 1, "Of Our Spiritual Strivings," see Du Bois, "Strivings of the Negro People," *Atlantic Monthly* 80 (August 1897): 194-198. For ch. 2, "Of the Dawn of Freedom," see Du Bois, "The Freedmen's Bureau," *Atlantic Monthly* 87 (March 1901): 354-365. For ch. 3, "Of Mr. Booker T. Washington and Others," see Du Bois, "The Evolution of Negro Leadership," *Dial* 31 (July 16, 1901): 53-55. For ch. 4, "Of the Meaning of Progress," see Du Bois, "A Negro Schoolmaster in the New South," *Atlantic Monthly* 83 (January 1899): 99-104. For ch. 6, "Of the Training of Black Men," see Du Bois, "Of the Training of Black Men," *Atlantic Monthly* 90 (September 1902): 289-297. For chs. 7 and 8, "Of the Black Belt" and "Of the Quest of the Golden Fleece," see Du Bois, "The Negro as He Really Is," *World's Work* 2 (June 1901): 848-866. For ch. 9, "Of the Sons of Master and Man," see Du Bois, "The Relationship of the Negroes to the Whites in the South," *Annals of the American Academy of Social and Political*

Science 18 (July 1901): 121-140. For ch. 10, "Of the Faith of the Fathers," see Du Bois, "The Religion of the American Negro," *New World* 9 (December 1900): 614-625. For additional information, see Herbert Aptheker, *"The Souls of Black Folk: A Comparison of the 1903 and 1952 Editions,"* *Negro History Bulletin* 34 (January 1971): 15-17.

10. Du Bois, *"The Souls of Black Folk," Independent* 57 (Nov. 17, 1904): 1152.

11. Du Bois, "The Talented Tenth," in Booker T. Washington *et al., The Negro Problem* (New York: James Pott, 1903), pp. 31-75.

12. See e.g. Herman Lotze, *Outlines of Psychology,* trans. and ed. George T. Ladd (Boston, 1886), pp. 91-130; James McCosh, *Psychology: The Cognitive Powers* (New York, 1891), p. 1.

13. William James, *The Principles of Psychology* (New York, 1890), I, 399.

14. Oswald Külpe, *Outlines of Psychology,* trans. Edward Bradford Titchener (New York, 1895), p. 217.

15. Bernard W. Bell, *The Folk Roots of Contemporary Afro-American Poetry* (Detroit: Broadside Press, 1974), pp. 16-31.

16. Du Bois, "The Relation of the Negroes to the Whites in the South," *Annals of the American Academy of Social and Political Science* 18 (July 1901): 121-140.

17. Ralph Ellison, *Invisible Man* (New York: Random House, 1952).

18. James Weldon Johnson, *Black Manhattan* (New York: Knopf, 1930), p. 134.

19. Samuel R. Spencer, Jr., *Booker T. Washington and the Negro's Place in American Life* (Boston: Little, Brown, 1953), p. 95.

20. "Talented Tenth," 31-75.

21. Booker T. Washington, "Industrial Education," in *The Negro Problem,* p. 28.

22. H. T. Kealing, "The Characteristics of the Negro People," in *The Negro Problem,* pp. 163-185.

23. Du Bois, "The Evolution of Negro Leadership," *Dial* 31 (July 16, 1901): 53-55.

24. William Hannibal Thomas, *The American Negro: What He Was, What He Is, and What He May Become* (New York: Macmillan, 1901), p. 180.

25. Du Bois, "The Storm and Stress in the Black World," *Dial* 30 (Apr. 16, 1901): 262-264.

26. Du Bois, "The Religion of the American Negro," *New World* 9 (December 1900): 614-625.

27. Louis R. Harlan, *Booker T. Washington: The Making of a Black Leader, 1856-1901* (New York: Oxford University Press, 1972), p. viii.

28. See William Dean Howells, "An Exemplary Citizen," *North American Review* 272 (August 1901): 280-288.

29. Louis R. Harlan, ed., *The Booker T. Washington Papers* (Urbana: University of Illinois Press, 1972), II, 260-261.

30. Booker T. Washington, *Up from Slavery: An Autobiography* (New York: Doubleday, Page, 1901), p. 119.

31. "Talented Tenth," p. 45. See also Houston A. Baker, Jr., "The Black Man of Culture," *Long Black Song: Essays in Black American Culture* (Charlottesville: University Press of Virginia, 1972), pp. 96-108.

5. The Mantle of the Prophet

1. W. E. B. Du Bois, "The Niagara Movement," *Voice of the Negro* 2 (September 1905): 619. See also Du Bois, "The Growth of the Niagara Movement," *Voice of the Negro* 3 (January 1906): 43-54.

2. *The Autobiography of W. E. B. Du Bois: A Soliloquy on Viewing My Life from the Last Decade of Its First Century,* ed. Herbert Aptheker (New York: International Publishers, 1968), p. 248.

3. Du Bois, "Possibilities of the Negro: The Advance Guard of the Race," *Booklover's Magazine* 2 (July 1903): 3-15.

4. Du Bois, "Debit and Credit: The American Negro the Year of Grace Nineteen Hundred and Four," *Voice of the Negro* 2 (Jan. 1, 1905): 677.

5. *Autobiography,* pp. 224-225.

6. See August Meier, "Booker T. Washington and the Negro Press," *Journal of Negro History* 38 (January 1953): 67-90; Meier, "Booker T. Washington and the Rise of N.A.A.C.P.," *Crisis* 61 (February 1954): 69-76, 117-123; Elliott M. Rudwick, "The Niagara Movement," *Journal of Negro History* 43 (July 1957): 177-200; Rudwick, *W. E. B. Du Bois: Propagandist of the Negro Protest* (New York: Atheneum, 1969), pp. 94-119; Louis R. Harlan, *Booker T. Washington: The Making of a Black Leader, 1856-1901* (New York: Oxford University Press, 1972) pp. 254-271.

7. For the charges against Washington, see Du Bois to Oswald Garrison Villard, Mar. 24, 1905; Villard to Du Bois, Apr. 18, 1905; Du Bois to Villard, Apr. 20, 1905, Villard Papers, Houghton Library, Harvard University.

8. See Herbert Aptheker, "The Washington-Du Bois Conference of 1904," *Science and Society* 13 (Fall 1949): 344-351. See also Aptheker, "The Niagara Movement," *Afro-American History: The Modern Era* (New York: Citadel Press, 1971), pp. 127-158.

9. Du Bois, "The Training of Negroes for Social Power," *Outlook,* Oct. 17, 1903, pp. 409-414.

10. Du Bois, "Credo," *Independent* 57 (Oct. 6, 1904): 787.

11. "Niagara Movement," p. 621.

12. Du Bois, "Niagara Address of 1906," in Herbert Aptheker, ed., *Documentary History of the Negro People in the United States* (New York: Citadel Press, 1951), II, 907-910.

13. Du Bois, "The Value of Agitation," *Voice of the Negro* 4 (March 1907): 109-110.

14. Rudwick, *Du Bois,* pp. 118-119.

15. *Autobiography,* p. 224.

16. *Moon,* Mar. 2 (Paul Laurence Dunbar Memorial Number), June 23, 1906.

17. Paul G. Partington, "*The Moon Illustrated Weekly*—Precursor of the *Crisis,*" *Journal of Negro History* 48 (July 1963): 206-216.

18. *Horizon* 1 (January 1907): 8.

19. *Horizon* 4 (November-December 1908): 13.

20. *Horizon* 3 (February 1908): 17.

21. *Horizon* 3 (March 1908): 7.

22. *Horizon* 5 (December 1909): 1-2.

23. *Horizon* 5 (February 1910): 2.

24. *Horizon* 1 (April 1907): 5.

25. *Horizon* 2 (October 1907): 10.

26. *Horizon* 5 (November 1909): 1.

27. Du Bois, "A Litany at Atlanta," *Independent* 61 (Oct. 11, 1906): 856-858.

28. *Horizon* 2 (November 1907): 3-5.

29. *Horizon* 1 (February 1907): 4-6.

30. *Horizon* 3 (January 1908): 5-6.

31. Du Bois, "A Hymn to the Peoples," *Independent* 70 (Aug. 24, 1911): 400.

32. Du Bois, *John Brown* (Philadelphia: George W. Jacobs, 1909), p. 15. All

parenthetical references in the text are to this edition.

33. *Autobiography,* pp. 251, 259.

34. Aptheker, *Afro-American History,* p. 48.

6. The Quest of the Silver Fleece

1. Du Bois, *The Gift of Black Folk: The Negroes in the Making of America* (New York: Washington Square Press, 1970), p. 167.

2. *The Gift of Black Folk,* p. 163.

3. George W. Cable, "What Shall the Negro Do?" in Arlin Turner, ed., *The Negro Question: A Selection of Writings on Civil Rights in the South by George W. Cable* (New York: W. W. Norton, 1958), pp. 153-165. For Du Bois' reply, "What the Negro Will Do," ms., Feb. 4, 1889, Du Bois Papers, see Francis L. Broderick, *W. E. B. Du Bois: Negro Leader in a Time of Crisis* (Stanford: Stanford University Press, 1959), p. 10.

4. Du Bois to Cable, Feb. 13, 1890, in Herbert Aptheker, ed., *The Correspondence of W. E. B. Du Bois, vol. I. Selections, 1877-1934* (Amherst: University of Massachusetts Press, 1973), p. 7.

5. *Crisis* 3 (December 1911): 77-78.

6. Du Bois, *The Quest of the Silver Fleece: A Novel* (Chicago: A. C. McClurg, 1911). All parenthetical references in the text are to this edition.

7. See Arlene A. Elder, "Swamp Versus Plantation: Symbolic Structure in W. E. B. Du Bois' *The Quest of the Silver Fleece,*" *Phylon* 34 (December 1973): 358-367.

8. Du Bois, *The Souls of Black Folk* (Chicago: A. C. McClurg, 1903), p. 195.

9. *The Souls of Black Folk,* p. 11.

10. Broderick, *Du Bois,* p. 52.

11. *The Souls of Black Folk,* p. 100.

12. *The Souls of Black Folk,* p. 202.

13. Du Bois, "My Evolving Program for Negro Freedom," in Rayford W. Logan, ed., *What the Negro Wants* (Chapel Hill: University of North Carolina Press, 1944), p. 49.

14. Frank Norris, "A Plea for Romantic Fiction," in Donald Pizer, ed., *The Literary Criticism of Frank Norris* (Austin: University of Texas Press, 1964), p. 76.

15. William James, *The Varieties of Religious Experience* (New York: Longmans, Green, 1902), pp. 31-32.

16. Arthur P. Davis, *From the Dark Tower: Afro-American Writers, 1900 to 1960* (Washington, D.C.: Howard University Press, 1974), pp. 22-23.

17. Du Bois, *Dusk of Dawn: An Essay Toward an Autobiography of a Race Concept* (New York: Harcourt, Brace & World, 1940), p. 269.

7. The Crisis and Politics

1. *The Autobiography of W. E. B. Du Bois: A Soliloquy on Viewing My Life from the Last Decade of Its First Century,* ed. Herbert Aptheker (New York: International Publishers, 1968), p. 258.

2. William English Walling, "The Race War in the North," *Independent* 65 (Aug. 20, 1908): 442-443; Oswald Garrison Villard, "The Call," ms., 1909, Villard Papers, Houghton Library, Harvard University.

3. See Minutes of the Board of Directors, NAACP, 1909-1910, Manuscript Division, Library of Congress.

4. Mary White Ovington, "Beginnings of the NAACP," *Crisis* 32 (June 1926):

77. For the history of the first decade of the association, see Charles Flint Kellogg, *NAACP: A History of the National Association for the Advancement of Colored People, vol. I. 1909-1920* (Baltimore: Johns Hopkins Press, 1967).

5. *Crusade for Justice: The Autobiography of Ida B. Wells,* ed. Alfreda M. Duster (Chicago: University of Chicago Press, 1970), pp. 323-327.

6. Du Bois to W. E. Walling, June 13, 1910, Records of the NAACP, Manuscript Division, Library of Congress.

7. J. E. Spingarn to Du Bois, Oct. 24, 1914, *The Correspondence of W. E. B. Du Bois, vol. I. Selections, 1877-1934,* ed. Herbert Aptheker (Amherst: University of Massachusetts Press, 1973), pp. 200-202.

8. See Villard to F. J. Garrison, Feb. 7 and 11, 1913; Villard to J. E. Spingarn, Mar. 20, 1913, Villard Papers.

9. Spingarn to Du Bois, Oct. 24, 1914, *Correspondence,* p. 202.

10. Ovington to Villard, Aug. 10, 1915, Villard Papers.

11. For Villard's review, see *Nation* 89 (Sept. 30, 1909): 302. See also Du Bois to The Editor of the *Nation* (Paul Elmer More), Nov. 6, 15, 20, 1909, *Correspondence,* pp. 154-158. For Villard's defense, see Villard to F. J. Garrison, Nov. 17, 1909, Villard Papers; Villard to Du Bois, Nov. 26, 1909, *Correspondence,* pp. 158-159.

12. Du Bois to J. E. Spingarn, Oct. 28, 1914, *Correspondence,* pp. 203-207.

13. Du Bois to M. W. Ovington, Apr. 9, 1914, *Correspondence,* pp. 188-191.

14. Du Bois, *Dusk of Dawn: An Essay Toward an Autobiography of a Race Concept* (New York: Harcourt, Brace, 1940), p. 255. See also B. Joyce Ross, *J. E. Spingarn and the Rise of the NAACP* (New York: Atheneum, 1972) p. 245.

15. Du Bois to Ovington, Apr. 9, 1914, *Correspondence,* p. 191.

16. Kellogg, *NAACP,* p. 97; Du Bois to Arthur Spingarn, Jan. 12, 1918, Arthur B. Spingarn papers, Manuscript Division, Library of Congress.

17. Board Minutes, NAACP, Apr. 1, 1913.

18. James Weldon Johnson to Du Bois, May 2, 1924, Records of the NAACP, Manuscript Division, Library of Congress.

19. Mary White Ovington to Du Bois, Mar. 4, 1925, Records of the NAACP.

20. See Annual Reports of the Director of Publicity and Research, Records of the NAACP.

21. Board Minutes, NAACP, July 9, 1934.

22. Memorandum, J. E. Spingarn to Walter White, May 10, 1933, Records of the NAACP.

23. Shirley Graham Du Bois, *His Day Is Marching On: A Memoir of W. E. B. Du Bois* (New York: Lippincott, 1971), p. 28.

24. J. Saunders Redding, "Portrait: W. E. Burghardt Du Bois," *American Scholar* 18 (Winter 1948-49): 93.

25. Henry Lee Moon, *The Emerging Thought of W. E. B. Du Bois* (New York: Simon and Schuster, 1972), p. 419. See also Moon, "History of *The Crisis,*" *Crisis* 70 (November 1970): 321-322, 383-385.

26. See Elinor D. Sinnette, "The Brownies' Book," *Freedomways* 5 (Winter 1965): 133-142.

27. *Crisis* 18 (September 1919): 235.

28. *Crisis* 3 (February 1912): 153.

29. *Crisis* 30 (May 1925): 7.

30. Du Bois, *The Negro* (New York: Oxford University Press, 1970), p. 145.

31. *Crisis* 2 (September 1911): 195.

32. O. G. Villard to F. J. Garrison, Feb. 7, 11, 1913, Villard Papers.

33. *Crisis* 2 (September 1911): 195.

34. *Crisis* 40 (February 1933): 46.

35. *Crisis* 7 (February 1914): 187.

36. Du Bois, "Marrying of Black Folk," *Independent* 69 (Oct. 13, 1910): 812-813.

37. *Crisis* 1 (January 1911): 21.

38. *Crisis* 25 (March 1923): 203.

39. *Crisis* 7 (December 1913): 84.

40. *Crisis* 19 (January 1920): 107.

41. *Crisis* 16 (July 1918): 111.

42. *Crisis* 16 (September 1918): 217.

43. Du Bois, "On Being Ashamed of Oneself: An Essay on Race Pride," *Crisis* 40 (September 1933): 199-200.

44. Marcus Garvey to Du Bois, Apr. 25, 1916, July 16, 1920, Du Bois to Garvey, Apr. 29, 1916, July 22, 1920, *Correspondence,* pp. 215-246.

45. Du Bois, "A Lunatic or a Traitor," *Crisis* 28 (May 1924): 8-9.

46. "On Being Ashamed of Oneself," p. 199.

47. Du Bois, "Back to Africa," *Century* 105 (February 1923): 539-548.

48. *Crisis* 23 (April 1922): 252.

49. Du Bois, *Darkwater: Voices from Within the Veil* (New York: Harcourt, Brace & Howe, 1920), p. 60.

50. Du Bois to James Weldon Johnson, May 21, 1929, Arthur B. Spingarn Papers, Library of Congress.

51. Du Bois, "The Pan-African Congress," *Crisis* 17 (April 1919): 271-274.

52. Du Bois, "My Mission," *Crisis* 18 (May 1919): 7-9.

53. Du Bois, "Manifesto of the Second Pan-African Congress: To the World." *Crisis* 23 (November 1921): 5-10.

54. *Crisis* 27 (April 1924): 273-274.

55. *Crisis* 28 (July 1924): 106.

56. *Autobiography,* p. 289.

57. *Autobiography,* p. 263.

58. *Crisis* 2 (August 1911): 157-158; see also Du Bois, "The Races Congress," *Crisis* 2 (September 1911): 200-209.

59. *Crisis* 22 (July 1921): 103.

60. *Crisis* 33 (November 1926): 8.

61. *Crisis* 37 (April 1930): 137-138.

62. *Crisis* 5 (November 1912): 29.

63. *Crisis* 28 (July 1924): 103.

64. See Margaret Deland to Du Bois, Dec. 3, Du Bois to Deland, Dec. 12, 1928, *Correspondence,* pp. 383-384.

65. *Messenger* 2 (April-May 1920): 10-11.

66. Elliott M. Rudwick, *W. E. B. Du Bois: Propagandist of the Negro Protest* (New York: Atheneum, 1969), pp. 221-222.

67. *Emerging Thought of W. E. B. Du Bois,* p. 15.

68. *Crisis* 14 (May 1917): 8.

69. Du Bois to Yolande Du Bois, Oct. 29, 1914, *Correspondence,* pp. 207-208.

70. *Crisis* 21 (November 1920): 5-6.

71. *Crisis* 40 (March 1933): 55-56; (May 1933): 103-104, 118.

72. Du Bois, "The Negro and Communism," *Crisis* 38 (September 1931): 313-315, 318-320.

73. Du Bois, "Education and Work," *The Education of Black People: Ten Cri-*

tiques by W. E. B. Du Bois, 1906-1960, ed. Herbert Aptheker (New York: Monthly Review Press, 1973), pp. 61-82; reported in *Crisis* 37 (August 1930): 280.

74. *Education of Black People,* p. 82.

75. *Crisis* 39 (March 1932): 102-103.

76. *Crisis* 39 (July 1932): 218.

77. Du Bois, "Health of Black Folk," *Crisis* 40 (February 1933): 31; "Color Caste," *Crisis* 40 (March 1933): 55-56; "Right To Work," *Crisis* 40 (April 1933): 93-94.

78. *Crisis* 40 (June 1933): 128-129, 140-142; Du Bois, "Our Class Struggle," *Crisis* 40 (July 1933): 164-165.

79. Du Bois, "The Field and Function of the Negro College," *Education of Black People,* pp. 83-102; reported as "The Negro College" in *Crisis* 40 (August 1933): 175-177.

80. *Crisis* 40 (September 1933): 199 200.

81. Du Bois, "Pan-Africa and New Racial Philosophy," *Crisis* 40 (November 1933): 247, 262.

82. *Crisis* 41 (April 1934): 115-117.

8. Darkwater

1. Du Bois, *Darkwater: Voices from Within the Veil* (New York: Harcourt, Brace & Howe, 1920), p. 23. All parenthetical references in the text are to this edition.

2. Oswald Garrison Villard, "Darkwater," *Nation* 110 (May 1920): 727.

3. See Du Bois, "The Shadow of Years," *Crisis* 15 (February 1918): 167-171.

4. Du Bois, "The Souls of White Folk," *Independent* 69 (Aug. 18, 1910): 339-342; and Du Bois, "Of the Culture of White Folk," *Journal of Race Development* 7 (April 1917): 434-437.

5. For "The Hands of Ethiopia," see Du Bois, "The African Roots of the War," *Atlantic Monthly* 115 (May 1915): 707-714.

6. See Du Bois, "The Burden of Black Women," *Horizon* 2 (November 1907): 3-5.

7. Du Bois, "A Hymn to the Peoples," *Independent* 70 (Aug. 24, 1911): 400.

9. The Crisis and Literature

1. Leslie Pinckney Hill, "Jim Crow," *Crisis* 1 (December 1910): 5.

2. *Crisis* 1 (April 1911): 21.

3. William Stanley Braithwaite, "Democracy and Art," *Crisis* 10 (August 1915): 186.

4. William Stanley Braithwaite, "Some Contemporary Poets of the Negro Race," *Crisis* 17 (April 1919): 275-276.

5. William Stanley Braithwaite, "The Negro in Literature," *Crisis* 28 (September 1924): 208-210.

6. Jessie Fauset, *The Chinaberry Tree* (New York: Negro Universities Press, 1969), p. ix.

7. Langston Hughes, *The Big Sea* (New York: Hill and Wang, 1963), p. 223.

8. Jessie Fauset, "The Debut of the Younger School of Negro Writers," *Opportunity* 2 (May 1924): 143.

9. Jessie R. Fauset to Jean Toomer, Feb. 17, 24, 1922, Jean Toomer Papers, Fisk University Library. I am indebted to Professor Hortense Thornton for granting access to her taped interview with Arna Bontemps, July 21, 1972. Bontemps'

first published poem was "Hope," *Crisis* 28 (August 1924): 126.

10. Arna Bontemps, *100 Years of Negro Freedom* (New York: Dodd, Mead, 1961), p. 221.

11. Du Bois, *Dusk of Dawn: An Essay Toward an Autobiography of a Race Concept* (New York: Harcourt, Brace, 1940), pp. 202-203.

12. *Crisis* 12 (June 1916): 69.

13. *Crisis* 12 (August 1916): 169.

14. *Messenger* 2 (July 1918): 27-28.

15. *Messenger* 2 (April-May 1920): 10-11.

16. *Messenger* 2 (October 1919): 8.

17. The *Survey Graphic* number formed the basis of Alain Locke, ed., *The New Negro: An Interpretation* (New York: Boni and Liveright, 1925).

18. Claude McKay to W. E. B. Du Bois, June 18, 1928, *The Correspondence of W. E. B. Du Bois, vol. I. Selections, 1877-1934,* ed. Herbert Aptheker (Amherst: University of Massachusetts Press, 1973), pp. 374-375.

19. *Crisis* 29 (November 1924): 26.

20. Du Bois, "Negro Art," *Crisis* 22 (June 1921): 55-56.

21. *Crisis* 25 (November 1922): 7-8.

22. Du Bois and Alain Locke, "The Younger Literary Movement," *Crisis* 27 (February 1924): 161-162.

23. "Younger Literary Movement," pp. 162-163.

24. *Opportunity* 2 (May 1924): 143.

25. See Patrick J. Gilpin, "Charles S. Johnson: Entrepreneur of the Harlem Renaissance," in Arna Bontemps, ed., *The Harlem Renaissance Remembered* (New York: Dodd, Mead, 1972), pp. 215-246.

26. Langston Hughes, "The Negro Artist and the Racial Mountain," *Nation* 122 (June 23, 1926): 692-694.

27. "Foreword," *Fire!!* 1 (November 1926).

28. Du Bois, "Our Book Shelf," *Crisis* 31 (January 1926): 141.

29. "A Questionnaire," *Crisis* 31 (February 1926): 165.

30. *Crisis* 32 (June 1926): 72.

31. *Crisis* 32 (May 1926): 36.

32. *Crisis* 31 (April 1926): 280.

33. *Crisis* 31 (March 1926): 220.

34. *Crisis* 31 (April 1926): 278, 280.

35. *Crisis* 32 (August 1926): 194.

36. See James Weldon Johnson, "Negro Authors and White Publishers," *Crisis* 36 (July 1929): 228-229.

37. Du Bois, "Criteria of Negro Art," *Crisis* 32 (October 1926): 290-297.

38. Du Bois, "Mencken," *Crisis* 34 (October 1927): 276.

39. Du Bois, "Books," *Crisis* 33 (December 1926): 81-82.

40. *Crisis* 34 (June 1927): 129.

41. Du Bois, "Harlem," *Crisis* 34 (September 1927): 240.

42. Du Bois, "Two Novels," *Crisis* 35 (June 1928): 202.

43. Du Bois, "The Browsing Reader," *Crisis* 38 (September 1931): 304.

44. George S. Schuyler, "Negro-Art Hokum," *Nation* 122 (June 16, 1926): 662-663.

45. *Messenger* 8 (September 1926): 279.

46. *Messenger* 10 (May-June 1928): 116-117.

47. Johnson, *Black Manhattan,* pp. 226-228.

48. *Crisis* 38 (July 1931): 230.

49. Memorandum, Du Bois to Walter White, September 1926, Records of the NAACP, Manuscript Division, Library of Congress.

50. Du Bois, "Toward a New Racial Philosophy," *Crisis* 40 (January 1933): 22.

51. Du Bois to Alfred Harcourt, Oct. 25, 1928, quoted in Herbert Aptheker's Introduction to Du Bois, *Dark Princess* (Millwood, N.Y.: Kraus-Thomson, 1974), pp. 20-21.

52. "Mencken," p. 276.

53. Du Bois, "The Negro College," *Crisis* 40 (August 1933): 176.

54. Francis L. Broderick, *W. E. B. Du Bois: Negro Leader in a Time of Crisis* (Stanford: Stanford University Press, 1959), p. 160; Robert A. Bone, *The Negro Novel in America* (New Haven: Yale University Press, 1965), p. 101.

55. George Santayana, *Interpretations of Poetry and Religion* (New York: Scribner's, 1900), pp. 166-216.

56. Nathan Irvin Huggins, *Harlem Renaissance* (New York: Oxford University Press, 1971), p. 30.

10. Dark Princess

1. W. E. B. Du Bois, *Dusk of Dawn: An Essay Toward an Autobiography of a Race Concept* (New York: Harcourt, Brace, 1940), p. 270.

2. For the background of the novel, see Herbert Aptheker's Introduction to Du Bois, *Dark Princess* (Millwood, N.Y.: Kraus-Thomson, 1974).

3. Du Bois, *The Negro* (New York: Oxford University Press, 1970), p. 146.

4. Du Bois, *Dark Princess: A Romance* (New York: Harcourt, Brace, 1928), p. 151. All parenthetical references in the text are to this edition. There is some discrepancy about the dating of the action in the novel. Part II is supposed to take place between September and December 1923 (p. 37). Yet a poster prepared by Perigua dates the lynching of Matthew's friend on December 16, 1926 (p. 87). This should have been December 16, 1923.

5. See R. Shamasastry, trans., *Kautilya's Arthaśāstra* (Mysore: Wesleyan Mission Press, 1923).

6. Du Bois to Margaret Deland, Dec. 12, 1928, *The Correspondence of W. E. B. Du Bois, vol. I. Selections, 1877-1934,* ed. Herbert Aptheker (Amherst: University of Massachusetts, 1973), p. 385.

11. The Coming Unities

1. *The Autobiography of W. E. B. Du Bois: A Soliloquy on Viewing My Life from the Last Decade of Its First Century,* ed. Herbert Aptheker (New York: International Publishers, 1968), p. 299.

2. Minutes of the Board of Directors, NAACP, July 9, 1934, Manuscript Division, Library of Congress.

3. *Autobiography,* p. 301.

4. Du Bois, "Apology," *Phylon* 1 (First Quarter, 1940): 3-5.

5. Du Bois, "Phylon: Science or Propaganda," *Phylon* 5 (First Quarter, 1944): 5-9.

6. *Autobiography,* pp. 324-325.

7. Rayford W. Logan, ed., *W. E. B. Du Bois: A Profile* (New York: Hill and Wang, 1971), p. 295.

8. Du Bois, "The Revelation of St. Orgne the Damned," *The Education of Black People: Ten Critiques, 1906-1960,* ed. Herbert Aptheker (New York: Monthly Review Press, 1973), pp. 103-126.

9. Benjamin Stolberg, "Minority Jingo," *Nation* 149 (Oct. 23, 1937): 437-439. For Du Bois' reply, see "A Forum of Fact and Opinion," Pittsburgh *Courier,* Dec. 4, 1937.

10. Du Bois, "As the Crow Flies," *Amsterdam News* (New York), Oct. 10, 1942.

11. *Amsterdam News,* Jan. 18, 1941.

12. Du Bois, "The Winds of Time," Chicago *Defender,* May 5, 1945; Du Bois, "What He Meant to the Negro," *New Masses* 55 (Apr. 24, 1945): 9.

13. *Amsterdam News,* Feb. 24, 1940.

14. Chicago *Defender,* Mar. 23, 1946.

15. *Amsterdam News,* Apr. 12, 1941.

16. Pittsburgh *Courier,* Dec. 19, 1936.

17. Chicago *Defender,* Sept. 15, 1945.

18. *Amsterdam News,* Aug. 19, 1944.

19. George Shepperson, "Introduction," in Du Bois, *The Negro* (New York: Oxford University Press, 1970), p. xiv.

20. Du Bois, *Black Folk Then and Now* (New York: Henry Holt, 1939), p. vii.

21. Du Bois, *The World and Africa: An Inquiry into the Part Which Africa Has Played in World History* (New York: Viking, 1947), p. xi.

22. For such revaluation of his own earlier work, see Du Bois, "The Browsing Reader," *Crisis* 39 (March 1932): 102-103; Du Bois, "Reading, Writing, and Real Estate," *Negro Digest* 1 (October 1943): 63-65; Du Bois, Fiftieth-Anniversary Introduction to *The Souls of Black Folk* (New York: Blue Heron, 1953).

23. Du Bois, *The Negro* (New York: Henry Holt, 1915), p. 24.

24. *The Negro,* pp. 74, 69.

25. *The Negro,* p. 137.

26. Wilson J. Moses, "The Poetics of Ethiopianism: W. E. B. Du Bois and Literary Black Nationalism," *American Literature* 47 (November 1975): 426. For a discussion of Ethiopianism, see St. Clair Drake, *The Redemption of Africa and Black Religion* (Chicago: Third World Press, 1970), pp. 41-53.

27. *The Negro,* p. 159.

28. Du Bois, *Dusk of Dawn: An Essay Toward an Autobiography of a Race Concept* (New York: Harcourt, Brace, 1940), p. 269.

29. Du Bois, "The Freedmen's Bureau," *Atlantic Monthly* 87 (March 1901): 354-365.

30. Du Bois, "Reconstruction and Its Benefits," *American Historical Review* 15 (July 1910): 781-799.

31. Du Bois, "The Reconstruction of Freedom," *The Gift of Black Folk: Negroes in the Making of America* (New York: Washington Square Press, 1970), pp. 95-140.

32. Memorandum, Du Bois to Board of Directors, NAACP, May 12, 1931, Records of the NAACP, Manuscript Division, Library of Congress.

33. *Gift of Black Folk,* pp. 134-135.

34. Du Bois, *Black Reconstruction in America: An Essay Toward a History of the Part Which Black Folk Played in the Attempt To Reconstruct Democracy in America, 1860-1880* (New York: Harcourt, Brace, 1935), p. 15.

35. Herbert Aptheker, *Afro-American History: The Modern Era* (New York: Citadel Press, 1971), p. 56.

36. *Black Reconstruction in America,* p. 381.

37. Du Bois to Benjamin Stolberg, Oct. 1, 1934, quoted in Aptheker, *Afro-American History,* p. 62.

38. Du Bois, "Reconstruction, Seventy Years After," *Phylon* 4 (Third Quarter, 1943): 205-212.

39. See e.g. Du Bois, "The Star of Ethiopia," *Crisis* 11 (December 1915): 91-93.

40. Howard K. Beale, "On Rewriting Reconstruction History," *American Historical Review* 45 (July 1940): 809.

41. *Black Reconstruction in America,* p. 726.

42. Herbert Aptheker, *Annotated Bibliography of the Published Writings of W. E. B. Du Bois* (Millbrook, N.Y.. Kraus-Thomson, 1973), p. 556.

43. *Dusk of Dawn,* pp. vii-viii. All parenthetical references in the text are to the 1940 edition.

12. The Wisdom of Age

1. *The Autobiography of W. E. B. Du Bois: A Soliloquy on Viewing My Life from the Last Decade of Its First Century*, ed. Herbert Aptheker (New York: International Publishers, 1968), pp. 326-339.

2. Du Bois, "As the Crow Flies," *Amsterdam News,* Aug. 9, 1944.

3. Du Bois, *Color and Democracy: Colonies and Peace* (New York: Harcourt, Brace, 1945), pp. 72, 122.

4. See Du Bois, ed., *An Appeal to the World: A Statement on the Denial of Human Rights to Minorities in the Case of Citizens of Negro Descent in the United States of America and an Appeal to the United Nations for Redress* (New York: NAACP, 1947), pp. 1-14.

5. Du Bois, "The Freeing of India," *Crisis* 54 (October 1947): 301-304, 316-317.

6. Du Bois, "The Greatest Man in the World," *Unity* 134 (May-June 1948): 25-26.

7. Du Bois, "The Winds of Time," Chicago *Defender,* Aug. 9, 1947.

8. Du Bois, *The World and Africa: An Enquiry into the Part Which Africa Has Played in World History* (New York: Viking, 1947), p. 24.

9. Du Bois, *Behold the Land* (Birmingham: Southern Youth Congress, 1946), pp. 7-15.

10. Arna Bontemps, "Nocturne at Bethesda," *Crisis* 33 (December 1926): 66.

11. Du Bois, "From McKinley to Wallace: My Fifty Years as a Political Independent," *Masses & Mainstream* 1 (August 1948): 12.

12. Chicago *Defender,* Oct. 5, 1946.

13. "From McKinley to Wallace," pp. 3-13.

14. New York *Times,* Sept. 9, 14, 1948.

15. See Shirley Graham Du Bois, *His Day Is Marching On: A Memoir of W. E. B. Du Bois* (New York: Lippincott, 1971), p. 99f.

16. Shirley Graham, "Why Was Du Bois Fired," *Masses & Mainstream* 1 (November 1948): 15-26.

17. Du Bois, *In Battle for Peace: The Story of My 83rd Birthday* (New York: Masses & Mainstream, 1952), p. 17.

18. Du Bois, "Peace: Freedom's Road for Oppressed Peoples," *Worker,* Apr. 17, 1949.

19. Shirley Graham Du Bois, *His Day Is Marching On,* p. 119.

20. *In Battle for Peace,* p. 186.

21. New York *Times,* July 17, 1950.

22. *In Battle for Peace,* p. 72.

23. *In Battle for Peace,* p. 119.

24. *In Battle for Peace,* p. 160.

25. Du Bois, "I Take My Stand," *Masses & Mainstream* 4 (April 1951): 10-16.

26. "A Negro Leader's Plea to Save the Rosenbergs," *Worker,* Nov. 16, 1952.

27. Du Bois, "The Rosenbergs," *Masses & Mainstream* 6 (July 1953): 10-12.

28. Du Bois, "This Man I Know," *Masses & Mainstream* 7 (February 1954): 43; Du Bois, "Testifying at Ben Gold's Trial," *Jewish Life,* May 1954.

29. Du Bois, "The Hard-Bit Man in the Loud Shirts," *National Guardian,* Jan. 22, 1953.

30. Du Bois, "On Stalin," *National Guardian,* Mar. 16, 1953.

31. *Autobiography,* p. 395.

32. New York *Times,* Oct. 6, 1950.

33. Du Bois, "The Choice That Confronts America's Negroes," *National Guardian,* Feb. 13, 1952.

34. Du Bois, "American Negroes and Africa," *National Guardian,* Feb. 14, 1955.

35. Du Bois, "The Negro in America Today," *National Guardian,* Jan. 16, 1956.

36. Du Bois, "Will the Great Gandhi Live Again?" *National Guardian,* Feb. 11, 1957.

37. Shirley Graham Du Bois, *His Day Is Marching On,* p. 301.

38. Du Bois, *The Story of Ben Franklin* (Vienna: World Peace Council, 1956).

39. *Autobiography,* p. 35.

40. See *Autobiography,* pp. 44-53.

41. Du Bois, "Ghana Calls," in John Henrik Clarke, Esther Jackson, Ernest Kaiser, and J. H. O'Dell, eds., *Black Titan: W. E. B. Du Bois: An Anthology by the Editors of Freedomways* (Boston: Beacon, 1970), pp. 299-302.

42. "Ghana Calls," in *Black Titan,* pp. 304-306.

43. New York *Times,* Nov. 23, 1961.

44. Rayford W. Logan, *Two Bronze Titans: Frederick Douglass and William Edward Burghardt Du Bois* (Washington, D.C.: Howard University, 1972).

45. Conversation with David Du Bois, Sept. 18, 1975.

46. Herbert Aptheker, "On the Passing of Du Bois," *Political Affairs* 42 (October 1963): 35-41.

47. Du Bois, "Forty-Two Years of the USSR," *National Guardian,* Sept. 7, 1959.

48. George Shepperson, "Introduction," in Du Bois, *The Negro* (New York: Oxford University Press, 1970), p. xii.

49. *The World and Africa,* p. 258.

50. *Worker,* June 23, 1957.

51. *National Guardian,* Aug. 15, 1960.

52. J. Saunders Redding, "W. E. Burghardt Du Bois," *American Scholar* 18 (Winter 1948-1949): 93-96.

53. Julius Lester, *The Seventh Son: The Thought and Writings of W. E. B. Du Bois* (New York: Random House, 1971), II, 707, I, 145.

13. The Black Flame

1. Du Bois, *The Ordeal of Mansart* (1957), *Mansart Builds a School* (1959), and *Worlds of Color* (1961), were issued by Mainstream Publishers of New York.

All parenthetical references in the text are to this edition, the volumes being referred to as I, II, and III.

2. For example, in *Mansart Builds a School,* Jean Du Bignon is called the great-granddaughter of Mère Du Bignon; but according to the record of births and marriages (pp. 112-116), Jean should be her great-great-great-granddaughter. Also, the old lady dies in "the ninety-ninth year of her life" (p. 123); yet she was born in 1816 (p. 112) and is alive in 1918 (p. 120).

3. Henry Steele Commager, *The American Mind: An Interpretation of American Thought and Character since the 1880's* (New Haven: Yale University Press, 1950), p. 269.

4. Du Bois, "As the Crow Flies," *Crisis* 39 (July 1932): 214.

5. Herbert Aptheker, *Afro-American History: The Modern Era* (New York: Citadel Press, 1971), p. 65.

6. Du Bois, "Bismarck," ms., 1888, Du Bois Papers, in F. L. Broderick transcripts, Schomburg Collection, New York Public Library.

7. Du Bois, "Jefferson Davis as a Representative of Civilization," ms., 1890, Harvard University Archives.

8. Du Bois, *The Souls of Black Folk* (Chicago: A. C. McClurg, 1903), pp. 263, 83, 214.

9. *The Autobiography of W. E. B. Du Bois: A Soliloquy on Viewing My Life from the Last Decade of Its First Century* (New York: International Publishers, 1968), pp. 422, 412.

10. *The Souls of Black Folk,* pp. 3-4.

11. *Autobiography,* pp. 422-423.

14. Africa Calls

1. Du Bois, "A Future for Pan-Africa: Freedom, Peace, Socialism," *National Guardian,* Mar. 11, 1957.

2. *The Autobiography of W. E. B. Du Bois: A Soliloquy on Viewing My Life from the Last Decade of Its First Century,* ed. Herbert Aptheker (New York: International Publishers, 1968), p. 401.

3. Quoted in Shirley Graham Du Bois, *His Day Is Marching On: A Memoir of W. E. B. Du Bois* (New York: Lippincott, 1971), pp. 336-337.

4. Shirley Graham Du Bois, *His Day Is Marching On,* p. 353.

5. *Autobiography,* p. 419.

6. Harold R. Isaacs, "Du Bois and Africa," *Race* 2 (November 1960): 8.

7. William Leo Hansberry, "W. E. B. Du Bois' Influence on African History," in John Henrik Clarke, Esther Jackson, Ernest Kaiser, and J. H. O'Dell, eds., *Black Titan: W. E. B. Du Bois* (Boston: Beacon, 1970), p. 113.

8. W. Alphaeus Hunton, "W. E. B. Du Bois: The Meaning of His Life," in *Black Titan,* p. 134.

9. William Branch, "Ghana Gives State Burial to Dr. Du Bois," *Amsterdam News* (New York), Sept. 7, 1963. For a review of work on the Encyclopedia Africana before and after Du Bois' death, see Clarence G. Contee, "W. E. B. Du Bois and Encyclopedia Africana," *Crisis* 77 (November 1970): 375-379. For other details of Du Bois' last days, see Leslie Alexander Lacy, *Cheer The Lonesome Traveller: The Life of W. E. B. Du Bois* (New York: Dell, 1972), pp. 122-153.

Index

Abolitionists, 2, 96, 106, 114, 236
Aborigines Protection Society, 161
Acheson, Dean, 253
Activism: of Du Bois, 47, 115, 133, 220; cost of, 96; inexperience in, 99; factors inhibiting, 109; in manifesto, 154. *See also* NAACP; Niagara Movement; Socialism
Addams, Jane, 43, 66, 134
Adler, Felix, 156
Adventures of Huckleberry Finn, The, 89
Africa, 100, 111, 227, 229; Du Bois' interest in, 57-58, 89; writings on, 58, 144, 146, 149, 150, 174-176; plans for, 151-155 *passim;* visits to, 154, 245, 261; last period in, 260, 288-293
African Mail, 101
African Methodist Episcopal Church, 11, 81
African peoples, 161; Du Bois' histories of, 58, 227-234. *See also* Africa; Pan-Africanism
"African Roots of the War," 262
Afro-America: Du Bois' impact on, 1; as a metaphor of, 17-18; parties of force and education in, 29; artistic creation of, 68, 88-90; two camps in, 81; Crummell a model for, 87; celebration of, 106, 169. *See also* Afro-Americans
Afro-American Council, 98
Afro-Americans: Du Bois and, 8-9, 12-18 *passim,* 31-32, 67, 147, 172; form of worship, 14; in *Philadelphia Negro,* 52-53; "truths" about, 56; definitive statement on, 61-62; *Souls* on, 68-69; literary needs of, 116; in *Quest,* 132; and *Crisis,* 138-139, 147; pride of, 145-147; criticize Du Bois, 147; lose interest in pan-Africanism, 155; progress of, 161-162, 181; and capitalism, 162; and self-segregation, 162, 163-168; 1933 proposed discussion of, 165, 198-199; in *Dark Princess,* 204-205, 217, 218; and *Phylon,* 221; decreasing interest in, 223, 224; and Roosevelt, 225; *Dusk of Dawn* on, 243, 244; urged to go South, 249; and Du Bois' indictment, 254; final revaluation of, 266, 274, 293. *See also* Activism; Harlem Renaissance; Litera-

ture; Race pride; Racial theory; Racism; Socialism
Age (New York), 10
All-Soviet Peace Conference, 252
American Dilemma, An, 51
American Historical Association, 235
American Labor party, 245
American Mercury, 190
American Missionary Association, 54
American Negro, The, 82-83
American Negro Academy, 61
American Negro Labor Congress, 158-159
American Socialist party, 156
Amsterdam News (New York), 223, 224
Ancestry, 9-10, 15-16, 17-18, 148; prophetic role of, 172-173
Anderson, Marian, 189
Anderson, Sherwood, 192, 195
"Appeal to the World," 248
Aptheker, Herbert, 68, 110, 240, 258, 261, 262
Arnold, Matthew, 1, 29, 39, 86, 87, 103
Art and music: European, 46-47, 249; *Souls* on black, 71-72, 89; in manifesto, 154; *Crisis* on black, 165, 188; and propaganda, 184, 185, 190-191; and white audience, 188, 193, 199-200; African, 230, 233
Artha-śāstra, 210
"As the Crow Flies," 141, 223
Atlanta, 100, 121, 156. *See also* Atlanta University
Atlanta Exposition address (1895), 62
Atlanta Riot (1906), 104, 145, 269, 272, 283
Atlanta University, 15, 16, 47, 99, 229, 265; career at, 48, 219; departures from, 65, 104, 133, 223, 245; *Souls* on, 70; and social studies program, 222
Atlanta University Conferences, 64, 66, 91, 222
Atlanta University Publications, 48, 54, 55-58, 134, 165, 221, 230
Atlantic Monthly, 61, 62, 64, 99, 235, 262
Autobiography, 260
Autobiography of an Ex-Colored Man, The, 68
Azikiwe, Nnamdi, 248, 260

317